Research Methodology and Applied Statistics

Research Methodology and Applied Statistics

D.N. Sansanwal
M.Sc. (Physics), M.Ed., Ph.D. (Education)

SHIPRA

(2023, First Published in 2020)

Rs. 1600, US$ 55

ISBN: 978-93-88691-54-3

2024 Impression

Research Methodology and Applied Statistics

Published by:
SHIPRA PUBLICATIONS
LG 18-19, Pankaj Central Market
I.P. Ext., Patparganj, Delhi 110092, India
11 2223 5152; 96500 28065, 9810522367
info@shiprapublication.com
www.shiprapublication.com

Dedicated to

My Mother Gyaso Devi

and

Father Behari Lal

Preface

The development of any nation depends to a large extent on the quality of researches conducted by its people. Quality of research further depends on understanding of different concepts of research and availability of required facilities. At present it is observed that researchers are not able to write Title and Objectives correctly. This is because no where students are taught how to write title and objectives. Not only this, even students are not able to decide whether Hypothesis is to be formulated or not. If formulated then which tense should be used. Should "significant" word be used in the wording of hypothesis? Different universities have a format of writing research proposal. As per the format of writing research proposal, the candidate is supposed to write hypothesis, list independent and dependent variables, etc. These cannot be written by researchers who want to do theoretical research or research in subjects like Philosophy, History, Languages, etc. Sampling techniques are not properly understood by researchers and hence unable to use it for selecting sample. It is observed that some researchers mention that Purposive Random Sampling Technique was used for selecting sample. It is technically wrong because Non-probability as well as Probability Sampling Techniques cannot be combined or used in an integrated fashion. The tools or instruments used in the research go a long way in deciding the quality of research. Majority of researchers mention that data were collected with the help of Questionnaire. Questionnaire can be used as a general word as well as technical word. In fact in research it should be used as a technical word. Further researchers must understand that questionnaire cannot be standardised as most of the information collected with its help is qualitative in nature which cannot be analysed with the help of statistical techniques. Researchers must understand the nature of the variable and decide the tool or instrument accordingly. In social science research, it is not possible to use standardised tool as in many researches qualitative information is required. The tool used for getting qualitative information has to be unstandardised. It is due to the use of unstandardised tool, the quality of research is in danger as it is not free from personal biased. The findings of experimental researches are of too much use by society but the quality comes in its way for wider use. Teaching of research methodology in classrooms has not changed in majority of institutions of higher education. It is a matter of great concern. Not only this even the data analysis and interpretation done by researchers is quite faulty. Last but not the least the research report written by the researcher in the form of thesis, dissertation or paper is weak. Thus, people concerned with the quality of research must think as how to improve its quality. This book is a small attempt in this direction. Hope researchers will be able to learn basics of research and use them during the process of conducting research and writing its report.

Chapters of tnis book have been read by many Research Fellows, Assistant Professors, Associate Professors, Professors and Deans of Faculties of different universities. Their suggestions have contributed a lot in improving its content. I thankfully acknowledge their untiring support. I wish to express my gratitude to my wife Urmila, daughter Aditi, Son Ankur, grand daughter Aarya, and son-in-law Daniel Sequoyah Tuell who allowed me free time to write this book. Special thanks to my In-laws Late Shri Gopal Singhji, and Mrs. Chandraji. At this stage I cannot afford to forget my mentors Late Prof. M.B. Buch and Late Prof. B.K. Passi who nurtured me to the extent that I could write this book. I am short of words to thank them. Last but not least I acknowledge the support of all those who directly or indirectly helped me in writing this book.

I do acknowledge the support of Mr. D. Kumar and his team who readily agreed to publish this book.

D.N. Sansanwal

Contents

1
Research: Concept, Types and Steps

INTRODUCTION

The progress of any nation to a great extent depends on the Research and Development. The explosion of information is due to the researches conducted in different areas. The technological development is also due to research. In a nutshell the research is the backbone of any country's progress and development. Thus, research is conducted in all disciplines. But it is observed that the society gets maximum benefit from researches conducted in different areas of Science, Medicine and Technology. The findings of researches in Social Sciences are not as useful as those of Science, Medicine and Technology. Further, in India, research methods are not taught in many disciplines although people do research. Now people are becoming conscious about the importance of Research Method. In this chapter, information is given related to concept of research, types and steps to be followed in conducting research in any discipline. After reading this chapter, you will be able to:

- Define research
- List characteristics of research
- Differentiate among discovery, invention and research
- Differentiate between different types of research
- List the steps to be followed in conducting research.

RESEARCH

It is a known fact that necessity is the mother of invention. The necessity comes in the form of a problem. The problem is the base of research. There is a problem and its solution also exists but the people may not be fully satisfied with the existing solution of the problem. It is this *dissatisfaction* that motivates people to find another solution of the same problem. It is also a fact that there is no absolute solution of the problem. Each solution of the problem leads to a new problem. Take the case of mobile. People wanted to be in contact during their travel. It was the need. The research gave mobile as the solution but there are many problems associated with it. The researches have indicated that there are many health hazards which were not there before the invention of mobile. Thus, research gives both the solution and a new problem.

It is a fact that there are many solutions of the same problem both in Sciences and Social Sciences. Due to this, it is not appropriate to say that the outcome of the research, that is, the solution is correct or incorrect. The solution of the problem has to be accepted as it comes. For getting the solution, some activities have to be carried out. Any activity can be carried out unsystematically or systematically. An activity is said to be carried out systematically when the probability of success is maximum. On the other hand, whenever the probability of success is not maximum, the activity is said to be done unsystematically. So in research, activities have to be carried out systematically. The word Systematic reflects that there are well defined steps arranged in predefined order/sequence. Whenever there are steps, it must be a Process. On the basis of above explanation, the research can be defined as:

Research refers to a *Process* wherein *Activities* are carried out *Systematically* to find *Solution* of the *Problem.*

This is the general definition of Research. From this the definition of research in different disciplines can be coined. A few are given below:

Research in Physics refers to a *Process* wherein *Activities* are carried out *Systematically* to find *Solution* of the *Problem related to some aspect of Physics.*

Research in Hindi refers to a *Process* wherein *Activities* are carried out *Systematically* to find *Solution* of the *Problem related to some aspect of Hindi.*

Research in Education refers to a *Process* wherein *Activities* are carried out *Systematically* to find *Solution* of the *Problem related to some aspect of Education.*

Research in Management refers to a *Process* wherein *Activities* are carried out *Systematically* to find *Solution* of the *Problem related to some aspect of Management.*

CHARACTERISTICS OF RESEARCH

The following are the characteristics of any research.

1. It is systematic in nature.
2. It is problem oriented.
3. It refers to a process.
4. It involves activities.
5. It leads to solution.

DIFFERENCE AMONG DISCOVERY, INVENTION AND RESEARCH

Let us take the example of X-Ray. X-Ray was discovered incidentally in 1895 by German Scientist Wilhelm Roentgen. India was also discovered incidentally by Vasco da Gama in 1497. No systematic efforts were made. Thus, discovery is not the outcome of activities carried out systematically. It is due to this that people cannot be trained for discovery. Thus, discovery is unsystematic.

The steam engine was invented by James Watt. Let us understand the process of inventing Steam Engine. James Watt saw that the steam coming out of the boiling water was able to lift the lid put over the vessel. It reflected that the steam has energy to push the lid upward. James Watt thought of using this idea and the Steam Engine was invented through activities carried out systematically. Thus, Steam Engine was the outcome of activities carried out systematically. Inventions are Applied Researches. So the invention may take place while some one is doing Research. Research as pointed out earlier is systematic in nature. So invention is systematic in nature and it may happen during conducting research. Thus, it is easy to differentiate among Discovery, Invention and Research.

TYPES OF RESEARCH

There are different types of research. The type of research depends on its base. The types of Researches along with their bases are given below.

Qualitative Research and Quantitative Research

The data/information can be Qualitative or Quantitative. In Languages, Philosophy, History, etc. mostly the qualitative data exist. The qualitative data can be converted into quantitative data but it should not be converted into quantitative data because there is a loss of information or data. To understand this let us take one example. Suppose there is a 10 marks question while checking the answer of this question, the teacher reads the answer which is in qualitative form and assigns say 6 marks out of 10 which is the maximum score for this question. So the qualitative data/information has been converted into quantitative data. Now from this quantitative data can one get back the Original qualitative data? The answer is no. It means there is a loss of information in transforming qualitative data into quantitative data. So while analysing the qualitative data one should not convert it into quantitative data. It should be used as qualitative data only. Thus, the basis for *Qualitative Research and Quantitative Research* is Types of data/information.

Philosophical Research, Historical Research, Survey Research, Experimental Research and Case Study Research

For conducting research, the researcher has to follow some steps. So there is a method or procedure to be followed in conducting a research. The method/procedure to be followed are different for different researches. Thus, on the basis of method/procedure followed, the types of research are: Philosophical Research, Historical Research, Survey Research, Experimental Research, and Case Study Research. *Thus Method/procedure followed is the basis of classifying researches into Philosophical Research, Historical Research, Survey Research, Experimental Research, and Case Study Research.*

Basic/Fundamental/Theoretical Research, Applied/Experimental Research and Action Research

The outcome of a research is in the form of solutions of the problem. It is also called findings. It is observed that sometime the findings of research are not usable. That is, society cannot benefit from the findings of all researches. Such researches are not required as the society cannot benefit from them. It is a well-known fact that the theory developed by a person is not only used by the people of his country but the whole World can benefit from the theory. Thus, the Basic/Fundamental/Theoretical Research has utility or applicability for all people of the world.

Fan, TV, Mobile, etc. are the outcomes of Applied/Experimental Research. Fan which is used in India requires 220 Volts but the Fan in Canada requires 110 Volts. It means that the Indian fan will not work in Canada and similarly Canada fan will not work in India. Mobile requires SIM card which differs from country to country. Thus, Applied/Experimental Researches have limited utility/applicability. So the degree of utility or applicability reduces.

Finally, you must have noticed that two people having fever may not get the same medicine. There are large number of medicine for fever. Whatever medicine suits to a person, the same medicine may not suit to another person. Similarly, if the students of College A go on strike and the College Authority negotiate with the students and find the solution of the problem. The students go back to their classes. Suppose after some time another College B students go on strike. The reason of going on strike by students of College A may or may not be the same as that of College B. So the solution of College A will not apply to College B. Separate solution has to be worked out. So the Degree of utility or applicability is too limited.

Thus, the base of Basic/Fundamental/Theoretical Research; Applied/ Experimental Research and Action Research is *the Degree of Utility or Applicability.*

STEPS OF RESEARCH

The research refers to a process which is scientific or systematic in nature. So its steps are also derived from the scientific process. These are as follows:

1. Identification of Problem
2. Formulation of Hypothesis
3. Data Collection
4. Data Analysis
5. Conclusion

The details of each step are given below:

Identification of Problem is the first step. Let us understand why the first step of research is Identification of Problem but not Selection of Problem? Identification word is to be used when the situation is heterogeneous and in homogeneous situation selection word is to be used. Take an example. Whenever one goes to the market to buy vegetable, one first find out which all types of vegetables are available. Naturally, there are different types of vegetables in the market. So it is heterogeneous situation. Suppose one decides to purchase potatoes. From potatoes one will select potatoes of nearly the same size. Here the word selection is used because one is taking potatoes from heap of potatoes which is homogeneous because all are potatoes. Thus, selection word is used whenever the situation is homogeneous and in heterogeneous situation identification word is to be used. This is because it is easy to select when the situation is homogeneous.

To understand the difference between Identification and Selection, let us take another example. There are subjects like, Economics, Political Science, Hindi, English, Management, Education, Psychology, Social works, Physics, Mathematics, Chemistry, etc. It is a heterogeneous situation. Suppose one wants to do research in Management. So the researcher has identified the subject in which he/she wants to do research. There are different areas in Management, like, Marketing, Finance, Advertising, Human Resource, etc. From these the researcher decides to do research related to Marketing. There are different marketing strategies. Among these one may decide to conduct research related to e-marketing. This is selection because the researcher started narrowing management to marketing than to e-marketing.

Now let us understand the word Problem. You have normal body temperature so it is not a problem. It becomes problem whenever body temperature changes. Suppose you want to buy Car. As there are varieties of cars, it may not be easy to choose one car. The decision about the car is not easy. Thus, more alternatives lead to problem as it delays the decision making process. A characteristic that has a tendency to change is called Variable. Thus, another name of problem is variable. In this step the researcher has to finally select the variable.

In this step, the researcher is supposed to select the Variable. After this, the title has to be written. The title should neither be too broad nor too specific. It should be narrow. The title should give information about the Variable(s) to be studied. The population of the study should also be reflected in the title. After reading the title the reader should also know the nature or type of research. Thus, an appropriate research title should give:

- Information about the variable(s),
- Population, and
- Type of research

Any title that does not give all these information is not complete. Further the Title cannot start with the word "To" because the title is not pinpointed. Also the title cannot indicate the direction. The objectives have to start with the word "To" because objectives are pinpointed and indicates the direction. After writing the title of research, the researcher should write the objectives. The objectives are research questions whose answers the researcher tries to get through the research. The objectives can be written in statement form or question form. In one research, both objectives as well as research questions should not be written.

Formulation of Hypothesis is the second step. Hypothesis is the tentative solution of the problem. Another definition is that hypothesis is the intelligent guess about the solution of the problem. Conjectural statement about the relationship between variables is another definition of hypothesis. From these definitions it is evident that Hypothesis is not the final Solution of the Problem. To get the final Solution, it has to be tested. The testing of hypothesis is to be done with the help of Statistical Technique. The statistical technique requires quantitative data. It means whenever in a research, quantitative data are not collected, the hypothesis cannot be tested. Hence, hypothesis should not be formulated in a research where qualitative data are collected. So, formulation of hypothesis step may not be there in some researches. Thus, it is an optional step.

The researcher must understand:

- How the hypothesis is to be worded?
- Should "Significant" word be used or not in the Statement of Hypothesis?
- What difference will it make if Significant word is not used in the Statement of Hypothesis?
- What is the base or rational of stating the Hypothesis?
- When should one state Null Hypothesis or Directional Hypothesis?
- When to use One Tailed Test or Two Tailed Test?
- What is the relationship between level of Significance and Type of Error?

Data Collection is the third step of research. To start with, the researcher should know from where the data are to be collected. That is, the population should be known in case of survey and experimental type of researches and source of data should be known in case of Philosophical and Historical Type of Researches. It may happen that the researcher is not able to collect information or data from each and every member of the population. Under such circumstances, the sample has to be taken from the population.

The process of selecting Sample from the Population is called Sampling. The Sample is the small representative portion of the population. The representation has to be with respect to the correlates of the variable under study. It is not possible to have truly representative sample of the population but efforts must be made to select Sample that can represent the population to the maximum extent. There are different sampling techniques. The sampling techniques have been classified into two categories:

- Non-Probability Sampling and
- Probability Sampling

The researcher must know which type of sampling technique is to be used in the current research or research in hand. This information is known from the researcher in deciding which sampling technique is to be used. Further, the researcher must know what sample size should be appropriate for the research. The sampling error must be known to the researcher.

After selecting the sample, the researcher should decide the tool or instrument to be used for collecting data. The tools are of various types, such as, Test, Scale, Inventory, Observation Schedule, Interview Schedule, and Questionnaire. Tools are standardised and unstandardised. Tests, Scales and Inventories can be standardised but interview schedule and questionnaire cannot be standardised. On the other hand, observation schedule cannot be standardised but inter observer reliability can be established. The researcher must know that tools have characteristics. The characteristics are Reliability, Validity, Objectivity, Sensitivity, and Usability. The characteristics of the tool will be imbibed in the data. That is, if the tool is reliable and valid, then data will also be reliable and valid. Consequently the finding will also be reliable. Thus, the researcher has to select tools carefully.

After selecting the tools/instruments, the researcher must decide the Method of Research to be followed in conducting research. The different methods of research are: Philosophical Method, Historical Method, Survey Method, Experimental Method and Case Study Method. Each method of research has well defined steps. The researcher has to follow the steps meant for the method of research which he/she is using.

Data Analysis is the fourth step of research. The data can be qualitative or quantitative. For analysing the qualitative data, the techniques available are: Content Analysis, Meta-Analysis and SWOT Analysis. Statistical techniques are available for analysing the quantitative data. The researcher must know the scale of measurement underlying the data and accordingly select the appropriate statistical technique. The statistical techniques have been classified into Parametric Statistics and Non-parametric Statistics. The choice of statistic is guided by the wording of the objective. It is due to this that the wording of objectives should be pinpointed.

Conclusion is the last step of research. Conclusions are nothing but Findings of the research undertaken by the researcher. It must be consistent with the objectives of research. Sometime researcher writes conclusion in four to five pages and even more. From these pages, it is difficult to know the conclusion. Sometime researcher writes findings. There should be a linkage between objectives and findings. If there is no objective corresponding to the finding, there cannot be a finding.

Take a Test*

1. Which of the following is not the Characteristic of a Research?
   A) It refers to a problem.
   B) It depends on review of related literature.

* For checking correct answers, see p. 294.

C) It is systematic in nature.
D) It leads to solution.

2. Which of the following is not the step of a Research?
A) Selection of problem B) Formulation of hypothesis
C) Data collection D) Data analysis.

3. Which of the following is not the step of a Research?
A) Formulation of hypotheses B) Data analysis
C) Review of related literature D) None of the above.

4. Research can be defined as:
A) a process of arriving at the solution of the problem.
B) a process of collection of data and arriving at the solution of the problem.
C) a solution oriented process.
D) a process wherein activities are carried out scientifically to find solution of the problem.

5. Which of the following statement is correct?
A) Problem is another name of a variable.
B) Discovery and invention words can be used interchangeably.
C) One can have patent for the discovery
D) During discovery, invention can take place.

6. Data Collection includes
A) Tools B) Sample
C) Method of research D) All of the above

7. Identification of problem should give information about
A) Title of the research
B) Objectives of the study
C) Variables involved in the research
D) All of the above.

8. On the basis of Degree of Utility, the type of Researches are:
A) Historical Research, Survey Research, Experimental Research and Case Study Research
B) Theoretical Research, Experimental Research and Action Research
C) Qualitative and Quantitative Research
D) None of the above.

9. The correct sequence of activities under Identification of Problem are:
A) Selection of Variable, Title writing and Objective writing
B) Title writing, Selection of Variable, and Objective writing
C) Title writing, Objective writing
D) Objective writing, Title writing and Selection of Variable.

10. The base for Qualitative and Quantitative Researches is:
A) Steps followed B) Applicability
C) Degree of utility D) Type of information.

2

Variables, Sources of Problem, Title and Objectives Writing

INTRODUCTION

By now you must have understood the general definition of research and the way it can be modified so as to suit the particular subject. Thus, you can now define research in any subject. Also you can list the characteristics of research. From the definition as well as characteristics of research, you must have understood that for doing Research one must confront with a Problem. That means without problem, research is not possible. Another name of problem is Variable. So both problem and variable can be used interchangeably. Once you understand variable or problem then you may be interested in knowing the Sources of Problem. In day-to-day life one comes across many problems related to different aspects of life. But still it is difficult to identify problem for the research. To help you as a researcher, the sources of problem are given which may be used to identify the problem. Once the problem is identified and selected then one should know how to write the Title of Research. All of us know that there are titles of books, papers, and research. All these differ in length and wordings. From the wording of the title one can make out whether it is the title of a research or not. Normally teachers under research methodology do not teach how to write title. Due to this the researchers make mistake in writing title. Sansanwal (2015) has pointed out this weakness in his paper entitled "Methodological Issues in Experimental Research". The same problem exists in other type of researches also. So, one has to be very careful in writing the title of the research. Thus, after reading this chapter, one will be able to:

- Define Variable.
- List different types of Variables.
- Differentiate between Continuous and Discontinuous Variables.
- Identify Independent Variable and Dependent Variable in the Experimental Research.
- List Intervening Variables in the Experimental Researches.
- Define Confounding Variable and Moderating Variable.

- List Confounding Variables as well as Moderating Variables in the Research Study.
- List different Sources of Problem and use them to Select the Problem for the Research.
- List the points to be kept in mind while selecting a problem.
- Write appropriate Research Title for Philosophical Research, Historical Research, Survey Research, and Experimental Research.
- Write pinpointed Objectives for different Types of Researches.

VARIABLE

You know that human beings differ in characteristics, like, weight, skin colour, hemoglobin, height, intelligence, aptitude, reading comprehension, vocabulary, gender, residential background, nationality, religion, age, etc. All these characteristics are variables. Characteristic which has a tendency to change is called Variable. In day-to-day life one may come across human beings with same age, height, weight, vocation, gender, etc. but side by side one may find people with different age, height, weight, vocation, gender, etc. So in general age, height, weight, vocation, gender, etc. are variables.

There are some characteristics which do not change at all, such as, number of days in a week, number of seconds in one minute, the sum of three angles of a triangle, the value of π, etc. Such characteristics are called Constant. Thus, constant is the characteristic which does not change at all. It means that the characteristic remain same everywhere and all the time.

Suppose a researcher wants to study the Intelligence of Females. In this, intelligence is a variable but gender is held constant because the intelligence of only females is studied but not of males. So it is possible to keep a variable constant in a research and the same may be a variable in another research. Thus, the basic nature of the variable cannot be changed permanently but temporarily change is possible.

For a variable, it is possible to have either Qualitative data or Quantitative data. From quantitative data one may calculate Mean and Standard Deviation. For a variable what should be the minimum value of Standard Deviation? To understand this let us take one example. Suppose we take Intelligence scores of 10 people and the scores were found to be 30, 30, 30, 30, 30, 30, 30, 30, 30 and 30. From this data one may find that the Mean is 30 and the value of Standard Deviation is ZERO because there is no variation in the intelligence scores. Thus, in this case, intelligence is not a variable. Suppose the intelligence scores of 10 people are 30, 30, 30, 30, 30, 30, 30, 30, 30 and 29. In this case, the value of Standard Deviation when computed will be greater than ZERO. Hence, intelligence is a variable in this case. Thus, for a variable the minimum value of Standard Deviation is greater than ZERO. Further Standard Deviation value will always be positive because Standard Deviation refers to the differences within the group which is the scalar quantity.

TYPES OF VARIABLE

Variables are of different types. These are given in the following:

Continuous and Discontinuous/Discrete Variables

Generally all variables can be classified either as Continuous Variable or Discontinuous/Discrete Variable.

Continuous Variable is one which can be expressed in whole as well as fractions. In other words a variable that is not restricted to particular values (other than limited by the accuracy of the measuring instrument or the tool used) is called Continuous Variable. For example, weight, height, academic achievement, power of a lens, time of running, intelligence, monthly expenses, height of a plant, room size, etc. are all Continuous Variables.

Discontinuous/Discrete Variable is one which can be expressed only in whole numbers. In other words, variables having only integer values are called Discrete/Discontinuous Variables. For example, vocabulary, number of words per line, RBC, gender, types of school, colours, marital status, school subjects, courses offered by the university, number of teachers, caste, religion, etc. are all Discontinuous/Discrete variable.

As stated earlier that research cannot be done without a variable, so the variable which the researcher has in his/her study will be either Continuous Variable or Discontinuous Variable. Researches in Philosophy, Literature, History, Sociology, Political Science, Social Work, Computer, Physics, Chemistry, Botany, Economics, Commerce, Education, Pharmacy, Mathematics, Mechanical Engineering, Civil Engineering, etc. cannot be done without having either Continuous Variable and/or Discontinuous/Discrete Variable.

Independent and Dependent Variable

Independent Variable is that variable which can bring change in another variable. It is also called *Manipulated Variable* as well as *Treatment Variable*.

Dependent Variable is one in which the variations are caused due to change in some other variable. In other words the values of the Dependent Variable depend upon another Variable, that is, the Independent Variable.

Let us take one example. All of us know that the variation in health can be brought by changing the quality of food. It means that health depends on quality of food. Thus, in this situation Quality of Food is the Independent Variable and Health is the Dependent Variable. It is a known fact that the Quality of Food depends on Monthly Income of the Family. In this situation monthly income is the Independent Variable and quality of food is the Dependent Variable. So in the previous situation quality of food was the Independent Variable but it is Dependent Variable in the second case. So a variable may be Independent Variable in one research and the same may become Dependent Variable in another research. It may, therefore, be said that Independent Variable and Dependent Variable are the relative terms but not absolute terms. Further the changes in the health may not be only due to the changes in quality of food. The changes in health may also be due to the working hours, environmental conditions, nature of work, etc. It means the changes in the health may be due to quality of food, and also due to working hours, environmental conditions, nature of work, etc. But the researcher is interested in studying the changes in the health only due to the quality of food but not due to working hours, environmental conditions, nature of work, etc. So working hours, environmental conditions, nature of work, etc. variables intervene in the process. So such variables are called Intervening Variables. So in the experimental researches attempts are made to know beforehand the Intervening Variables so that one can decide the various ways or methods of controlling Intervening Variables. It is important to mention that it is not possible to know beforehand all the Intervening Variables and thus impossible to control all the Intervening Variables. If all Intervening variables are controlled then there cannot be a failure.

Let us take one more example from the classroom. In a class whenever the teacher teaches with the help of a Method of Teaching, all students do not understand to the same extent. In this example, understanding depends on method of teaching used by the teacher. So Method of Teaching is the Independent Variable and Understanding is the Dependent Variable. In this case the Intervening Variables might be intelligence, study habits, comprehension, stress, family background, noise outside the classroom, light intensity, foul smell in the classroom, etc. because these can bring change in the understanding in the presence of method of teaching.

> ***Caution:*** *The Independent Variable and Dependent Variable words can be used only in experimental researches. Therefore, Independent Variable and Dependent Variable words should not be used in survey researches, philosophical researches, historical researches and case study researches. Hence, except experimental research, in all other researches* ***Criterion Variable*** *word should be used in place of* ***Dependent Variable****.*

Intervening Variables are those which might be in the process or outside the process but bring change in the dependent variable in the presence of independent variable. This occurs only in the experimental research. Sometime *Intervening Variables* are also called *Mediating Variables* or *Intermediary Variables.*

The intervening variables might be in the process or outside the process of research but do bring change in the dependent variable in the presence of independent variable. Those intervening variables which are in the process but bring change in the dependent variable in the presence of independent variable are called *Intrinsic Variables or Endogenous Variables.* On the other hand, those intervening variables which are outside the process but bring change in the dependent variable in the presence of independent variable are called *Extrinsic Variables* or *Exogenous variables.*

In the example of method of teaching and understanding of students, different intervening variables mentioned are intelligence, study habits, comprehension, stress, family background, noise outside the classroom, light intensity, foul smell in the classroom, etc. Of these, the *Intrinsic Variables* are intelligence, study habits, comprehension, stress, family background, etc. but noise outside the classroom, light intensity, foul smell in the classroom, etc. are the *Extrinsic Variables*.

Confounding Variable is an *extraneous variable* whose presence affects the variables being studied so that the results one get do not reflect the actual relationship between variables under investigation. The confounding variables might be in the experimental research and correlational survey research and are large in number. It is very difficult to control all confounding variables in the experimental research.

Moderating Variable is one that influences or moderates the relationship between two variables and thus produces an interaction effect.

SOURCES OF PROBLEM

Normally it is said that the young researcher is Problem Blind. It means that although there are so many problems around him/her but he/she is unable to see. So it is important to introduce young researcher systematically to different sources of problem. The sources of problem are given below.

Review of Related Literature

Review of Related Literature is one of the sources of problem. Here literature means journals, e-Journals, dissertation abstract international (DAI), doctoral thesis, etc. Related refers to the chosen aspect of the area in which one wants to do research. If one wants to do research related to e-marketing, one has to see researches related to marketing strategies. There might have been many researches related to marketing strategies. So the researcher has to review the researches related to marketing strategies. This is the meaning of review of related literature. This is one of the important source of identification of problem. In all subjects, the researcher has related literature. It can depict whether any research has been conducted or not. If no research has been conducted, it means that gap exists. Then the researcher can identify the problems or variables related to that aspect where no research has been conducted till date. In case a few researches have been conducted, then also the researcher can identify problems related to that variable because no generalisation can be made from the findings of a few researches. In case large number of researches have been conducted, there might be consistency or inconsistency in findings. In case there is a consistency in findings no more researches are required because one has reached at a stage where generalisation can be made. In other words one can put fourth theory or formulate laws. But if there is inconsistency in findings, more researches are required. In this way the review of related literature can help the researcher in identification of problems for the research. From the identified problems, one can finally select the problem for the research. The review of related literature starts helping the researchers from the beginning. So it is a part and parcel of first step– identification of problem but it is not a separate step of research.

Unutilised/Underutilised Theory

It is a fact that there are theories in different subjects, like, Physics, Chemistry, Mathematics, Economics, Psychology, Education, etc. The theories are developed so that people can use them to make their life comfortable. One must have experienced that in school the teacher might have said good, excellent, etc. whenever one has given the correct answer. When one listens such words, one get motivated and try to do better. That means reward motivates individuals. There might be different ways of giving rewards for motivating people to do better. Thus, there is a scope of doing researches related to Theories of Motivation.

Let us take one more example. Bruce Joyce and M. Weil (1985) found that there were theories related to teaching, learning, evaluation, motivation, administration, decision-making, etc. But the available theories have not been fully utilised. One of the reasons was that people did not know how to use them. So Bruce Joyce and M. Weil (1985) translated the unutilised theories and gave Models of Teaching. Now researchers can conduct researches related to different models of teaching.

So it can be said that researches can be conducted related to the Unutilised/Underutilised Theories. Thus, Unutilised/Underutilised Theory becomes another Source of Problem.

Seminars/Conferences

Seminars/conferences are organised in all subjects. These may be organised at state level, national level, and international level. In seminars/conferences the researchers present their researches related to the theme of the seminar/conference. Generally there is a lead speaker who gives talk related to the seminar/conference theme. The talk is generally very rich in ideas and covers all the sub-aspects of the seminar/conference. While listening to the talk one may get an idea related to which the research can be conducted. Further, the participants also present their research work. One may get interested in idea presented through the paper and think of conducting research. In this way seminar/conference may become a source of problem. Sometime the researcher gets feedback on his/her presentation. The researcher may like to modify the presented paper and like to send it to some journal for the publication. If so, it becomes the part of review of related literature. Thus, seminars/conferences may be another source of problem.

Informal Source: Newspaper, Radio, TV, etc.

We get information of government policies related to education, health, finance, etc. through newspaper, radio, TV, etc. During Congress regime it was decided that there will be no formal annual examination up to Class VIII and all students will be promoted to the next class. As a researcher one may like to study the reaction toward No Examination Policy of the government of parents, teachers, and social workers. For this problem the Source is Newspaper.

Let us take another example. While traveling in a train or bus you might have experienced that co-passenger may start conversation by asking what do you do? In case you say that I am a teacher. On listening this he may start expressing his opinion about teachers. While expressing his opinion, he may say that these days teachers do not teach; teachers do tuitions; teachers do not take classes regularly and so on. After this experience, you as a conscious researcher, may like to study the opinion toward teachers of parents. For this problem, the source is personal experience.

One should know that Informal Source is not a very good Source of Problem. One may use it to do a research for writing paper but not for conducting research leading to some degree.

POINTS TO BE KEPT IN MIND WHILE SELECTING A PROBLEM

Using the Sources of Problem mentioned earlier, one may come across many problems but the researcher has to select only one problem for conducting research. The following points are to be kept in mind while selecting a problem for conducting research.

- The researcher should have interest in the aspect of area related to which he wants to do research.
- He should have funds for conducting research.
- The researcher should have time.
- The facilities, like, equipment, library, experts' help, etc. required for conducting research should be available.
- The outcome of the research should be useful to the society.
- The researcher should have necessary specialisation required for conducting research.
- In some cases, the availability of the guide or guiding teacher who will help the researcher during the process of research.
- The researcher must have patience for doing research and should not get frustrated fast.

TITLE WRITING

After selecting the problem, one has to write title. Normally the title writing is not taught to the students. The various reasons are: it is not given in the books of Research Methodology. Title writing is not a part of the syllabus. Teachers teaching Research Methodology do not teach how to write title for the research. Title writing remains very weak. Research is systematic and title writing is a part of it, so title writing should also be systematic and researcher should be trained in writing title for the research.

Researcher must know the answer to the following questions:

- Should the research title be Broad vs Narrow vs Specific?
- Which all information should a researcher gives in the research title?
- Can the research title begin with "To"?
- Can a title have full stop at the end of it?

To understand the answer of above mentioned questions, let us select *Stress* as a variable for doing research. The process of Title Writing is as follows:

1. A comparative study
2. A comparative study of Stress
3. A comparative study of Stress of male and female students
4. A comparative study of Stress of male and female students of Class IX
5. A comparative study of Stress of male and female students of Class IX of Government schools
6. A comparative study of Stress of male and female students of Class IX of Government schools of India
7. A comparative study of Stress of male and female students of Class IX of Government schools of Madhya Pradesh
8. A comparative study of Stress of male and female students of Class IX of Government schools of Indore
9. A comparative study of Stress of male and female students of Class IX of Malwa Kenya Higher Secondary School of Indore

The title 1 is too broad, so it is vague. One cannot make out anything from the title 1. So the title of a research cannot be too broad. By comparing title 2 with title 1, one can see that title 2 is little narrow as the word Stress is mentioned. Stress is a Variable. So title 2 has a Variable while it is missing in title 1. Still title 2 is not complete as it does not say anything about whose Stress is to be compared. By comparing title 3 with title 2, one can see that the Stress of male and female students is to be compared. Thus, in title 3, some information about the Population is given but it is too broad. By comparing title 4 with title 3, one can see that Class IX has been added. So the population as evident from title 4 is "male and female students of Class IX" but still the population is broad as it does not tell the Type of School to which the students belong. By comparing title 5 with title 4, one can see that in title 5 Government schools is mentioned. This information has further narrowed down the Title. Still title 5 is not complete as it does not say anything about the country or place to which the Government schools will belong. This information one gets from title 6 where India is mentioned. So "male and female students of Class IX of

Government schools of India" is the information related to population of the research. This population is still broad. By comparing title 7 with title 6, one can note that title 7 is further narrowed as Madhya Pradesh is mentioned in place of India. Madhya Pradesh is too big it has to be further narrowed. In title 8, Indore is mentioned in place of Madhya Pradesh. Looking at title 9, one can say that the population is too specific because the name of the school is given. The title 9 is too specific. Such a title is not appropriate for the research. Amongst the given 9 titles, title 7 or 8 may be appropriate. Title 7 may be appropriate because while writing the report of the research, the researcher may mention the name of the place from where the sample was taken. From title 7 and 8 one knows that the Method of Research will be Survey Research. Thus, an appropriate title should give information about the Variable, Population and Method of Research. Any research title lacking in these information will be technically incorrect. Now you can answer first two questions given above related to title of research.

You know that the title is narrow but not pinpointed. It does not give direction to the research. Thus, "To" cannot be used in the beginning of the title of a research. "To" comes in the beginning of objectives only because objectives are pinpointed and give direction to the researcher as how to proceed further. Not only Research Title but title of a book as well as research paper should not have "To" in the beginning.

Sometime it is observed that full stop is put at the end of title or caption heading. It is wrong because title or caption heading is not a complete sentence. Full stop is put only at the end of the sentence.

Let us understand the process of writing title for survey research with the help of other example where *Stress* is the variable.

1. A Study of
2. A Study of Stress
3. A Study of Stress in relation to
4. A Study of Stress in relation to Anxiety, Tension and Monthly Expenses
5. A Study of Stress in relation to Anxiety, Tension and Monthly Expenses of Teachers
6. A Study of Stress in relation to Anxiety, Tension and Monthly Expenses of College Teachers
7. A Study of Stress in relation to Anxiety, Tension and Monthly Expenses of College Teachers of India
8. A Study of Stress in relation to Anxiety, Tension and Monthly Expenses of College Teachers of Uttar Pradesh
9. A Study of Stress in relation to Anxiety, Tension and Monthly Expenses of College Teachers of Lucknow, Uttar Pradesh
10. A Study of Stress in relation to Anxiety, Tension and Monthly Expenses of Banarsi Lal College of Teachers Education of Lucknow, Uttar Pradesh

Now you can say that the most appropriate Research Title amongst the above given 10 titles are Title 8 and Title 9. Title 10 is too narrow and its finding may not add to the existing information. So Title 10 is not appropriate for Research. Such title should not be written.

Let us understand Title Writing for Experimental Research where *Stress* is the Variable.

1. Effectiveness
2. Effectiveness of Yoga
3. Effectiveness of Yoga in terms of Stress
4. Effectiveness of Yoga in terms of Stress of IT Sector
5. Effectiveness of Yoga in terms of Stress of IT Sector Middle Level Managers
6. Effectiveness of Yoga in terms of Stress of IT Sector Middle Level Managers of India
7. Effectiveness of Yoga in terms of Stress of IT Sector Middle Level Managers of Maharashtra
8. Effectiveness of Yoga in terms of Stress of IT Sector Middle Level Managers of Mumbai
9. Effectiveness of Yoga in terms of Stress of Wipro Middle Level Managers of Mumbai

Title 1 is too broad as one cannot understand whose effectiveness is to be studied. Title 1 is vague. By comparing Title 2 with Title 1, one can note that in Title 2, Yoga word has been added. Title 2 is slightly narrower than Title 1 but still it is not complete because it is not mentioned on what basis the effectiveness of Yoga is to be studied. In Title 3, it is mentioned that "Effectiveness of Yoga in terms of Stress". In Title 3, name of Variable Stress appears. Still Title 3 is incomplete as the information about the population is not given. By comparing Title 4 with Title 3, one can see that "IT Sector" is mentioned in Title 4 which gives little information about the population. In IT sector people are working at different levels from peon to CEO. More information about population is given in Title 5 where Middle Level Managers is mentioned. From Title 5, one can see that "IT Sector Middle Level Managers" gives information about the population. Information about population has been narrowed but still it is broad. The population is further narrowed as evident from Titles 7 and 8. In Title 9, population is too narrow. Title 9 is appropriate for Action Research. Thus, Title 7 or Title 8 is appropriate Title. From Titles 7 and 8, one can note that Stress is the Variable; IT Sector Middle Level Managers of Maharashtra or Mumbai refers to population and "Effectiveness" reflects that it is experimental study. So the information about method of research is also given. Hence, from Titles 7 and 8, one can get information related to variable, population and method of research. Therefore, the appropriate Titles are 7 and 8. This is how the Title for an Experimental Research should be written.

It has been observed that sometime researcher wants to use "Effect" word in the Title of Experimental Research. Using the word "Effect" Title 8, can be written as:

10. A study of Effect of Yoga on Stress of IT Sector Middle Level Managers of Mumbai

In Title 10, "A study of" is meaningful because it helps the reader in understanding the Title. "A Study of" will not be appropriate if used in Title 8. If "A Study of" is used in the beginning of Title 8, these words will be redundant. A title should not have redundant words because redundant words do not add to the meaning.

By now it is clear as how to write Research Title for Survey Research and Experimental Research. Let us understand how to write Title for Historical Research.

1. A Study of
2. A Study of System of Education
3. A Study of System of Education during British Period
4. A Study of System of Education during British Period in India

Amongst the four Titles, Title 4 is the most appropriate. In this title, "System of Education" is the Variable, "British Period" refers to the Time, and Method of Research is Historical. In Title 4, "A Study of" is not redundant word but meaningful word. Title for Historical Research may start with "A Study of" words. Thus, the Historical Research should give information related to variable, time period and method of research.

By now it is clear as how to write Research Title for Survey Research, Experimental Research and Historical Research. Let us understand how to write Title for Philosophical Research.

1. A Study of
2. A Study of Educational Thoughts
3. A Study of Educational Thoughts of Mahatma Gandhi

Amongst the three Titles, Title 3 is the most appropriate. In this title, "Educational Thoughts" is the Variable, "Mahatma Gandhi" refers here as Philosopher, and Method of Research is Philosophy. In Title 3, "A Study of" is not redundant word but meaningful word. Title for Philosophical Research may start with "A Study of" words. Thus, the Philosophical Research should give information related to Variable, Philosopher and Method of Research.

Thus, one can write Research Title for Survey Research, Experimental Research, Historical Research, and Philosophical Research.

OBJECTIVES WRITING

It has been observed that researchers are not able to write pinpointed Objectives.

Researchers begin the Objectives with words, such as, "To Find out"; "To Evaluate"; "To Examine"; "To Assess", etc. These are not appropriate words to begin with. The most appropriate words are "To Study" and "To Compare". Objectives can be worded in Sentence form or Question form. The meaning is the same. So there is no need of writing objectives both in sentence form as well as question form. It will be repetition and not of any help to the researcher. In this book the objectives are written in sentence form. Let us take the following title of Survey Research and understand how to write pinpointed Objectives.

➤ A Comparative Study of Stress of Male and Female Students of Class IX of Government Schools of Indore

For the given title let us consider the following Objectives:

1. To compare Stress of Male and Female Students.
2. To compare mean scores of Stress of Male and Female Students.

The Objective 1 is vague because the base of comparison of Stress of Male and Female Students is not known. From Objective 2, it is evident that the researcher wants to compare mean scores of Stress of Male and Female Students. Further from Objective 1, one cannot understand how the data related to Stress are to be analysed. But from Objective 2 it is evident that mean scores of stress of male and female students are to be compared and for the comparison of mean scores a statistical technique known as t-Test is to be used. So the wording of Objective 2 is appropriate as it helps in deciding the Data Analysis Technique.

The following Objectives can be written for the given Research Title.

1. To compare mean scores of Stress of Male and Female students.
2. To compare adjusted mean scores of Stress of Male and Female students by considering their Anxiety as covariate.
3. To study the influence of Gender, Residential Background and their interaction on Stress of students.
4. To study the influence of Gender, Residential Background, Monthly Income and their various interactions on Stress of students.
5. To study the influence of Gender, Residential Background and their interaction on Stress of students by considering their Anxiety as covariate.
6. To study the influence of Gender, Residential Background, Monthly Income and their various interactions on Stress of students by considering their Anxiety as covariate.

Above mentioned Objectives 1 to 6 are pinpointed and it is easy to decide the Statistical Technique to be used for analysing the data. For analysing the data related to Objective 1, t-Test or Independent Samples t-Test should be used provided the data satisfies the assumptions of t-Test. One Way ANCOVA be used for analysing the data related to Objective 2. For Objectives 3 and 4, Two Way ANOVA and Three Way ANOVA respectively will be used for analysing the collected data. Finally, for Objectives 5 and 6, Two Way ANCOVA and Three Way ANCOVA respectively will be used for analysing the collected data.

Let us take the following Research Title and write some of the Objectives.

➢ A Study of Stress in relation to Anxiety, Tension and Monthly Expenses of College Teachers of Lucknow, Uttar Pradesh

For this Research Title, the following Objectives can be written

1. To study the inter-correlation among Stress, Anxiety, Tension and Monthly Expenses of College Teachers.
2. To study the correlation between Stress and Anxiety by partialling out the effect of Tension and Monthly Expenses of College Teachers.
3. To study the correlation between Stress and Tension by partialling out the effect of Anxiety and Monthly Expenses of College Teachers.
4. To study the correlation between Stress and Monthly Expenses by partialling out the effect of Anxiety and Tension of College Teachers.
5. To study the joint contribution of Anxiety, Tension and Monthly Expenses in predicting Stress of College Teachers.
6. To study the individual contribution of Anxiety, Tension and Monthly Expenses in predicting Stress of College Teachers.
7. To establish Regression Equation for predicting Stress on the basis of Anxiety, Tension and Monthly Expenses of College Teachers.

The wording of all the seven Objectives is pinpointed. The data related to Objective 1 can be analysed with the help of Product Moment Correlation. Partial correlation should be used for analysing data related to Objectives 2, 3 and 4. For analysing the data related to Objective 5, Multiple Correlation should be used. The Regression Analysis can be used for analysing the data related to Objectives 6 and 7.

Let us take the following Research Title and write some of the Objectives.

➢ Effectiveness of Yoga in terms of Stress of IT Sector Middle Level Managers of Mumbai

For this Research Title, the following Objectives can be written.

1. To compare mean scores of Stress of Yoga Group and Non-Yoga Group.
2. To study the effect of Physical Exercise, Gender and their interaction on Stress of Middle Level Managers.
3. To study the effect of Physical Exercise, Gender, Family Size and their various interactions on Stress of Middle Level Managers.
4. To compare adjusted mean scores of Stress of Yoga Group and Non-Yoga Group by considering their Anxiety and Tension as covariates.
5. To study the effect of Physical Exercise, Gender and their interaction

on Stress of Middle Level Managers by considering their Anxiety and Tension as covariates.

6. To study the effect of Physical Exercise, Gender, Family Size and their various interactions on Stress of Middle Level Managers by considering their Anxiety and Tension as covariates.
7. To study the trend of effect of Yoga on Stress of Middle Level Managers.

The wording of all the six Objectives is very specific. The data related to Objective 1 can be analysed with the help of t-Test or Independent samples t-test. The data related to Objectives 2 and 3 can be analysed with the help of Two Way ANOVA and Three Way ANOVA respectively. Data related to Objectives 4, 5 and 6 can be analysed with the help of One Way ANCOVA, Two Way ANCOVA and Three Way ANCOVA respectively. Finally, Trend Analysis should be used for analysing data related to Objective 7.

By now it must have been clear that the Objectives should be worded pinpointed and give information about the Data Analysis.

Take a Test

1. Which of the following is a variable?
   A) Male B) Urban Area
   C) Salt intake D) Red colour.
2. Which of the following is a continuous variable?
   A) Reasoning B) Reaction towards ETV Programme
   C) Power of a lens D) All of the above.
3. Which of the following statement is not correct?
   A) Discontinuous Variable cannot be made Continuous.
   B) Intervening Variable can be in Survey Research.
   C) A Variable may be Independent in one research and Dependent in another research.
   D) An Intervening Variable is always Continuous.
4. Which of the following is the correct title of the research?
   A) Relationship between Study Habits and Achievement in Hindi of Class IX students
   B) A study of effect of Computer Aided Instruction on Achievement in Physics of Class X students of Government Schools of Jaipur
   C) Effect of Computer Aided Instruction on Achievement in Physics
   D) Study of Values of Mahatma Gandhi
5. Which of the following is the correct wording of the Objective?
   A) To compare Self-confidence of Male and Female students.
   B) To investigate the relationship between Self-confidence and Gender.
   C) To compare mean scores of Self-confidence of Male and Female students.
   D) To explore the relationship between Self-confidence and Gender.
6. Another name of Intervening Variable is:
   A) Mediating Variable B) Intermediary Variable
   C) Both A as well as B D) None of the above.

7. Which of the following statement(s) is/are correct?
   A) Extraneous Variable is also called Confounding Variable.
   B) Confounding Variable is one type of Intervening Variable.
   C) Confounding Variables are in Survey Researches also.
   D) All of the above.
8. The researcher has to select a .... for Research.
   A) Problem B) Variable
   C) Both A or B D) Neither A nor B.
9. Which of the following is not a Source of Problem?
   A) Review of Literature
   B) Unutilised Theory
   C) Papers presented in Conferences
   D) Review of Related Literature.
10. Which of the following is the correct wording of Objective of Research?
    A) To compare Stress of Urban and Rural students.
    B) To study the differences in Stress of Urban and Rural students.
    C) To compare mean scores of Stress of Urban and Rural students.
    D) All of the above.
11. Which of the following is correct title of Experimental Research?
    A) Effect of Computer Aided Instruction on Achievement in English of Class VIII students
    B) Effectiveness of Computer Aided Instruction in terms of Achievement in English of Class VIII students of Central Schools of Delhi
    C) Influence of Computer Aided Instruction on Achievement in English of Class VIII students of Central Schools of Delhi
    D) All of the above.
12. Which of the following is the title of Historical Research?
    A) Education System during British Period
    B) A study of British Period in Australia
    C) Business System and British Period
    D) A study of School Curriculum during British Period in India
13. While studying Review of Related Literature one may come across:
    A) Inconsistencies in Findings of Researches.
    B) A few Researches have been conducted.
    C) No research has been conducted.
    D) All of the above.
14. Research Title must give information related to:
    A) Only Variable.
    B) Only Population.
    C) Variable, Population and Type of Research.
    D) Only Method of Research.
15. Philosophical Research Title must give information related to:
    A) Name of the Philosopher B) Name of Variable
    C) Both A as well as B D) None of the above.

3
Hypothesis

INTRODUCTION

By now you are in a position to write Research Title as well as Objectives. Objectives point out the types of data. In chapter-1, you have studied that there are two types of data-Qualitative Data and Quantitative Data. It is only the quantitative data that can be analysed with the help of statistical technique. So formulation of hypothesis will be the second step of research provided one is able to get quantitative data. After reading this chapter, you will be able to:

- Define Hypothesis.
- Write basis of formulating a Hypothesis.
- Differentiate between Research Hypothesis, Statistical Hypothesis and Operational Hypothesis.
- Formulate Research Hypothesis, Statistical Hypothesis and Operational Hypothesis for the given Objective in Null Form and Directional Form.
- Decide when to Formulate Hypothesis in Null Form and Directional Form.
- Justify the tense in which the Hypothesis is to be formulated.
- Define the Degree of Freedom and answer questions related to it.
- Define Level of Significance.
- Justify which level of significance is high and why.
- Test the given Hypothesis.
- Differentiate between One Tailed Test and Two Tailed Test.
- Differentiate between Type I Error and Type II Error.

DEFINITION OF HYPOTHESIS

Hypothesis can be defined in any of the three ways.

1. Hypothesis is the tentative solution of the problem.
2. Hypothesis is the intelligent guess about the solution of the problem.
3. Hypothesis is the conjectural statement about the relationship between variables.

From these definitions it is evident that hypothesis is not the final solution but a tentative one. To get the final solution, one has to test the hypothesis. For testing the hypothesis, statistical technique is to be used. So the data should be quantitative. In case the data are qualitative, hypothesis cannot be formulated because it cannot be tested with the help of statistical technique. On the other hand, if the qualitative data are converted into quantitative than hypothesis can be formulated because it can be tested with the help of statistical technique. Thus, formulation of hypothesis is the second step only in Correlational Survey Researches and Experimental Researches.

BASIS AND FORMS OF HYPOTHESIS

The researcher cannot state Hypothesis in any form he/she likes. There are basis of formulating a hypothesis. The basis will guide the researcher when to write hypothesis either in Null Form or Directional Form. The researcher has a choice to formulate any one of the three types of hypothesis but there are basis of formulating a hypothesis. The two major basis of formulating a Hypothesis are Review of Related Literature and Theory. Each one of these is detailed below.

1. Review of Related Literature: Here Literature means journals, e-Journals, dissertation abstract international (DAI), thesis, etc. and Related means the area of the research. For example, if a researcher wants to undertake research related to e-Marketing, than the researches conducted related to marketing will be reviewed. While reviewing researches one may find that no research has been conducted related to e-Marketing. Under such circumstances the researcher has to formulate Hypothesis in the Null Form (H_0). On the other hand, if a few researches have been conducted, it is difficult to give any direction as the base is not strong. Thus, under such situation also hypothesis should be stated in Null Form only.

In case large number, say 6000 researches have been conducted. There will be two options. Firstly, there might be consistency in findings. In this condition, no research will be conducted and so no need of formulating a hypothesis. Suppose there are inconsistencies in findings. For example, there is large number of researches where the Intelligence of Males and Females was compared. Suppose a researcher might find that 80% of researches reported that males were found to be significantly more intelligent as compared to females. In 5% researches, females were found to have significantly higher intelligence as compared to males and remaining 15% reported that both males and females were found to be equally intelligent. Under such a situation, the researcher has to formulate a hypothesis in Directional Form. The direction should be as evident from the findings of 80% of researches. There might be another situation where 40% of researches reported that males were found to be significantly more intelligent as compared to females. In 45% researches, females were found to have significantly higher intelligence as compared to males and remaining

15% reported that both males and females were found to be equally intelligent. In this situation no clear direction is forth coming. Hence, the researcher should formulate hypothesis in Null Form (H_0).

So on the basis of Review of Related Literature, the researcher will state hypothesis in Null Form (H_0) only as the base for Direction or Alternative Form is not be very strong. On the other hand, in case Review of Related Literature indicates the direction, the hypothesis should be formulated in the Directional form only. The direction has to be as reflected by the Review of Related Literature.

2. Related Theory: A researcher may undertake a research which is based on some theory. If a researcher wants to study the effect of Reward on Memorisation of Spellings by Grade 2 students, in this regard the Skinner's Theory of Operant Conditioning will be helpful in formulating hypothesis. The researcher should formulate hypothesis in Direction Form (H_1) only as Related Theory is the base. The hypothesis in Null Form cannot be stated.

Thus, there are two basis of formulating a hypothesis. These are Review of Related Literature and Related Theory. The two forms in which the hypothesis can be formulated are Null Form (H_0) and Directional Form (H_1). The hypothesis should be stated in the Present Tense as there are basis for formulating a hypothesis.

TYPES OF HYPOTHESIS

Hypotheses are of three types. These are Research Hypothesis, Statistical Hypothesis and Operational Hypothesis. These three types of hypothesis differ in wordings. The researcher can formulate any one of these but the statistical technique can test directly Statistical Hypothesis or Operational Hypothesis but not Research Hypothesis. The Research Hypothesis can be tested only through the Statistical Hypothesis. To understand the formulation of three Types of hypothesis, let us take one objective.

Suppose the Objective is: To compare mean scores of Stress of Male and Female College Teachers.

For the given *Objective*, the *Research Hypothesis* can be stated as:

- There is no significant relationship between Stress and Gender of College Teachers.

The *Statistical Hypothesis* can be stated as:

- There is no significant difference in mean scores of Stress of Male and Female College Teachers.

The *Operational Hypothesis* is stated as:

- There is no significant difference in mean scores of Stress of Male and Female College Teachers when Stress is assessed with the help of Stress Scale developed by XYZ.

Let us take second example. Suppose the Objective is: To compare mean scores of Hemoglobin of Urban and Rural Females of 25 years of age.

For the given *Objective*, the *Research Hypothesis* can be stated as:

- There is no significant relationship between Hemoglobin and Residential Background of Females of 25 years of age.

The *Statistical Hypothesis* can be stated as:

- There is no significant difference in mean scores of Hemoglobin of Urban and Rural Females of 25 years of age.

The *Operational Hypothesis* is stated as:

- There is no significant difference in mean scores of Hemoglobin of Urban and Rural Females of 25 years of age when Hemoglobin is tested in XYZ Pathology Lab.

Let us take third example. Suppose the Objective is: To study the correlation between Stress and Work Efficiency of IT Professionals.

For the given *Objective*, the *Research Hypothesis* can be stated as:

- There is no significant relationship between Stress and Work Efficiency of IT Professionals.

The *Statistical Hypothesis* can be stated as:

- There is no significant correlation between Stress and Work Efficiency of IT Professionals.

The *Operational Hypothesis* is stated as:

- There is no significant correlation between Stress and Work Efficiency of IT Professionals when Stress is assessed with the help of XYZ tool and Work Efficiency by LMP tool.

From above examples it is evident that in the statement of Research Hypothesis, "Relationship" word should be used. In Statistical Hypothesis, statistical words like "mean, correlation, multiple correlation, etc." should be used. The use of statistical words in the formulation of hypothesis differentiates Statistical Hypothesis from Research Hypothesis. Lastly, in case of Statistical Hypothesis, if the name of the tool to be used in collecting data is mentioned, it becomes Operational Hypothesis.

> ***Caution:*** *The researcher has to write only one type of hypothesis for one objective. It is only the statistical hypothesis in null form that can be directly tested with the help of statistical technique.*

TESTING OF HYPOTHESIS

The hypothesis can be tested through the use of statistical technique which requires quantitative data. In case there are qualitative data which can be converted into quantitative, the Hypothesis can be stated and tested. The quantitative data must satisfy the assumptions of the statistical technique to be used for analysing the given data. The assumptions to be satisfied by the statistical techniques have been given along with them in separate chapters of this book. To understand the testing of hypothesis, one must understand concepts, like, Degree of Freedom and Level of Significance. Without understanding them, one may not be able to explain as to how the hypothesis is to be tested.

Degree of Freedom: Freedom commonly means the total available options or alternatives. People cannot have infinite options. The options will be limited. So total available options or alternatives are always finite. By adding Degree, the Freedom should get reduced. That is, there are some restrictions. Thus, Degree of Freedom can be expressed as:

Degree of Freedom (df) = Total available options/alternatives – Total restrictions imposed

Philosophically no one in this world has complete freedom as there are rules which restrict the freedom. Everyone has to obey rules. Doing this will limit ones freedom. Hence, there is Degree of Freedom. In India while driving on road, one has to keep to left. This rule reduces ones Degree of Freedom. The traditions, religion, customs, etc. do limit the freedom of human beings. To understand it further, let us take one example. Choose any four numbers so that Mean = 4. What is the df? In this total options are 4 because one can choose any four numbers and the total restriction is 1 and that is of the Mean. Thus, df = 4–1 = 3.

Total restriction imposed cannot be equal to total available options. If so than there is no freedom. In the absence of freedom, there cannot be any Degree of Freedom (df). Thus, df cannot be zero. Further, Total options and total restrictions are always in whole number as these are counts or frequencies. Thus, conceptually the df will be in whole number. But mathematically df can be in fraction.

Level of Significance: Normally while travelling in a bus it is possible that one may hit someone. If the person who was hit says something to the person who hit him than the person says sorry. It means that the person did not hit intentionally but it was by chance. Sometimes we say that by chance he met me on the road. By chance it rained today. It means that the event may occur by chance or may not be by chance. *So the fine line which discriminates between occurrences of event by chance and not by chance is called Level of Significance.* Whenever the event occurs by chance, it means that it is due to some error. It is commonly observed that whenever we wash our hands with soap and see hands through microscope one may find some germs. It is due to some error. Sometime due to some error the rocket launching may fail. The source of error is not known beforehand. If known than people can make corrections to prevent the happening of error. It means errors are unavoidable. Therefore, scientists decided to allow maximum 5% error. It means that if a research is repeated 100 times without changing anything, than 95 times one may get same finding/result and 5 times the finding/result may differ which may be due to error. So this constitutes 5% Error and the Level of Significance will be 0.05. Similarly, if a research is repeated 100 times without changing anything, than 99 times one may get same finding/result and once the finding/result may differ which may be due to error. So this constitutes 1% Error and the Level of Significance will be 0.01.

Level of significance and % of Error are inversely related. That is, more the % of Error, low will be the Level of Significance and vice-versa. The Level of Significance indicates the percentage of error to be tolerated by the researcher at the time of testing the hypothesis. As mentioned earlier that the maximum allowed error is 5%. But the researcher may increase the allowed error as per the situation. Suppose a researcher is trying to develop a medicine for blood cancer. While trying out the medicine, he may find that amongst those who used the medicine for blood cancer, 60% of them survived. Should this medicine be made available to blood cancer patients in the absence of no other better medicine? I think most of the reader will agree that his medicine should be made available till the better one is made available. If so than the allowed percentage of error is 40% and the level of significance is 0.40. Normally, the maximum allowed error is 5% and level of significance is 0.05. In Science subjects the percentage of allowed error should be as low as the situation supports because the instruments are sensitive and better control.

To know the % of Error one has to analyse the data with the help of the appropriate statistical technique. One gets the value of the statistic. This value is to be compared with the appropriate value given in the statistical table under 0.05 level against the given df. For the given df, if the calculated value of the statistics is less than the table value, than the calculated value is not significant. On the other hand, for the given df, if the calculated value is equal to or greater than the table value given under 0.05 level but less than the table value given under 0.01 level, than the calculated Value is significant at 0.05 level because it contains error equal to or less than 5% but more than 1%. On the other hand, for the given df if the calculated value is equal to or greater than the table value given under 0.01 than the calculated value is significant at 0.01 level because it contains error equal to or less than 1%.

To understand it better, let us take one example as given below:

Suppose the *Objective* is: ***To compare mean scores of Stress of Male and Female College Teachers.***

For the given Objective, the Statistical Hypothesis in Null Form is: There is no significant difference in mean scores of Stress of Male and Female College Teachers.

Suppose the data are collected in respect of Stress from 70 Male Teachers and 52 Female Teachers. The data are analysed with the help of t-test and suppose t-value was found to be 1.12. This calculated t-value is compared with the Table t-value given against df = 70 + 52 − 2 = 120 under 0.05 and 0.01 Level of Significance. From t-Table 1, it can be seen that the Table t-values given against df = 120 under 0.05 and 0.01 Level of Significance are 1.980 and 2.617 respectively. The calculated t-value, that is, 1.12 is less than the Table value of 1.980 given under 0.05 level. Thus the calculated t-value has error more than 5%. So the calculated t-value is not significant at 0.05 level. It shows that the two calculated mean scores of Stress of Male and Females Teachers do not differ significantly. Therefore, the null hypothesis that there is no significant difference in mean scores of Stress of Male and Female College Teachers is not rejected. Once the researcher says that the Null Hypothesis is rejected or not rejected, it means the given Hypothesis has been tested.

Let us take another example: Suppose the Objective is: To compare mean scores of Hemoglobin of Urban and Rural Females of 25 years of age.

For the given Objective, the Statistical Hypothesis in Null Form is: There is no significant difference in mean scores of Hemoglobin of Urban and Rural Females of 25 years of age.

Suppose the data are collected in respect of *Hemoglobin* from 22 Urban Females and 20 Rural Females. The collected data are analysed with the help of t-Test and suppose t-value found to be 2.356. This calculated t-value is to be compared with the table t-value given against df = 22+20-2 = 40 under 0.05 and 0.01 Level of Significance. From Table 1, it can be seen that the table t-values given against df = 40 under 0.05 and 0.01 Level of Significance are 2.021 and 2.704 respectively. The calculated t-value, that is, 2.356 is greater than the table value 2.021 given under 0.05 level but less than the table value 2.704 given under 0.01 level. Thus, the calculated t-value has error less than 5% but more than 1%. So the calculated t-value is significant at 0.05 level. It shows that the two calculated mean scores of *Hemoglobin* of Urban Females and Rural Females differ significantly. Therefore, the null hypothesis that *there is no significant difference in mean scores of Hemoglobin of Urban and Rural Females of 25 years of age is rejected.* Once the researcher says that the null hypothesis is rejected or not rejected, it means the given hypothesis has been tested.

ONE TAILED TEST AND TWO TAILED TEST

As stated earlier that the Hypothesis can be formulated either in Null Form or Directional Form. Whenever the Hypothesis is formulated in Null Form, the 5%

error is to be equally divided into two Tails of the Normal Probability Curve. If so than this refers to the Two Tailed Test. On the other hand, whenever the whole error is kept on one side of the Tail, it is called One Tailed Test. Thus, at the time of testing the hypothesis in the Null Form, one has to compare the calculated statistical value with the table value given for the Two Tailed Test. In case the hypothesis is formulated in the Directional Form, one should compare the calculated statistical value with the table value given for the One Tailed Test. It is important to note that the formula used for calculating the statistical value will be the same for One Tailed Test and Two Tailed Test but the table values with which the calculated value is to be compared to know whether the calculated value is significant or not will differ. For the given df, the table value given under 0.05 level for Two Tailed Test will be higher than that given for One Tailed Test. This is because in One Tailed Test the whole error is on one side of the tail and the same error in divided in two equal parts in case of Two Tailed Test. Thus, less the error the higher will be the Table Value.

TYPE I ERROR AND TYPE II ERROR

To understand Type I Error and Type II Error, let us consider one hypothesis in the Null Form. Suppose the Statistical Hypothesis in Null Form is: *There is no significant difference in mean scores of Stress of Male and Female College Teachers.*

Suppose the data are collected in respect of *Stress* from 30 Males and 32 Females. The data are analysed with the help of t-Test and t-value is found to be 1.789. This calculated t-value is to be compared with the table t-value given against df = 30+32-2 = 60. From Table 1 (given in the appendix), it can be seen that the table t-value given against df = 60 under 0.05 level of significance is 2.000. The calculated t-value, that is, 1.789 is less than the Table Value of 2.000. Thus, the calculated t-value is *not significant.* It shows that the two mean scores of *Stress* of Males and Females do not differ significantly. So the hypothesis in Null Form should *not be rejected.* Thus, the finding is that both Males and Females were found to have *Stress* to the same extent. If the same t-value is compared with the Table t-value given under 0.1 level than from Table 1 it can be seen that against df = 60 under 0.1 level the Table value is 1.671. So the calculated t-value of 1.789 is greater than the Table Value of 1.671. Thus, the calculated t-value of 1.789 is significant at 0.1 level with df = 60. It indicates that the mean scores of *Stress* of Males and Females differ significantly. So the hypothesis in Null Form should *be rejected.* From here it can be said that t-value of 1.789 is not significant at 0.05 level but it is significant at 0.1 level. It means that a non-significant value can be made significant by increasing the error or lowering the level of significance. This is Type I Error. Thus, when the *Hypothesis in the Null Form should not be rejected but the researcher decides to reject it is called Type I Error or α-Error.*

Let us take another hypothesis to understand Type II Error. Suppose the Statistical Hypothesis in Null Form is: *There is no significant difference in mean scores of Hemoglobin of Urban and Rural Females of 25 years of age.*

Suppose the data are collected in respect of *Hemoglobin* from 22 Urban Females and 20 Rural Females. The collected data are analysed with the help of t-Test and suppose t-value is found to be 2.356. This calculated t-value is to be compared with the table t-value given against df = 22+20-2 = 40 under 0.05 and 0.01 Level of Significance. From Table 1, it can be seen that the table t-values given against df = 40 under 0.05 and 0.01 Level of Significance are 2.021 and 2.704 respectively. When df = 40, the calculated t-value, that is, 2.356 is greater than the Table Value 2.021 given under 0.05 level but less than the Table Value 2.704 given under 0.01 level. Thus, the calculated t-value has error less than 5% but more than 1%. So the calculated t-value is significant at 0.05 level. It shows that the two calculated mean scores of *Hemoglobin* of Urban Females and Rural Females differ significantly. Therefore, the null hypothesis that *there is no significant difference in mean scores of Hemoglobin of Urban and Rural Females of 25 years of age is rejected.* This is the result when the Hypothesis in the Null Form is tested by taking 0.05 Level of Significance. Suppose the researcher wants to test this Hypothesis at a higher level of significance, that is, 0.01 level. In this case the calculated t-value is to be compared with the Table t-value given at 0.01 level with df = 40. The Table value is 2.704 and the calculated t-value is 2.356. This calculated t-value is less than the Table t-value given under 0.01 level with df= 40. It means the calculated t-value is not significant at 0.01 level. It reflects that the two calculated mean scores of *Hemoglobin* of Urban Females and Rural Females do not differ significantly. Therefore, the null hypothesis that *there is no significant difference in mean scores of Hemoglobin of Urban and Rural Females of 25 years of age is not rejected.* From here it can be said that t-value of 2.356 is significant at 0.05 level but it is not significant at 0.01 level. It means that a significant value can be made non-significant by decreasing the error or increasing the level of significance. This is Type II Error. Thus, when the *Hypothesis in the Null Form should be rejected but the researcher decides not to reject it is called Type II Error or β-Error.*

Take a Test

1. In Statistical testing of Hypothesis, what happens to the region of rejection when the level of significance α is reduced?
   A) The answer depends of the value of β.
   B) The rejection region is reduced in size.
   C) The rejection region is increased in size.
   D) The rejection region is unaltered.
2. Which of the following is NOT correct?
   A) The probability of Type I Error is controlled by the selection of the level of significance α.

B) The probability of Type II Error is controlled by the sample size (n).
C) The power of a test depends on sample size and the distance between the Null Hypothesis and Alternative Hypothesis.
D) The p-value measures the probability that the Null Hypothesis is true.

3. In testing the Statistical Hypothesis which of the following statement(s) is false?
A) The p-value measures the probability that the Null Hypothesis is true.
B) The critical region is the value of the test statistics for which the Null Hypothesis is to be rejected.
C) The level of significance is the probability of Type I Error.
D) In testing $H_0 : \mu = \mu_0, H_1 : \mu \# \mu_0,$ the critical region is two sided.

4. Since α = the probability of Type I Error then $1-\alpha$
A) Probability of rejecting H_0 when H_0 is true.
B) Probability of not rejecting H_0 when H_0 is true.
C) Probability of not rejecting H_0 when H_1 is true.
D) Probability of rejecting H_0 when H_1 is true.

5. Which of the following statement is correct?
A) The p-value measures the probability that the hypothesis is true.
B) The p-value measures the probability of making Type II Error.
C) An extremely small p-value indicates that the actual data differ significantly from the expected if the Null Hypothesis is true.
D) The larger the p-value, the stronger the evidence against the Null Hypothesis.

6. The following are percentages of fat found in 5 Samples of each of two brands of baby food:
Sample 1: 5.7, 4.5, 6.3, 6.2, 7.3
Sample 2: 6.3, 5.7, 5.9, 6.4, 5.1
Which of the following statistical technique is appropriate to test the hypothesis of equal average fat content in the two type of ice cream?
A) Paired Samples t-test with df = 5.
B) Sign Test.
C) Paired Samples t-test with df = 4.
D) Independent Samples t-test with df = 8.

7. Rejection of Null Hypothesis is a conclusive proof that the Alternate Hypothesis is
A) True B) False
C) Neither True nor False D) None of the above

8. The level of significance can be viewed as the amount of risk that an analyst will accept when making a .... decision.
A) Correct B) Incorrect Decision
C) Correct or incorrect decision D) None of the above

9. By taking a level of significance of 5%, it is same as saying that
A) One is 5% confident that the results have not occurred by chance.
B) One is 95% confident that the results have not occurred by chance.
C) One is 95% confident that the results have occurred by chance.
D) None of the above is correct.

10. One or Two Tail test will determine
    A) If two extreme values of the sample need to be rejected.
    B) If the hypothesis has one or possibly two conclusions.
    C) If the region of rejection is located in one tail of the distribution.
    D) If the region of rejection is located in one or two tails of the distribution.
11. Two types of error associated with hypothesis testing are Type I and Type II. Type II error is committed when
    A) When one rejects the Null Hypothesis while the Alternate Hypothesis is true.
    B) One rejects the Null Hypothesis when it is true.
    C) One accepts the Null Hypothesis when it is not true.
    D) One accepts the Null Hypothesis when it is true.
12. Conjectural statement about the relationship between variables is called
    A) Hypothesis B) Hypothesis Testing
    C) Level of Significance D) None of the above
13. Any hypothesis which is tested for the purpose of rejection under the assumption that it is true is called
    A) Operational Hypothesis B) Directional Hypothesis
    C) Null Hypothesis D) Statistical Hypothesis
14. A statement about the value of a population parameter is called
    A) Null Hypothesis B) Statistical Hypothesis
    C) Directional Hypothesis D) Research Hypothesis
15. The probability of rejecting the Null Hypothesis when it is true is called
    A) Power of a test B) Confidence interval
    C) Level of significance D) Either B or C
16. Different types of Hypothesis are
    A) Statistical Hypothesis B) Research Hypothesis
    C) Operational Hypothesis D) All of the above
17. If the critical region is located equally on both sides of sampling distribution of test statistic, the test is called
    A) One Tailed Test B) Two Tailed Test
    C) Right Tailed Test D) Left Tailed Test
18. If H_0 is true and the researcher rejects it is called
    A) Type–I Error B) Type–II Error
    C) Neither of the above D) Any one of A or B
19. A failing student is passed by an examiner, it is an example of
    A) Difficult to tell B) Type–I Error
    C) Type–II Error D) Neither Type–I error nor Type–II Error

4
Sampling

INTRODUCTION

By now you might have understood how the Research Title and Objectives are to be worded. One has to collect data related to the variables of the research in hand. In case of Philosophical Researches one has to read the original writing of the person. For example, if someone wants to study the Educational System proposed by Mahatma Gandhi, this information one will get from the Mahatma Gandhi's writing about educational system. In Philosophical Research, one has to use only the original source to get the required data/information. On the other hand in Historical Researches, one can get the required data/information either from the primary source and/or secondary source. So there will be sampling of the required information only. The information about Primary Source and/or Secondary Source is being given in the chapter on Historical Research.

In Survey Research and Experimental Research, the researcher has to collect data from some portion of the population and so sampling has to be done. It is important for researchers to understand sampling. After reading this chapter, one will be able to:

- Differentiate between Universe and Population.
- Define Population, Sample, Frame, Sampling, Sampling Bias, and Sampling Error.
- Differentiate between Non-Probability Sampling and Probability Sampling.
- List different Non-Probability Sampling Techniques.
- List different Probability Sampling Techniques.
- Decide the Sampling Technique to be used in the research..
- List advantages and disadvantages of different Non-Probability as well as Probability Sampling Techniques.
- List points to be kept in mind while selecting a Sample.
- Decide the Sample Size required for the research.

UNIVERSE

Whatever exists on this planet is the part of Universe. The universe comprised different populations, such as, population of plants, population of animals, population of minerals, population of chemicals, population of people, etc. It means universe is heterogeneous. Each researcher has to have well defined small portion of the universe for the study.

POPULATION

Well defined small portion of the Universe is called Population. In Survey Research as well as Experimental Research, the researcher has to define the population in terms of its characteristics. If the population size is not too large, one can take the whole population. That is, one may collect data from each and every member of the population. In case the population size is too large, then it is not possible to collect data from each member of the population. Under such circumstances, one has to take a small portion of the population.

SAMPLE

Well defined small representative portion of the Population is called Sample. It is not possible to have a sample which truly represents the population. Only in case of homogeneous population, it is possible to have a sample which truly represents the population. In majority of researches sample may not truly represent the population.

FRAME

Listing all members of the Population is called a Frame or Sampling Frame. There are situations where it is possible to make a list of all members of the population but there might be situations where it is not possible to list all members of the population. Let us take an example. Suppose a researcher wants to study the daily routine of Drug addicts of New Delhi. It is not possible to make a list of all drug addicts of New Delhi because there is no source from where the information about all drug addicts is available. It is not possible to know the total number of drug addicts of New Delhi. Thus, in case of drug addicts, Frame is not available.

Let us take another example. Suppose one wants to study Problems of Street Children of Pune. There is no demarcated area where all street children are found. In this case also it is not possible to make a list of all street children of Pune. It is not possible to know the total number of street children of Pune. Thus, the Frame is not available.

Let us consider another situation. Suppose one wants to compare Study Habits of Male and Female Students of Class IX of Government Schools of Indore. In this case, it is possible to make the list of all male and female students of Class IX studying in government schools of Indore. However, listing all male and female students of Class IX studying in government schools of Indore may take more time. So, the researcher can find the total number of male and female students of Class IX studying in Government Schools of Indore. Thus, in this case the Frame is available.

Suppose one wants to study the Stress of Middle Level Managers of IT Sector of Bangalore. It is possible to list all Middle Level Managers working in different IT organizations, like, TCS, Wipro, E & Y, Dell, Apple, etc. situated in Bangalore. So the researcher can find the total number of Middle Level Managers of IT Sector of Bengaluru. Thus, the Frame is available in this case also.

Thus, the researcher may have a Frame or may not have a Frame for the research.

SAMPLING

Sampling refers to the procedure of selecting sample from the Population.

SAMPLING BIAS

Sampling Bias refers to situation where the sample does not reflect the characteristics of the target Population.

SAMPLING TECHNIQUES

Sampling refers to the procedure of selecting sample from the population. In researches the size of population is known but in some researches the size of population is not known. In other words, the researcher may have a Frame or may not have a Frame for the research. In case the Frame is not known, the Sampling Technique to be used is called Non-Probability Sampling. On the other hand, if the Frame is known, then the Sampling Technique is called Probability Sampling. Thus, the Sampling Techniques are classified into two categories—Non-Probability Sampling and Probability Sampling.

> ***Caution:*** *Researchers should not use both Non-Probability Sampling and Probability Sampling Techniques in a research.*

Non-Probability Sampling Techniques

Non-Probability Sampling Technique is to be used only if it is impossible to list all members of the population. That is, frame is not available. Different Non-Probability Sampling Techniques available are as follows:

- Purposive Sampling
- Judgement Sampling
- Convenience Sampling
- Quota Sampling
- Snowball Sampling

Purposive Sampling is Non-Probability Sampling Technique where sample is selected based on the knowledge of a population and the purpose of the study. The subjects are selected because of some characteristic. Field researchers are interested in studying extreme or deviant cases—that is, cases that do not fit into regular pattern of attributes and behaviours. By studying the deviant cases, researcher can often gain a better understanding of the more regular pattern of behaviour. So it should be used when one wants to access a particular sub-set of people. A researcher may have a specific group in mind, such as, high level business executive; toppers in the university examination; workplace packages that include dental benefits; etc. In such researches, one can use Purposive Sampling Technique.

One research title where sample is selected with the help of Purposive Sampling Technique is as given below:

➢ A Study of Study Habits of Distinction Holders in Mathematics of Class XII students of Central School, No. I of Indore

For this study, the sample will comprise only students of Class XII of Central School, No.1, Indore who got distinction in Mathematics. Students of Class XII of the same school getting distinction in other subjects will not be the part of the sample. For this research, the researcher has to use only Purposive Sampling Technique. While selecting the sample, reject subjects who do not fit a particular profile or sub-set of subjects. In case study researches, only Purposive Sampling Technique is the most appropriate to be used.

Advantages of Purposive Sampling Technique

1. It ensures balance of group sizes when multiple groups are to be selected.
2. It is appropriate for qualitative research.
3. It is easy to use.
4. It is less costly.
5. It is less time consuming.
6. It ensures high participation rate.
7. Generalisation is possible to similar subjects.
8. It adds credibility to qualitative research.
9. Assures receipt of needed information.

Disadvantages of Purposive Sampling Technique

1. It can be subject to bias and error.
2. Samples are not easily defensible as being representative of population due to potential subjectivity of researcher.
3. It is difficult to generalise to other subjects.
4. Less representative of an identified population.
5. Findings dependent on unique characteristics of the sample.

Judgement Sampling is Non-Probability Sampling Technique where researcher selects subjects to be sampled based on their knowledge or professional judgement. It is used when a sample is taken based on certain judgements about the overall population. The underlying assumption is that the researcher will select subjects that are characteristic of the population. The critical issue here is Objectivity: how much can judgement be relied upon to arrive at a typical sample?

It is the only viable sampling technique to be used in obtaining information from a very specific group of people. It is also possible to use judgement sampling if the researcher knows a reliable professional or authority that one thinks is capable of assembling a representative sample. The researcher uses one's own judgement to select what seems like an appropriate sample. This sampling technique is often used in exploratory studies. Researchers also prefer to use this method in laboratory settings where the choice of experimental subjects (i.e. animal, plants, vegetable, human, etc.) reflects the researcher's pre-existing beliefs about the population.

Further, sampling is not done on a random basis. There is no determination of a sampling error, nor any statistical conclusions about precision or confidence level.

To understand it further, let us consider the following title of the research.

➢ A Study of Causes of Unrest among Teachers of Aligarh Muslim University

In this study the researcher may like to collect information from Vice-Chancellor, Registrar, and executive members of Teacher's Association of Aligarh Muslim University because these may be able to give the relevant information. So these will be the members of the sample. Thus, in this case Judgement Sampling Technique may be used for selecting sample.

Advantages of Judgement Sampling Technique

1. It is easy to understand and use.
2. No special knowledge of statistics is required.
3. It is time saving.
4. It is not costly.

Disadvantages of Judgement Sampling Technique

1. It is unscientific.
2. It is wasteful and usually too large samples are selected.
3. One cannot extrapolate the results to the population as a whole as the samples are not representative.
4. Personal bias in selecting the sample is unavoidable.
5. There is no logic to the selection of the sample or its size.
6. The sample selection is too erratic that it cannot be said to have applied to all members of the population in the year.

7. The conclusions reached are usually vague.
8. Low level of reliability.

Convenience Sampling is a Non-Probability Sampling Technique where subjects are selected because of ease of their availability and proximity to the researcher. If a researcher has to complete the study in short time, Convenience Sampling is mostly used and therefore the sample may not be sufficiently representative of the entire population. Some time for Survey researches one may use Convenience Sampling Technique and may collect data from the neighborhood. To understand it further, let us consider the following title of the research.

- A Study of Quality of Treatment given by Doctors in Clinics Situated in R.K. Puram, New Delhi

R.K. Puram is vastly spread and divided into large number of sectors. In each sector there are many clinics. If the researcher stays in R.K. Puram Sector 3, he may collect data about quality of treatment from patients of Sharma Clinic of Sector 3 because it is near to his home and easy to approach the patients who come to Sharma Clinic for the treatment. For such studies, Convenience Sampling Technique may be used for selecting sample.

Advantages of Convenience Sampling Technique

1. The availability and quickness with which the data can be collected.
2. It is inexpensive.
3. It is easy to use and subjects are easily available.
4. Participation rate is high.

Disadvantages of Judgement Sampling Technique

1. The sample does not represent the population as a whole so results cannot speak of the whole population.
2. It might be biased by volunteers.
3. It is less representative of an identified population.
4. Results dependent on unique characteristics of the sample.

Quota Sampling is a Non-probability Sampling Technique where researcher selects subjects according to some fixed quota. That is subjects are selected on the basis of pre-specified characteristics so that the total sample has the same distribution of characteristics assumed to exist in the population being studied. In India, quota system exists for admission in schools and colleges, in jobs, etc. The quota is decided by the government. At the time of admission in colleges, students belonging to different castes are admitted as per the quota fixed by the government. If researcher decides to select subjects belonging to different castes, he may select them on the basis of quota.

In Quota Sampling, the researcher wants to represent the major characteristics of the population by sampling a proportional amount of each characteristic. Suppose a researcher wants to obtain a proportional Quota Sample of 100 college students based on gender. First, one needs to find out the proportion of population of males and the proportion of population of females. This information is available from the office. From the record available in the office of the college, if one finds from the admitted students that 40% are females and 60% males. One starts sampling and continues until one gets those proportions as decided earlier and then one should stop. If one gets 40 females for the sample, but not 60 males, one will continue to sample males and discard any legitimate female respondents that come along. One does not need females because one has already met the quota. One has to decide in advance the specific characteristics on which the researcher will base the quota. Quota can be as per gender, age, education, religion, etc.

Suppose one wants to conduct a study whose title is as given below:

- A Study of Job Preferences of Males and Females Post Graduate Students of Government Arts and Commerce College, Indore

From the office of Government Arts and Commerce College, Indore the number of post graduate students can be obtained and proportions of male and female students can be worked out. Suppose there are 300 postgraduate students of which females are 30% and males 70%. As a researcher you decide to take only 100 postgraduate students, then one has to collect information from 30 female students and 70 male students of postgraduate courses. The researcher can stand at the main gate of the Government Arts and Commerce College, Indore and stop student to find out whether he/she belongs to the desired population. If yes, than the required information about job preferences and the gender are collected. The researcher will continue till the required information is collected from 30 female students and 70 male students. The sample thus obtained is through the use of Quota Sampling Technique.

Advantages of Quota Sampling Technique

1. It is less costly.
2. It is less time consuming.
3. It is easy to use.
4. It ensures high participation rate.
5. It ensures more representative of population than Purposive or Convenience Sampling Technique.

Disadvantages of Quota Sampling Technique

1. It is more time consuming than Purposive or Convenience Sampling Technique.
2. Less representative of an identified population.

3. The selection of subjects within a given category of the quota may be biased even though the proportion of the population is accurately calculated.
4. Results depend on the unique characteristics of the sample.
5. One cannot generalise from the findings.

Snowball Sampling is a Non-probability Sampling Technique that is used by researchers to identify the potential subjects in studies where subjects are hard to locate or very rare or limited to a very small subgroup of population. This type of sampling works like chain referral. Once the researcher gets one subject who belongs to subgroup of the population, then this subject helps in identifying another subject with the similar characteristics. This chain continues till the researcher gets the required number of subjects. To understand it further, let us consider the following title of the research.

➢ A Study of Home related Problems of Illegal Drug Users of Lucknow

There is no one place or colony where all Illegal Drug Users are staying in Lucknow. It is hard to locate them. If the researcher finds one Illegal Drug User, the information about Home related Problems is collected. After collecting the information, he may be requested to give reference of other Illegal Drug Users known to him. After knowing about other Illegal Drug Users, the required information about home related problems may be collected. This process may continue till one gets the desired number of Illegal Drug User. For the problem, Snowball Sampling Technique has been used for selecting Sample. Snowball Sampling Technique is very useful in Social Works subject.

Advantages of Snowball Sampling Technique

1. It helps in locating hidden population.
2. It helps in locating people with specific population (i.e. homeless, users of illegal drugs, street children, etc.)
3. It is less costly.

Disadvantages of Snowball Sampling Technique

1. It is inexact and can provide varied and inaccurate results.
2. Sample is not selected randomly.
3. It is inevitable in social system.
4. There is no way to know the total size of the population.
5. The lack of definite knowledge as to whether or not the sample is an accurate reading of the target population.
6. Lack of control over the sampling method.

Probability Sampling Techniques

Probability Sampling Technique is to be used only if it is possible to list all members of the population. That is, if frame is available. Probability Sampling Technique can be used for selecting sample from the population. Different Probability Sampling Techniques available are as follows:

- Random Sampling
- Systematic Sampling
- Stratified Random Sampling
- Stratified Proportionate Random Sampling
- Cluster Sampling
- Multistage Sampling

Population of the research might be widely spread or not widely spread. In case the population is not widely spread, the population might be homogeneous or heterogeneous. Whenever the population of the research is homogeneous and not widely spread, Random Sampling and Systematic Sampling are the most appropriate sampling techniques to be used. On the other hand, if the population of the research is heterogeneous and not widely spread, Stratified Random Sampling or Stratified Proportionate Random Sampling is the most appropriate sampling technique to be used. If the population is widely spread, the most appropriate sampling techniques to be used are Cluster Sampling and Multistage Sampling. Let us understand each of Probability Sampling Techniques one by one.

Random Sampling Technique is useful only if the population is homogeneous and not widely spread. Also the frame must be available. Let us take one research title as mentioned in Chapter 2. The same is reproduced here for the benefit of readers.

- A Study of Stress in Relation to Anxiety, Tension and Monthly Expenses of College Teachers of Lucknow, Uttar Pradesh

From the research title it is evident that the population is all college teachers of Lucknow. Here it is possible to make a list of all college teachers of Lucknow. So the population is homogeneous and not widely spread. Thus, Random Sampling Technique is the most appropriate for selecting sample.

There are different ways of selecting sample through Random Sampling Technique. These are as given below:

- Fish Bowl or Chit or Lottery Procedure
- Random Number Table
- Computer Generated Random Numbers

Fish Bowl or Chit Procedure is more useful when the size of population is not too large so that it is not difficult to make chit for each and every member of the population. One can use common sense to decide whether it is possible and easy to make chit for each and every member of the population. All chits must be identical in respect of size, colour, folds, and shape so that there is no biasing in selecting member from the population of the research. Suppose the population size is 100. The researcher wants to select only 30 members out of 100 members of population. One can give serial numbers and write each serial number on a separate chit. Fold the chit and keep it in a container. In this way fold all 100 chits separately and keep all of them in a container. The container must be big enough to accommodate all the 100 chits. Now shake well the container so that all chits are mixed up. Now take out one chit and write its number on a separate paper. Suppose the number of the selected chit is 42. So the member of the population having Serial number 42 has been selected and is the member of sample. The probability of selecting chit number 42 is 1/100. Refold the chit and keep it in the same container along with the other chits so that the number of chits in the container remains 100. Shake the container so that all chits are mixed up. Now take out another chit from the container. Suppose this time the chit having serial number 4 is selected. The probability of selecting chit having serial number 4 is also 1/100. Thus, the researcher has so far selected two members for the sample out of a population of 100 members. These two selected members have serial numbers 42 and 4. Repeat this procedure till you get all 30 members from the population of 100. In this case after selecting the member, the chit is to be replaced back so that the total chits remain same in the container. If the number of total chits is the same, the probability of selecting each member is also the same. It is possible that during this process, the same chit appears again and again. This has to be ignored because it has already been included in the sample. In this way one can use chit technique to select the sample from the given population. This is selection by replacement where probability of selecting each member remains same. If the population size is too large, then chit technique is not very useful for selecting sample from the large population. In case of large population size, it is better to use Random Number Table for selecting sample of required size.

Random Number Table is one where each digit from 0 to 9 appears equal number of times in rows as well as columns. It is very useful for selecting sample from a large homogeneous population. To start with, each and every member of the population is to be numbered. One may start numbering each member of the population from any number. It is not compulsory to start numbering them from serial number 1. One may start from zero also. The population members need not to be arranged in any sequence. One may number them as they appear. Suppose one wants to select 500 Class IX students from a population of 10,000 students. As a researcher if you want to use chit method in this case, then you may find that it is very difficult to make 10,000 chits. So the lottery or chit procedure is not appropriate when the population size is large. For selecting sample from large population, one may use Random Number Table.

To start with, each member of the population is to be numbered. The researcher can identify the member of the population from its serial number. Suppose one wants to select 50 members from a population of 589. The Random Number Table is to be used. One assigns number starting from 1 and the last number is 589. One has to decide the number of rows or columns to be used. Here the last number is of three digits, so one may start using either the three rows or columns. If one uses only one column at a time then one always gets one digit number, the members having serial numbers in two or three digits can never be selected. Thus, total number of rows or columns to be considered at a time depends upon the total number of digits of the last serial number. Suppose one decides to use columns. One can start using any three columns of Random Number Table because the last serial number is 589 which is of three digits. A sample of Random Number Table is given in Table 4.1.

Table 4.1: Random Number Table

7	3	7	3	5	4	5	9	6	3	7	8	1	3	4	6	3	8	7	3
0	2	9	6	5	5	8	3	0	3	9	0	7	0	8	2	0	0	2	5
9	8	8	5	9	2	3	8	5	1	2	7	9	6	5	6	2	3	9	4
3	3	6	6	6	6	2	5	7	0	6	4	7	7	5	7	8	4	2	8
8	1	6	6	6	2	6	4	4	0	2	0	4	2	2	0	5	7	2	0
1	5	8	3	8	4	7	1	7	4	7	6	8	6	6	1	4	3	3	0
8	9	7	9	3	3	4	3	7	8	0	8	7	3	0	5	6	5	2	2
7	8	1	5	5	2	2	4	6	6	8	1	9	7	8	5	7	3	2	3
1	6	3	8	1	6	6	2	0	7	1	1	6	9	8	9	9	3	1	4
7	5	0	0	2	8	0	8	2	7	5	3	8	6	7	3	7	7	9	7
9	9	9	8	2	2	7	6	0	1	6	2	6	8	6	4	4	7	1	1
8	4	5	4	3	8	7	4	4	2	5	0	0	3	3	1	4	0	2	1
7	7	7	5	7	5	4	0	4	3	4	6	1	7	6	4	2	3	9	1
8	0	8	7	1	3	2	7	9	2	8	7	9	8	9	7	2	2	4	8
3	0	5	0	0	2	8	2	2	0	1	2	4	4	4	7	1	8	4	0

One can select any column and starts from anywhere. Suppose one decides to use 2, 3 and 4 columns and starts from fourth number which is 366. The member at serial number 366 is selected and is a part of the sample. The next number in the sequence is 166. The member at serial number 166 is also selected. The next number in the sequence is 583; the member with serial number 583 is also selected. So the sample has members with serial numbers 366; 166 and 583. Next number in the sequence is 979. There is no member with serial number 979. Thus, 979 number is to be ignored. Further there are no members with serial numbers 815 as well as 638. One has to leave these serial numbers. The member with serial number 500 is selected for the sample. The next serial number is 998. It should also be ignored. The members having serial numbers 454, 087 and 050 are also included in the sample. So far sample will have members with serial numbers 366; 166; 583; 500; 454; 087 and 050. Like this one can continue using the columns till the end and after that one can continue with next three columns. In this case one can start using 5, 6 and 7 columns. The member with serial number 545 is also selected. Now the members with serial numbers 366; 166; 583; 500; 454; 087; 050 and 545 will be members of the sample. Like this one should continue using Random Number Table till one selects the required number. In this example, one wanted 50 members but so far only eight members have been selected for the sample. Thus, one should continue using Random Number Table till one gets a Sample of 50 which is the required number decided by the researcher.

Computer Generated Random Numbers is way to generate random numbers with the help of Computers. There are many software's available for generating random numbers. One can use Google for searching the software. In Google one can type "Computer Generated Random Numbers Table" and a list of different sites will appear. One may choose Random Number Generator/Random Number Table. It will require the following information.

- How many random numbers?
- Minimum value
- Maximum vale
- Allow duplicate entries: True/False

After giving the above required information, one can click on calculate. This software will calculate the required numbers for the sample.

There are other software available for Computer Generated Random Numbers, such as, Stat Trek's Random Number Generator; GraphPad Software, etc. Anyone can be used.

Advantages of Random Sampling Technique

1. It represents the target population and eliminates sampling bias.
2. Easy to analyse and interpret results.
3. It is easy to understand and use.

Disadvantages of Random Sampling Technique

1. It is very difficult to use when the population is too large and widely spread.
2. It requires numbering of each subject in the population.
3. Larger sampling error as compared to stratified random sampling.
4. It is time consuming.
5. It is costly.

6. Minority subgroups of interest in population may not be present in the sample in sufficient number.

Systematic Sampling is to be used only if the given population is logically homogeneous, because systematic sample units are uniformly distributed over the population. It is a Probability Sampling Method in which sample members from a larger population are selected according to a random starting point and a fixed periodical interval. This interval, called sampling interval, is calculated by dividing the population size by the desired sample size. The researcher must ensure that the chosen sampling interval does not hide a pattern. Any pattern would threaten randomness. Despite the sampling population being selected in advance, systematic sampling is still thought of as being random provided the periodic interval is determined beforehand and the starting point is random.

Suppose More Supermarket wants to study buying habits of their customers, then using Systematic Sampling they can choose either 10th or 15th customer entering the More Supermarket and conduct the study on this sample.

Let us take another example to understand the procedure of selecting sample through the use of Systematic Sampling Technique. Suppose one wants to understand about the career goals of students at University of Mumbai, Mumbai. Let us say that the University of Mumbai has about 10,000 students. These 10,000 students is the researcher population (N). In order to select a Sample (n) of students, one may use Systematic Sampling Technique. Suppose one wants to select 400 students. The sample size is 400 and is denoted by n. This is chosen because it reflects the limit of researcher budget and time. The researcher has the list of students enrolled in different Departments of University of Mumbai. Each student is assigned consecutive number from 1 to N, next to each of the students. In this case one will assign a consecutive number from 1 to 10,000 (i.e. N = 10,000, population of students at University of Mumbai). Assuming that one has to choose a sample size of 400 students, the sampling starts by selecting a subject from the list at random and then every kth subject from frame is selected, where k is the sampling interval and is calculated as given below:

$$k = N/n = 10000/400 = 25,$$

where n is the sample size and N the population size

It means that every 25th student from the population of 10,000 students at the University of Mumbai is to be selected. One needs to select the first student, which starts the process of selecting sample. Suppose the first student selected is 10th on the list of 10,000. The second student will be 35th, fourth student 60th, next 85th, etc. Now continue like this till one gets 400 students from the list of 10,000 students. This is how a sample is selected using Systematic Sampling Technique.

Since Systematic Sampling is a Probability Sampling, one must ensure that all members of the population have equal chance of being selected as the starting point or the interval subject.

One must be certain that the chosen constant interval between subjects do not reflect a certain pattern of traits present in the population. If a pattern in the population exists and it coincides with the interval set by the researcher, randomness of the Sampling Technique is compromised.

One risk when using Systematic Sampling involves how the list used with the sampling interval is organised. If the population placed on the list is organised in a cyclical pattern that matches the sampling interval, the selected sample may be biased.

Advantages of Systematic Sampling Technique

1. It is simple to use.
2. It allows the researcher to add a degree of system or process into the random selection of subjects.
3. The population is evenly sampled.
4. Selected sample usually represents the population.
5. There exists a chance of Random Sampling that allows a clustered selection of subjects. This is systematically eliminated in Systematic Sampling.

Disadvantages of Systematic Sampling Technique

1. The process of selection can interact with a hidden periodic trait within the population.
2. If sampling technique coincides with the periodicity of the trait, the Sampling Technique will no longer be random and representative of the sample is compromised.

Stratified Random Sampling Technique is useful only if the population is heterogeneous and not widely spread. Let us take a Research Title and its Objectives as mentioned in Chapter 2. The same is reproduced here for the readers benefit.

➢ A Comparative Study of Stress of Male and Female students of Class IX of Government Schools of Indore

For this title following objectives can be written:

1. To compare adjusted mean scores of Stress of Male and Female students by considering Anxiety as covariate.
2. To study the influence of Gender, Residential Background and their interaction on Stress of students.
3. To study the influence of Gender, Residential Background, Monthly Income and their various interactions on Stress of students.

From the title it is evident that the population is Male and Female Students of Class IX of Government Schools of Indore and suppose it is 10,000. From Objectives 1 to 3, it is evident that the sample should represent Gender, Residential Background and Monthly Income. This means that the population should be first split on the basis of Gender. Suppose out of 10,000 students, there are 6000 male students and 4000 female students. Both male and female population should be divided on the basis of Residential Background. Out of 6000 male students, 4000 male students are from urban area and 2000 male students from rural area. Similarly, out of 4000 female students, 2000 female students belong to urban area and 2000 female students belong to rural area. So far the population has been divided into four strata. These are Urban Males; Rural Males; Urban Females and Rural Females. Each stratum is further divided on the basis of Monthly Income. Suppose students belong to Middle and Low Income Groups. Out of 4000 Urban Males, there are 2000 Urban Males belonging to Middle Income Group and 2000 Urban Males to Low Income Group. Out of 2000 Rural Males, there are 500 Rural Males belong to Middle Income Group, and 1500 Rural Males belong to Low Income Group. Similarly, out of 2000 Urban Females, 1000 Urban Females belong to Middle income Group and another 1000 Urban Females belong to Low Income Group. Lastly, out of 2000 Rural Females, 500 Rural Females belong to Middle Income Group and remaining 1500 Rural Females belong to Low Income Group. In this way there are eight strata. The population distribution in eight strata are 2000 Urban Males Middle Income Group; 2000 Urban Males Low Income Group; 500 Rural Males Middle Income Group; 1500 Rural Males Low Income Group; 1000 Urban Females Middle Income Group; 1000 Urban Females Low Income Group; 500 Rural Females Middle Income Group; and 1500 Rural Females Low Income Group. In terms of percentages, the Population comprised of 20% Urban Males Middle Income Group; 20% Urban Males Low Income Group; 5% Rural Males Middle Income Group; 15% Rural Males Low Income Group; 10% Urban Females Middle Income Group; 10% Urban Females Low Income Group; 5% Rural Females Middle Income Group; and 15% Rural Females Low Income Group. Out of 10,000 students, one wants a Sample of 2000 students. Thus, this will comprise 400 Urban Male Middle Income students; 400 Urban Male Low Income students; 100 Rural Male Middle Income students; 300 Rural Male Low Income students; 200 Urban Female Middle Income students; 200 Urban Female Low Income students; 100 Rural Female Middle Income students; and 300 Rural Male Low Income students. Now after dividing the population into eight strata, in the present example, one selects students randomly from each stratum as each stratum is homogeneous. This selection is in proportion to each stratum in the population. Hence, it is called *Stratified Proportionate Random Sampling Technique.*

On the other hand if the researcher decides to select equal number of subjects from each stratum, the procedure is *Stratified Random Sampling*

Technique. In the present example, a researcher wants to select 2000 students belonging to eight Strata. From each stratum one has to select 250 students randomly. Here one has selected 2000 students out of 10,000 students using Stratified Random Sampling Technique.

Advantages of Stratified Random Sampling Technique:

1. The sample should be highly representative of the target population.
2. One can generalise from the results obtained.
3. It can provide greater precision than Random Sample of the same size.
4. Because it provides greater precision, a Stratified Random Sample often requires a smaller sample, which saves money.

Disadvantages of Stratified Random Sampling Technique:

1. It is time consuming and difficult.
2. It may require more administrative effort than Random Sampling.
3. It is not useful when the population cannot be exhaustively partitioned into disjoint subgroups.

Cluster Sampling is very useful when the population is wide spread and normally divided into well-defined clusters or groups. India is divided into States and Union Territories. There are 29 States and seven Union territories. Suppose one wants to conduct a research where Principals of Middle Schools of whole India is the population. In this research one cannot use Random Sampling Technique and Stratified Random Sampling Technique for selecting Principals because it is impossible to list all Principals of Middle Schools of India. India has been divided into well-defined states and the list of states is available. From the list of states, one can select one or more states or clusters randomly and all Principals of Middle Schools within the chosen cluster(s) are the member of sample. In this situation Cluster Sampling Technique is the most appropriate to be used for selecting sample.

Further the population within a cluster should ideally be as heterogeneous as possible, but there should be homogeneity between cluster means. Each cluster should be a small-scale representation of the total population. The clusters should be mutually exclusive and collectively exhaustive. A Random Sampling Technique is then used to select clusters from which the subjects should be included in the study. In single stage cluster sampling, all subjects from each of the selected clusters are part of the sample to be used for conducting the research. In two-stage Cluster Sampling, a Random Sampling technique is used to further select subjects randomly from the selected subjects.

The main difference between Cluster Sampling and Stratified Sampling is that in Cluster Sampling the cluster is treated as the sampling unit so analysis is done on population of clusters (at least in the first stage). In the Stratified

Random Sampling, the analysis is done on subjects within strata. In Stratified Random Sampling, a random sample is drawn from each of the strata, whereas in Cluster Sampling only the subjects of selected clusters are studied. The main objective of Cluster Sampling is to reduce cost by increasing sampling efficiency. This contrasts with Stratified Random Sampling where the main objective is to increase precision.

To understand the whole process of Cluster Sampling Technique, let us take the following title:

➢ A Study of Problems in Managing Mid-day Meal by Principals of Middle Schools of Madhya Pradesh State

From the above mentioned research title, it is evident that the population for this research is Principals of Middle Schools of Madhya Pradesh State. Madhya Pradesh comprised 48 Districts. The Middle Schools are in each and every District. As the population for this research is wide spread, so Cluster Sampling Technique is the most appropriate for selecting sample. As the list of Districts is available, so to start with the Districts are selected randomly. Madhya Pradesh has 48 Districts. From these Districts, say 15 Districts are selected randomly. From each selected District, Principals of all Middle Schools are members of the sample. This is the first stage of selecting sample using Cluster Sampling Tcchnique. Sometime if the Sample size is large, one can further select Principals randomly from the selected districts. This is the second stage of Cluster Sampling Technique. One should not go beyond the two stages. If one goes beyond two stages, Cluster Sampling Technique in no longer applicable. Another Sampling Technique known as Multistage Sampling Technique is to be used.

Although Cluster Sampling and Stratified Random Sampling bear some superficial similarities, they are substantially different. In Stratified Random Sampling, a random sample is drawn from all the strata, where in Cluster Sampling only the selected clusters are studied, either in single or two stages.

Advantages of Cluster Sampling Technique

1. Generating sampling frame for Clusters is economical, and sampling frame is often readily available at Cluster level.
2. Most economical form of sampling.
3. Larger sample for a similar fixed cost.
4. Less time for listing and implementation.
5. Also suitable for survey of institutions.

Disadvantages of Cluster Sampling Technique

1. The sample may not reflect the diversity of the population.
2. Other elements in the same cluster may share similar characteristics.
3. Provides less information per observation than Stratified Random Sampling of the same size.

4. Standard errors of the estimates are high as compared to other sampling techniques with the same sample size.

Multistage Sampling is very useful when the population is wide spread and it is not possible to list all members of the sampling unit. It is a complex form of Cluster Sampling. Cluster Sampling is a type of sampling which involves dividing the population into groups or clusters. Then one or more clusters are chosen at random and everyone within the chosen cluster is sampled. Cluster Sampling sometime involves selecting samples in two stages but Multistage Sampling involves more than two stages of selecting sample.

To understand the whole process of Multistage Sampling Technique, let us take the same title which was used for explaining Cluster Sampling Technique:

- A Study of Problems in Managing Mid-day Meal by Principals of Middle Schools of Madhya Pradesh State

In this study the sampling unit is Principals of Middle Schools of Madhya Pradesh State. To select the sample of Principals of Middle Schools, first one should select Districts. Suppose one decides to select 15 Districts randomly out of 48 Districts. From the selected Districts, one may not be able to take all Principals of Middle Schools as the number is too large. At first stage Districts are selected randomly. At the second stage, the Middle Schools from selected Districts are selected randomly. From Principals of selected Middle Schools, the Principals are selected randomly. This is how the sample of Principals of Middle Schools is selected in three stages. In this case the sample is selected using Multistage Sampling. In Multistage Sampling, after having selected Principals randomly, one can divide the Sample of Principals as per their gender, namely, males and females. At the fourth stage one can use Stratified Random Sampling Technique. Thus, during the process of selecting sample through the use of Multistage Sampling, one can also use Stratified Random Sampling Technique at the appropriate stage. Thus, Multistage Sampling Technique involves selecting sample randomly in more than two stages.

Advantages of Multistage Sampling Technique

1. It is cost effective.
2. It is feasible.
3. It is easy to find sampling unit.
4. It is normally more accurate than Cluster Sampling of the same size.

Disadvantages of Multistage Sampling Technique

1. It is not as accurate as Random Sampling Technique, if sample is of same size.
2. More testing is difficult to do.
3. Further analysis is difficult.

Points Kept in Mind while Selecting a Sample

The researcher must keep the following points in mind while selecting a Sample from the Population.

1. The subjects of the study should be clearly described, and the description should be specific and detailed. The demographic characteristics of subjects such as, age, gender, socio-economic status, family background, grade level, etc. should be clearly indicated. Also the unique characteristics such as gifted students, volunteers, etc. should also be reported while describing the sample of the study.
2. The population of the study should be clearly defined. It is specifically important to provide specific definition of the population in studies using Probability Sampling. Vague description such as retired teachers, high ability students, creative students, etc. should be avoided. The characteristics of each stratum in a Stratified Sampling Technique should be included.
3. The sampling procedure should be clearly described. The specific type of sampling procedure, such as, Random Sampling, Stratified Random Sampling, Cluster Sampling, Multi-stage Sampling, Convenience Sampling, etc. should be described in sufficient details to enable other researchers to replicate the study.
4. Whenever a researcher collects data with the help of questionnaire, it is important to report the percentage of filled in questionnaires received. If the return is less than 60%, the researcher should analyse the implications of excluding a significant portion of the population. This step is accomplished by comparing the non-respondents to those who fiiled in the questionnaire to determine if there are significant differences between the groups.
5. The selection of subjects should be free of bias. The procedure and criteria for selecting subjects should not result in systematic error. Bias is more likely when a researcher is "proving" something to be true, with convenience samples, and when volunteers are used as subjects.
6. Selection procedure should be appropriate for the problem being studied. If the problem is to study Science Attitude of Middle School students, it should be inappropriate to use high school students as member of the sample. If the researcher wants to study the Characteristics of Effective Teaching, the work of student-teachers would probably not be very representative of Effective Teaching behaviours.
7. There should be an adequate number of subjects. If the Sample is selected from a Population, the Sample size should be large enough to represent the Population accurately. There must be sufficient number of subjects in each subgroup that is analysed. Studies with small samples that report no differences or no relationships should be viewed with

caution since a higher number or a better selection of subjects may result in meaningful differences or relationships. Researches that have a very large number of subjects may report "significant" differences or relationships that are of little practical utility.

8. Qualitative studies should have informative and knowledgeable subjects, since the purpose of qualitative research is to understand a phenomenon in depth. It is important to select subjects that will provide the in-depth information. The researcher should indicate the criteria used to select subjects, the reasons why these particular individuals were selected, and strategies used for selecting subjects during the study.

SAMPLING ERROR

Whenever a Sample is selected from a Population, there is always some degree of Sampling Error. Sampling Error is the error caused by collecting data from a sample instead of the whole population. Also Sampling Error is the difference between a Sample Statistics used to estimate a Population parameter and the actual but unknown value of the parameter.

There are different causes of Sampling Error. Most frequent cause of Sampling Error is a biased sampling procedure. Every researcher must try to take a sample that is free from bias and is representative of the entire population. If this is done, the researcher is able to minimise Sampling Error.

Another possible cause for Sampling Error is chance. Probability Sampling is done to minimise Sampling Error but it is possible that sample may not be representative of the population.

The most common result of Sampling Error is Systematic Error wherein the results from the sample differ significantly from the results of the entire population. It may be because the sample does not represent the entire population; the results from it will most likely differ from the results of the data collected from the entire population.

SAMPLE SIZE

An important consideration in judging the credibility of a research is the size of sample. In most of the researches there are restrictions that limit the number of subjects or sample size, although it is difficult to know when the sample is too small. Formal Statistical Techniques can be used to determine the number of subjects needed, but in most studies these techniques are not used.

Determining the sample size to be selected is an important step in research study. For example, suppose that researcher wants to study Prevalence of Eye Problems in school children of Indore and wants to conduct a survey. The important question to be answered is "How many students should be chosen for the survey?" However the answer cannot be given without considering the Objectives and the Population.

Decision about the sample size depends on non-statistical considerations and statistical considerations. The non-statistical considerations may include availability of resources, manpower, budget, ethics, administrative concerns and sampling frame. The statistical concerns will include the desired precision of the estimate, confidence level, and variability within the population or subpopulation of the study. Along with these, the following three criteria need to be specified to determine the appropriate sample size.

1. *The level of Precision or Sampling Error:* It is the range in which the true value of the population lies. This range is expressed in percentage points. Thus, if a researcher finds that 70% of people from the rural area have started using mobiles with a precision rate of ±5%, then the researcher can conclude that between 65% and 75% of people in the population have adopted the new technology.
2. *The Confidence Level:* It is the statistical measure of the number of times out of 100 that results can be expected to be within a specified range. For example, a confidence interval of 95% means that 95 out of 100 samples will have the true population value within range of precision. This is according to the Central Limit Theorem which states that when a population is repeatedly samples, the average value of an attribute obtained is equal to the true population value.
3. *Degree of Variability:* Depending upon the target population and attributes under consideration, the degree of variability varies considerably. The more heterogeneous a population is, the larger the sample size is required to get an optimum level of precision. Note that a proportion of 55% indicates a high level of variability than either 10% or 80%. This is because 10% and 80% means that a large majority does not or does, respectively, have the attribute or characteristic under consideration.

There are number of approaches to determine the sample size including: using a census for smaller populations, using published tables, imitating a sample size of similar studies, and applying formula to calculate a sample size.

For the benefit of researchers, Table 4.2 and Table 4.3 are given which may be used for determining the required sample size for the research in hand. The researcher should know approximately the size of population and after that Table 4.2 can be used to decide the size of sample. For Table 4.2, the level of significance is 0.05 and Margin of Error is 5.0%. The researcher should note that beyond population size of 1000000, the sample size will still be 384. From Table 4.2, it is evident that when the population size is 5000, the sample size should be at least 357 but not less than 357. The researcher may decide to have sample more than 357. If the researcher wants to decide the sample size when the level of significance is 0.01 and Margin of Error is 5.0%, the Table 4.2 can be used.

Caution: *The Sample size calculated using Tables 4.2 or Table 4.3 does not guaranty the representation of the population.*

Table 4.2: Determining Sample Size from the Population when Level of Significance is 0.05 and Margin of Error is 5.0%

N	n	N	n	N	n	N	n	N	n
10	10	100	80	280	162	800	260	2800	338
15	14	110	86	290	165	850	265	3000	341
20	19	120	92	300	169	900	269	3500	346
25	24	130	97	320	175	950	274	4000	351
30	28	140	103	340	181	1000	278	4500	354
35	32	150	108	360	186	1100	285	5000	357
40	36	160	113	380	191	1200	291	6000	361
45	40	170	118	400	196	1300	297	7000	364
50	44	180	123	420	201	1400	302	8000	367
55	48	190	127	440	205	1500	306	9000	368
60	52	200	132	460	210	1600	310	10000	370
65	56	210	136	480	214	1700	313	15000	375
70	59	220	140	500	217	1800	317	20000	377
75	63	230	144	550	226	1900	320	30000	379
80	66	240	148	600	234	2000	322	40000	380
85	70	250	152	650	242	2200	327	50000	381
90	73	260	155	700	248	2400	331	75000	382
95	76	270	159	750	254	2600	335	1000000	384

Where N is the Population size and n the Sample Size

Table 4.3: Determining Sample Size from the Population when Level of Significance is 0.01 and Margin of Error is 5.0%

N	*n*	*N*	*n*	*N*	*n*	*N*	*n*	*N*	*n*
10	10	200	154	800	363	5000	586	250,000	662
20	19	250	182	1000	399	7500	610	500,000	663
30	29	300	207	1200	427	10,000	622	1,000,000	663
50	47	400	250	1500	460	25,000	646	2,500.000	663
75	67	500	285	2000	498	50,000	655	10,000,000	663
100	87	600	315	2500	524	75,000	658	100,000,000	663
150	122	700	341	3500	558	100,000	659	300,000,000	663

Where N is the Population size and n the Sample Size

Take a Test

1. Interviewing all members of a given population is called
   A) A sample B) A Gallup poll
   C) A Census D) None of the above

2. Sampling means following a sequence of stages. Which one of the following stages should come before the others?
   A) Proceed with the field work.
   B) Find suitable source for the population members.
   C) Define the people of interest.
   D) Examine the objective of the study.
3. Which one of the following sampling methods is the Probability Sampling Method?
   A) Quota Sampling B) Random Sampling
   C) Purposive Sampling D) Incidental Sampling
4. For Sampling which one of the following should be up-to-date, complete and affordable?
   A) A census B) Population
   C) Sampling Frame D) Respondents
5. Which one of the following is the benefit of using Random Sampling?
   A) One can calculate the accuracy of results.
   B) The results are always representative.
   C) Researcher can choose respondents freely.
   D) Subject can refuse to participate in the research.
6. Which ONE of the following is the main problem of using Non-probability Sampling method?
   A) The expense. B) The results are never representative
   C) Human judgement error. D) Subject can refuse to participate.
7. Which one of the following is the best but often unused way to decide the sample size?
   A) By using Industry standards B) By calculation
   C) By building blocks D) As per the available budget
8. Which one of the following methods is generally used in qualitative research?
   A) Random dialing Sampling B) Quota Sampling
   C) Stratified Random Sampling D) Cluster Sampling
9. Cluster Sampling, Stratified Random Sampling and Systematic Sampling are
   A) Non-Probability Sampling B) Probability Sampling
   C) Neither A nor B D) All the above
10. Listing of elements in Population with Identifiable number is classified as
    A) Regulatory Experimental Frame
    B) Indirect Experimental Frame
    C) Direct Experimental Frame
    D) Frame for Experiment
11. Type of Sampling in which each member of Population has equal chance of being selected is called
    A) Random Sampling B) Incidental Sampling
    C) Convenient Sampling D) Judgement Sampling
12. Quota Sampling, Judgement Sampling and Convenience Sampling are part of
    A) Random Sampling B) Direct Sampling
    C) Probability Sampling D) Non-Probability Sampling
13. Non-probability Type of Sampling is
    A) Snowball Sampling B) Random Sampling
    C) Cluster Sampling D) Multistage Sampling

14. Standard Deviation of Sampling Distribution of any Statistics is called
    A) Sampling Error B) Type–I Error
    C) Standard Error D) Non-Sampling Error
15. The list of all units in a population is called
    A) Frame B) Parameter
    C) Statistics D) All the above
16. Any numerical value calculated from sample data is called
    A) Error B) Mean
    C) Standard Deviation D) Statistic
17. Sample is subset of
    A) Population B) Itself
    C) Universe D) Data
18. In Sampling with replacement a Sampling Unit can be selected
    A) Only once B) More than one time
    C) Less than one time D) None of the above
19. Non-Sampling error is reduced by
    A) Increasing Sample Size B) Decreasing Sample Size
    C) Reducing amount of data D) None of the above
20. Any numerical value calculated from population data is called
    A) Statistics B) Parameter
    C) Error D) Sampling error
21. In Random Sampling, the probability of selecting an item from the population is
    A) Unknown B) One
    C) Known D) Zero
22. The difference between Statistic and Parameter is called
    A) Error B) Standard Error
    C) Standard Deviation D) Sampling Error
23. Sampling in which a sampling unit can be repeated more than once is called
    A) Sampling without replacement B) Random Sampling
    C) Sampling with replacement D) None of the above
24. When each member of a population has an equally likely chance of being selected, this is called:
    A) A nonrandom sampling method B) A quota sample
    C) A snowball sample D) An Equal probability selection method
25. A study of relationship between Self-confidence and Anxiety of Science Teachers of Government Schools of Haryana
    For the above mentioned title, the population for this research is
    A) Science Teachers
    B) Teachers of Government Schools
    C) Science Teachers of Government Schools of Haryana
    D) Teachers of Government Schools of Haryana

5
Tools/Instruments

INTRODUCTION

From Chapter 2, you must have come to know how to write Title for the research. From the Title of research, one can know the Population from where the data are collected but the Variables with respect to which data are to be collected is known only from the Objectives. In case of Philosophical Researches and Historical Researches, normally Tools are not required because the data are to be collected from the existing sources or documents. But Tools are required for Survey Researches, Experimental Researches and Case Study Researches. Researchers from the discipline of Science, Medical Science, Agriculture, Physical Education, etc., use Instruments for collecting data from the members of Sample. They may also use Tools. Thus, selection of Tools or Instruments is the part of Data Collection. After reading this chapter, one will be able to:

- List different Characteristics of Tools or Instruments.
- Define Validity, Reliability, Objectivity, and Sensitivity.
- Differentiate between Measurement and Assessment.
- Distinguish between Standardised Tools and Unstandardised Tools.
- List different Types of Tools.
- Differentiate between Test, Scale, and Inventory.
- Develop and Standardise the Tools required for the research in hand.
- List different Methods of establishing Reliability and Validity.
- Tell different factors which affect the Reliability and Validity of the Tool.
- Explain which Method of Reliability is to be used for establishing Reliability of the Tool.
- Explain which Method of Validity is to be used for establishing Validity of the Tool.
- Define Norm and write the procedure of its development.
- Tell names of unstandardised tools.
- List advantages and disadvantages of Interview Schedule.

- Describe Structured as well as Unstructured Interview Schedule.
- List phases of using Interview Schedule.
- List the points to be kept in mind while preparing and using Interview Schedule.

CHARACTERISTICS OF TOOL/INSTRUMENT

It is important to understand that the characteristics of data depend on the characteristics of the Tools or Instruments used. If one sits on a dirty chair with clean clothes on, the clean clothes will become dirty. Here the characteristic of chair has been passed on to the clothes and becomes the characteristic of clothes. In the same way the characteristics of tool or instrument will be passed on to the data collected with the help of the tool or instrument used. So it is important to know different desirable characteristics of the tool or instrument so that the researchers can keep them in mind while selecting the tools or instruments. The desirable characteristics of tools or instruments are as follows:

1. *Validity:* Validity denotes the extent to which a tool or an instrument is measuring what it is supposed to assess or measure. Whenever a tool or an instrument is developed, it is always to assess or measure a particular characteristic or variable. Instruments are used in Sciences, Medical Science, Pharmacy, Engineering, etc. and have higher degree of validity but this is not so in case of Social Sciences and Languages. This is because in Social Sciences, variables are complex and can have different definitions. The tools used in research must be valid.
2. *Reliability:* Reliability of a tool or an instrument refers to the consistency with which it assesses or measures what it is intended to assess or measure. Suppose one takes weight several times over a short period of time using the same weighing machine, the reading will be same. If so than the weighing machine is said to be reliable. Let us take another example. Suppose a watch is 10 minutes ahead, and always it is so, the watch is said to be reliable but it is not valid as it does not give the correct time. Thus, a tool or an instrument may be reliable but may not be valid. On the other hand, if a tool or an instrument is valid than it has to be reliable. It can be said that validity ensures reliability but vice-versa is not true. Thus, the tools used in research must be reliable.
3. *Objectivity:* A tool or an instrument is said to be objective if it is free from personal bias in scoring the responses. It is a well-known fact that if the answer of an Essay Type Question is checked by the same examiner again and again or by different examiners, the marks given by them will differ. This shows that there is subjectivity in awarding the marks or assessing the answer. Thus, there is less Objectivity but more Subjectivity in assessment of Essay Type Question Papers. On the other hand, if there is paper with Multiple Choice Type items and the

answer of one candidate is checked by many examiners or by the same examiner again and again, the marks given by them will not differ. This is due to objectivity in scoring. Objectivity is one of the most primary pre-requisites required for maintaining all other qualities of a good tool or instrument. Thus, the tools or instruments used in research must be objective.

4. *Sensitivity:* Sensitivity refers to the tendency of a tool or an instrument to assess or measure the smallest change that has occurred in the characteristic or variable that it purposes to assess or measure. Suppose a person takes his weight using a weighing machine before taking lunch and he again takes his weight with the help of the same machine after taking lunch. If the weighing machine is able to record the change in weight before and after the lunch, the weighing machine is said to be sensitive. Sensitivity is an important characteristics of instruments used in Sciences, Medical Science, Pharmacy, Engineering, etc. The least count of the Instrument refers to its' sensitivity. This characteristic is absent in case of tools used in Social Sciences and Languages.
5. *Practicability or Usability:* A tool however well it satisfies all the above characteristics, may be useless unless it is not practically feasible or usable. For example, suppose, in order to ensure comprehensiveness, it was felt that one thousand items should be given to be answered in ten hours. This may yield valid result, but from practical point of view it is quite impossible to use such a test. Thus, the tool or instrument should be practicable so that the researcher is able to use it.

Difference between Measurement and Assessment

For a researcher it is important to understand the difference between Measurement and Assessment so that one can use these words appropriately. Measurement and assessment cannot be used interchangeably. Taking weight of a person with the help of weighing machine is measurement because it gives the complete information about the weight of the person at that point of time. Similarly, if a doctor takes the temperature of a patient with the help of thermometer, thermometer gives the complete information about the temperature of the patient at that point of time. So temperature is measured but not assessed. There are instruments which give the complete information about the status of the variable at a point of time. Such instruments are used for measurement purpose. A researcher will always do the measurement of variables, such as, weight, height, temperature, blood pressure, head circumference, volume of a cube, RBC, hemoglobin, power of a lens, distance between to cities, speed, etc. Thus, in Sciences, Medical Science, Pharmacy, Engineering, Physical Education, etc. instruments are used for measurement purpose.

On the other hand, in the examination, question paper does not cover the complete content of the subject. Whatever the marks a student gets, it only gives information about part of the content but not whole of it. In this case assessment is done. If a researcher administers an Intelligence Test on Class IX students, the marks of intelligence only give partial information about the intelligence of each student because it is difficult to have an Intelligence Test which can encompass the whole concept of intelligence. So in subjects like, Education, Economics, History, Philosophy, Political Science, Psychology, etc., mostly assessment is done but not measurement. A researcher will always do the assessment of variables, such as, Intelligence, Anxiety, Interest, Stress, Job Satisfaction, Tolerance of Ambiguity, Personality, Tension, Fear of Failure, Competency, Reaction towards Educational Television Programme, Scholastic Achievement, Educational Problems, Home related Problems, Social Intelligence, Spiritual Intelligence, Emotional Intelligence, etc. Thus, assessment always gives the partial information about the characteristic or variable.

From above it is evident that measurement is always quantitative while assessment can be both quantitative and qualitative. Further measurement gives the complete information about the variable at a point of time while assessment always gives the partial information about the variable at a point of time. Lastly, instruments are used for measurement while tools are used for assessment.

TYPES OF TOOLS

Basically tools are of two types, namely, Standardised and Non-standardised. Standardised Tools include Tests, Scales and Inventories while Observation Schedule, Interview Schedule, and Questionnaire are Non-standardised Tools. In this chapter, questionnaire includes checklist. In case of a test, the response of the student can be categorised as correct or incorrect but it is not so in case of scales and inventories. Further test and questionnaire are technical terms and should not be used as a general terms in any research. There are different tests, such as, Intelligence Test, Differential Aptitude Test, Vocabulary Test, Reading Comprehension Test, Achievement in Physics Test, Reasoning Test, etc. Scales are as Scientific Attitude Scale, Reaction towards Educational Television Programme Scale, Reaction towards Programmed Learning Material Scale, Self-Confidence Scale, etc. Inventory can be as Interest Inventory, Kuder-Preference Record, Vocational Interest Inventory, etc. The differences between Standardised and Non-standardised Tools are given separately in next caption.

DIFFERENCE BETWEEN STANDARDISED AND NON-STANDARDISED TOOLS

It is well known fact that all examination papers at schools and colleges passed by us were Non-standardised. Marks obtained by an individual do not indicate anything about his/her learning. Many-a-time it has been noticed that a student gets 70% marks in the School Board examination and he fails in the University examination. Many students have cleared National Eligibility Test (NET) conducted by University Grants Commission, New Delhi but have not been able to get through the interview and are without job. Since the marks obtained by a candidate do not speak anything about his/her abilities, people responsible for the recruitment do pay attention to the percentage of marks but have their own criteria of selection. Institutes like, IITs, IIMs, AIIMS, etc. take their own entrance examination and use the School Board examination percentage to decide whether a candidate is eligible or not for the entrance test. Although Non-standardised Tests are not of much use, still people continue to use them. It is mainly because Non-standardised papers are easy to prepare and use.

There are differences between Standardised and Non-standardised tools that are given in the following Table.

Basis	*Standardised Tool*	*Non-standardised Tool*
Preparation	It is difficult to prepare.	It is easy to prepare.
Time	More time is required for its preparation.	Less time is required for its preparation.
Cost	It involves more money.	It involves less money.
Utility	More useful	Less useful
Objectivity	More Objective	Less Objective
Reliability	Reliability is known.	Reliability is not known.
Validity	Validity is known.	Validity is not known.
Norms	Norms can be developed.	Norms cannot be developed.

Non-standardised Tools are in use for a long time and continue to be used. If the researcher can Standardise the Tool to be used for his/her research, he/she should do so. Tools like Test, Scale and Inventory can be standardised but Observation Schedule, Interview Schedule and Questionnaire cannot be standardised. Therefore, researchers are bound to use Non-standardised tools also.

PROCEDURE OF DEVELOPMENT AND STANDARDISATION OF TOOL

As stated earlier, Test, Scale and Inventory can be standardised while Observation Schedule, Interview Schedule and Questionnaire cannot be standardised. Researchers from a long time have been conducting researches and have developed and standardised large number of tests, scales and inventories. Due to rapid change in the social system, some of the tools developed earlier are not relevant at present. Under such circumstances researchers have to develop new tools or modify the existing tools. Not only this even the tools developed for a particular target group cannot be used as it is, so some modification is required. Modification may be in respect of language, number of items, types of items, instructions, time of responding, sequence of items, etc. In case researcher decides to develop and standardise tools, one should know the procedure of tool development and standardisation. The steps used for developing and standardising tools are as given below:

Step I: Giving Operational Definition

Tool is developed for assessing a variable. Each variable can be defined in several ways. So the researcher has to define the variable for which the tool is to be developed. This definition has to be operational definition. It means the variable is to be defined in such a way so that the researcher is able to observe and assess or measure the variable in terms of its' attributes or characteristics. Further the operational definition describes exactly what the variable is and how it is to be assessed or measured within the context of the study.

For example, if a researcher wants to study the effect of Sleep Deprivation on Driving Performance in Mumbai, one would need to operationally define what one means by Sleep Deprivation and Driving Performance. The researcher might define Sleep Deprivation as getting less than seven hours of sleep at night and define Driving Performance as how well a participant does on a driving test.

Thus, an Operational Definition is clear, concise and detailed definition of a measurement or an assessment. The need of Operational Definition is fundamental when collecting all types of data. When collecting data, it is essential that everyone in the system has the same understanding and collect data in the same way. Operational Definitions should therefore be made at the time of developing the tool or instrument.

The researcher has to give Operational Definition of variable for which the tool or instrument is to be developed. For developing an Operational Definition, one should keep the following points into mind:

- Identify the characteristic of interest. The researcher must identify the characteristic(s) to be assessed or measured with the help of the tool that is to be developed.
- Select the assessment tool. The researcher has to decide in the beginning whether to use Test, Scale or Inventory for the assessment.
- Describe the test method. The test method is the actual procedure used for taking assessment or measurement. When measuring time, the start and finish points of the test need to be specified. When taking any measurement, the degree of accuracy also needs to be stated. For example, it is important to know whether time will be measured in hours, minutes, or seconds. For assessing achievement in Mathematics, one has to decide whether achievement in Mathematics scores should be only in whole numbers or decimals also. If decimals, place of decimal should be decided before hand and followed through the study accordingly.
- Document the Operational Definition. Operational Definition should be written so it can be used in different stages of the tool development.
- Test the Operational Definition. It is essential to test the Operational Definition before using it. Operational Definition should make the task

clear and easy to perform. The best to test an Operational Definition is to ask different people to give their responses on several items by following the Operational Definition. Find out whether they are completing the tool as expected? Are the results consistent?

Also identify one or more specific observable events or conditions so that any other researcher can independently measure or assess. For example, a researcher assessing Happiness and Depression among college students of Kanpur decides to use a ten-item Happiness Scale to assess positive outlook of the subjects. In other words, the Operational Definition of Happiness in this case is a given subject's score on the scale.

Step II: Item Writing

Item is a technical word and used in case of test, scale or inventory. Sometime people use question in case of a test, statement in scale and list in inventory. The choice of the word "item", in preference to "question" is because items often are not in question format and each item is independent in the tool. The quality of response of an individual depends upon the structure of items. While writing items, the following points are to be kept in mind.

- Use good grammar, punctuation, and spelling consistently.
- Express item as precisely, clearly, and simply as possible
- The language in which the members of the target group are proficient.
- The background of the target population for whom the tool is being developed.
- Minimise examinee reading time in phrasing each item.
- Keep the vocabulary consistent with the examinee's level of understanding.
- Each item should focus on a single dimension/component of the variable for which the tool is to be developed.
- Do not take item verbatim from any textbook.
- Ensure that the directions in the stem are clear, and that wording lets the examinee know exactly what is being asked.
- Use multiple choice type items to assess higher level of thinking.
- Include the central idea and most of the phrasing in the item.
- In case of scale, there should be equal number of positive and negative statements.
- In case of scale, avoid the use of humor.
- In case of a test, make sure that there is only one correct answer.
- Avoid jargon and textbook language.
- Eliminate irrelevant sources of difficulty.
- Instruction regarding the mode of response should be clear.
- Write items double the number required.

By keeping above mentioned points in the mind, items are written. Along with items instruction for the subjects should be written. Instruction must give information about what the tool intends to assess, how to give the response, what is the time limit, scoring procedure, etc. The clear instruction will help subjects in giving genuine responses which will go a long way in improving validity and reliability. After writing item along with the instruction, the next step is to Tryout the items. The Tryout is at two stages, Initial Tryout and Final Tryout. Each one of these is explained below.

Step III: Initial Tryout

After writing items, it is important to do the Tryout. The first Tryout is called Initial Tryout. The main purpose of Initial Tryout is to find out the suitability of the language for the target group, the extent to which the items are able to assess the variable under study, and item analysis. In case of test, the responses can be designated as correct or incorrect. Thus, in case of test, item analysis is done on the basis of Difficulty Level and Discrimination Index. The Discrimination Index is also called Validity Index. On the other hand, in case of scale and inventory, item analysis is done by computing only discrimination index as the responses cannot be categorised as correct or incorrect. Initial Tryout is done at three levels, namely, Expert Tryout, Individual Tryout, and Group Tryout. The data received from Expert Tryout, and Individual Tryout help in knowing the suitability of the language. Data from experts also help in understanding the extent to which the items are able to assess the variable under study. This is on the basis of content of the tool and it is also referred as content validity. Each of these is detailed as given below:

Experts Tryout: Normally researcher finds it difficult to decide who is an Expert. In fact there is no list of experts. An expert is one who has developed the tool for the variable under study and/or a person who is an expert in research methodology, especially Tool development. The number of experts cannot be large. Normally the researcher may identify 10 to 15 Experts from anywhere on the planet because an expert may be approached through e-mail. After having identified Experts, the researcher must take their consent for critically examining the tool developed by him/her. On receiving the consent, the researcher must send the tool along with operational definition, name of dimensions/components and dimension-wise serial number of items to the expert with a request to examine each item carefully in the light of the operational definition, dimension, and language. If the tool is sent through post than the researcher must send along with the tool a self-addressed stamped envelope so that the expert need not to pay for the postage. Self-addressed stamped envelope is not required if the tool is emailed. Some experts may send their observations fast but a few needs push up. Those experts who have not responded to your mail, you need to follow them. Continue following the experts till you get the observations from majority of them. Now examine each item in the light of observations of each expert. If majority of experts suggest change on an item, the item should be revised in the light of suggestions of experts. Further on any item even if one expert suggests modification, it should be carefully examined and modify the item as suggested if the researcher agrees with the suggestion of the expert. Thus, on the basis of experts tryout, some of the items may be dropped or modified. The researcher must do the suggested modification in the tool. Experts have also examined each item in the light of operational definition. If majority of experts agree that the tool can assess for which it is developed, the content validity of it is established.

Individual Tryout: After modifying the items as per Experts Tryout, now it is time for Individual Tryout. The main purpose of Individual Tryout is to assess the suitability of items with respect to the language. That is whether the subjects are able to understand the item. To know this the researcher should do the Individual Tryout on individuals belonging to that population on which it is to be used for collecting data. These individuals may be selected randomly or purposively. The number of individuals may be between 20 to 25 subjects. It cannot be large as it is time consuming because the tool has to be tried out on one subject at a time. On a day the researcher may not be able to do individual tryout on more than three or four individuals because on one individual it may take one hour or more. To begin with, the researcher will approach the individual who has given his consent to be part of the Individual Tryout. The rapport is to be established with the subject. He should be told the purpose of this tryout and what is expected of her/his. On agreeing this, the subject is asked to read instruction. He should be asked whether the instruction is clear. In case the subject points out some problem, the researcher should modify the instruction and take the opinion of the subject about the suitability of instruction. If yes, the researcher should note the modification on a separate paper and to be used later on in modifying the tool. Now the first item is given to him to read and tell whether he has understood it or not. In case of any problem, the researcher should immediately modify the item and check whether the modified item is within comprehension level of the subject. This process will continue till all items are read by the subject. The procedure is to be repeated with all subjects one by one till all individual of the Individual Tryout have been covered.

On the basis of Individual Tryout, the researcher should find out items where modifications are required. Now do the modification as per the data gathered through the individual tryout. It may happen that some of the items may be dropped because the subjects did not understand them. Whatever Items are cleared through Individual Tryout, are to be used for Group Tryout.

Group Tryout: The main purpose of Group Tryout is to do item analysis. As mentioned before, item analysis for Test is to be done on the basis of difficulty level and discrimination index. On the other hand for scale and inventory, the item analysis is to be done on the basis of only discrimination index. Item analysis represents the tool. All the things of the tool depend on items. Item analysis is very important as the quality of the tool depends to a great extent on it. So importance of item analysis is:

1. There can be little doubt that item analysis is a vitally important operation in the development of a new tool, such as, test, scale, and inventory. It should invariably be carried out unless special circumstances.
2. Both validity and reliability of any tool depend ultimately on the characteristics of its items. High validity and reliability can be built into the tool in advance through item analysis.
3. Tools can be improved through the selection, substitution or revision of item analysis.
4. Item analysis makes it possible to shorten a tool and at the same time to increase its validity and reliability.

Thus, after the Individual Tryout, the selected items are put in the proper format along with the instruction. Now the tool is ready for the Group Tryout whose main purpose is item analysis. For Group Tryout, a large sample is taken and subjects used at initial tryout are not included in this sample. The sample size will depend on the size of population. The sample is to be selected in such a way so that it approximately represents the population on important characteristics. The characteristics are to be decided on the basis of variable for which the tool is being developed. Suppose you as a researcher decide to have 500 subjects for the Group Tryout. These subjects belong to different places and institutes. The researcher has to take permission from the head of the institute for administering the Tool on subjects belonging to their institute. If the permission is not given to the researcher by the head of the institute, he cannot take sample from that institute and has to select another institute. Once the institutes are selected by the researcher, and suppose he goes to an institute where there are 20 subjects. The researcher will first establish rapport with the subject by telling the purpose of his/her coming to the institute. After this the subjects are given one copy of the tool to each student so that they go through the tool independently and give their individual responses. They are asked to read instruction carefully. In case of any problem in understanding the instruction, the researcher will help the subjects in understanding the instruction. After making sure that all subjects have understood the instruction, the researcher can ask subjects to start responding the items given in the tool and can take as much time as they like but do not spend much time on an item. As soon as subjects start responding, the time is noted. Subjects will proceed at their own speed. The subject who completes all the items can return the response sheet along with the test booklet to the researcher. The booklets are reusable so the subjects are asked not to write anything on the booklet.

The time of completion of the tool is also noted for each subject on their answer sheet. The researcher knows the starting time and completion time for each subject. From this data, the average time required for the tool can be calculated for later use. The calculation of time is not required in case of scale and inventory but is very useful in test. Most of the tests are used as speed test where there is a fixed time for completion of the test for all subjects. In case of power test, there is no restriction of time. Subjects are asked to take their own time but must answer all items.

Item Analysis for Scale and Inventory: The main purpose of item analysis is to determine discriminant index for each Item. For scale and inventory, difficulty level cannot be determined as the responses cannot be categorised as right or wrong. As stated earlier there are both positive and negative statements in equal number in scale. The researcher can have a Three Point Scale, Five Point Scale, Seven Point Scale, etc. Normally, researchers have Five Point Scale. The Five Points can be as, Strongly Agree (SA), Agree (A), Undecided (U), Disagree (D), and Strongly Disagree (SD); Very Helpful, Helpful, Neutral, Not Helpful, and Not Helpful At All; etc. These alternatives depend on the structuring of items in the scale. Scale should always have odd points but not even points because even points cannot have neutral point in it where as it is compulsory to have neutral point. In case of scale, weightages of responses on positive statements are 5, 4, 3, 2, and 1 for SA, A, U, D, and SD respectively. The scheme of assigning weightages is reversed in case of negative statements. For negative statements, 1, 2, 3, 4, and 5 is assigned for SA, A, U, D, and SD respectively. It is not compulsory to assign weightages in whole numbers. It may be in infraction but it is important to have intervals of equal length. When one assigns weightages as 1, 2, 3, 4, and 5, the intervals between two consecutive numbers is 1. It may be ½, or ¾, etc. but the intervals should be of equal length. Normally fractions are not used because the addition becomes difficult. Following this scoring system, each response is assigned a score. In case of Five Point Scale, on one statement, the score of a subject is between 1 and 5. Some of the scale developers start assigning weightage of 4, 3, 2, 1, and 0 for positive statements and it is reversed in case of negative statement. In Social Sciences, it is difficult to assign a weightage of Zero to the response because the response has occurred. Thus in the Scale, one should not assign a weightage of Zero to any point. If the scale contains 40 statements and has Five Point Scale, the minimum score can be 40 and maximum 200. Thus, the score of each individual lies between 40 and 200. After following this scoring scheme, each individual total score is calculated. As mentioned earlier the Group Tryout is done on 500 subjects. So there are scores of 500 subjects. Theses scores can be arranged in ascending or descending order. Suppose researcher decides to arrange total scores of subjects in descending order. Subjects belonging to top 27% group and bottom 27% group are computed. In the present example, 27% of 500 is 135. There are 135 subjects in top 27% group and equal number in bottom 27%

group. The total scores of 46% of subjects are left out from the calculation. This is because the scores of middle 46% of subjects do not vary to a great extent and may not help in determining Discrimination Index. Secondly, the computation becomes easy as group size reduces. The data of 135 subjects belonging to top 27% and 135 belonging to bottom 27% were analysed for, suppose, seven items to determine the Discrimination Index of items and suppose the results are as given in Table 5.1.

Table 5.1: Item-wise M, SD, N and t-values

Item Number	*M1*	*SD1*	*M2*	*SD2*	*t-value*	*Remark*
1.	3.15	1.41	1.92	1.07	4.38**	Selected
2.	2.10	1.13	1.85	0.89	1.10	Rejected
3.	2.35	1.21	2.87	1.45	1.76	Rejected
4.	2.12	1.19	3.35	1.35	4.39**	Selected
5.	2.01	1.05	2.97	1.37	3.30**	Selected
6.	2.35	1.21	3.10	1.33	2.63**	Selected
7.	2.50	1.34	3.10	1.33	2.01*	Selected

** Significant at 0.01 Level, * Significant at 0.05 Level

From Table 5.1, it is evident that t-values for Items at serial numbers 1, 4, 5, 6, and 7 are significant either at 0.01 or 0.05 level. These items are found to discriminate between subjects belonging to top 27% and bottom 27%. Thus, items 1, 4, 5, 6, and 7 have been selected while items at 2 and 3 have been rejected because the t-values are not significant. It means the items 2 and 3 do not discriminate between subjects belonging to top 27% and bottom 27%. So items 2 and 3 should be rejected and not used in the scale.

The researchers can do item analysis by following the procedure as illustrated above and select items which can discriminate between top 27% group and bottom 27% group. The selected items are to be used for establishing the validity and reliability which has to be done through final tryout.

Item Analysis for Test: In case of test, the Item Analysis is to be done by computing Difficulty Level and Discrimination Index. Test has items whose responses can be categorised either as correct or wrong because each item has one and only one correct answer. In test, the items are of multiple-choice with four or five options. Out of the given options, only one is the correct answer. The remaining options must act as distractors. Distractor is an important part of the item because there is a relationship between the distractors subjects chosen and total score on the Test. The quality of distractors influences subjects' performance on an Item. Although the correct answer must be truly correct, it is important that the distractors be incorrect. Distractors should appeal to low scorers who have not mastered the material whereas high scorers should infrequently select the distractors. Reviewing the options can reveal optional errors of judgement and inadequate performance of distractors. The poor distractors can be revised, replaced, or removed.

As mentioned before, the developed test tried out on 500 subjects. For each item there are four or five options. For each item the number of subjects selecting the given option is computed. So for each item option-wise frequency table is prepared. This table tells researcher the number and/or per cent of students that selected a given distractor. Distractors that are selected by a few or no students should be removed or replaced. These kinds of distractors are likely to be so implausible to students that hardly anyone selects them. Keeping distractors in view, some items are deleted or modified. One has to proceed further with the remaining items for computing Difficulty Index and Discrimination Index.

As mentioned earlier, subjects belonging to top 27% group and bottom 27% group are separated. There are 135 subjects in top 27% group and 135 subjects in bottom 27% group. For each item, one should calculate the number of subjects answering the item corrected from top 27% group and bottom 27% group. Suppose the data are as given in Table 5.2.

Table 5.2: Item-wise Number of Correct Answer, Difficulty Index and Discrimination Index

Item No.	*Top 27%*	*Bottom 27%*	*Difficulty Index*	*Discrimination index*	*Remark*
1.	100	40	100+40/135+135 = 0.52	100-40/135 = 0.44	Selected
2.	20	60	20+60/135+135 = 0.30	20-60/135 =-0.30	Rejected
3.	130	120	130+120/135+135 = 0.92	130-120/135 = 0.07	Rejected
4.	120	78	120+78/135+135 = 0.73	120-78/135 = 0.31	Selected
5.	100	20	100+20/135+135 = 0.44	100-20/135 = 0.58	Selected

One should first consider values of Discrimination Index. If the Item does not discriminate then it has to be dropped irrespective of value of Difficulty Index. As a rule higher the value of Discrimination Index the more discriminating the item. A highly discriminating item indicates that the subjects who have high scores got the item correct whereas subjects who have low scores got the item incorrect. Further items with discrimination index near or less than zero must be removed from the test. This indicates that subjects who overall did poorly on the test did better on that item than subjects who overall did well. The item may be confusing for better scoring subjects. From Table 5.2 it is evident that items number 2 and 3 have been rejected because their discriminating indices are –0.30 and 0.07 which are negative or near zero. Further, item numbers 2, 4, and 5 have been selected as their discrimination index is positive and more than zero.

Step IV: Final Tryout

The last step in development and standardisation of tool is Final Tryout. The main purpose of Final Tryout is to establish reliability, validity and norms. Using Group Tryout data, the items are selected as explained earlier. The selected items are put in the proper format along with the instruction so that they may be used at Final Tryout. For Final Tryout a large sample is selected from the target population. For many of the tools available in the market for use, Final Tryout was done on 20,000 subjects belonging to the defined population. It only indicates that a large sample is to be selected from the population for which the tool is being developed. The sample should be selected in such a way so that it approximately represents the target population. It is important to understand that it is difficult to standardise a tool which is applicable to whole of India or USA or UK or Canada, etc. population. It is because of this reason large number of tools has been developed by researchers belonging to different countries and places within a country. The developed tool is normally for a small population. The Sample size to be taken for Final Tryout depends on the spread of the population, availability of time, cost, purpose for which tool is to be used, etc.

For Final Tryout a large sample, say, of 800 subjects is to be selected by using Probability Sampling Technique in such a way so that it approximately represents the target population. The sample is spread all over the population. After selecting the sample, the researcher goes to selected institute, a place from where the sample has been taken. The researcher has to take permission from the head of the institute for administering the tool on subjects belonging to their institute. If the permission is not given to the researcher by the head of the institute, he cannot take sample from that institute and has to select another institute. Once the institutes are selected by the researcher and taken permission from the head of institutes, suppose he goes to an institute where there are 45 subjects. The researcher first establishes rapport with the subject by telling the purpose of his/her coming to the institute. After this the subjects are given one copy of the tool to each student so that they go through the tool independently and give their individual responses. They are asked to read instruction carefully. In case of any problem in understanding the instruction, the researcher can help the subjects in understanding the instruction. After making sure that all subjects have understood the instruction, the researcher can ask subjects to start responding the items given in the tool and can take as much time as they like but do not spend much time on an item. In case of speed test, the time to be taken by subjects for answering the items should be told to all subjects. As soon as subjects start, the time is noted. Subjects will proceed at their own speed. The subject who completes all the items can return the response sheet along with the test booklet. The booklets are reusable so the subjects are asked not to write anything on the booklet. This procedure is used uniformly throughout the Final Tryout. Now is time to establish reliability, validity and norms of the tool. The procedure used for these is given separately in the following.

METHODS OF RELIABILITY

Different methods of establishing reliability available are: Test-retest Method,

Split-half Method, Parallel Forms or Alternative Forms or Equivalent Forms Method, Kuder-Richardson Formula 20, and Formula 21, and Cronbach's Alpha.

There are factors which affect the Reliability. These are as given below:

- Measurement errors can be caused by examinee specific factors, like, motivation, concentration, fatigue, boredom, momentary lapse of memory, carelessness in writing answer, and luck in guessing.
- Measurement error can be caused by test-specific factors, like, ambiguous or tricky items, and poor direction.
- Measurement error can be caused by scoring specific factors, like, non-uniform scoring guidelines, carelessness, and counting or computational errors.

Different methods of reliability are explained as under.

Test-retest Method of Reliability: As the name indicates, the same tool is to be administered at two points of time on larger portion of the population for which it is to be used later on. The following conditions need to be fulfilled in the establishment of Test-retest Reliability:

- The same tool should be used both at testing as well as retesting stages and under the same conditions.
- The same researcher should use the same tool both at testing as well as retesting stages.
- The location and timings of testing as well as retesting must be same.
- The retesting should be done over a short period of time.

Keeping above mentioned points in the mind, the same tool is to be administered on the same group at two points of time. As mentioned earlier, the researcher decides to take 800 subjects for establishing reliability of the tool. 800 subjects are from different portion of the population spread over a particular area. To start with suppose the tool is administered on 40 subjects from an institute in the morning. On another group from another institute, the same tool may be administered in the evening. The first testing should continue till it is administered on all 800 subjects. If researcher decides to do retesting at the gap of 10 days, the same tool has to be administered on same subjects under similar conditions as were at the time of first testing. The time difference between two administrations should be such so that there is no natural change among subjects with respect to the variable for which the tool is developed. The conditions of administration of tool at both test and retest stages must be as identical as possible. After administering the tool, the scoring of both the administrations is done and total score of those subjects who were present at both test and retest testing's is computed. The sample size may reduce as some of the subjects might drop out at the second testing. So take scores of all those subjects who were present at both the first test and the retest and compute Person Product Moment Correlation. The correlation coefficient is called Reliability Coefficient. If the reliability coefficient is 0.7 or higher, then the tool is said to have good Test-Retest Reliability. Generally the Test-Retest Reliability coefficient is lower in value as compared to Split-Half Reliability coefficient and Parallel Form Reliability coefficient because in Test-Retest Method the assessment is done at two points of time with gap between two administrations.

In Test-Retest Method, the repeatability coefficient is a precision measure which represents the value below which the absolute difference between two repeated test results may be expected to lie with a probability of 95%. The standard deviation under repeatability conditions is part of precision and accuracy because the same Tool is administered twice and every test is parallel with itself. Differences between scores on the test and scores on the retest should be due to solely measurement error. This is quite probably true for many physical measurements. However, it is often inappropriate for Psychological or Social assessment, because it is often impossible to consider the second administration of a test a parallel measure to the first. The second administration might yield systematically different scores than the first administration due to the following reasons:

- The attribute that is being measured or assessed may change between the first test and the retest if the time interval is large. A low test-retest correlation reflects that there is a real change in the attribute itself.
- The experience of taking the test itself can change subject's true score.
- There can be a carryover effect, if the interval between test and retest is short. When retested, subjects may remember their original responses, which could affect the responses on the second administration.

Test-Retest Method of Reliability can be used for establishing reliability of tests, scales and inventories. This method is most frequently used by researchers as there are no strict conditions for its use.

Split-Half Method of Reliability: Test-Retest Method may be expensive or inconvenient to administer the tool twice on the same group of subjects to estimate its reliability. Also, practice effect or other changes between time 1 and time 2 might invalidate Test-Retest estimates of reliability. An alternate approach is to administer the tool on a group of, say, 800 subjects only once. After administering divide the whole tool into two equivalent parts in such a way so that each part has items of same difficulty level, assessing the same dimension of the variable, has equal number of items, same discrimination index, etc. The researcher may keep these points in the mind while arranging the items in the tool. The researcher may arrange items in such a way so that all odd items and even items may assess the same aspect of the variable; have same difficulty level and discrimination index; equal number of items; etc. Thus, Odd-Even Method of Reliability is another name of Split-Half Method of Reliability.

Now from score of subjects on these two halves, the correlation is computed and is called the Half-Test Reliability Coefficient denoted by r_{hh}. This halves reliability estimate is then stepped up to the full length by using Spearman-Brown correction as given below.

$$r_{11} = 2\ r_{hh}/1 + r_{hh}$$

Where r_{11} = Reliability coefficient of the whole tool
r_{hh} = Half-Test Reliability Coefficient

Advantages of Split-Half Method:

1. It requires only one test session.
2. It eliminates the possibility that the variable being measured will change between measurements.
3. The effect of memory does not operate in Split-half Method.
4. The Split-halves are usually cheaper and more easily obtained than over time data.

Disadvantages of Split-half Method:

1. There is no guarantee that the two 'split-halves' are equivalent. If not, then this method underestimates the reliability of the tool.
2. The correlation between two halves will vary slightly depending on how the items are divided.

Split-half Method of reliability can also be used for establishing reliability of tests, scales, and inventories provided the researcher is able to write items for the tool so that it can be split into two equivalent halves. Wherever this condition is not satisfied Split-half Method of establishing reliability cannot be used but Test-Retest Method can be used.

Parallel Forms Method: The other names of Parallel Forms Method are Alternative Forms or Equivalent Forms Method. The researcher must decide before hand which Method of Reliability is most appropriate for establishing the reliability of the tool. In cases of multiple assessments of the same subjects, the researcher has to use different forms of the same tool. If so then the reliability has to be established with the help of Parallel Forms Method as other Methods of establishing reliability, such as, Test-Retest Method, and Split-half Method are of no use. So the key to this method is the development of Alternate Forms of the same tool. The Alternate Forms must be equivalent in terms of content, number of items, types of items, difficulty level, discrimination index, duration of the test, response processes, etc. so that subject's true score on Form A would be identical to their true score on Form B. If both forms of the tool are administered on the same subjects, then differences between scores on Form A and Form B may be due to errors in measurement only. Further Parallel Forms Method is very similar to Split-half Method. The major difference is that the

Parallel Forms are developed so that the two forms can be used independent of each other and considered equivalent measures. With Split-half Reliability one has a tool that one wishes to use as a single measurement tool and only split the tool in two halves for the purpose of estimating the reliability coefficient.

In case the researcher decides to use Parallel Forms Method for establishing reliability of the tool, to start with one has to write more than double the number of items required. Suppose the researcher decides to develop a tool with 30 items, one has to select 60 items after the Group Tryout. In order to have 60 items, the researcher has to write more than 60 items. The items must be written in such a way so that each form has items equivalent in terms of content, number of items, types of items, difficulty level, discrimination index, duration of the test, response processes, etc. If this is not met than Parallel Forms cannot be developed, so Parallel Forms Method cannot be used for establishing reliability of the tool. At the time of item analysis the researcher has to selects 30 items for Form A and another 30 items for Form B. Now the researcher has to administer first either Form A or Form B to a group of subjects. As mention earlier, a sample of 800 subjects is taken for establishing reliability. Suppose the researcher decides to administer Form A first on a group of 40 subjects from an institute. If possible on the same day with a difference of a few hours or on the following day, the Form B should be administered. The time difference between the two administrations should be short, but it needs to be long enough so that subjects' scores are not affected by fatigue. During administration of the Form A as well as Form B, all conditions, such as, duration of administration, time of administration, conditions of administration, etc. should be as similar as possible. The researcher should administer both forms of the tool on all 800 subjects. It takes time. After administering both the forms of the tool, the scoring has to be done. Take scores of all those subjects who were present during administrations of Form A as well as Form B. Now compute the correlation between the total scores of subjects on Form A and Form B. The obtained coefficient is called the coefficient of stability or coefficient of equivalence. If the correlation is 0.7 or higher, the tool is said to have good Parallel Forms Reliability. This reliability coefficient tells the researcher that both forms of the tool are reliable and one can use any form of the developed tool.

The Parallel Forms Method provides a partial solution to many of the problems inherent in the Test-Retest Method of Reliability. For example, since the two forms of the tool are different, carryover effect is less of a problem. Reactivity effects are also partially controlled; although taking the first form of the tool may change the responses to the second form of the tool. However, it is reasonable to assume that the effect will not be as strong with alternate forms as with the two administrations of the same tool.

There are disadvantages of Parallel Forms Method. These are:

- It may be very difficult to create several alternate forms of tool for a variable.
- One may not be able to write lots of items that reflect the same construct.
- It may also be difficult, if not impossible, to guarantee that the two alternate forms of a Tool are parallel measures.

Kuder-Richardson Method: Reliability is to be established of tests, scales and inventories. The responses on test items can be categorised as correct or incorrect. This is not so in case of scales and inventories. The essential condition of using Kuder-Richardson Method is that the responses should be categorised as correct or incorrect. This is possible only in case of test. Thus, Kuder-Richardson Method can be used only in case of tests but not scales and inventories. There are two Kuder-Richardson Formulas, namely, Kuder-Richardson Formula 20 (K-R 20) and Kuder-Richardson Formula 21 (K-R 21). Kuder-Richardson Formula 20 is to be used only when each response is scored as correct and incorrect, and items are with a range of difficulty levels. Items can be of multiple-choice, fill in the blanks, or short answer questions provided the answers of short answer type questions can be scored as correct and incorrect. The Kuder-Richardson Formula 20 is as given below:

$$KR_{20}: [n/(n\text{-}1)]\ [\sigma_t^2 - \sum pq/\sigma_t^2]$$

Where KR_{20} = estimated reliability of the full length test
n = number of items in the test
σ_t^2 = variance of the whole test
p = proportion of correct answer on an item
q = proportion of wrong answer on an item
$\sum pq$ = sum of product of pq for all n items of the test

Kuder-Richardson Formula 21 is to be used only when each response is scored as correct and incorrect, and all items are about the same difficulty level. Items can be of multiple-choice, fill in the blanks, or short answer questions provided the answers of short answer type questions can be scored as correct and incorrect. The Kuder-Richardson Formula 21 is as given below:

$$KR_{21} = [n/(n\text{-}1)]\ [1 - M\ (n\text{-}M)/n\ \sigma_t^2]$$

Where KR_{21} = estimated reliability of the full length test
n = number of items in the test
σ_t^2 = variance of the whole test
M = mean score on the test

As mentioned earlier, the researcher decides to take 800 subjects for establishing reliability of the Test. 800 subjects are from different portion of the population spread over a particular area. To start with suppose the test is administered on 40 subjects from an institute in the morning. On another group from another institute, the same test may be administered in the evening. The testing should continue till it is administered on all 800 subjects. Test may have items with different difficulty levels or same difficulty level. In case, the test has items with different difficulty levels, Kuder-Richardson Formula 20 is to be used for calculating the Reliability of the test. On the other hand, if items are of same difficulty level, reliability can be computed using Kuder-Richardson Formula 21.

Cronbach's Alpha Method: It is used as a measure of internal consistency or reliability of a Scale. Mostly information gathered in Social Sciences, Marketing, Medicine, Business, etc. relate to attitude, reaction, opinion, anxiety, personality, and description of people involves the use of Likert Type Scale. As individuals attempt to quantify constructs which are not directly measurable they often use multi-item scales and summated ratings to quantify the construct(s) of interest. Likert Scale has equal number of favourable and unfavourable statements concerning the attitude or reaction or opinion scale, is given to a group of subjects. The subjects are asked to respond to each statement in terms to their own degree of agreement or disagreement. Typically, subjects are asked to select one of five responses: Strongly Agree, Agree, Undecided, Disagree, and Strongly Disagree. The specific responses to the items are combined so that the individuals with most favourable attitude or reaction or opinion will have the highest scores while individuals with unfavourable attitude or reaction or opinion will have the lowest scores. While not all summated scales are created according to Likert's specific procedures, all such scales share the basic logic associated with the Likert Scaling.

However, when items are used to form scale they need to have internal consistency. The items should all assess the same thing, so they should be correlated with one another. Cronbach's Alpha generally increases when the correlations between the items increase. For this reason, the coefficient also indicates the internal consistency or reliability of the scale.

The four characteristics that make a scale a summated rating scale, are as follows:

- A scale must contain multiple items. The use of summated in the name implies that multiple items will be combined or summed.
- Each individual item must measure something that has an underlying, quantitative measurement continuum. In other words it measures the property of something that can vary quantitatively rather than qualitatively. An attitude, for example, can vary from being very favourable to being very unfavourable.
- Each item has no "right" answer, which makes the rating scale different from multiple-choice test. Thus, summated rating scale cannot be used to test for knowledge or ability.
- Each item in the scale is a statement, and the respondents are asked to

give rating about each statement. This involves asking subjects to indicate which of several response choices best reflects their response to the item.

As mentioned earlier, the researcher decides to take 800 subjects for establishing reliability of the scale. 800 subjects are from different portion of the population spread over a particular area. To start with, suppose the Scale is administered on 40 subjects from an institute in the morning. On another group from another institute, the same Scale may be administered in the evening. After collecting data from all 800 subjects, it can be analysed to get Cronbach's Alpha Reliability Coefficient with the help of SPSS. The researcher can also calculate Cronbach's Alpha Reliability using the following formula.

$$\alpha = [n/n-1] [\sigma_t^{2} - \sum \sigma_t^{2}/\sigma_t^{2}]$$

Where α = estimated reliability of the full length Scale; n = number of items

σ_t^{2} = variance of the whole Scale; and $\sum \sigma_t^{2}$ = sum of variance for all n items

The Cronbach's Alpha Reliability Coefficient normally ranges between 0 and 1. However, there is actually no lower limit to the coefficient. The closer Cronbach's Alpha coefficient is to 1.0 the greater the internal consistency of items in the scale. As a thumb rule, if the Cronbach's Alpha Reliability coefficient is either equal to or greater than 0.7, the scale is said to be reliable. However, an Alpha of 0.8 is probably reasonable. While increasing the value of Alpha is partially dependent upon the number of items in the scale that has diminishing returns. It should be noted that while a high value of Cronbach's Alpha indicates good internal consistency of the items in the scale, it does not mean that the scale is unidimensional.

The following are the problems associated with the Cronbach's Alpha Reliability.

- The problem is that alpha is dependent not only on the magnitude of the correlation among items, but also on the number of items in the scale. A scale can be made to look more 'homogeneous' simply by doubling the number of items, even though the average correlation remains the same.
- If the researcher has two scales which each assess a distinct aspect, and combine them to form one long scale, Alpha would probably be high, although the merged scale is obviously tapping two different attributes.
- If Alpha is too high, then it may suggest a high level of item redundancy; that is, a number of items asking the same thing in slightly different ways.

METHODS OF VALIDITY

Only establishing reliability of the developed tool is not enough, a tool must also be valid for its use. Thus, validity has also to be established. Different Methods of establishing Validity are: Face Validity, Content Validity, Predictive Validity, Concurrent Validity, Construct Validity, Factorial Validity, and Criterion Validity. Each of these is explained in the following.

Face Validity: It refers to the extent to which a tool is subjectively viewed as covering the concept it purports to measure or assess. It refers to the transparency or relevance of a test, scale, or inventory as it appears to test participants. In other words, a test, scale, or inventory can be said to have Face Validity if it "looks like", it is going to measure or assess what it is supposed to measure or assess. Suppose one prepares a test to assess whether students can perform multiplications. The title of the test is Multiplication Test. Anyone who reads the title, thinks that this test is for assessing knowledge of Multiplications. This refers to Face Validity.

Many a time in the Board examination, the sealed question papers are sent and to be opened only on the day of the examination. Suppose the students are to take examination of English. The Centre Superintendent will take out all envelops on which English Test is written. From this title, it is assumed that envelop contains English Test papers but on opening it was found that the envelop contained Physics Test papers. Here on the face of the envelop it appeared that it contains English Test paper but it was not so. The face may not really reflect what this tool is supposed to assess. Sometime one may purchase a book looking to the title only but after reading one may know that the content is not related to the Title. While looking at the face of a person, one may think that he/she is tired but it may not be so. Thus, Face Validity is not a good method of establishing Validity. This is one of the weakest methods of establishing Validity. Researchers should avoid this method.

Content Validity: It is also known as Logical or Rational Validity. The Content Validity is different from Face Validity which refers not to what the tool actually assesses but to what it superficially appears to assess. Content Validity requires the use of recognised Subject Matter Experts to evaluate whether tool items assess defined content. Content Validity is most often addressed in academic and vocational testing, where test items need to reflect the knowledge actually required for a given area (e.g. Physics, History, Mathematics, English, etc.) or job skill (e.g. accounting, teaching, research, etc.). In clinical settings, Content Validity refers to the correspondence between test items and symptom content of a syndrome.

As explained earlier that first step in the development of Tool is to write Operational Definition of the Variable for which the Tool is to be developed. The researcher even has to write the components or dimensions of the variable for which the tool is to be developed. After this, the items are to be written.

These items must represent the population of items which can be written for the variable. The items along with the operational definition of the variable should be given to the Subject Matter Expert (SMEs) raters to judge how well the items assess the variable for which these are written. C.H. Lawshe (1975) developed a method of measuring Content Validity. It is essentially a method of gauging agreement among raters or judges regarding how essential a particular item is. Lawshe proposed that each of the SMEs on the judging panel respond to the question for each item, that is, "Is the skill or knowledge measured or assessed by this item 'essential,' 'useful, but not essential,' or 'not necessary' to the performance of the construct?" According to Lawshe if more than half the experts indicate that an item is 'essential', that item has at least some Content Validity. Greater levels of Content Validity exist as larger number of experts agrees that a particular item is 'essential'. Lawshe developed a formula termed as Content Validity Ratio (CVR) and is as given below:

$$CVR = (n_e - N/2)/(N/2)$$

Where CVR = Content Validity Ratio;

n_e = Number of Subject Matter Expert Raters indicating 'essential'

N = Total Number of Subject Matter Expert Raters

This formula yields value which ranges from –1 to + 1; positive values indicate that at least half the Subject Matter Expert rated the item as 'essential'. The mean CVR across items may be used as an indicator of overall Tool Content Validity.

Predictive Validity: It refers to the extent to which performance on a Test or Scale is related to later performance that the Test or Scale was designed to predict. That is, it addresses how well a specific tool predicts future performance or behaviour. Predictive Validity must be established for all tools used for selecting subjects for the study or jobs.

It is a well-known fact that entrance or selection tests have been conducted by different organisations, and subjects scoring high on these tests are selected for job or admission into the course. Entrance Tests are being conducted by Indian Institutes of Management (IIM), Indian Institutes of Technology (IIT), Union Public Service Commission (UPSE), State Public Service Commission (PSC), University Grants Commission (UGC), All India Institute of Medical Sciences (AIIMS), etc. Some of the popular tests are Graduate Record Examination (GRE), National Eligibility Test (NET), Combined Aptitude Test (CAT), etc. Even different Universities conduct entrance tests for admission into different courses. For all entrance examination or selection tests, it is essential to establish Predictive Validity so that the entrance or selection tests become more useful. Normally, Predictive Validity of entrance or selection tests used by different organisations is not established. That is why many-a-time people do not have faith on results of different entrance or selection tests. The procedure of establishing Predictive Validity is as given below.

Suppose one lakh students appeared in CAT examination conducted by, say, IIM Indore. Through CAT examination subjects are evaluated in terms of their Numerical Ability, Language Ability, and Reasoning Ability because subjects scoring high on these abilities are likely to benefit more through course than those who score less in CAT examination. On the basis of performance in the CAT examination and interview conducted by IIM faculty members, the merit list is prepared. The students are admitted on the basis of merit list. Now the researcher is interested in studying the Predictive Validity of Combined Aptitude Test (CAT). These selected students are taught the subjects of Management for one semester. Their performance on different tests is noted and a composite score for each admitted subject is computed. Now the researcher has scores for all subjects or students on Combined Aptitude Test as well as in the first semester examination. The correlation between these two sets of scores is computed. Higher correlation coefficient indicates that those subjects or students who scored high in Combined Aptitude Test have also scored high on the first semester examination. That is the future performance of subjects could be predicted on the basis of performance in Combined Aptitude Test. Thus, the test has higher degree of Predictive Validity. On the other hand, if the correlation coefficient is low, it indicates low degree of Predictive Validity.

Predictive Validity is more expensive and time consuming, and as a result fewer selection tools are available for the users with information on Predictive Validity. But Predictive Validity provides more useful data or information about test validity because it has greater fidelity to the real situation in which the test will be used. After all, most tests are administered to find out something about future behaviour of subjects.

It is important to note that as with many aspects of Social Science, the magnitude of the correlation obtained from Predictive Validity is usually not high. A typical Predictive Validity for an employment test might obtain a correlation around 0.35. Higher values are occasionally seen and lower values are very common. Nevertheless the utility (that is the benefit obtained by making decision using the test) provided by a test with a correlation of 0.35 can be quite substantial.

Advantage of Predictive Validity Method: The following is the advantage of Predictive Validity Method.

- Predictive Validity demonstrates relationships between test scores and future criterion (such as Job Performance, Achievement in Examination, etc.). Thus, it is well suited to tests used in selection or admission into a course of study.

Disadvantage of Predictive Validity Method: The following are the disadvantages of Predictive Validity Method.

- There is a delay in obtaining results and so it is time consuming.
- Criterion related validities are highly susceptible to the problems of restriction in range and poor quality of criterion reliability.
- It does not test all of the available data, and individuals who are not selected cannot, by definition, go on to produce a score on that particular criterion.
- In education setting, it is difficult to collect information or data from students who failed to attend the institute due to poor performance on tests, personal preference or financial concerns. This leaves a hole in the data, and the Predictive Validity relies upon this incomplete data set, so the researcher must always make some assumptions.
- In education system, if the students with the highest score in the entrance examination score higher after the first semester or year at the university examination, and the students who just scraped in get the lowest, one may assume that non-attendees would score lower still. This downwards extrapolation might be incorrect, but Predictive Validity has to incorporate such assumptions.

Concurrent Validity Method: It is a measure of how well a particular test or scale correlated with a previously validated measure. There are large numbers of tests, scales and inventories have been standardised by different researchers all over the world. At the time of developing the tool, researcher has to give Operational Definition of the construct. This definition does indicate different components or dimensions. The operational definition of the variable for which the tool is to be developed might be close to the operational definition of already standardised tool. If so, than Concurrent Validity Method can be used for establishing the validity of the newly developed tool. In the absence of already standardised tool Concurrent Validity Method cannot be used. This method is commonly used in Social Science, Psychology, Education, etc.

Suppose a researcher wants to develop an Intelligence Test for Class IX students. The researcher writes the Operational Definition. Based on the operational definition, items are written. On the basis of Group Tryout, items are selected as explained earlier under Group Tryout. The researcher decides to establish Concurrent Validity as there are already standardised Intelligence Tests available, such as, Patel Intelligence Test, Verbal Intelligence Test, Raven's Standard Progressive Matrices, Stanford-Binet Intelligence Scale, Wechsler Intelligence Scale for Children, Wechsler Adult Intelligence Scale, Woodcock-Johnson III Test of Cognitive Abilities, etc. Keeping the operational definition in mind, researcher tries to find a standardised Intelligence Test whose operational definition is quite close to the Intelligence Test whose Concurrent Validity is to be established. It is important to note that it is very difficult to have already Standardised Tool which resembles to a great extent with to be standardised Tool of the same variable. Suppose the researcher wanted to establish Concurrent

Validity of the Non-Verbal Intelligence Test which he has developed for Class IX students. He/she decides to take Raven's Standard Progressive Matrices. The researcher administered both the Intelligence Test on a group of, say, 800 students. Both the Intelligence Tests can be administered on the same day or two different days. After administering both the Intelligence Tests to all 800 students, the scoring is done, and correlation is computed between the scores of both the Intelligence Tests. If the correlation coefficient is either 0.7 or more, the developed Intelligence Test is said to have Concurrent Validity.

*Advantages of Concurrent Validity Method***:** The following are advantages of Concurrent Validity Method.

- It provides an excellent means by which a validation coefficient can be obtained. There is no delay in obtaining the data.
- It is highly appropriate means of validating tools used for assessment of current attributes.
- Concurrent Validity is a stalwart of Education and Employment Testing, where it can be a good guide for new testing procedures. Ideally, researcher initially tests Concurrent Validity and then follows up with a Predictive Validity to make their findings strong.

Disadvantages of Concurrent Validity Method: The disadvantages of Concurrent Validity Method are as follows:

- If test is intended for use in selection, Concurrent Validity Method is theoretically less appropriate than Predictive Validity Method because a concurrent validation result cannot show that the test is related to future performance. Concurrent Validity Method is therefore less suited to tools used to assess potential, rather than current attributes.
- Concurrent Validity is regarded as a fairly weak type of validity and is rarely accepted on its own. The problem is that the benchmark test may have some inaccuracies and, if the new tool shows a correlation, it merely shows that the new tool contains the same problem.

Construct Validity Method: Creativity, Intelligence, Emotional Intelligence, Motivation, Anxiety, Fear of Failure, Self-Confidence, Tension, etc. are all examples of Constructs. A construct is a skill, attribute, or ability that is based on one or more established theories. Constructs exist in the human brain and are not directly observable. For example, though one may know that a person is intelligent by the way he speaks, gives logical explanations, uses appropriate words, etc. but one cannot directly observe intelligence. Further one can say that someone is anxious if he is trembling, sweating, and restless, but one cannot directly observe anxiety. Thus, there are large number of behaviours which cannot be observed directly but can be felt through their behaviours. So all complex and abstract concepts cannot be observed directly but can be observed indirectly through behaviours.

Construct Validity can be defined as the experimental demonstration that a test or scale is measuring the construct it claims to be measuring. Such an experiment could take the form of a differential-groups study, wherein the performances on the test are compared for two groups: one that has the construct and one that does not have the construct. If the group with the construct performs better than the group without the construct, that result is said to provide evidence of the Construct Validity of the test. An alternative strategy is to do an experiment wherein a group that is weak in the construct is measured using the test, then taught the construct, and measured again. If a non-trivial difference is found between the pretest and posttest, than that difference can be said to support the Construct Validity of the Test.

Suppose a researcher is developing a Tool to assess Fear of subjects. Fear is a construct which can be manipulated through some intervention. Fear scale developed by the researcher is administered to a group of, say, 50 subjects and scores for each subject is computed and called Pretest Fear Scores. This group is shown a horror move so that the fear of subjects can be changed. Once the researcher feels that subjects fear has changed, the same Fear Scale is again administered on same 50 subjects. Responses are scored and called Posttest Fear Scores. The mean scores of Fear at Pretest and Posttest are compared with the help of Correlated t-test. If the t-value comes out to be significant and mean score of Fear at Posttest stage is significantly higher than mean score of Fear at Pretest stage. It indicates that the Fear Scale does assess fear. Thus, the Construct Validity of Fear Scale has been developed.

In this method it is important to understand that those construct or variables which cannot be manipulated, Construct Validity cannot be established. Construct Validity is valuable in Social Sciences, where there is a lot of subjectivity in defining the construct.

Threats to Construct Validity: There are a large number of ways in which Construct Validity is threatened. Some of the threats are as follows:

- Hypothesis guessing is when the subject guesses the intent of the Test or Scale consciously or subconsciously alters their behaviour.
- Evaluation apprehension threat is based upon the tendency of humans to act differently when under pressure. In individual testing, normally subject tries to move fast. This can improve or hinder performance.
- Researcher expectancies and bias is another threat. Researchers are human beings and may give cues that influence the behaviour of subject. Humans may give clue through body language, and subconsciously smiling when subject gives a correct answer or frowning at an undesirable response, all have an effect. This effect can lower Construct Validity by clouding the effect of the actual research variable. To reduce this effect, interaction should be kept to a minimum.

- Poor construct definition is another threat. Construct Validity is all about semantics and labeling. Defining a construct in too broad or too narrow terms can invalidate the tool. For example, a researcher intends to assess Depression but actually assesses Anxiety.
- Construct confounding can vitiate Construct Validity. It occurs when other constructs mask the effects of measured construct. For example, Self-esteem is affected by Self-Confidence and Self-worth. The effect of these constructs needs to be incorporated into the research.
- The data obtained through the use of test or scale may be unreliable. Anxiety Scale in English and Hindi when administered on the same subjects may not give the same result. The difference in result may be due to language rather than Anxiety.

Factorial Validity Method: It is concerned with the internal structure of Tests, Scales and Inventories. It is used to establish Validity of Tests, Scales and Inventories. Many tools are multidimensional, that is they tap a number of different but related dimensions of the variable being assessed. For example, Adjustment Inventory by Hugh M. Bell contains four dimensions—Home Adjustment, Health Adjustment, Social Adjustment, and Emotional Adjustment. Cattel's 16 Personality Factor Questionnaire has 16 dimensions of Personality—Warmth (A), Reasoning (B), Emotional Stability (C), Dominance (E), Liveliness (F), Rule Consciousness (G), Social Boldness (H), Sensitivity (I), Vigilance (L), Abstractedness (M), Privateness (N), Apprehension (O), openness to Change (Q_1), Self-Reliance (Q_2), Perfectionism (Q_3), and Tension (Q_4). There are many tools which have items belonging to different dimensions. For tools comprising of different related dimensions, the most appropriate method of establishing validity is Factorial Validity. The statistical technique used to establish Factorial Validity is Factor Analysis. Factor Analysis is advanced technique used to determine how the items making up a multidimensional instrument are actually related to the different dimensions being assessed. The dimensions are referred to as Factors or Latent Variables and the tool items as manifest or observed are variables. The dimensions are called Latent because they are not directly observable; they are hypothetical constructs. The researcher only observes subjects responses to a set of items and from that he/she can infer their level on the variable for which the tool is developed. The common observation is that majority of researchers developing tools having different related dimensions but do not establish Factorial Validity. Reasons might be vague Operational Definition, defective language of items, unclear instruction, unconcerned subjects who are involved in testing, etc.

Suppose a researcher develops Adjustment Inventory having items related to dimensions, like, Home Adjustment, Health Adjustment, Social Adjustment, and Emotional Adjustment. After selecting items through Group Tryout, suppose the Adjustment Inventory contains 140 items. Out of 140 items, each dimension has 35 items. Items are arranged randomly. The researcher knows which items are related to which dimension of adjustment. Suppose items related to Home Adjustment dimension are 1, 5, 8, 10, 15, 16, 30, 35, 44, 53, 58, 63, 66, 69, 73, 77, 83, 85, 88, 95, 99, 100, 104, 108, 110, 113, 117, 119, 122, 127, 129, 133, 136, 137, and 140. Similarly, researcher knows which items are related to the other three dimensions of adjustment. For establishing validity, the Adjustment Inventory is administered on 800 high school students belonging to different schools of Rajasthan. There was no time limit for giving the responses by the subjects. So subjects were asked to take as much time as they want but do not spend much time on any item of the Adjustment Inventory. After the data collection, scoring is done and for each student the score is obtained on each item. These data are analysed through Factor Analysis. There are different methods of Factor Analysis. Mostly Varimax Rotation Method is used for establishing Factorial Validity. For Factor Analysis, SPSS package can be used. From the output of the analysis, if one gets only Four Factors with maximum cumulative % of Total Variance explained show that the tool comprised four dimensions, and each Factor has items only measure the dimension they are supposed to measure. If one of the extracted Factors has highest Factor Loading on Items 1, 5, 8, 10, 15, 16, 30, 35, 44, 53, 58, 63, 66, 69, 73, 77, 83, 85, 88, 95, 99, 100, 104, 108, 110, 113, 117, 119, 122, 127, 129, 133, 136, 137, and 140 which are related to Home Adjustment as claimed by the researcher, this extracted Factor is named as Home Adjustment. Factor Loading refers to the correlation of the variable with the Factor. Similarly, the other three extracted factors can be named. If the items belong to the dimension of the Adjustment Inventory as thought to be by the researcher, then the Adjustment Inventory is said to have Factorial Validity. The researcher can follow the above mentioned procedure to establish Factorial Validity.

Criterion Validity Method: It is concerned with the degree to which variable scores from an instrument or tool correlate with scores on some relevant criterion variable. This method is used when scores of a variable on a new instrument or tool are correlated with scores of a variable on an older instrument or tool. For example, a researcher has developed an Achievement in Mathematics Test. He/she knows that Achievement in Mathematics is positive and highly correlated with intelligence. Thus, the researcher may take intelligence as a criterion to establish Criterion Validity of Achievement in Mathematics Test. The researcher administers both Achievement in Mathematics Test and an Intelligence Test on 800 students. Both may be administered one after the other either on the same day or on the following day. After scoring both the tests, the correlation is computed. If the correlation coefficient comes out to be positive and high, the researcher may say that Achievement in Mathematics Test is Valid. This is how the Criterion Validity is developed.

There are two problems with this method. First, how big does the correlation need to be to indicate validity? There is no simple answer to this. It depends on the context and judgement has to be made by the researcher as to whether a particular correlation is big enough. Second, if the old instrument or tool is not very valid (that is, it is not a valid measure of the thing that the new instrument is designed to measure or assess) but the new one is valid, why should they correlate anyway? So this approach is rather weak, but it is better than nothing.

NORMS

After establishing the Reliability and Validity of Tests, Scales, and Inventories, the researcher may establish Norms as the raw scores on Tests, Scales, and Inventories do not mean anything. In order to make raw score on test, scale or inventory meaningful, one needs norm for the tests, scales, and inventories. So norms provide a useful frame of reference for interpreting test, scale, or inventory scores. In other words, norms provide basis of comparing an individual with the group. One may compute percentiles. Percentile scores indicate the percentage of subjects/candidates who scored below a given score. For example, a percentile score of 70 is well above average; it indicates the subject/candidate scored better than 70% of candidates in the comparison group. Percentiles range from 1 to 99, with a percentile score of 50 being average.

Normally the Tool developers develop their own norms reflecting the characteristics of their population. For developing norms administer the tool to a large sample of subjects belonging to the population for which it is being developed. The minimum number of subjects depends upon the number of percentile points that are to be computed (e.g., percentiles 1-99, deciles, quartiles). As a general rule, the sample for establishing norm should be large enough to have a representative sample of the population.

Suppose a researcher has developed an intelligence test for students of Delhi belonging to age group of 14 to 17 years. For developing norms, the intelligence test should be administered on a large number, say, 5000 students in the age group of 14 to 17 years belonging to different schools of Delhi. It must be ensured that the Sample represents the Population in terms of Gender, Location, and Types of School or any other variable which researcher feels is important in developing Norms for the Tool. Administer the developed Intelligence Test on a group of subjects from a school selected by the researcher. Continue administering the same intelligence test on subjects belonging to different schools of Delhi till it covers 5000 students in the age range of 14 to 17. While administering the intelligence test all precautions should be kept in mind. Now score all the answer sheets and get a composite score on the test for each subject. If the researcher is interested in developing percentiles norms for males and females separately, then different percentiles are computed for male and female students separately.

The researcher may also think of establishing other types of norm which may be more appropriate and useful in the context of the test, scale, or inventory.

NON-STANDARDISED TOOLS

There are many tools which cannot be standardised because the collected data are qualitative in nature. Qualitative data can be analysed with the help of content analysis. From this data only percentages can be computed because the scale of measurement is nominal. Item analysis cannot be done when data are on nominal scale. Similarly, reliability and validity cannot be established. Thus, the tool remains non-standardised.

Types of Non-Standardised Tools

- Schedule and Questionnaire are two types of Non-standardised tools.
- Observation Schedule and Interview Schedule are two types of Schedule.
- Open Ended Questionnaire and Close Ended Questionnaire are two types of Questionnaire.

OBSERVATION SCHEDULE

Observation schedules have been developed by different researchers all over the globe. These have been compiled and titled as Mirrors for Behaviours whose editors are Anita Simon and E. Gil Boyer (1967). Mirrors for Behaviour are available only in Department of Education, Devi Ahilya University, Indore. Different observation schedules available in Mirrors for Behaviours are as given in Table 5.3.

Table 5.3: Observation Schedules with Objectives and Author(s)

S. No.	*Name of Schedule*	*Objective*	*Author(s)*
1.	Amidon system (modified category system, MCS)	Interaction Analysis: Recent Developments	Edmund J. Amidon
2.	Cmidon-Hunter system (verbal interaction category system, VICS)	Verbal Interaction Category System (VICS)	Edmund J. Amidon & Elizabeth Hunter
3.	Aschner-Gallagher system	Aschner-Gallagher System for Classifying Thought Processes in the Context of Classroom Verbal Interaction	Mary Jane Aschner, James J. Gallagher, Joyce M. Perry, William Jenne, Sibel S. Afsar & Helen Farr
4.	Flanders system (Flanders system of interaction analysis, FSIA)	Interaction Analysis in the Classroom: A Manual for Observers	Ned A. Flanders

5.	Flanders system (Flanders extended system)	Subscripting Interaction Analysis Categories: A Twenty-two Category System	Ned A. Flanders
6.	Gallagher system (topic classification system)	A System of Topic Classification Classroom Interaction Study	James Gallagher, Faye Shaffer, Sondra Phillips, Sandra Addy, Mary Ann Rainer & Thomas Nelson
7.	Honigman system (multidimensional analysis of classroom interaction, MACI)	Multidimensional Aanalysis of Classroom Interaction, MACI	Fred K. Honigman
8.	Hough system	An Observational System for the Analysis of Classroom Instruction	John B. Hough
9.	Hough system	The Teacher in Action: A Guide for Student Observers in Elementary Classrooms	Robert Gilstrap
10.	Joyce system	Instructional Flexibility Training	Bruce R. Joyce & Richard E.Hodges
11.	Lindvell system (student observational form)	Student Observational Form	C.M.Lindvell, J. L.Yeager, M. Wang & C. wood
12.	Medley system (observation schedule and record, OSC AR 4V)	Coding Teachers' Verbal Behaviour in the Classroom	Donald M.Medley, Joseph T. Impellitter & Lou H. Smith
13.	Miller–Hughes system	The Collaboration Scale for the Analysis of Teaching: Responsive–Directive Dimension	George M. Miller
14.	Moskowitz system (foreign language interaction system, FLINT system)	The FLINT System: An Observational Tool for the Foreign Language Class	Gertrude Moskowitz
15.	Oliver–Shaver system	The Analysis of Public Controversy: A Study in Citizenship Education	Donald W. Oliver & James P. Shaver
16.	Openshaw–Cyphert system (taxonomy of teacher behaviour)	The Development of a Taxonomy for the Classification of Teacher Classroom Behaviour	M. Karl Openshaw & Frederick R. Cyphert,
17.	Simon–Agazarian system (sequential analysis of verbal interaction, SAVI)	Sequential Analysis of Verbal Interaction (SAVI)	Anita Simon & Yvonne Agazarian
18.	Smith system (logic)	A Study of the Logic of Teaching	B. Othanel Smith & Milto O.Meux
19.	Smith system (strategies)	A Study of Strategies of Teaching	B. Othanel Smith, Milto O.Meux, Jerrold Coombs, Graham Nuthall & Robert Precians

20.	Spaulding system (coding analysis schedule for educational setting, CASES)	An Introduction to the Use of the Coping Analysis Schedule for Educational Setting (CASES)	Robert L. Spaulding
21.	Spaulding system (spaulding teacher activity rating schedule, STARS)	The Spaulding Teacher Activity Rating Schedule (STARS)	Robert L. Spaulding
22.1	Taba system	Coding Scheme	Hilda Taba
22.2	Taba system	The Use of Teaching Module to Study High Level Thinking in the Social Studies	Anthony H. McNaughton, Norman E. Wallen, Shu-Kie Ho & William R. Crawford
22.3	Taba system	Informal Evaluation of Listening, Categorising & Labeling Skills (Exercise A)	Anthony H. McNaughton
22.4	Taba system	Test Exercises in Listening, Grouping, Labeling & Generalising Skills (Exercise B)	Anthony H. McNaughton
22.5	Taba system	Informal Tests on Concepts & Generalisations (Exercise C)	Anthony H. McNaughton
22.6	Taba system	Informal Evaluation of the Ability to Interpret Data in Written Materials & Make Inferences From Them (Exercise D)	Anthony H. McNaughton
22.7	Taba system	Measuring Cognitive Elements in Attitudes (Exercise E)	Anthony H. McNaughton
22.8	Taba system	A Generalisation is a Generalisation	Anthony H. McNaughton
22.9	Taba system	One Model for Disseminating Curriculum Innovations; Problems, Processes & Possibilities	Hilda Taba
23.1	Withall system (social–emotional climate index)	Social Emotional Climate Index	Johan Withall
23.2	Withall system (social–emotional climate index)	The Development of a Technique for the Measurement of Social-Emotional Climate in Classroom	Johan Withall
24.	Wright system	Teacher-Pupil Interaction in the Mathematics Classroom: A Sub-Project Report of the Secondary Mathematics Evaluation Project	E. Muriel J. Wright
25.	Wright–Proctor system	Systematic Observation of Verbal Interaction as a Method of Comparing Mathematics Lessons	E. Muriel J. Wright and Virginia Proctor

26.	Bellack system	The Language of the Classroom (Separately Boxed)	Arno A. Bellack, Herbert M. Kliebard, Ronald T. Hyman, & Frank L. Smith, Jr.
27.1	Adams–Biddle system	An Analysis of Classroom Activities	Bruce J. Biddle & Raymond S. Adams
27.2	Adams–Biddle system	A Sociological Approach to Classroom Research	Raymond S. Adams
27.3	Adams–Biddle system	Realities of Teaching	Raymond S. Adams & Bruce J. Biddle
28.	Altman system (science observation system)	A Science Observation System	Harold Altman
29.	A. Anderson system	An Analysis of Instructor-Students Classroom Interaction	Alexander S. Anderson
30.	H.H. Anderson system	The Management of Domination & Socially Integrative Behaviour in Teachers' Contacts with Children	Harold H. Anderson
30.1	Argyris system	Organisation and Innovation	Chris Argyris
30.2	Argyris system	Interpersonal Barriers to Decision Making	Chris Argyris
31.1	Bales system (interaction process analysis)	Personality & Interpersonal Behaviour	Robert F. Bales
31.2	Bales system (interaction process analysis)	A Set of Categories for Analysis of Small Group Interaction	Robert F. Bales
31.3	Bales system (interaction process analysis)	Task status and Likeability as a Function of Talking and listening in Decision Making Groups	Robert F. Bales
31.4	Bales system (interaction process analysis)	How People Interact in Conferences	Robert F. Bales
31.5	Bales system (interaction process analysis)	In Conferences	Robert F. Bales
32.1	Barnes system	Language in the Secondary Classroom: An Introduction to the Analytical Instrument	Dougias Barnes
32.2	Barnes system	Language in the Secondary Classroom	Dougias Barnes
33.	Blumberg system	A System for Analysing Supervisor-Teacher Interaction	Arthur Blumberg
34.	Borgatta system (behaviour scores system, BSS)	A Workbook for the Study of Social Interaction Processes	Edgar F. Borgatta & Betty Crowtner
35.1	Brown system (teacher practices observation record, TPOR)	Pluralism in the Analysis of Classroom Behaviour	Jeaninne Nelson Webb & Bob Burton Brown

35.2	Brown system (teacher practices observation record, TPOR)	Establishing Reliability & Validity estimates of Systematic Classroom Observation	Jeaninne Nelson Webb & Bob Burton Brown
35.3	Brown system (teacher practices observation record, TPOR)	Teacher practices Observation Record	Bob Burton Brown
35.4	Brown system (teacher practices observation record, TPOR)	Measurement of Experimentalism	Bob Burton Brown
35.5	Brown system (teacher practices observation record, TPOR)	Follow Through Tasks: The Candy Cane Experiment	Bob Burton Brown
35.6	Brown system (teacher practices observation record, TPOR)	Teacher Competence Research Project	Bob Burton Brown
35.7	Brown system (teacher practices observation record, TPOR)	An Investigation of Observer-Judge Ratings of Teacher Competence	Bob Burton Brown
35.8	Brown system (teacher practices observation record, TPOR)	Congruity of the Belief & the Practices of Student Teachers with Dewey's Philosophy	Bob Burton Brown
36.1	Brown-Ober-Soar-Webb system (Florida taxonomy of cognitive behaviour, FTCB)	Florida Taxonomy of Cognitive Behaviour: Directions	Bob Burton Brown, Richard L. Ober, Robert Soar, & Jeaninne Nelson Webb
36.2	Brown-Ober-Soar-Webb system (Florida taxonomy of cognitive behaviour, FTCB)	The Florida Taxonomy of Cognitive Behaviour: A Working Mannual	Jeaninne Nelson Webb
36.3	Brown-Ober-Soar-Webb system (Florida taxonomy of cognitive behaviour, FTCB)	Follow-Through Tasks: Taxonomy of Cognitive Behaviour	Jeaninne Nelson Webb
37.1	Buehler–Richmond system	Interpersonal Communication Behaviour Analysis: A Research Method	Roy E. Buehler, and Jo F. Richmond
37.2	Buehler–Richmond system	The Reinforcement of Behaviour in Instructional Settings	Roy E. Buehler, C.R Patterson, & J.M. Furnise
37.3	Buehler–Richmond system	Communication Behaviour and Education	Roy E. Buehler, and Jo F. Richmond
38.	Clements system	Question Types, Patterns, and Sequences Used by Arts Teachers in the Classroom	Robert Donald Clements
39.	Cooperative educational research laboratory, inc, system (CERLI)	CERLI Verbal Behaviour Classification System (CVC)	Cooperative Educational Research Laboratory, Inc.

40.1	Denny-Rusch–Ives system (Denny, Rusch, Ives classroom creativity observation schedule, CCOS)	Classroom Creativity Observation Schedule: Direction Manual	David A. Denny
40.2	Denny-Rusch–Ives system (Denny, Rusch, Ives classroom creativity observation schedule, CCOS)	Identification of Teacher Classroom Variables Facilitating Pupil Creativity Growth	David A. Denny
40.3	Denny-Rusch–Ives System (Denny, Rusch, Ives classroom creativity observation schedule, CCOS)	Teacher Characteristic, Teacher Behaviour, and Changes in the Pupil Creativity	Richard L. Turner, & David A. Denny
41.1	DODL system	Pupil Questioning Behaviour in the Context of Classroom Interaction	Norman R. Dodl
41.2	DODL system	Questioning Behaviour of Elementary Classroom Groups	Norman R. Dodl
42.	Fuller system (Fuller affective interaction records, Fair 33)	FAIR System Manual: Fuller Affective Interaction Records	Frances F. Fuller
43.1	Galloway system	A Description of Teacher Behaviour: Verbal and Non-Verbal	Charles Galloway
43.2	Galloway system	Nonverbal Communication	Charles Galloway
44.	Hall system (Notation of Proxemic behaviour)	A System for the Notation of Proxemic Behaviour	Edward T. Hall
45.1	Herbert system (System for analysing lessions, SAL)	Analysis of Lessons: A New Development in the Analysis of Teaching and a Research Report	John Herbert
45.2	Herbert system (System for analysing lessions, SAL)	Charting the Lesson and Some Uses of Lesson Analysis	John Herbert
45.3	Herbert system (System for analysing lessions, SAL)	Record of Lesson Observation: Lesson 4	John Herbert
46.1	Hill system (Hill interaction matrix, HIM)	Learning Through Discussion (LTD)	William Fawcett Hill
46.2	Hill system (Hill interaction matrix, HIM)	HIM: Hill Interaction Matrix & Annotated Bibliography	William Fawcett Hill
45.3	Hill system (Hill interaction matrix, HIM)	HIM: Hill Interaction Matrix Scoring Manual	William Fawcett Hill
46.4	Hill system (Hill interaction matrix, HIM)	It all has to do with Identity	Terry M. MaCarty

47.	Honigman-Stephens System (Student activity profile, SAP)	Student Activity Profile	Fred K. Honigman & James B. Stephens
48.	Hunter system (revised verbal interaction category system–science, revised VICS)	The Effect of Training in the use of New Science Programme upon the Classroom Verbal Behaviour of First Grade Teachers as they Teach Science	Elizabeth Hunter
49.1	Jansen system	Background Information for the Registration Form-Danish	Mogens Jansen
49.2	Jansen system	A Discourse of the Formulation of the Registration Form-Danish	Mogens Jansen
50.1	Jason system (medical instruction observation record: MIOR)	Instruction for the use of MIOR	Hilliard Jason
50.2	Jason system (medical instruction observation record: MIOR)	Medical Instruction Observation Record	Hilliard Jason
50.3	Jason system (medical instruction observation record: MIOR)	A Study of Medical Teaching Practices	Hilliard Jason
50.4	Jason system (medical instruction observation record: MIOR)	A Description of Teaching Programs in Psychiatry	John R. Graham
51.	Kowatrakul system	Some Behaviours of Elementary School Children Related to Classroom Activities & Subject Areas	Surang Kowatrakul
52.1	Longabaugh system (resource-process coding system, R-P)	Resource-Process Coding 1969: Its' Relevance to the Classroom	Richard Longabaugh
52.2	Longabaugh system (resource-process coding system, R-P)	A Resource-Process Coding Manual	Richard Longabaugh & Stanley Eldred
52.3	Longabaugh system (resource-process coding system, R-P)	A Working Paper: Coding Interaction as Social Exchange: A Modified Perspective	Richard Longabaugh
52.4	Longabaugh system (resource-process coding system, R-P)	The Resource–Process Category System	Richard Longabaugh
52.5	Longabaugh system (resource-process coding system, R-P)	Supplementary Notes	Richard Longabaugh
53.	Macdonald-Zaret system	Report of a Study of Openness in Classroom Interaction	James B. Macdonald & Esther Zaret

54.1	Matthews system (science curriculum assessment system, SCAS–teacher & students)	Handbook for the Application of the Science Curriculum Assessment System	Charles C. Matthew, & Darrell G. Phillips
54.2	Matthews system (science curriculum assessment system, SCAS–teacher & students)	Child–Structured Learning in Science: A Research & Development Project of the Department of Science Education, Florida State University	Charles C. Matthew
55.	Melbin system	Field Methods and Techniques: An Interaction Recording Device For Participants Observers	Murray Melbin
56.1	Mid-continent regional educational laboratory system, (MCREL) (MCREL interaction analysis system, MIA)	Overview of the Development of the MCREL Interaction Analysis System	Wilford A. Weber
56.2	Mid-continent regional educational laboratory system, (MCREL) (MCREL interaction analysis system, MIA)	Indicators and Determinants of Self-Directed Learning: Towards a Behavioural Definition	Richard Bingman et al.
56.3	Mid-continent regional educational laboratory system, (MCREL) (MCREL interaction analysis system, MIA)	Teacher Behaviour Relevant to Student Self-Directed Learning: Towards a Behavioural Definition	Sibel Afsar et al.
56.4	Mid-continent regional educational laboratory system, (MCREL) (MCREL interaction analysis system, MIA)	Selection of the Flanders System of Interaction Analysis of MCREL Adaptation	Wilford A. Weber, Larry Havlicek & Sibel Afsar
56.5	Mid-continent regional educational laboratory system, (MCREL) (MCREL interaction analysis system, MIA)	MCREL Interaction Analysis Categories	Wilford A. Weber
57.	Mills system (Sign process analysis, SPA)	Group Transformation: An Analysis of Learning Group	Theodore M. Mills
58.	Moustakas-Sigel-Schalock system	An Object Method for the Measurement & Analysis of Child-Adult Interaction	Clark E. Moustakas, Irving E. Sigel & Henry D. Schalock
59.	Ober system (reciprocal category system, RCS)	The Reciprocal Category System: RCS	Richard L. Ober
60.	Parakh system (verbal pupil-behaviour category system, VPBCS)	A Study of Relationship Among Teacher Behaviour, Pupil Behaviour, and Pupil Characteristics in High School Biology Classes	Jal S. Parakh

61.	Perkins system (teacher behaviour observation system)	-A Procedure for Assessing the Classroom Behaviour of Students & Teachers -Classroom Behaviour & Underachievement	Hugh V. Perkins
62.	Ribble-Schultz system (social substantive schedule)	The Social Substantive Schedule: a Language for the Assessment of Congruence Between Operationally Stated Objective & Instructional Implementation	Robert B. Ribble & Charles B. Schultz
63.	Riskin system (family interaction scales)	Family Interactions Scales: A Preliminary Report	Jules Riskin
64.1	Roberson system (instrument for coding teacher verbal and nonverbal behaviour)	An Approach to Teacher In-Service: Teacher Self-Appraisal	E. Wayne Roberson
64.2	Roberson system (instrument for coding teacher verbal and nonverbal behaviour)	Teacher Verbal and Nonverbal Classroom Behaviour (An Observation System for Self-Appraisal	E. Wayne Roberson
64.3	Roberson system (instrument for coding teacher verbal and nonverbal behaviour)	The Preparation of An Instrument for the Analysis of Teacher Classroom Behaviour	E. Wayne Roberson
64.4	Roberson system (instrument for coding teacher verbal and nonverbal behaviour)	The Effect of Alternative Techniques for Modifying Teacher Behaviour (An Abstract)	Elbert D. Brooks
65.	Roberson system (models of communication)	Models of Communication: a Model of Studying Teacher-Student Interaction	William Lloyd Roberts
66.1	Schalock system (teacher research system, T-R)	An Overview of the Teaching Research System for the Description of Teaching Behaviour	H. Del Schalock, Clark Smith, Frances Vogel & Sidney Micek
66.2	Schalock system (teacher research system, T-R)	The Category System	H. Del Schalock
67.1	Schusler system (Classroom interaction management analysis record, CIMAR)	The CIMAR a Method of Categorizing Interaction in the Classroom	Richard A. Schusler
67.2	Schusler system (classroom interaction management analysis record, CIMAR)	The Principal as a Supervisor—A New Approach Through Structured Observation	Mary Catherine Meehan and Richard A. Schusler
68.	Snyder system	An Investigation of the Nature of Non-Directive Psychotherapy	William U. Snyder

69.1	Solomon system (Taxonomy of image provocation profile, TIP)	A System for Planning and Assessing Imagery in the Classroom Teaching-Learning Situation	Gerard O. Solomon
69.2	Solomon system (taxonomy of image provocation profile, TIP)	Taxonomy of Image Provocation Profile	Gerard O. Solomon
70.1	Steinzor system	Direction for Categorizing Statements	Bernard Steinzor
70.2	Steinzor system	The Development & Evaluation of a Measure of Social Interaction, Part–1: The Development & Evaluation of Reliability	Bernard Steinzor
70.3	Steinzor system	The Development & Evaluation of a Measure of Social Interaction, Part–II: The Development & Evaluation of Validity	Bernard Steinzor
71.	Stukat--Engstrom system (Didactic process analysis)	TV–Observations of Teacher Activities in the Classroom	Karl-Gustal Stukat & Ragnar Engstrom
72.	Tyler system	The Utilization of Psychoanalytic Concept for Assessing Classroom Transaction	Louise L. Tyler
73.1	Waimon system	The Study of Teaching Behaviour by Prospective Teachers	Morton D. Waimon
73.2	Waimon system	Helping Prospective Teachers Classify & Study Teaching Behaviour	Morton D. Waimon & Henry J. Hermanowicz
73.3	Waimon system	Teaching Behaviour: The Observation Instrument	Morton D. Waimon
74.1	Wallen-Moohr-Hall-Weisberg system (Step observation schedule, STEPOS)	San Francisco State College, Sausalito School District. San Francisco Teacher Education Project-Monograph # 1	Norman E. Wallen & James E. Bixler
74.2	Wallen-Moohr-Hall-Weisberg system (step observation schedule, STEPOS)	Sausalito Teacher Education Project: Final Report	Norman E. Wallen, Marilyn Moohr, S. Pike Hall & Karel Weisberg
75.1	Withall-Lewis-Newell system (classroom communication observational categories)	Trends in Observing and Recording Classroom Interaction	John Withall
75.2	Withall-Lewis-Newell system (classroom communication observational categories)	Mental Health in the Classroom	John Withall and M. Vere DeValut

75.3	Withall-Lewis-Newell system (classroom communication observational categories)	Summary and Implications: Mental Health and Communication	M. Vere DeValut, Dan W. Anderson, John Withall and Eleanore Larson
75.4	Withall-Lewis-Newell system (classroom communication observational categories)	The Wisconsin Project: Appendix H–Wisconsin Teacher Education Research Project Papers, Listed Chronologically	John Withall
75.5	Withall-Lewis-Newell system (classroom communication observational categories)	An Analysis of Classroom Patters of Communication	W. W. Lewis, John M. Newell and John Withall
76.	Wragg system	Collecting Interaction Data in the Foreign Language Classroom	E. C.Wragg
77.	Flanders (additional materials for Flanders system of interaction analysis, FSIA)	Analysing Classroom Interaction	Ned A. Flanders
78.	Simon-Agazarian (additional materials for sequential analysis of verbal interaction, SAVI)	A Theory of Verbal Behaviour and Information Transfer	Yvonne Agazarian

In India, mostly Flanders Interaction Category System (FICS) has been used by different researchers for studying the classroom behaviour of teachers. Rest of the above mentioned systems have not been used. There might be different reasons of not using. One is the non-availability of literature. It was difficult to use them in the classroom because of their complexity. Due to technological advancement, now it is possible to use them. Researchers can video record the classroom teaching. This video recording can be analysed by using the appropriate Observation Schedule as available in Mirrors for Behaviour. The findings of such researches may guide teachers for better interaction in the classroom. The findings may also help National Council for Teacher Education to revamp different Teacher Training Programmes. It may also help in improving the classroom interaction between teacher and students, and among students.

Researchers may also develop their own Observation Schedule as per the requirement of research. For developing Observation Schedule, one has to be careful in deciding what to observe and its use in the research.

INTERVIEW SCHEDULE

Interview Schedule is to be used by researcher when s/he is interested in collecting information about different aspects of the organisation, institute, or system. This information can be provided only by the head of the organisation as he is supposed to be the custodian of all information related to different aspects of organisation. In other words whenever the information is to be obtained from the person who is at the top of the hierarchy, Interview Schedule is the best tool available for research.

Interview Schedule can be structured or unstructured. Structured Interview Schedule is to be used only when one wants to collect information related to different aspects or dimensions of the problem under study. In case one wants to go deep into an aspect or wants detailed information, Unstructured Interview Schedule is the best. In Structured Interview Schedule the researcher has to decide the aspects in advance related to which the information is to be taken and these are listed in the form of questions. While listing the questions, the sequence of questions may be decided by the researcher. On the other hand, in Unstructured Interview Schedule the researcher can decide the first question which s/he wants to ask. The other questions depend on the response of the previous question. Thus, the researcher cannot list the question to be asked while using Unstructured Interview Schedule.

Advantages of Interview Schedule

The advantages of Interview Schedule are as follows:

1. An Interview Schedule facilitates the conduct of interview because the questions to be asked have already been listed in the most desired sequence.
2. It increases the likelihood of collecting accurate and required information or data. This is because the questions are thought and worded beforehand.
3. The rate and amount of responses are higher. Often the interviewer is given limited time during which the researcher can take all required information. Since the researcher prepares questions before hand, so the available time is properly utilised.
4. It allows researchers to get more information, since they can ask follow-up questions or seek more information. Thus, the information gathered is relevant and useful.
5. It offers flexibility and may be used when interviewing different people. The interviewer can prepare the questions keeping in mind the respondent.

Disadvantages of Interview Schedule

The disadvantages of Interview Schedule are as follows:

1. It is time-consuming especially if it is for an extensive or in-depth interview. To save time it is important to ask pinpointed and relevant questions.
2. There is a high risk that the interview and its results may suffer from the bias of the interviewer, as he is the one that will choose the questions to be asked during the interview.
3. Variability may be high when the interview schedule is used by

multiple interviewers. This may result to unreliable information gathered during the interviews.

4. It is difficult to get objective responses or information.
5. It cannot be used when the sample is large. In such cases questionnaire is the best tool to be used.

Types of Interview Schedules

There are two major types of interview schedule, namely, Structured Interview Schedule and Unstructured Interview Schedule.

Structured Interview Schedule

The Structured Interview Schedule contains questions through which the researcher wants the relevant information for his/her research. This type of interview schedule is often compared with questionnaire because of their similarities. The difference lies in the usage. Obviously, the Structured Interview Schedule is used by the interviewer during a face-to-face interaction, while the questionnaire is simply filled out by the respondent.

Structured Interview Schedule is well planned. The researcher should use it if s/he wants information related to different aspects or dimensions. It is more appropriate for wider coverage. It contains questions that will be asked, and the interviewer will have to either record the answers to those questions or video tape the whole interview session. For video recording the permission of the interviewee is a must. Essentially, the process of preparing an interview schedule for a Structured Interview is the same as preparing a questionnaire.

For more flexibility, however, some interviewers combine the features of these two types when they prepare their interview schedule. It would really be up to the interviewer, and what he deems to be most effective in achieving his objectives.

Unstructured Interview Schedule

It is very useful for obtaining in-depth information. It is more useful for sensitive issues. The questions are open-ended and the interviewer can ask for clarification or further information if necessary. Normally answer of one question leads to another question. It is a chain of questions which takes the researcher to the bottom of the problem. In this, the interviewee is given more room to talk about all the topics that will crop up during the interview, so s/he is free to use his own words and let the ideas flow out of him/her easily. The key characteristics of Unstructured Interview Schedule are as listed below.

- The schedule contains indications of the interviewee's awareness of the purpose of the interview and how long it will take.
- The questions must be worded to provide answers relevant to the topic or issue. It should answer the main problem of the research.
- All questions should be relevant. Remove any irrelevant questions, or those with answers that won't be of any use to the researcher.

- Questions must be pinpointed so that each question is meant to tackle only one issue, instead of addressing several issues all at one. If not pinpointed than it has a tendency to confuse not only the interviewee, but also the interviewer, and result in the latter losing control of the direction of the interview.
- Instead of using questions answerable with a Yes or No, the questions are open-ended, which can be used as a starting or reference point for more questions. In this way, the interviewer can go deeper in getting information he needs.
- The questions are neutral, avoiding leading questions that have the potential to dictate the answer to the interviewee.

Phases of Using Interview Schedule

There is no single standard procedure for using interview schedule. Generally, the format will depend on the type and purpose of the interview being conducted, as well as the target respondents or interviewees. However, the interview schedule must have three major phases:

Phase I: Opening/Warm-up session

Some researchers call this as the "warm-up" phase, where the objective is to create an atmosphere that will accommodate the open and free flow of ideas between the interviewer and interviewee, whether it is one-on-one.

To start with, the interviewer should welcome the interviewee and make an effort to put him/her at ease. If the respondent is relaxed, the interview is likely to go smoothly. The interviewer will then proceed to inform the interviewee of the following:

- *Objectives of the interview*: The interviewee deserves to know why the interview is taking place, and why s/he is involved. S/He should be told clearly the objectives of one's research and how the information taken from him/her is to be used and kept confidential.
- *The topics or points that will be discussed in the course of the interview*: This is to make the interviewee comfortable, and a chance to collect relevant information.
- *The estimated length or duration of the interview:* The interviewee must be told about the approximately total time required for the interview. In case it is a long interview, it may be conducted in different sittings. The date and time must be decided in consultation with the interviewee and the researcher must stick to it.

The interviewee may also feel that s/he will benefit in some way from this interview, if so it would definitely help to answer the questions properly and accurately. If you don't, s/he may not be inclined to answer the questions, or give the required information.

This part of the interview schedule may be formatted in such a way that fits the interviewer's personality, and even that of the interviewee. The questions, related to which the information is required, may be given in advance to the interviewee so that s/he may be ready with the required information. It will save time and make the researcher task easy.

Phase II: Body/Core Discussion

This phase is very important because the interview starts from this phase. As planned the interviewer starts taking information by way of asking questions. The responses of the interviewee are to be noted down by the interviewer or may be video recorded by the permission of the interviewee. It will help at the time of analysis and arriving at the solution of the problem. If need be, clarification maybe sought in between the interview. Care to be taken not to miss any important information given by the interviewee. This phase may not get over in one meeting. In case it continues for another day, the time must be decided in consultation with the interviewee. During the interview both Structured and Unstructured Interview Schedules may be used as per the situation. That is, while Structured Interview is in progress and the researcher wants to get more information about an aspect, s/he may use Unstructured Interview Schedule. The Unstructured Interview Schedule will allow the researcher to go deep into the problem and get the required information which one may not get during Structured Interview. The main thing that one should never overlook is that the questions should fulfill the objective of the interview.

Phase III: Closing

The interview is about to be wrapped up. The reason that it is included in the interview schedule is to ensure that the interview will not end abruptly, which may come across as rude to the interviewee. The closing will cover the main points, in summary, that were talked about during the interview, followed by a brief discussion on the next steps that will be taken after the interview.

Tips in Preparing and Using an Interview Schedule

The main concern in the preparation of an interview schedule is on the questions. What should be asked, and how should they be asked? But that is not all. Even the order or sequence of asking the questions also matters, which is why it should also be reflected on the interview schedule.

Remember the following tips when preparing the Interview Schedule that one may use for the interview.

- *Do not start probing into any personal information of the interviewee.* One can start things off by asking the interviewee about his expertise in the field that you are interviewing him about. Do not ask him personal questions about his family or similar topics.

- *Start with the "lighter" questions*, or those that will not immediately put the interviewee or respondent on his guard. The interviewer should be able to answer the question easily, then you can move on gradually to the more sensitive or difficult topics. If you start it with a controversial question, or something that will make the interviewee uncomfortable, that will set a grim tone for the rest of the interview.
- *The general rule is to arrange the questions in a logical order or manner***.** One can start with general questions, and move towards the specific questions later on. Of course, one may have to be flexible at times, especially when a general question may be followed by a specific question in order to clarify something.
- For variety and a more natural flow, *if one is using both Structured and Unstructured Interview Schedule, it is important to use them appropriately* instead of using Structured Interview Schedule in the beginning and Unstructured Interview Schedule at the end. Normally one starts with Structured Interview Schedule and Unstructured Interview Schedule is used at appropriate time during the process.
- *Keep the respondents in mind while preparing the questions.* In research, the Interview Schedule is to be used to get information from the person who is at the top of the system. The time is very important in such cases. So take information which one may not get from other sources and it is important in the research.
- *The wording of the questions must be clear.* Avoid using complicated and highly technical terms, unless you are completely sure that the respondent is familiar with them. Try using simple language and layman's terms to avoid confusion. Stay away from colloquial terms and jargon, especially when there are better–easier to understand–alternatives that you can use. Sentence structure is also important. Questions structured into long and run-on sentences may confuse you both and the interviewee may miss the main point that you are asking about. As earlier mentioned, as much as possible, each question should address a single issue. Avoid placing too many questions in a single sentence, to be read in one breath.
- *Provide adequate time for video recording or writing the answers or responses to each question.* There is an option to use a recorder during the interview, in case there are some points that you fail to record on the interview schedule. If you are going to use one, you have to inform the interviewee about it at the start of the interview, and get his consent to video recording the interview.
- *As interviewer, you have to familiarise yourself with the interview schedule.* You want the interview to flow naturally, and you definitely don't want to sound stilted when asking the questions or, worse, as if

you rehearsed it. Well, you probably have, but you don't want to make that apparent to the interviewee. You have to exude confidence; after all, you are the one asking the questions. Once you have prepared the interview schedule, you have to know its inside out.

QUESTIONNAIRE

Another unstandardised tool is Questionnaire. There are two types of Questionnaire, namely, Open Ended and Close Ended. In Open Ended Questionnaire, the respondent is free to construct his/her response. There is no restriction on length of the response. The respondent must have a good written expression power. Mostly Open Ended Questionnaire is easy to use with educated subjects. In case the subjects are illiterate, the responses are either to be written by the researcher or to be recorded for further use. On the other hand, in Close Ended Questionnaire, the researcher writes the items and against each item three choices are given. The three choices are Yes, Undecided, and No. The responses of neither Open Ended nor Close Ended Questionnaire cannot be quantified. At the most one can compute frequencies of responses. That means the Nominal Scale data can be generated from the responses. The data from Questionnaire can be analysed with the help of appropriate Non-Parametric Statistics because data do not satisfy assumptions of Parametric Statistics.

Advantages of Questionnaire

The following are the advantages of questionnaire.

1. It is easy to develop questionnaire.
2. The large information can be collected from large sample in short time.
3. Both qualitative and quantitative information can be collected with ease.
4. These days data can be collected online or through mail.
5. It is not necessary that the researcher has to collect data himself/herself. In fact, through questionnaire, data can be collected by any one.
6. The data analysis can be done manually or through the use of already available software.
7. The respondent can take as much time as s/he likes.
8. Questionnaire is self-administered.
9. The subjects need not to give responses in the presence of researcher.
10. The subjects may give responses either in one or multiple sittings.

Disadvantages of Questionnaire

The following are the disadvantages of questionnaire.

1. Questionnaire cannot be used for collecting data related to all types of behaviours.
2. Questionnaire cannot be standardised.

3. Data collected through questionnaire are subjective rather than objective.
4. Data collected through questionnaire are not on Interval or Ratio Scale and so cannot be analysed with the help of Parametric Statistics.
5. Responses of subjects cannot be compared if the questions are too vague.
6. The findings arrived at through analysis of questionnaire data may not help in generalisation.
7. Findings have limited use in suggesting solution of problem arrived at by analysing the data collected through the use of questionnaire.
8. Data collected through questionnaire is difficult to analyse and there is too much subjectivity in the interpretation.
9. It is difficult to get back the filled-in-questionnaire from all members of sample.
10. In case of Open-ended Questionnaire, sometime it is difficult to understand responses of subjects due to their bad handwriting.
11. The facts may be withheld by the subjects.
12. Filled-in-questionnaire may not represent the population of the research.

Points to be Kept in Mind while Developing and Using Questionnaire

The following points must be kept in mind while developing a questionnaire.

1. The items must be written in the language which subjects of the study understand.
2. The items must be worded in simple language.
3. Vague words should not be used.
4. Instead of complex sentence, simple sentence should be written.
5. Instead of long sentences, short sentences should be written.
6. If researcher does not want to use Gender information than it should not be asked. So collect only the relevant information.
7. The instruction must be clear and to the point. It should be mentioned clearly that the responses will be kept confidential and used only for research purpose.
8. There should not be fixed time for giving the responses to the questions.
9. For capturing the variation in responses, open ended as well as close ended questions must be given.
10. For getting the filled in questionnaire, many a time, reminders are to be sent to subjects. Try to get responses from as many subjects as possible.
11. The researcher should send questionnaire to larger subjects because the percentage of returned filled in questionnaires is not too high.
12. Don't ask question which may hurt the feeling of subjects or put him/her in a tight shoes.

13. In this age of Information Technology, questionnaire should be sent through email and follow up is required only in those cases where filled in questionnaire is not received. It is easy to send reminder through email or Whatsapp.
14. Printed questionnaire is not suitable for Blind subjects, it should be either printed in Braille language or put it on audio tape. The subjects' response may also be recorded on tape or CD or using mobile phone.
15. At any point of time, if a respondent seek any clarification then it should be immediately provided, else the item may remain unanswered or may get vague response.

Take a Test

1. The quality of Research depends to a large extent on
   A) Identification of Problem B) Naming the Variable
   C) Formulation of Hypothesis D) Tool/Instrument used.
2. The desired characteristics of Tools are
   A) Usability B) Reliability
   C) Validity D) Objectivity
   E) All the above.
3. Which of the following Tools cannot be standardised?
   A) Observation Schedule B) Scale
   C) Inventory D) Test .
4. Which of the following is not the Method of Reliability?
   A) Kuder-Richardson Formula–20 B) Odd-Even Method
   C) Parallel Form Method D) Predictive Method.
5. Which of the following Method of Validity is not very useful?
   A) Content Validity B) Face Validity
   C) Concurrent Validity D) Criterion Validity.
6. A researcher wants to study the reasons of failure in Mathematics. He should not collect data from
   A) Teachers of Mathematics B) Students
   C) Social Workers D) Parents.
7. Which of the following statement is correct?
   A) Reliability Coefficient is always positive.
   B) Validity Coefficient can be positive or negative.
   C) Reliability Coefficient can be negative.
   D) B and C.
8. Through Questionnaire, the nature of collected data is
   A) Only qualitative B) Only quantitative
   C) Both qualitative as well as quantitative D) Not sure.
9. The data collected through Questionnaire is on
   A) Nominal Scale B) Ordinal Scale
   C) Interval Scale D) Ratio Scale.

10. The data collected through Achievement Test is on
    A) Nominal Scale B) Ordinal Scale
    C) Interval Scale D) Ratio Scale.
11. Which of the following statement is correct?
    A) Validity ensures Reliability.
    B) Reliability ensures Validity.
    C) Validity does not ensure Reliability.
    D) Reliability does not ensure validity.
12. For getting different types of information from Head of the Organisation, the most appropriate tool is
    A) Questionnaire B) Scale
    C) Interview Schedule D) Observation Schedule.
13. Which of the following tool cannot be standardised?
    A) Observation Schedule B) Interview Schedule
    C) Questionnaire D) All the above.
14. Which of the following is best Method of establishing Validity of an Entrance Test?
    A) Content Validity B) Predictive Validity
    C) Concurrent Validity D) Criterion Validity.
15. In case of Scientific Attitude Scale, the item analysis is to be done by computing
    A) Validity Index B) Difficulty Index
    C) Validity Index as well as Difficulty Index D) None of the above.
16. Which of the following is a Schedule?
    A) 16 PF B) TAT
    C) Galloway System D) DAT.
17. Which of the following statement is correct?
    A) Data collected through questionnaire are subjective rather than objective.
    B) The facts can be withheld by the respondent.
    C) Subjects may not give information always in the presence of researcher.
    D) All the above.
18. Which of the following tools can be standardised?
    A) Interest Inventory B) Structured Interview Schedule
    C) Observation Schedule D) Questionnaire.
19. Stock register is a type of
    A) Questionnaire B) List
    C) Inventory D) Scale.
20. CVT stands for
    A) Construct Validity Ratio B) Content Validity Ratio
    C) Concurrent Validity Ratio D) Covalent Validity Ratio.

6
Historical Method

INTRODUCTION

Researches are being conducted in different subjects. During the conduct of research, researchers do follow a method which is most suited to their research. Different methods of research available are Philosophical Method, Historical Method, Survey Method, Experimental Method and Case Study Method. Each method of research has its' utility. No method of research is superior to others. The appropriateness of the method is the key point to be taken into cognizance while selecting the method of research. In this chapter, information related to Historical Method is given. After reading this chapter, one will be able to:

- Define Historical Research.
- Write year of origin of Historical Method.
- Tell nature of Historical Research.
- State purposes of Historical Research.
- List characteristics of Historical Method.
- List advantages and disadvantages of Historical Method.
- Tell different sources of information: Primary Source and Secondary Source
- Check the credential of the information.
- Explain steps followed in conducting Historical Research.

DEFINITION

Historical Research is a qualitative type of research, which involves examining past events to draw conclusions and make predictions about the future.

ORIGIN

The origin of Historical Method is 1835-1845.

NATURE

The unique characteristic of Historical Research is that it focuses exclusively on the past events. Events which have already taken place are studied systematically so as to understand why, what and how of the event understudy.

PURPOSES OF HISTORICAL RESEARCH

- Researchers conduct historical studies for a variety of reasons, but perhaps the most frequently cited is to help people learn from past failures and successes.
- When well-designed and carefully executed, historical research can unfold the reasons underlying the event.

CHARACTERISTICS OF HISTORICAL METHOD

Different characteristics of Historical Method are:

1. It is not a mere accumulation of facts and data or even a portrayal of past events.
2. It is a flowing, vibrant report of past events which involves an analysis and explanation of these occurrences with the objective of recapturing the personalities and ideas that influenced these events.
3. Conducting Historical Research involves the process of collecting and reading the research material collected and writing the manuscript from the data collected. The researcher often goes back-and-forth between collecting, reading, and writing. That is, the process of data collection and analysis are done simultaneously and are not two distinct phases of research.
4. It deals with data that already exists and does not involve collection of data using structured tools.
5. It is analytical in that it uses logical induction.
6. It has a variety of foci such as issues, events, movements and concepts.
7. It records and evaluates the accomplishments of individuals, agencies or institutions.

ADVANTAGE OF HISTORICAL METHOD

- It throws light on present and future trends.
- It enables understanding of and solutions to contemporary problems to be sought in the past.
- It can illuminate the effects of key interactions within a culture or sub-culture.
- It allows for the revaluation of data in relation to selected theories and generalisations that are presently held about the past and present.
- It permits investigation of topics and questions that can be studied in no other fashion.
- It can make use of more categories of evidence than most other

methods (with the exception of case studies and ethnographic studies).

- It is the only research method that can study evidence from the past.
- Researcher is not physically involved in the problem under study.
- There is no danger of Experimenter-Subject interaction.
- Documents are located by the researcher, data are gathered, and conclusions are drawn out of the data.

DISADVANTAGE OF HISTORICAL METHOD

- It cannot control for threats to internal validity.
- Limitations are imposed due to content analysis.
- Researchers cannot ensure representation of the sample.
- Bias in interpreting historical sources.
- Interpreting data is very time consuming.
- Source of historical research may be problematic.
- Lack of control over external variables.

SOURCES OF INFORMATION

In conduct of the research, the data collection is the most important step. In Survey Research and Experimental Research data are collected from the field. This is not the case in Historical Research where the information has to be collected from documents, newspaper, video, archaeology, etc. Researchers have to collect information from two sources, namely, Primary Source and Secondary Source. Before discussing particular types of source material *it must be very clearly recognised that all sources are biased.* Therefore, the researchers must recognise the outlook of the source and take it into account when using it as evidence. The major types of sources recognised by historians can be classified as follows:

Primary Source: A primary source is one prepared by an individual who was a participant in, or a direct witness to, the event that is being described. The raw material used by other writers to provide them with information and data. Original documents; Relics; Remains; and Artifacts are the Primary Sources. In using primary source it is important to recognise the value judgement made by the people who wrote them and the intent of the author in writing the original document.

Types of Primary Sources: (1) Original handwritten documents, early copies of original documents, letters, diaries, and book manuscripts; (2) Printed documents, published books; (3) Personal documents, private documents, government documents, public documents; (4) Pictures, photographs and film; (5) Archaeological evidence; statistical data derived from documents; (7) Oral evidence and (8) capturing the happening of the event or incident in the mobile.

Secondary Source: A secondary source is a document prepared by an individual who was not a direct witness to an event, object, or condition but who obtained his or her description of the event from someone else. It gives information about the subject either from a great distance or on the basis of second-hand or even more remote information. Textbooks; Encyclopedias; Newspapers; Periodicals; Review of research and other references are Secondary Sources. Secondary sources provide interpretations and make judgements about primary sources. When using secondary sources it is important to realise that the account they give, even when it involves lengthy quotations from primary sources, may not be accurate. Secondary sources can be used to understand primary sources but must not be confused with them. Several cautions need to be observed when using secondary sources. The most important are:

1. Secondary sources as Primary sources: Sometimes a secondary source may be used as a primary source for information about the period when the secondary source was written. Thus, Mill's *History of India* is a secondary source for Indian History but a primary source for anyone wanting to understand James Mill's thinking about India.
2. Are anthologies primary or secondary sources?
   Anthologies such as *History of Education* in India by Ram Nath Sharma and Rajendra Kumar Sharma contains short extracts from a large number of published primary sources, such as, Report of the Education Commission (1964-1966) by D.S. Kothari; Sargeant Report on Education 1944; Acharya Narendra Dev Committee 1939-1953. As such it is very useful to students but it must be used with great care and not confused with true primary sources. The problem is that the reader must trust the author(s) of the book.
3. Translations: Although it is often necessary to work with translated materials but translations must never be treated as an original Primary source.

CHECKING CREDENTIALS OF DATA

By now it must have been clear that there are Primary and Secondary Sources from where data are collected in Historical Research. The findings will depend on the quality of information. Before using the information, it is important to scrutinise the data. This is done on the basis of External Criticism and Internal Criticism. External and internal criticism provides the basic methodology of modern historical research. The researcher first checks the authenticity of information and then moves to study the reliability of authenticated source.

External Criticism: *It refers to a process by which historians determine whether a source is authentic by checking the validity of the source.* To authenticate a source, historians examine whether or not the language conforms to language used during the period under study. They also investigate to see if the purported author exhibits ignorance of things that someone during that time would know or, conversely, demonstrates knowledge of things not yet known at the time. External criticism applies "science to a document". It involves physical and technical test such as dating of paper on which document is written but it also involves knowledge of when certain things existed or were possible, e.g. when zip codes were invented.

Internal Criticism: *It looks at the reliability of an authenticated source after it has been subjected to external criticism.* Internal criticism looks within the data itself to try to determine truth—facts and "reasonable" interpretation. It includes looking at the apparent or possible motives of the person providing the data. Also it asks if the source is accurate, was the writer or creator competent, honest, and unbiased? How long after the event happened until it was reported? Does the witness agree with other witnesses?

Establishing the Genuineness of a Document of Relic

1.	Does the language and writing style conform to the period in question and is it typical of other work done by the author?
2.	Is there evidence that the author exhibits ignorance of things or events that man of his training and time should have known?
3.	Did he report about things, events, or places that could not have been known during that period?
4.	Has the original manuscript been altered either intentionally or unintentionally by copying?
5.	Is the document an original draft or a copy? If it is a copy, was it reproduced in the exact words of the original?
6.	If manuscript is undated or the author unknown, are there any clues internally as to its origin?

Checking the Content of a Source of Information

In Historical Research it is important to check the content of a Source of Information. This is more important in case the Information is from Secondary Source. While using the information from the Secondary source, one should check the content keeping in mind the following two questions.

What was meant by the author by each word and statement?
How much credibility can the author's statements be given?

This has to be done meticulously. It depends on the researcher's competency and understanding. It involves extensive reading of the material related to the variable under study. As far as possible the researcher should collect maximum information from Primary Source.

STEPS OF HISTORICAL RESEARCH

Historical Research is a process, so there are steps which the researcher should follow while doing Historical Research. The steps of Research have been given in Chapter-I. The steps of Historical Research are as follows:

- Identification of Problem
- Data Collection
- Data Analysis
- Conclusion

Step 1: Identification of Problem

Under Identification of Problem, the researcher has to first select a Variable, and then write the Title and Objectives. In case of Historical Research in Education, the variable has to be related to some aspect of education. If one undertakes Historical Research in Economics, the variable has to be related to some aspect of Economics; in Management, the variable has to be related to some aspect of Management and so on. After selecting the variable, one has to write the title of the problem. In Historical Research, the title of problem must include the variable and the period. A few titles are given below:

1. A study of Educational Administration in India from 1600 AD to 1920 AD
2. A study of Management of Educational Systems in Odisha during British Period
3. A study of Development of Modern Education in India from Curzon to 1947
4. A study of Development of Education in Manipur from 1947 to 1968
5. A study of Development of Tribal Education in Odisha from 1947 to 1990

In all the above titles, it is evident that Variables and Time or Period are given. Now the researcher should write the Objectives. For title "A study of Educational Administration in India from 1600 AD to 1920 AD", the objectives can be as given below:

1. To study the procedure of appointing Principals at School and Higher Educational levels.
2. To study the Educational responsibilities of Principals at School and Higher Educational levels.
3. To study the System of inspection of education at School and Higher Educational levels.

4. To study the Structure of Educational Administration at School and Higher Educational levels.

Step 2: Data Collection

From Step 1, it is evident that the data have to be collected in respect of procedure of appointing Principals: Educational responsibilities of Principals; System of inspection of education; and Structure of educational administration. Data related to these variables should be in the context of School and Higher Educational levels from 1600 AD to 1920 AD. The information has to be collected from the Primary Sources. The Primary Sources which the researcher uses are: (1) Original handwritten documents, early copies of original documents, letters, diaries, and book manuscripts; (2) Printed documents, published books; (3) Personal documents, private documents, government documents, public documents; (4) Pictures, photographs and film; (5) Archaeological evidence; statistical data derived from documents; and (7) Oral evidence. Before using the information, it is important to scrutinise the data. This is done on the basis of External Criticism and Internal Criticism. External and Internal criticism provides the basic methodology of modern Historical Research. The researcher first checks the authenticity of information and then moves to study the reliability of authenticated source.

Step 3: Data Analysis

After checking the authenticity of information and the reliability of authenticated source, data are to be analysed. Most of the data are qualitative but there may be quantitative information also. The appropriate data analysis technique is Content Analysis. So the qualitative data is to be analysed with the help of Content Analysis. Mostly the quantitative data are on Nominal Scale which can be analysed by computing percentages.

Step 4: Conclusion

On the basis of data analysis, the Objective-wise finding or conclusion can be written.

Take a Test

1. Which of the following is the appropriate title of Historical Research?
   A) A Study of Science Text Books of Class VIII Students
   B) A Study of Classroom Practices during 1900 to 2000 in India
   C) A Study of Reasons of Absenteeism of Students of Class X of Delhi
   D) Effectiveness of Computer Aided Instruction in terms of Achievement in Mathematics of Class XII students of Hyderabad

2. In Historical Research
   A) Only Qualitative data are obtained.
   B) Only Quantitative data are obtained.
   C) Both Quantitative and Quantitative data are obtained.
   D) None of the above
3. Which of the following statement is correct?
   A) Primary is a Source of data. B) Secondary is a type of data.
   C) Primary is a type of data. D) All the above
4. Which of the following statement is correct?
   A) Authenticity is used for internal criticism of data.
   B) Authenticity is used for external criticism of data.
   C) Authenticity is not used for external criticism of data.
   D) None of the above
5. Data of Historical Research are always on
   A) Nominal Scale B) Ordinal Scale
   C) Interval scale D) Ratio Scale
6. Which of the following cannot be step of Historical Research?
   A) Identification of Problem B) Formulation of Hypothesis
   C) Data Collection D) Data Analysis
7. Which of the following can be a Primary Source of data?
   A) Personal Documents B) Archaeological data
   C) Oral recorded conversation D) All of the above
8. Which of the following is the Disadvantage of Historical Research?
   A) Bias in interpretation. B) Lack of control over External variables.
   C) Both A and B D) Neither A nor B
9. Which of the following statement is correct?
   A) Historical Research can be done in Science.
   B) Historical Research can be done in Hindi subject.
   C) Historical Research can be done in Economics.
   D) Both A and C
10. Which of the following is/are the advantage(s) of Historical Research?
   A) It helps in understanding contemporary problems.
   B) It is the only research method that can study evidence from the past.
   C) There is no physical involvement of researcher in the problem under study.
   D) A, B as well as C

7
Experimental Method

INTRODUCTION

By now it must have been clear that a researcher has to follow a Method of Research which is best suited to the research problem. Different methods of research available are Philosophical Method, Historical Method, Survey Method, Experimental Method and Case Study Method. Historical Research Method has been given in detail in the previous chapter. For studying the effectiveness of the treatment, one has to conduct experimental study. For this the Experimental Method has to be used. The present chapter is devoted to the Experimental Method. After reading this chapter, one will be able to:

- Define Experimental Design.
- Write principle of Experimental Design.
- List characteristics of Experimental Method.
- Explain different Methods of Controlling Intervening Variables.
- Define Internal Validity of Experimental Design.
- List different factors which vitiate Internal Validity of Experimental Design.
- Define External Validity of Experimental Design.
- List different factors which vitiate External Validity of Experimental Design.
- Differentiate between Pre-Experimental Design, Quasi-Experimental Design, and True Experimental Design.
- Name, give layout and other operational details of all Pre-Experimental Designs.
- Explain Internal Validity and External Validity of each Pre-Experimental Design.
- Name, give layout and other operational details of all Quasi-Experimental Designs.
- Explain Internal Validity and External Validity of each Quasi-Experimental Design.
- Name, give layout and other operational details of all True Experimental Designs.

- Explain Internal Validity and External Validity of each True Experimental Design.

EXPERIMENTAL DESIGN

In Experimental Research, Independent Variable or Treatment, Intervening Variable, and Dependent Variable words are to be used. When the researcher decides to conduct an experiment, he/she has to select subjects. Subjects may be selected randomly or taken as an intact group(s) from the field. In social science research, mostly intact group(s) is/are taken because randomisation is not practical as well as feasible. After the selection of group(s) the treatment has to be assigned. In case of Single Group, there is no option of assigning the treatment. But in case of two or more groups, the researcher has to take decision regarding the assignment of treatment. Mostly it is done randomly. Thus, treatments are assigned randomly to groups. Next the researcher has to take decision regarding the control of Intervening or Confounding Variables. It is important to exercise rigorous control on intervening variables otherwise the researcher cannot say with confidence that the observed change in dependent variable is due to the treatment. The researcher must understand that it is difficult to know all the intervening variables in advance and their methods of control. It is a known fact that some time the patient dies on the operation table due to excess flow of blood because doctors could not locate the source from where the blood is flowing. Similarly, sometime rocket does not reach to the designated position in the space. All this is due to inability of experimenters to control all the Intervening or Confounding Variables. Lastly, the decision has to be taken regarding the assessment of dependent variable. That is, when and how many times the dependent variable is to be assessed. Thus, in order to design an experiment, one has to select the group(s), assign the treatment, decide the methods of controlling intervening or confounding variables, and lastly the assessment of dependent variable.

Hence, the Experimental Design refers to selecting the group(s), assigning the Treatment, controlling the Intervening Variables, and assessing the Dependent Variable.

PRINCIPLE OF EXPERIMENTAL DESIGN

Let us take one example. Suppose the researcher wants to study the effect of Physical Exercise on Weight of IT professionals of Gurgaon. It is evident that the change in Weight might be due to Physical Exercise, work stress, diet, duration of work, etc. That means the Change in Weight is equal to Change due to Physical Exercise + change due to diet + change due to duration of work + change due to work stress, etc. The researcher here is not interested in studying the change in weight due to diet, due to duration of work, due to work stress, etc. So the change in weight due to diet, duration of work, work stress, etc. is considered change due to Error. One can say that change in weight is equal to variance due to physical exercise and variance due to error. In other words, Change in Dependent Variable is equal to Treatment Variance and Error Variance. In order to study the change in Dependent Variable one has to maximize the Treatment Variance and minimize the Error Variance. Thus, the principle of Experimental design is maximization of Treatment Variance and minimization of Error Variance.

CHARACTERISTICS OF EXPERIMENTAL METHOD

The methods of research are Philosophical Method, Historical Method, Survey Method, Experimental Method, and Case Study Method. All these methods of research have their own characteristics. Here only the Characteristics of Experimental Method are given. These are as follows:

Presence of Independent and Dependent Variables: In Chapter 2: Variable, Sources of Problem, Title and Objective Writing, it is mentioned that Independent Variable and Dependent Variable words should be used only in case of Experimental Research. In Experimental Research, the experimenter intentionally brings in the Treatment whose effect on Dependent Variable he wants to study. Suppose a researcher takes up an experimental study entitled "Effectiveness of Computer Aided Instruction on the basis of Achievement in Mathematics of Class IX students of Public Schools of Indore". Normally, it is observed that Mathematics teachers teach Mathematics through Lecture Method. For the experiment, the researcher has to develop Computer Aided Instruction (CAI) in Mathematics or takes already developed CAI in Mathematics. He takes two sections of Class IX either from one school or two schools. He selects randomly one group/section and decides to teach this section through CAI in Mathematics and another section through Lecture Method. The same topics should be taught to both the sections for the same duration. In this example, the independent variable is Method of Teaching which has two levels, namely, CAI in Mathematics and Lecture Method. Achievement in Mathematics is the dependent variable. Thus, an experimental research should have at least one Independent Variable and one Dependent Variable.

Manipulation of Variable: Normally, the independent variable has to be brought intentionally in the process so as to study its' effect on the dependent variable. It is observed these days that many young people suffer from Blood Pressure (BP). There are various reasons for it. One of them is salt intake. When the person visits the doctor, after examining, doctor asked him to reduce the salt intake. In this case doctor is manipulating the salt intake of the person. Similarly, Mathematics is normally taught through Lecture Method. If the researcher decides to teach Mathematics through Computer Aided Instruction in Mathematics, then he is said to manipulate Method of Teaching–the independent variable. Thus, experiment cannot be done without manipulating a variable. In other words, there has to be an Independent Variable in the Experimental Research.

Control of Intervening Variables: While explaining Experimental Design, it is mentioned that there are intervening variables in the experimental research. The intervening variables should be controlled in order to get the effect of treatment on dependent variable. Uncontrolled intervening variables can increase the error variance and true effect of treatment may not be visible. To understand it further, let us consider the title "Effectiveness of Computer Aided Instruction on the basis of Achievement in Mathematics of Class IX students of Public Schools of Indore". From this title it is evident that the dependent variable is Achievement in Mathematics. From the Review of Related Literature, one may find that different correlates of Achievement in Mathematics are intelligence, study habits, stress, anxiety, tension, fear of failure, etc. The researcher decides to take two sections of Class IX students. One section is randomly selected and taught Mathematics through CAI while another section is taught the same topics for the same duration of time through Lecture Method. At the end of the treatment, Achievement in Mathematics of both the groups is assessed by administering the same Achievement in Mathematics Test. On comparison, one may find that CAI in Mathematics group has achieved significantly higher in Mathematics as compared to Lecture Method group. This may be because CAI in Mathematics group has students who have high intelligence, better study habits, less stress, anxiety, tension and fear of failure. These factors might have helped CAI in Mathematics group to have higher Achievement in Mathematics than those of Lecture Method group. These factors and the like should have been controlled by the researcher. If control is exercised, than the result might have been different. Thus, in order to get the true effect of treatment, it is essential to control intervening variables. One must understand that it is impossible to know all intervening variables in advance and also the researcher cannot control all intervening variables. Thus there has to be some percentage of error in each experimental research which is beyond the control of the researcher.

Random Assignment of Subjects and Treatments to Groups: For experiment one has to select subjects from the field. Subjects belong to a population. Suppose the researcher wants to do a research whose title is "Effectiveness of Computer Aided Instruction on the basis of Achievement in Mathematics of Class IX students of Public Schools of Indore". From this title it is apparent that this experimental research is to be conducted on Class IX students of Public Schools of Indore. There are many public schools in Indore. The researcher may list all Class IX students studying in different public schools situated in Indore. From this he can select students randomly and form groups randomly as per the requirement of the study. This is not easy but feasible. In case the researcher decides to select students randomly than they will belong to different Public Schools of Indore. The selected students are further divided into two groups randomly and designate them as experimental group and control group. The students of experimental group will belong to different Public Schools spread all over Indore. It is impossible to go to different Public Schools to assign treatment to the selected students. Normally researcher may not select subjects randomly and divide them randomly into groups. Instead researcher selects school(s) randomly and takes subjects as available in schools in the form of sections. Subjects belonging to specific section may have some initial differences with respect to their abilities and characteristics. Such differences are natural because human beings are not endowed with similar characteristics. Such initial differences among groups of students may affect Achievement in Mathematics of students. The initial differences need to be checked. The same can be achieved if the subjects are randomly assigned to the groups. It means that the researcher can take all available Class IX students from one school and divide them into two groups randomly. In random assignment each subject has equal chance of being selected in a group. This procedure prevents the researcher from consciously or unconsciously assigning better subjects to a particular group. This helps in attaining experimental equivalency which removes the initial differences between or amongst the groups, if any. Therefore, achieving the experimental equivalency by assigning the subjects randomly to the groups is the essential characteristics of experimentation.

After forming equivalent groups, the researcher has to assign the treatment to groups. In case of only one group, the researcher does not have any option. The treatment has to be given to that group only. In case of more than one group, the researcher has a choice to assign treatment and it is done randomly. Thus, the treatments can be assigned randomly to groups. In other words, the groups may be assigned randomly to treatments.

Verification of Experimental Results through Replication: Experiments involving a variable are conducted by many researchers with the aim of knowing whether the findings are same or different. In case the findings are same, generalisation is made. Generalisation helps in formulating a theory, law or principle. So replication helps in verification of experimental results and generalisation.

METHODS OF CONTROL

The quality of experiment depends to a large extent on the control of intervening variables. Better the control, the less the error and more pronounce the treatment effect. There cannot be an experiment without using control mechanism because of the presence of intervening variables. It is also clear that there cannot be an experiment where there is no error because all intervening variables cannot be controlled. Sometime it is difficult to know beforehand all the intervening variables that may play their role during the conduct of an experiment. Different Methods of Control are: Physical Manipulation, Selective Manipulation, and Statistical Manipulation.

Physical Manipulation can be accomplished by elimination and constancy of intervening variables. To understand them, let us take an example. Suppose a researcher intends to compare Programmed Learning Material with Lecture Method on the basis of Achievement in Geography of Class IX students of Mumbai. The researcher takes two sections of Class IX students from a school. He decides to teach Geography to one section through Programmed Learning Material and another group through Lecture Method. In the classroom where Programmed Learning Material Group sits, there might be charts and geographical maps exhibited on the walls. When students sit in this type of classroom and study through Programmed Learning Material, they may refer to these charts and maps, although students are not instructed to do so. In such a situation, charts and maps may help students in comprehending the content presented through Programmed Learning Material. The Achievement in Geography of Programmed Learning Material Group reflects the joint effect of Programmed Learning Material and charts and maps related to the content taught through Programmed Learning Material. On the other hand, the group taught the same content through Lecture Method where charts and maps related to the content taught are not present. On comparing the mean scores of Achievement in Geography of Programmed Learning Material and Lecture Method Groups, one may find that the mean score of Achievement in Geography of Programmed Learning Material Group may be significantly superior to that of Lecture Method Group. This may be because of the presence of intervening variables, such as, charts and maps. It is important to control such intervening variables before starting the experiment. Under such circumstances it is easy to remove charts and maps from the classroom where Programmed Learning Material Group sits. Removing intervening variables from the experimental situation is called Elimination. Thus, one way of controlling intervening variable is Elimination of Intervening Variables from the experimental situation.

It is a common observation that most of the students learn faster when they are fresh. Later on due to fatigue the learning slows down. Similarly, if students are taught Geography through Programmed Learning Material in the first period when they are fresh, they are likely to concentrate more. Consequently, they learn faster. On the other hand, if students are taught the same topic from Geography through Lecture Method in the last period when they are tired, anxious to go home, etc. they are likely to concentrate less. Consequently their learning slows down. On comparison, Programmed Learning Material Group may found to have higher Achievement in Geography than those of Lecture Method Group. This may not reflect the superiority of Programmed Learning Material over Lecture Method rather it might have been due to different timings of teaching or treatment. Thus, the time of treatment may affect the Achievement in Geography. The effect of such variables is to be controlled in order to get the effect of Treatment on Achievement in Geography. This can be done by deciding the particular time of the treatment and keeping it same throughout the experiment. Here time factor has been controlled by keeping it constant throughout the experiment. Thus, another way of controlling intervening variable is constancy of condition during experimentation.

By now it must have been clear as how to control some of the intervening variables through physical manipulation. Similarly, many other variables, such as, size of class, presence of observer, presence of mechanical gadgets, outside noise, outside foul smell, comfortableness sitting, etc. may affect the dependent variable along with the independent variable or treatment. Such variables can be controlled either through elimination and/or constancy of conditions depending upon their nature. Thus, Elimination and Constancy of Conditions are two methods of Physical Manipulation.

Selective Manipulation is another method of controlling intervening variables. It can be achieved through Randomisation, Matching and Counterbalancing. The Counterbalancing is of three types, namely, Complete Counterbalancing, Incomplete Counterbalancing and Random selection of treatment combinations. The details are as follows.

Control can be employed by random assignment of subjects to groups or treatments. Suppose the researcher wants to compare effectiveness of ETV Programmes with Lecture Method on the basis of Achievement in Physics of Class IX students. The researcher takes a school where two sections of Class IX students are available. He decides to teach one section by ETV Programmes and another section through Lecture Method. The same topics for the same duration are taught to the two groups. At the end the same Achievement in Physics test is administered to both the groups. On comparing the mean scores of Achievement in Physics of the two groups, one may find that the mean score of Achievement in Physics of ETV Programme group is significantly higher than that of Lecture Method group. This difference might not have been due to the treatment only but might be due to initial differences in the groups with respect to intelligence, interest, study habits, achievement motivation, stress, anxiety, etc. because all these variables are related to Achievement in Physics. In order to study the effect of treatment (Method of Teaching), the researcher should control above mentioned factors or variables. One method is random assignment of subjects to groups or treatments. That is, the researcher may pool all students of both the sections and then divide them randomly using Random Number Table or Chit Method. The two groups thus obtained are said to be comparable on intervening variables. That is, the Achievement in Physics of both the groups gets affected by intervening variables to the same extent because both the groups are equivalent with respect to intervening variables. On comparing the mean scores of Achievement in Physics, the effect of intervening variables will be nullified. On the other hand the "Constant Error" and "Random Error" are not eliminated by randomisation, but only transformed "Constant Error" (which is bias) into "Random Error" which then can be eliminated through statistical estimation process. Thus, the effect of intervening variables can be controlled by random assignment of subjects to groups or treatment.

Intervening variables can be controlled by having the groups where individuals are matched case by case. Let us continue with the same example where the researcher wants to compare effectiveness of ETV programmes with Lecture Method on the basis of Achievement in Physics of Class IX students. Through Review of Related Literature, it is evident that there are many correlates of Achievement in Physics. One of them is Intelligence, as Intelligence and Achievement in Physics are positively and significantly correlated. Thus, the researcher decides to control the influence of Intelligence on Achievement in Physics. For this he administers, suppose, Raven's Progressive Matrices to all Class IX students available in the school selected randomly. In this case, the researcher needs to have two groups. He selects two students having similar scores on Intelligence Test and then randomly assigns one student to ETV programmes group and another to Lecture Method group. He proceeds to select another two students having similar scores on Intelligence Test. Of these one is to be assigned to ETV programmes group and another to Lecture Method group. The researcher continues like this to have sizable number of students in both the groups. In this way individuals are matched Case by Case and formed two groups. The method of formation of groups in this way is called "Matched Pair Method". The groups so formed have equivalence with respect to Intelligence. Since the groups have students who are similar in respect of Intelligence, the Achievement in Physics is likely to be influenced to the same extent in both the groups. It indicates that the influence of Intelligence can be controlled by having matched pair of subjects in the groups. Thus, some intervening variables can be controlled by forming matched pair groups. Now, suppose the researcher wants to control Intelligence as well as Interest because both these variables are related with Achievement in Physics and thus can influence the Achievement in Physics of students. The researcher after assessing Intelligence and Interest of students, he selects two students who have similar scores on Intelligence and Interest. It is quite possible that he may get a pair of students who have similar scores on Intelligence but different scores on Interest. Under such circumstances it is difficult for the researcher to get many pairs of subjects or students having similarity on Intelligence and Interest. Now one can imagine how difficult it is for the researcher, if he has to have subjects in groups who have similarity on many variables, like Intelligence, Interest, Stress, Motivation, Aptitude, etc. This shows the limitation of controlling intervening variables by using Matched Pair Method.

Controls can be employed by having groups matched on intervening variables. To understand this, let us continue with the above mentioned example. For matching the groups on Intelligence, administer the Intelligence Test on students of two existing groups. The mean score of Intelligence is computed for the two groups separately. Suppose one group has a mean score of

Intelligence as 100 and another group as 110. To make them equivalent on Intelligence, students from one group are shifted to another group till both groups have a mean score of Intelligence as 105. It indicates that both the groups on the whole have been matched on intelligence. This procedure of having equivalent groups is called Group Matching. This method is not appropriate for controlling many intervening variables. There is another problem with this method. It is possible that in one group the Intelligence scores may range from 90 to 140 while in another group it may range from 100 to 120. The average score of Intelligence of both the groups may be 105 but within each group the spread of Intelligence scores is different. This procedure of matching groups is questionable. However, the important point is that if the two groups are quite close in respect of Central Tendency and Variability, groups' equivalence seems to have been achieved.

Control can be achieved by holding intervening variables constant throughout experimentation. Review of Related Literature reveals that Achievement in Mathematics of Class IX students may be influenced by Residential Background, Type of school, Size of class, etc. In order to control the influence of Residential Background of students, the experimenter may select two groups of students either belonging to Urban Area or Rural Area. It is also possible to have equal number of students from Urban and Rural Areas in both the groups. By doing this the influence of Residential Background on Achievement in Mathematics of Class IX students of experimental as well as control groups is likely to be quite similar. On comparing the mean scores of Achievement in Mathematics of Class IX students of Experimental and Control Groups, the influence of Residential Background is nullified and only the effect of Treatment is depicted. Thus, intervening variables can be controlled by holding them constant throughout the experimentation. It is important to note that many intervening variables cannot be held constant in one experimental study.

To understand more methods of controlling intervening variables, let us take another example. Suppose the researcher is interested in studying the effect of different Types of Reward on Hand Writing Skill of Class VI students. Suppose the three types of Rewards are Material, Praise and Positive Remarks by the teacher. For this experimental study, three groups of Class VI students are taken from a school or taken from three different schools situated in the same city. The three groups to which Class VI students belong are "A", "B" and "C". The three rewards are randomly assigned to three groups of students. Suppose Group A is given Material Reward, Group B the Praise Reward and Group C the Positive Remarks by the teacher. Now the researcher rotates the Reward Treatment in such a way that each group gets each type of reward treatment only once. In this process the differences among the individuals get controlled because students of three groups are equally exposed to the three treatments although the sequence of treatment differs. When the group receives, say, Material treatment first followed by Positive Remarks by teacher, the time lapse between the administration of two treatments is so small that the effect of first treatment might not have been erased when the second treatment is given. In other words the effect of one treatment is carried over to the other treatment. The carry over effect may be different when treatments are given in different sequences. Thus, the carry over effect in case of Group A where rewards are given in sequence as Material, Positive Remark by teacher and Praise may be different from carry over effect in case of Group B where sequence followed is Praise, Material and Positive Remark by teacher. The effect which is attributed to order or sequence in which treatments are given is called Sequence effect. Thus in this study, two types of effect occur, namely "Carryover" and "Sequencing" when groups of subjects are exposed to multiple treatments. These effects bring change in dependent variable, that is, Hand Writing Skill which needs to be controlled in order to get the true effect of treatment. In other words carryover and sequencing effects must be controlled in order to find the true effect of treatment.

Carryover Effect and Sequencing Effect can be controlled through Counter Balancing. Suppose the researcher wants to study the effect of Meditation on Stress of Class XII students of CBSE affiliated schools of Indore. He selects two sections of Class XII students. One randomly selected section A is treated through Meditation (X) for three months and called Experimental Group while another section B is not given any specific treatment (Y) and called Control Group. After three months both A and B Groups are administered Stress Scale for assessing the Stress of students. Scores of Stress (O_1) of Meditation Group A depict the effect of Medication (X, treatment) and individual differences because the groups were not matched on intervening variables before starting the experiment. Also the scores of Stress (O_2) of Control Group reflect the effect of no treatment (Y) and individual differences. In order to control individual differences, the researcher rotates the treatment between groups. Now the students of Section A are not given any treatment (Y) and acts as Control Group. On the other hand, students of section B are treated through Meditation (X) for three months and acts as Experimental Group. At the end of three months, students of both the groups are administered the same Stress Scale as used earlier. Scores of Stress (O_3) of section A reflects the effect of no treatment, carryover effect of X on Y and individual differences. On the other hand scores of Stress (O_4) of section B reflects the effect of treatment (Meditation), carryover effect of Y on X and individual differences. The same can be shown as given below:

O_1 = Effect of X on dependent variable + Individual differences within group A

O_2 = Effect of Y on dependent variable + Individual differences within group B

O_3 = Effect of Y on dependent variable + Carryover effect of X on Y + Individual differences within group A

O_4 = Effect of X on dependent variable + Carryover effect of Y on X + Individual differences within group B

O_1 and O_4 can be added because these are the corresponding observations of experimental groups A and B treated through Meditation while O_2 and O_3 can be added because these are the corresponding observations of control groups B and A without any treatment. To find the effect of treatment (Meditation), the sum of scores of dependent variable of O_1 and O_4 are subtracted from the sum of scores of dependent variable of O_2 and O_3. For this the underlying assumptions are: (1) the carryover effect of treatment over other in both the groups is similar; and (2) the intensity of interaction of individual differences with the treatment in both groups is similar. Thus, the sum of scores of dependent variable of O_1 and O_4 are subtracted from the sum of scores of dependent variable of O_2 and O_3, the carryover effect and individual differences are cancelled out as per the stated assumptions. The net result reflects the effect of treatment on dependent variable.

From here it is clear that the sequence of giving treatments in both the groups is different. Because of a particular sequence (Sequencing effect) of treatment followed in each group, the effect of first treatment might have been carried over to second treatment (Carryover effect). By rotation of treatment between or among groups, the Carryover effect has been cancelled out. As Carryover effect is cancelled, the Sequence effect is also cancelled because Sequence effect gives rise to Carryover effect. The way of rotating the treatment between or among groups is called Counter Balancing. Counter Balancing helps in controlling Sequence effect and Carryover effect.

There are three ways of Counter Balancing. These are Complete Counter Balancing, Incomplete Counter Balancing, and Randomize Counter Balancing. Administration of all possible combinations of treatments to groups is called Complete Counter Balancing. Suppose the researcher is interested in studying the effect of Types of Reward on Reading Comprehension of Class V students of Government Schools of Delhi. There are, say, three Types of Reward, namely, Material Reward (X), Praise Reward (Y), and Positive Remarks by Teachers (Z). All possible combinations of Types of Reward are six. These are XYZ, XZY, YXZ, YZX, ZXY and ZYX. For studying all possible combinations of Types of Reward, six groups are required. It may not be possible to get six sections of Class V students from a school. Six sections of Class V students are to be taken from different Government Schools of Delhi. All combinations of Types of Reward are assigned randomly to six groups. One group receives only one combination of reward. Group I is first given Material Reward (X) followed by Praise Reward (Y) and then Positive Remarks by Teachers (Z). Group II gets first Material Reward (X) followed by Positive Remarks by Teachers (Z) and then Praise Reward (Y). Group III gets Praise Reward (Y) followed by Material Reward (X) and then Positive Remarks by Teachers (Z). Group IV gets Praise Reward (Y) followed by Positive Remarks by Teachers (Z) and then Material Reward (X). Group V gets Positive Remarks by Teachers (Z) followed by Material Reward (X) and then Praise Reward (Y). Lastly Group VI gets Positive Remarks by Teachers (Z) followed by Praise Reward (Y) and then Material Reward (X). The duration of each Type of Reward is to be decided by the researcher and must be kept same for all Types of Reward. Also at the end of each Reward, the dependent variable must be assessed with the help of a tool to be decided by the researcher and must be same in all the six possible combinations of rewards. From these groups it is evident that each treatment appears in each position only once. In this type of experiment both Sequencing Effect and Carryover Effects are controlled. Also in case of three treatments, total combinations are 6 (3X2X1). For four treatments the total combinations are 24 (4X3x2X1). Thus, 24 groups are required which may be difficult if not impossible to have them from the field. With increase in number of treatments the total combinations of treatment also increase. Thus, Complete Counter Balancing is practicable only in case of small number of combinations of treatments.

Each treatment appears equal number of times in each ordinal position helps in achieving counter balancing is called Incomplete Counter Balancing. As presented before, in case of three treatments, there are six combinations, namely XYZ, XZY, YXZ, YZX, ZXY and ZYX. Of these there are three combinations, such as XYZ, YZX and ZXY where each treatment appears an equal number of times in each ordinal position. It is evident that the number of combinations is equal to number of treatments. Similarly, in case of four treatments, X, Y, Z and M, there are four combinations of treatments, such as XYZM, YZMX, ZMXY and MXYZ where each treatment appears once in each ordinal position. So the researcher needs only four groups so that one combination of treatments is administered randomly to each group. Such experiments can be conducted where each treatment appears equal number of times in each ordinal position. In such a situation, the Sequencing effect is controlled. So the Carryover effect is also controlled.

Random selection of treatment combinations for each group helps in Counter Balancing Sequencing as well as Carryover effects. By now it is evident that the researcher can have six possible combinations of three treatments X, Y and Z. The six combinations are XYZ, XZY, YXZ, YZX, ZXY and ZYX. Of these the researcher can select randomly the number of treatment combinations as per the number of groups available. If the researcher has only two groups of students, he can select randomly two combinations of treatments and assign them randomly to the groups. In this, each group has equal chance to be selected, so the sequencing effect and carryover effect get randomly distributed among groups. Thus, randomization helps in controlling sequencing effect and carryover effect. The confidence in sequencing and carryover effects being controlled increases if the number of groups and subjects increase because the chances of each combination of treatment being selected increase. Thus, when treatment combinations are randomly selected as well as randomly assigned to groups is called randomised counterbalancing.

Statistical Manipulation also helps in controlling intervening variables. Statistical technique can help in controlling those intervening variables for which quantitative information is available. Variables like gender, types of school, residential background, school related problems, home related problems, size of family, type of family, cast, religion, etc. cannot be controlled using statistical technique. For controlling such variables, one may use Physical Manipulation and/or Selective Manipulation as per the requirement of the experiment. Let us take one example to understand the use of statistical technique for controlling intervening variables. Suppose the researcher wants to study the effectiveness of Concept Attainment Model on the basis of Achievement of Mathematical Concepts of Class X students of Government Higher Secondary Schools of Jaipur. The researcher selects randomly two groups of Class X students either from the same school or two different schools situated in the same city. He decides to teach Mathematical Concepts to one group through the use of Concept Attainment Model and the same Mathematical Concepts are taught to another group through Lecture Method. The duration of teaching remains same in both the groups. Through Review of Related Literature it is known that variables like Intelligence, Mathematical Aptitude, Study Habits, Stress, Fear of Failure, etc. are significantly related to Achievement of Mathematical Concepts. The students of both the groups may have differences with respect to Intelligence, Mathematical Aptitude, Study Habits, Stress, and Fear of Failure. In order to get the true effect of Concept Attainment Model, it is important to control these variables. The researcher has interval or ratio scale data related to Intelligence, Mathematical Aptitude, Study Habits, Stress, and Fear of Failure. All these can be controlled by analysing data with the help of Analysis of Covariance where the covariates are Intelligence, Mathematical Aptitude, Study Habits, Stress, and Fear of Failure. The researcher gets the adjusted mean scores of Achievement of Mathematical Concepts of Concept Attainment Model Group and Lecture Method Group when Intelligence, Mathematical Aptitude, Study Habits, Stress, and Fear of Failure are taken as covariates. In fact it is impossible to control all intervening variables although there are different methods of controlling intervening variables, and each method of control has its own limitation. Thus, another method of control is Statistical Manipulation.

Hence, different methods of controlling intervening variables are Physical Manipulation, Selective Manipulation and Statistical Manipulation. The Physical Manipulation can be accomplished by Elimination and Constancy of intervening variables. Selective Manipulation includes Randomization,

Matching and Counterbalancing. The different methods of matching are Paired Matching, Group Matching and holding intervening variable Constant. The Counterbalancing includes Complete Counter Balancing, Incomplete Counter Balancing and Randomised Counter Balancing. Lastly Statistical Manipulation helps in controlling intervening variables through the use of Analysis of Covariance Technique and Partial Correlation.

INTERNAL VALIDITY

In experimental research, the changes in the dependent variable may be due to treatment and extraneous variables. The confidence with which the experimenter is able to say that the changes in the dependent variable are due to treatment only refers to Internal Validity of experimental design. Extraneous variables present threats to internal validity because they offer competing explanations for the observed relationship between the independent and dependent variables; that is, they interfere with cause-and-effect inferences. True Experimental Designs have the highest Internal Validity because of the controlling properties of randomisation and control groups. The factors which vitiate the Internal Validity of Experimental Design are History, Maturation, Selection, Testing, Instrumentation Effects, Statistical Regression, Experimental Mortality, and Selection–Maturation interaction, etc.

History refers to the confounding effect of specific events, other than the experimental treatment, that occurs after the introduction of the Independent Variable/Treatment between Pretest and Posttest. For example, if one studies the differential effect of two forms of Physical Exercises on Muscular strength, history effect may include some subjects participating in other athletic activities that affect Muscular strength. History can also refer to more global events. For example, if one wants to study the effect of educational programmes for increasing the use of seat belt by teenagers. If the state passes a law mandating seat belt use during the course of the study that represents a history effect.

Suppose the researcher wants to study the effect of Remedial Teaching Programme in Mathematics on Achievement in Mathematics of Class VIII students of Government Higher Secondary Schools of Delhi. The Remedial Teaching Programme in Mathematics was organised for those students who did not get passing marks in half-yearly examination. It is a known fact that Remedial Teaching Programme in Mathematics is not a regular feature in majority of schools in Delhi. The researcher selects students from a school and starts giving them Remedial Teaching Programme in Mathematics for four months continuously. During the period of the treatment it is possible that some of the students might also take tuition at home, parents may help their child, students may start paying attention and do home-work regularly, etc. All these along with Remedial Teaching Programme in Mathematics may go a long way in improving the achievement in Mathematics of students when tested with the help of the same achievement in Mathematics Test which was used earlier. The improved achievement in Mathematics might be due to the treatment and special events happened during experimentation. The researcher may think that improvement in achievement in Mathematics of students is due to the treatment, that is, Remedial Teaching Programme in Mathematics but in fact it may be due to special events taking place during experimentation. The special events occurring during experimentation is beyond the control of the experimenter. Thus, occurrence of special events during experimentation gives rise to error and is called History Effect.

History may not be as serious a concern in studies where data collection is completed within a short period, such as a single session. The effect of conversation, moving around, or other disturbances in the environment may introduce History effect.

Maturation is another threat of internal validity which concerns processes that occur simply as a function of passage of time and are independent of external events. Maturation effect may cause subjects to respond differently on a second measurement or assessment because they have grown older, stronger, and healthier, more experienced, tired or bored since the first measurement or assessment.

It is a common observation that a child is not able to count or recite the tables but after a year he/she starts counting or reciting tables without error. This might be because the child has grown or matured. During experimentation, the researcher may think that the changes in the children or subjects are due to the treatment or different method of teaching used by the teacher but it might have been due to maturation along with the method of teaching used by the teacher. Thus, maturation might be another source of error.

Selection refers to differences that may exist between experimental groups prior to data collection on the basis of differential selection. This selection effect is obviously controlled when random assignment is used; however, it becomes an issue when intact groups are used or when the independent variable is an attribute variable. The design that does not allow randomisation is considered Quasi-experimental Design, in that differences between groups cannot be balanced out. Researchers can exert some degree of control for this effect when specific extraneous variables can be identified that vary between the groups. The strategy of matched pair or ANCOVA may be able to control initial group differences.

Selection bias is the bias introduced by the selection of individuals, groups or data for analysis in such a way that proper randomisation is not achieved, thereby ensuring that the sample obtained is not representative of the population intended to be analysed. It is sometimes referred to as the selection effect. The phrase "selection bias" most often refers to the distortion of a statistical analysis, resulting from the method of selecting samples. If the selection bias is not taken into account, then some conclusions of the study may not be accurate.

Testing concerns the potential effect of pretesting or repeated testing on the dependent variable. In other words, the mere act of collecting data changes the response that is being measured or assessed. Testing effects can refer to improved performance or increased skill that occurs because of familiarity with tool used for measurements or assessments. For example, in educational tests, subjects may actually learn information by taking a pretest, thereby changing their responses on a posttest, independent of any instructional intervention.

Tests that have the potential for changing the response they are measuring are called reactive measurements. Reactive effects occur when the testing process stimulate change, rather than acting as a passive record of behaviour. For example, place a video camera in room to record the reaction of the parents during interaction with the teacher; it may alter the response of parents because they know that the interaction is being recorded. It can be minimised by having the video camera all the time during interaction with parents.

Instrumentation Effects are concerned with the reliability of measurement or assessment. Changes that occur in calibration of hardware or shift in criteria used by human observers can affect the magnitude of the dependent variable, independent of any treatment effect. Observers can become more experienced and skilled at measurement or assessment between pretest and posttest. This threat to internal validity can be addressed by calibration and documenting test-retest and rater reliability.

Statistical Regression is also associated with the reliability of a test or tool or instrument. When measures are not reliable, there is a tendency of extreme scores on the pretest to regress toward the man on the posttest. This effect occurs even in the absence of intervention or treatment. Extremely low scores tend to increase; extremely high scores tend to decrease; and scores that fall around the average tend to stay the same. Statistical Regression (also called Regression toward the mean) is of great concern when the groups are selected on the basis of extreme scores. The amount of Statistical Regression is directly related to the degree of measurement error in the dependent variable. Therefore, this effect is minimised when reliability is strong.

Experimental Mortality refers to the differential loss of subjects from comparison groups; that is, dropouts occur for specific reasons related to the experimental situation. Suppose researcher wants to compare two methods of teaching Mathematics on the basis of achievement in Mathematics. Random assignment of subjects to the two methods may result in having less motivated students in experimental as well as control groups. In case less motivated students drop out from the experimental group, this loss can change the original balance of the experimental group. On comparing mean scores of achievement in Mathematics of experimental and control groups, one may find that experimental group might have significantly higher mean score of achievement in Mathematics as compared to control group. The experimental group's mean score of achievement in Mathematics reflects the joint effect of treatment and dropping out of subjects from the experimental group. The dropping of subjects from the experimental setting is called Experimental Mortality. Thus, another source of error is Experimental Mortality.

Selection–Maturation interaction etc.: Some of the foregoing threats to internal validity may interact with selection to produce changes in the dependent variable that may look like treatment effect. When subjects are not assigned randomly to groups or when randomisation fails, Maturation, History or Instrumentation threats may affect the groups differentially.

Selection-Maturation interaction effects occur when the experimental groups experience maturational change at different speeds. For example, if one compares changes in motor learning skills following a course of therapy in 3- and 10-year olds, one can expect a different rate of development change that could confound treatment effect.

Selection-History interaction effects result when experimental groups come from different settings so that local history of each group influences responses. This is especially important in multicenter studies or when groups are chosen to represent different geographical areas.

Selection-Instrumentation interaction occurs when the average scores for the various groups represent different points on the measuring instrument and when the instrument does not register equal intervals across the full range of measurement. These effects are often called "floor" and "ceiling" effects because the measurement scale is incapable of accurately recording values above or below a certain level. This can happen in extremely heterogeneous groups.

EXTERNAL VALIDITY

External Validity refers to the extent to which the results of a study can be generalised beyond the internal specifications of the study sample. Whereas internal validity is concerned specifically with the relationship between independent and dependent variables within a specific set of circumstances, external validity is concerned with the usefulness of that information outside the experimental situation. Threats to external validity involve the interaction of treatment with the specific type of subjects tested, the specific setting in which the experiment is carried out, or the time in history when the study is done. Different threats to external validity are Interaction of Selection and Treatment, Interaction of Testing and Treatment, Interaction of Setting and Treatment, Interaction of History and Treatment, Reactive Effects of Experimental Arrangements, and Multiple Treatment Interference.

Interaction of Selection and Treatment: One major goal of research is to apply results to a target population, that is, to individuals who are not experimental subjects but who are represented by the sample of the study. If subjects are sampled according to specific characteristics, such as, subjects may be restricted to a limited age range, one gender, only urban area, or a defined level of function. When samples are confined to certain types of subjects, it is not reasonable to generalise results to those who do not have these characteristics.

External validity is threatened when documented cause-and-effect relationship do not apply across subdivisions of the target population, that is, when specific intervention result in differential treatment effects, depending on the subjects' characteristics. Suppose the researcher wants to demonstrate the benefits of Concept Attainment Model for teaching science concepts to Class IX students of Government Schools of Delhi. The effect of Concept Attainment Model may not be generalisable across groups that exhibit various levels of specificity, those belonging to rural area, studying in Private schools, belong to educated family, etc. Studies are especially vulnerable to this threat when volunteers are used as subjects. Those who choose to volunteer may do so because of certain personal characteristics that ultimately bias the sample. When studies demonstrate conflicting results, it is often because of the differences within the accessible population.

Interaction of Testing and Treatment: External Validity may be affected due to Interaction of Testing and Treatment. In some designs, the researcher administers a pretest to get the present status of the group on the dependent variable under study. Now this group is given the treatment as decided by the researcher and at the end of the treatment, the same test is administered again to the group and it constitutes the posttest. The performance on the posttest is the resultant of interaction between treatment and pretest. So the finding of this group cannot be generalised to the population where pretesting is not done.

Interaction of Setting and Treatment: Suppose the researcher demonstrates a causal relationship between Concept Attainment Model and concept understanding of Class IX students of Government Schools of Delhi. Can the finding of this study be generalised to students of other states, students from urban area, different family structure, personality and schools, etc.? This can only be answered by replicating the same research in different settings. Further all situational specifics e.g. treatment conditions, time, location, lighting, noise, treatment administration, investigator, timing, scope and extent of measurement, etc. of a study potentially limit generalisability.

Interaction of History and Treatment: This threat to external validity concerns the ability to generalise the results to different periods of time in the past or future. For example, if one looks at the results of nutritional studies of reducing cholesterol in the diet, results may be quite different today from the results obtained 20 years ago, when knowledge about the effect of diet and exercise on cardiovascular fitness was less developed, and when the society and the media were less involved in promoting fitness and health. This type of generalisation is supported when results are replicated in future studies and previous research corroborates the established causal relationship.

Reactive Effects of Experimental Arrangement: An effect that is simply due to the fact that subjects know that they are participating in an experiment and experiencing the novelty of it—the Hawthorne effect. An experiment in remedial reading instruction has an effect that does not occur when the remedial reading programme, which is the experimental treatment, is implemented in the regular programme.

Experimental Bias or Hawthorne Effect: Construct validity concerns biases that are introduced into a study by expectations of either the subjects or the experimenter. Subjects often try their best to fulfill the researcher's expectation or to present themselves in the best way possible, so that responses are no longer representative of natural behaviour. This fact was documented in classical studies performed from 1924 to 1927 at the Hawthorne Works, a division of the Western Electric Company in Chicago. Researchers were interested in studying how various levels of illumination affected workers' output. What they found was that no matter what they did, lowering light or raising light, the workers increased production. This phenomenon became known as the Hawthorne effect, which is the tendency of persons who are singled out for special attention to perform better merely because of the expectations created by the situation.

Experimenters may also have certain expectancies that can influence how subjects respond. They may react more positively to subjects in the experimental group or give less attention to those in the control group, because of an emotional or intellectual investment in their hypothesis. Rosenthal described several types of *experimenter effects* in terms of the experimenter's active behaviour and interaction with the subject, such as, verbal cues and smiling, and passive behaviour, such as those related to appearance. This threat can be avoided by employing testers who are blinded to subject assignment and the research hypothesis.

Placebo Effect: A placebo is anything that seems to be a "real" medical treatment—but isn't. It could be a pill, a shot, or some other type of "fake" treatment. What all placebos have in common is that they do not contain an active substance meant to affect health. For instance, some people in a study might be given a new drug to lower cholesterol. Others would get a placebo. None of the people in the study will know if they got the real treatment or the placebo. Researchers then compare the effects of the drug and the placebo on the people in the study. That way, they can determine the effectiveness of the new drug and check for side effects.

Sometimes a person can have a response to a placebo. The response can be positive or negative. For instance, the person's symptoms may improve. Or the person may have what appear to be side effects from the treatment. These responses are known as the "placebo effect". The *placebo effect* refers to the phenomenon in which some people experience some benefit after the administration of a placebo. A placebo is a substance with no known medical effects, such as sterile water, saline solution or a sugar pill. In short, a placebo is a fake treatment that in some cases can produce a very real response. The expectations of the patient play a significant role in the placebo effect; the more a person expects the treatment to work, the more likely they are to exhibit a placebo response.

Multiple-treatment interference: When the same subjects receive two or more treatments as in a repeated measures design, there may be a carry-over effect between treatments, such results cannot be generalised to single treatment. For example, in a drug experiment the same animals are administered four different drug doses in some sequence. The effects of the second through fourth doses cannot be separated from the possible delayed effects of preceding doses.

DIFFERENCES AMONG DiFFERENT TYPES OF EXPERIMENTAL DESIGN

As per Campbell and Stanley (1963), experimental designs can be classified into three categories, namely, Pre-Experimental Design, Quasi-Experimental Design, and True Experimental Design. The differences among them are as follows:

Basis	*Pre-Experimental Design*	*Quasi-Experimental Design*	*True Experimental Design*
Selection of Subjects	Subjects as available in the field	Subjects as available in the field	Subjects are randomly selected
Assignment of Treatment	No scope of random assignment of treatment	Treatment is assigned randomly	Treatment is assigned randomly
Control	Poor control	Better control	Best control
Internal Validity	Poor	Better	Best
External Validity	Poor	Better	Best
Assessment of dependent variable	As per requirement of experimental design	As per requirement of experimental design	As per requirement of experimental design

PRE-EXPERIMENTAL DESIGNS

The Pre-experimental Designs are of three types, namely, One Shot Case Study, One Group Pretest-Posttest Design, and Static Group Comparison. The details are as follows:

One Shot Case Study

In One Shot Case Study, one intact group is taken from the field and given the treatment for a specific period. At the end of the treatment, the dependent variable was assessed. The layout of this design is as follows:

X O

As evident from the layout, there is no control group. This design is introduced here as a minimum reference point. Basic to scientific evidence is the process of comparison of recording differences or contrast. Any appearance of absolute knowledge, or intrinsic knowledge about singular isolated objects, is found to be illusory upon analysis. Securing scientific evidence involves making at least one comparison. For such a comparison to be useful, both sides of comparison should be made with the help of same tool administered under similar conditions. The researcher gets quantitative data. From this data mean, standard deviation, and coefficient of variation can be computed. The outcome of One Shot Case Study should be carefully compared with other evidences casually observed and remembered. The inferences are based upon general expectations of what the data would have been, had the treatment (X) not given. Such studies often involve collection of specific details, careful observation, testing, etc. and in such cases there are chances of error of misplaced precision. Researches using One Shot Case Study design are not of much value and one should avoid using this design. It is difficult to justify the finding of One Shot Case Study as there might be many reasons of it.

Internal Validity of One Shot Case Study Design

History refers to the confounding effect of specific events, other than the experimental treatment that occurs after the introduction of the Independent Variable/Treatment. Suppose the researcher wants to study the effectiveness of ETV programme on the basis of Achievement in Chemistry of Class XI students of Government Higher Secondary Schools of Delhi. He starts teaching Chemistry with the help of ETV programme in one of the schools. During the treatment period, students of the group may read the same topics from books, take help of teachers, attend tuition classes, etc. At the end of the treatment, an achievement in Chemistry test developed by the researcher is administered. The performance of students on the achievement in Chemistry test reflects the joint effect of treatment, that is, ETV Programme, and confounding effect of specific events occurring during the period of treatment. Thus, One Shot Case Study Design is not valid against the criterion of History.

During the period of treatment, students might mature mentally as well as physically. Students might start paying attention during teaching, develop positive attitude towards the subject, understand importance of better achievement, etc. This type of change in subjects refers to maturation and it affects the dependent variable along with the treatment. Thus, it gives rise to error due to maturation. Thus, One Shot Case Study Design is not valid against the criterion of Maturation.

As mentioned earlier, the researcher takes one intact group of students from the school. The students of the class might belong to family with high SES, have better facilities at home as well as school, parents provide all possible help to their child, etc. The achievement of this group is likely to be different if the same experiment is done with students having different characteristics. The dependent variable reflects the combined effect of treatment and selection of the group or subjects. Thus, One Shot Case Study Design is not valid against the criterion of Selection.

It is observed that students dropout during the process of experimentation. Dropping out of students/subjects from experimentation is called Mortality. When the treatment of ETV programme is being given, and some poor performing students miss many classes due to some reason, this gets reflected in the assessment of dependent variable, that is, achievement in chemistry. If poor performing students do not dropout, the final outcome is going to be different. So dropping out of subjects from the experimentation can change the outcome. Thus, One Shot Case Study Design is not valid against the criterion of Mortality.

External Validity of One Shot Case Study Design

In this experimental design, the researcher selects a school and administers the treatment to the students already admitted by the school. Researcher has no freedom of selecting students randomly but he has to take an intact group from the school. The selected students may not represent the population to which they belong. The result of interaction of Selection and Treatment of this group cannot be generalised to the population as the selected group does not represent the population to which it belongs. Thus, One Shot Case Study Design lacks External Validity with respect to criterion of Interaction of Selection and Treatment.

One Shot Case Study Design lacks Internal Validity with respect to History, Maturation, Selection and Mortality. It also lacks External Validity with respect to Interaction of Selection and Treatment.

Data Analysis of One Shot Case Study Design

The data can be analysed with the help of One Sample t-Test

One Group Pretest-Posttest Design/Pretest-Posttest Single Group Design

As the name indicates, the researcher takes a group as available in the field and assesses the dependent variable. It constitutes the Pretest (O_1). Now the Treatment is given to the group for a specific period of time. At the end of treatment the dependent variable is assessed again with the help of the same test as used at the Pretest stage. This constitutes Posttest (O_2). The layout of One Group Pretest-Posttest Design is as follows:

$$O_1 \quad X \quad O_2$$

Suppose researcher wants to study the effect of Cognitive Research Trust (CoRT) Strategy on Verbal Creativity of Class XII students of Public Schools of

Indore. One school is taken for this experiment. From this school all admitted students of Class XII were first administered Torrance Test of Creative Thinking for assessing Verbal Creativity of all students of this group. It constitutes Pretest (O_1). After this one exercise per day for a period of three months was given using CoRT Strategy. At the end of three months, Torrance Test of Creative Thinking was administered for assessing Creativity of all students of this group. It constitutes Posttest (O_2). The Internal Validity and External Validity of One Group Pretest-Posttest Design are discussed in the following.

Internal Validity of One Group Pretest-Posttest Design

History refers to the specific events that may take place and affect the Verbal Creativity (dependent variable) of experimental group. Suppose students start doing the same type of exercises at home with the family members, or friends as done in the class. Students may start reading content related to creativity from the Internet, etc. Whatever students do in addition to the exercises given in the class may affect the Verbal Creativity of students if related to facilitation of Verbal Creativity. There is no mechanism of controlling such factors. The Posttest (O_2) indicates the joint effect of treatment and History factors. By comparing mean scores of Verbal Creativity at the Pretest and Posttest stages, the researcher cannot say that the difference in mean scores of Verbal Creativity is due to CoRT Strategy because it reflects the combined effect of History and CoRT Strategy. Thus, One Group Pretest-Posttest Design is not valid against the criterion of History.

Maturation refers of natural changes in physical and cognitive aspects of subjects. The treatment continued for three months. During this period, there is bound to be changes in biological and psychological aspects of the subjects of this study and these get reflected in Posttest (O_2). So the Posttest (O_2) will reflect the combined effect of Maturation and CoRT Strategy (Treatment). By comparing mean scores of Verbal Creativity at the Pretest and Posttest stages, the researcher cannot say that the difference in mean scores of Verbal Creativity is due to CoRT Strategy because it reflects the combined effect of Maturation and CoRT Strategy. Thus, One Group Pretest-Posttest Design is not valid against the criterion of Maturation.

In One Group Pretest-Posttest Design, the experimental group is pretested (O_1) with the help of a test. Through pretesting students get to know the types of items and the responses required. This experience may make students interested in the subject, improve their attention span, concentrate during the exercises, etc. This might not have been the case in the absence of Pretest. After the treatment, the same test is administered again to the subjects of the same group and it constitutes Posttest (O_2). The scores on Posttest reflect the combined effect of Testing and Treatment. By comparing mean scores of Verbal Creativity at the Pretest and Posttest stages, the researcher cannot say that the difference in mean scores of Verbal Creativity is due to CoRT Strategy because it reflects the combined effect of Testing and CoRT Strategy. Thus, One Group Pretest-Posttest Design is not valid against the criterion of Testing.

It is a fact that no tool is 100% reliable and valid. In this design the subjects of the group are pretested (O_1) with the help of a test. This might have made them more experienced and skilled at assessment between pretest and posttest. This is because students know the items, type of response required, time given for the response, etc. The acquaintance with the test at the pretest stage may get reflected at the posttest (O_2) stage. So the performance of students at the posttest (O_2) reflects the joint effect of Instrumentation and Treatment. By comparing mean scores of Verbal Creativity at the Pretest and Posttest stages, the researcher cannot say that the difference in mean scores of Verbal Creativity is due to CoRT Strategy because it reflects the combined effect of Instrumentation and CoRT Strategy. Thus, One Group Pretest-Posttest Design is not valid against the criterion of Instrumentation.

Another confounding variable in some of the experimental researches is Regression. Suppose students are selected for an experiment because their Achievement in Mathematics was poor which was assessed with the help of an Achievement in Mathematics Test. It constitutes Pretest (O_1). Without giving treatment to the group, if the same Achievement in Mathematics Test or a parallel test is administered which is called posttest (O_2) the mean score of Achievement in Mathematics at the posttest is likely to be higher than mean score of Achievement in Mathematics at the pretest. This is due to imperfect correlation between (O_1) and (O_2). Errors of inference due to overlooking regression effects have been so troublesome in educational research that the fundamental insight into their nature is frequently missed. Thus, the internal validity of One Group Pretest-Posttest Design in respect of Regression is doubtful.

In this design, only one group is taken and pretested using a test. This group is then given the treatment for a specific period of time. At the end of the treatment the same test is administered again to the same group of subjects. The different characteristics of the members of the group taken for the experimentation get reflected equally in the pretest as well as posttest. On comparing the mean scores of dependent variable at pretest (O_1) and posttest (O_2) get cancelled. The net result reflects only the effect of treatment. Thus, One Group Pretest-Posttest Design is valid against the criterion of Selection.

In this design the dependent variable is assessed before the treatment and after the treatment. The treatment might be of a longer duration. During this period, it is possible that some subjects might dropout due to some valid reasons. In this design the scores of those subjects are used for calculation who were present both at the pretest as well as posttest. Thus, dropping out of subjects during experimentation does not get reflected in the posttest. The pretest (O_1) and posttest (O_2) scores are only of those subjects who were present throughout the period of experimentation. So Mortality has no effect on the outcome of the experiment. Thus, One Group Pretest-Posttest Design is valid against the criterion of Mortality.

In One Group Pretest-Posttest Design, one intact group is taken from the field as there is no chance of randomisation. The selected group has its own characteristics and might be heterogeneous. Among the selected subjects, some might be more matured in comparison to others. So there is likely to be interaction of Selection and Maturation, etc. and there is no way to control this interaction. The net result reflects the confounding effect of treatment interaction of Selection and Maturation, etc. Thus, One Group Pretest-Posttest Design is not valid against the criterion of interaction of Selection and Maturation, etc.

External Validity of One Group Pretest-Posttest Design

It is evident from the description of Internal Validity, that one intact group is taken for experimentation. This group is pretested with the help of a test. This constitutes Pretest (O_1). While taking pretest students/subjects get acquainted with the type of question, difficulty they faced, duration of time, etc. They might not have been able to answer all question of pretest correctly. During the treatment they might have concentrated and paid attention. Due to this they might have got the answers and improved their performance on the posttest (O_2) which was administered at the end of the treatment. Posttest performance of students/subjects reflects the effect of interaction of Testing and Treatment. The finding of this study cannot be generalised to the population to which the experimental group belongs because the group taken for the experiment does not represent the population of the study. Thus, One Group Pretest-Posttest Design lacks external validity against the criterion of interaction of Testing and Treatment.

In this design, the characteristics of the group are unknown as intact group is taken from the field. By chance if the selected group is intelligent, curious, hardworking, etc., the members of this group will benefit from treatment differently than those of less intelligent, less curious, less hardworking, etc. It means there is interaction of Selection and Treatment and it get reflected in the finding. The finding of One Group Pretest-Posttest Design cannot be generalised to the population to which the experimental group belongs because the group taken for experiment does not represent the population. Thus, One Group Pretest-Posttest Design lacks external validity against the criterion of interaction of Selection and Treatment.

One Group Pretest-Posttest Design lacks Internal Validity with respect to History, Maturation, Testing, Instrumentation, and Interaction of Selection and Maturation, etc. but this design has a strong Internal Validity in respect of Selection and Mortality. It also lacks External Validity with respect to

Interaction of Testing and Treatment, and Interaction of Selection and Treatment.

Data Analysis of One Group Pretest-Posttest Design

The data of One Group Pretest-Posttest Design can be analysed with the help of Correlated t-test or Paired Samples t-test.

Static Group Comparison Design

This is the last design that belongs to Pre-experimental Designs. Suppose a researcher intends to conduct an experimental study whose title is "A study of effect of Supervised Library Study on Achievement in Mathematics of Class IX students of Government Higher Secondary Schools of Delhi". For this study, two available intact sections of Class IX students are taken from a school. It means students are not selected randomly. The two sections of students are comparable with respect to class, locality of institution, age of student, type of school, syllabus, etc. but do not have equivalence with respect to intelligence, study habits, adjustment, personality, previous academic achievement, etc. Of the two selected sections, one section is randomly given the treatment of Supervised Library Study. The other section is not given any treatment but students continued with their usual classroom teaching. This experiment continued for a period of three months at the rate of one hour per working day. At the end of the treatment students of both sections are administered same Achievement in Mathematics test. The layout of Static Group Comparison Design is

$$
\begin{array}{cc}
X & O_1 \\
\hdashline
 & O_2
\end{array}
$$

From the layout it is clear that there are two groups separated by dotted line which indicates that the two groups are not equivalent. X represents the treatment of Supervised Library Study and called experimental group. The absence of X in the second group reflects that no specific treatment is given rather the group continued with the normal teaching. This group is called control group.

Internal Validity of Static Group Comparison Design

History refers to the specific event taking place during experimentation. As mentioned earlier that the treatment continued for three months. During this period it is possible that the Mathematics teacher might have taken extra class, given home work as well as class work, made students to solve extra numerical problems, arranged debates, etc. All these are special events that may take place during experimentation and affect Achievement in Mathematics of students of both experimental and control groups. The effect of all above mentioned activities gets reflected in Achievement in Mathematics. O_1 of experimental group indicates effect of history and treatment. O_2 of control group indicates the effect of history and absence of treatment. On comparison the effect of history is cancelled out leaving behind the effect of treatment. Thus, Static Group Comparison Design is valid against the internal validity criterion of History.

In the experiment under discussion, both groups of subjects belong to the same class. There may be little variation in their age. In other words, students of both the groups are considered to have matured to the same extent. So the maturation of subjects may affect Achievement in Mathematics of students equally. In case this does not happen, Achievement in Mathematics of experimental and control groups may get affected by their maturation. If so, this gets reflected in the Achievement in Mathematics of students. So this design may or may not have internal validity against the criterion of Maturation.

In Static Group Comparison Design, no pretesting is done. So no learning experience has been provided to the subjects of experimental as well as control groups. Due to this the testing of both the groups at the end of the treatment is in no way get affected by the testing procedure. While comparing the mean scores of Achievement in Mathematics of experimental and control groups, the result will indicate the effect of the treatment only. The finding is free from effect of testing effect. Thus, Static Group Comparison Design is valid against internal criterion of Testing.

As presented above, the researcher used same Achievement in Mathematics Test for assessing Achievement in Mathematics of students of experimental and control groups. It means types of item, number of items, duration of test, difficulty level, discrimination index, reliability, validity, etc. are same and will have almost similar effect on Achievement in Mathematics of experimental and control groups. While comparing the mean scores of Achievement in Mathematics of experimental and control groups, the result will indicate the effect of the treatment only. The finding is free from effect of Instrumentation. Thus, Static Group Comparison Design is valid against internal criterion of Instrumentation.

Another confounding variable in some of the experimental researches is Regression. In Static Group Comparison Design, no pretest was given. Regression effect is not there on the test administered after the treatment. Thus, Static Group Comparison Design is valid against internal criterion of Regression.

As mentioned above, two intact groups were taken from the field. One of the groups is given treatment of Supervised Library Study for a period of three months and the other group is allowed to continue with the Lecture Method. At the end of the treatment both groups are tested by administering an Achievement in Mathematics Test. The two intact groups taken from the school may not be equivalent in respect of intelligence, study habits, interest in Mathematics, stress, previous achievement in Mathematics, etc. These variables might have influenced Achievement in Mathematics along with the treatment. Thus, Static Group Comparison Design is not valid against internal criterion of Selection.

From above example it is evident that the treatment of Supervised Library Study continued for a period of three months. During this period, there might be some students who drop out from the experimentation due to some personal or other reasons. It is not possible that the dropout subjects have similar characteristics. If students with less intelligent, poor study habits, lack of interest in Mathematics, etc. dropout from one of the groups or from both the groups in different numbers, the mean scores of Achievement in Mathematics of the groups is likely to be different provided there is no drop out from any group. The significance of difference in mean scores of Achievement in Mathematics cannot be attributed to the treatment because if dropout would not have been there, the result would have been different. Dropping out of subjects during experimentation is called Mortality. So the finding has been influenced by Mortality of subjects. Thus, Static Group Comparison Design is not valid against internal criterion of Mortality.

It has been mentioned that the experiment involving Supervised Library Study and Lecture Method is conducted on Class IX students of two sections of a Government Higher Secondary School of Delhi. The two sections are taken from the field as existed. Students have not been selected randomly. Students of the two sections might not make the groups equivalent. The students of the two groups differ in respect of intelligence, achievement in Mathematics, study habits, self-concept, stress, etc. These differences are attributed to Selection. It is a known fact that the behaviour of the subject is the resultant of interaction of Selection and Maturation etc. In Static Group Comparison Design there is no way to control this interaction. The net performance of students on the Achievement in Mathematics test reflects the outcome of treatment as well as interaction of Selection and Maturation etc. The researcher cannot say with confidence that the performance of students on the test is purely due to treatment. Thus, Static Group Comparison Design is not valid against the internal criterion of interaction of Selection and Maturation etc.

External Validity of Static Group Comparison Design

The experiment involving Supervised Library Study and Lecture Method is conducted on Class IX students of two sections of a Government Higher Secondary School of Delhi. In this experiment two intact groups of students are taken. The students of these groups may not represent Class IX students studying in different Government Higher Secondary Schools of Delhi. Further these students may have interest in Mathematics, less stress, good adjustment in school, favourable attitude towards Mathematics, etc. Such a group of students if treated through Supervised Library Study may benefit differently than those taught through Lecture Method. The findings of this experiment cannot be generalised to the population to which the students of this study belong. Thus, Static Group Comparison Design is not valid against the external criterion of interaction of Selection and Treatment.

Hence, Static Group Comparison Design is having internal validity against criteria of History, Testing, Instrumentation, and Regression but lacks internal validity against criteria of Selection, Mortality, and interaction of Selection and Maturation, etc. The findings of this design cannot be generalised to the population of the experimentation. This design thus lacks external validity against the criterion of interaction of Selection and Treatment.

Data Analysis of Static Group Comparison Design

The data can be analysed with the help of t-test if its' assumptions are fulfilled otherwise Mann-Whiney U Test can be used for analysing the data.

In nutshell the *Internal and External Validity* of all Pre-Experimental Designs are as follows:

S.No.	*Name of Design*	*Source of Internal Validity*	*Source of External Validity*
1.	One Shot Case Study	---NIL---	---NIL---
2.	One Group Pretest-Posttest Design	Selection and Mortality	---NIL---
3.	Static Group Comparison Design	History, Testing, Instrumentation and Regression	---NIL---

In nutshell the *Internal and External Invalidity* of all Pre-Experimental Designs are as follows:

S. No.	*Name of Design*	*Source of Internal Invalidity*	*Source of External Invalidity*
1.	One Shot Case Study	History, Maturation, Selection, Mortality	Interaction of Selection and Treatment
2.	One Group Pretest-Posttest Design	History, Maturation, Testing, Instrumentation, Interaction of Selection and other Factors	Interaction of Testing and Treatment; Interaction of Selection and Treatment
3.	Static Group Comparison Design	Selection, Mortality, Interaction of Selection and other Factors	Interaction of Selection and Treatment

QUASI-EXPERIMENTAL DESIGNS

The prefix quasi means "resembling". Thus Quasi-experimental Design resembles the True Experimental Design but it is not True Experimental Design. Although the independent Variable is manipulated but subjects or participants are not randomly assigned to conditions or order of conditions. Because the independent variable is manipulated before the dependent variable is measured or assessed, Quasi-experimental Design eliminates the directionality problem. But because the participants are not randomly assigned—making it likely that there are other differences between conditions-Quasi—experimental Design does not eliminate the problem of confounding variables.

Quasi-experiments are most likely to be conducted in field settings in which random assignment is difficult or impossible. They are often conducted to evaluate the effectiveness of a treatment—perhaps a type of psychotherapy or an educational intervention. Different types of Quasi-experimental Designs are: Time Series Design, Equivalent Time Samples Design, Equivalent Materials Design, Non-equivalent Control Group Design, Counterbalanced Designs, Separate Sample Pretest-Posttest Design, Separate Sample Pretest-Posttest Control Group Design, and Multiple Time Series Design. It is not possible to give full details of all Quasi-Experimental Designs. Thus, only Time-Series Design, Equivalent Time Samples Design, and Non-equivalent Control Group Design are discussed in this chapter.

Time Series Design

Many research questions that deal with the effects of treatment on Psychological, Environmental, Educational, Medical, etc. variables are concerned with how those effects are manifested over time. Time Series Design is based on the application of multiple measurements or assessments, before and after the treatment so as to study the pattern or trend of dependent variable. This design has been adopted by behavioural analysts for the study of single subjects' responses over time. It is generally advisable to keep intervals equally spaced so as to avoid confounding by extraneous temporal factors. Also there should be minimum three measurements or assessments of dependent variable before as well as after the Treatment. The layout is as follows:

$$O_1 \quad O_2 \quad O_3 \quad O_4 \quad X \quad O_5 \quad O_6 \quad O_7 \quad O_8$$

Suppose a researcher wants to study the trend of effect of Yoga on weight of females of 20 years of age. Say the researcher takes a sample of 50 females as existed in the field, say, a Yoga Centre, New Delhi and measures their weight at intervals of 20 days. The researcher measures the weight of each subject four times before the treatment of Yoga. Now each subject practised Yoga once a day for one hour and continues for a period of 60 days. At the end of the treatment, the weight of each subject was measured. Again their weight is measured three more times at an interval of 20 days. So the weight of each subject was measured four times before the treatment and four times after the treatment is over. The sample size across such study must be the same and only data of those subjects are considered for analysis that were present throughout the experimentation. Such experimental researches are very important for studying the Trend of effect of Treatment (say Yoga) on Dependent Variable (say weight).

Time-Series design is distinguished from repeated measures designs by the large number of measurements that are taken continuously across baseline and intervention or treatment phase. It is also distinguished from the one-way repeated measures design in the number of observations over time, and repetitive monitoring of performance throughout the time frame of the study.

The research question concerns trends across these time intervals. The number of observations can vary, depending on the stability of the dependent variable. This design may be considered an extension of the Single Group Pretest-Posttest Design. Time Series Design offers more control because multiple pretests and posttests act as a pseudo-control condition, demonstrating maturational trends that naturally occur in the data or the confounding effects of extraneous variables.

Internal Validity of Time Series Design

The greatest threat to Internal Validity in the Time Series Design is History. There is no control over the possible coincidental occurrence of some extraneous event at the same time that treatment is initiated. That is, if some of the subjects of the study also do physical exercises at home or in gym during treatment period, it may also bring change in the weight of subjects. There is no mechanism of controlling such events. On analysis, the researcher cannot say with confidence that the change in dependent variable is only due to treatment. Thus, the Time Series Design in not valid against Internal Validity Criterion of History.

In Time Series Design, if all subjects taken belong to a small range of age so that they have similar maturity. In such a situation, maturity may not vitiate the effect of treatment on the dependent variable. On the other hand, subjects with different maturity also will not vitiate the effect of treatment on dependent variable because of multiple assessment or measurement before and after the treatment. On comparison difference, if any, will cancel out. Thus, Time Series Design is valid against the Internal Validity Criterion of Maturation.

In Time Series Design, the same tool is used before as well as after the treatment. Also the number of times testing is done before and after the treatment will be same. Different characteristics of tool used will remain same throughout the experiment. Also the measurement of dependent variable is done multiple times before and after the treatment. In case there is some effect of testing on the dependent variable, it will cancel out during the analysis of data. So the Testing effect, if any, is controlled. Thus, Time Series Design is valid against the Internal Validity Criterion of Testing.

In the Time Series Design, the testing of dependent variable is done multiple number of times before and after the treatment with the help of the same tool. The group may not have subjects with extreme performance. Even if there are subjects with extreme performance, the number will be small and they also tend to perform so as to regress towards the mean. In case there is some effect of regression on the dependent variable, it will cancel out during the analysis of data. So the regression effect, if any, is controlled. Thus, Time Series Design is valid against the Internal Validity Criterion of Regression.

In the Time Series Design, only one group of subjects from one institution is taken. The institutions may be selected randomly but the subjects are not selected randomly but all available subjects in the selected institution are taken for experimentation. The characteristics of subjects remain same before and after the treatment. In case there is some effect of selection on the dependent variable, it will cancel out during the analysis of data. So the selection effect, if any, is controlled. Thus, Time Series Design is valid against the Internal Validity Criterion of Selection.

In Time Series Design, the dependent variable is assessed number of times before as well as after the treatment. The scores of all those subjects are considered for analysis that were present throughout the period of experimentation. In case some subjects were not present at the time of any testing, their scores are not considered for the analysis. Only those subject scores are considered who were present throughout the experiment. So the mortality does not vitiate the result. Thus, Time Series Design is valid against the Internal Validity Criterion of Mortality.

In Time Series Design intact group is taken for experimentation. The selection procedure is the same as only one group of subjects is taken. The subjects of the intact group will be of the same maturity level. In case there is any interaction of selection and maturation, etc. will remain same throughout the experimentation. So the effect of interaction of selection and maturity, etc. is controlled. Thus, Time Series Design is valid against the Internal Validity Criterion of interaction of selection and maturity, etc.

Thus, Time Series Design has Internal Validity against the criterion of Maturation, Testing, Regression, Selection, Mortality, and interaction of Selection and Maturation, etc. but this design does not have Internal Validity against the criterion of History.

External Validity of Time Series Design

External Validity of the Time Series Design is limited to situations when repeated testing takes place. In Time Series Design, pretesting is done at equal intervals before assigning the treatment. This might make subjects conscious and may benefit from the treatment. Testing is likely to interact with the treatment. This restricts the generalisability of finding. Thus, Time Series Design does not have External Validity against the criterion of Interaction of Testing and Treatment.

Data Analysis of Time Series Design

The collected data can be analysed with the help of Trend Analysis and a graph may also be plotted for studying the Trend.

Equivalent Time Samples Design

The Equivalent Time Samples Design is a Quasi-experimental Design where the treatment or intervention is administered several times and it is taken away several times. The dependent variable is assessed after each administration of treatment and after each time period where the treatment is taken away or withdrawn. This design is very useful where the effect of experimental variable is anticipated to be of transient or reversible character. While the logic of the experiment may be seen as an extension of Time Series experiment but the statistical analysis is more typically similar to that of two group experiment in which the significance of difference between means of two sets of measures is employed. The layout of Equivalent Time Samples Design is as follows.

$$O_1 \quad X_1 O_2 \quad X_0 O_3 \quad X_1 O_4 \quad X_0 O_5 \quad X_1 O_6 \quad X_0 O_7$$

In the above layout, X_1 represents the assignment of treatment and X_0 represents the withdrawal of treatment. O represents the assessment of dependent variable.

It is important to note that the number of observations and experimental and control conditions varies in different studies, and the experimental and control conditions are normally alternated randomly rather than systematically. Gains or changes induced by the experimental condition are compared with those induced by the control condition to see if the former is more influential. This design minimizes the effect of History as a potential threat to internal validity, but is likely to increase the impact of Maturation, Mortality, Testing and unstable Instrumentation.

Suppose the researcher wants to study the effect of Yoga on Stress of Class XII students of Private Schools of Gurgaon, Haryana. The researcher selects one school randomly and takes all available students for experimentation. Stress of all students is assessed with the help of a Stress Scale and is labeled as O_1. The researcher demonstrates a few exercises of Yoga and asks students to do Yoga for 15 days at the rate of 30 minutes per day. At the end of 15 days, the same Stress Scale is administered on all subjects of the group and is labeled as O_2. The treatment of Yoga is withdrawn for 15 days and at the end of 15 days the same Stress Scale is administered on all subjects of the group and is labeled as O_3. Now the subjects are asked to do the same Yoga exercises for another 15 days at the rate of 30 minutes per day. At the end of 15 days, the same Stress Scale is administered on all subjects of the group and is labeled as O4. Now the treatment of Yoga is withdrawn for 15 days and at the end of 15 days the same Stress Scale is administered on all subjects of the group and is labeled as O_5. Thus, the assignment of treatment and withdrawal of treatment along with assessment of dependent variable continues till the time the experiment comes to an end.

Internal Validity of Equivalent Time Samples Design

As stated above, Equivalent Time Samples Design belongs to Quasi-experimental Designs. In this intact group is taken from the field as existed. The treatment is administered and withdrawn at equal intervals many a time. In case any special event occurs during the process of experimentation, it will effect equally to all subjects of the group. On comparison, the effect of History if any will cancel out. Thus, Equivalent Time Samples Design is valid against the criterion of History.

Treatment in Equivalent Time Samples Design is of long duration. The subjects of the group do not change but remain same throughout the experimentation. The dependent variable is assessed in the beginning of the experiment as well as many a time during the process of experimentation when the treatment is given as well as it is withdrawn. This design results in two groups, namely, Experimental and Control Groups because the treatment is given for a specific period of time and withdrawn for the same period of time. On comparison, the effect of maturation if any will cancel out. Thus, Equivalent Time Samples Design is valid against the criterion of Maturation.

In Equivalent Time Samples Design, the dependent variable is assessed multiple number of times. Whatever change occurs in subjects due to testing remains both with the Experimental and Control Groups because the subjects remain same it is only the treatment which is given and withdrawn. On comparison, the effect of testing, if any, will cancel out. Thus, Equivalent Time Samples Design is valid against the criterion of Testing.

In Equivalent Time Samples Design, the Dependent variable is assessed multiple number of times with the help of same instrument or tool. The different characteristics of instrument remain same for all subjects. Whatever the change is likely to occur in all the subjects, it will cancel out on comparison of subjects who received the treatment and those for whom the treatment is withdrawn. The duration of assigning treatment and withdrawing the treatment remain same. Thus, Equivalent Time Samples Design is valid against the criterion of Instrumentation.

In Equivalent Time Samples Design, subjects are tested many a times before as well as after the treatment. The subjects with extreme performance are likely to tend towards the average of the group. The tendency of extreme subjects moving towards to average of the group refers to the Regression. In this design, regression effect, if present, will balance out on comparison of mean scores of dependent variable of group with treatment and without treatment or withdrawal of treatment. Thus, Equivalent Time Samples Design is valid against the criterion of Regression.

In Equivalent Time Samples Design, intact group of subjects is taken for experimentation. The selection procedure is same for all the subjects. Due to selection whatever differences exist within the group remain same throughout the experimentation. If any difference exists, it will balance out on comparison of mean scores of dependent variable of group with Treatment and without treatment or withdrawal of Treatment. Thus, Equivalent Time Samples Design is valid against the criterion of Selection.

All of you know about mortality. It refers to dropping of subjects during experimentation. In Equivalent Time Samples Design, the scores of those subjects are considered for analysis who were present throughout the experimentation. Therefore, mortality, if any, will not affect the net result of the experiment because the score of those subjects who dropped out during experimentation are not considered at the time of analysing the data. Thus, Equivalent Time Samples Design is valid against the criterion of Mortality.

In Equivalent Time Samples Design, one intact group is taken from the field. The same group continues wherein the treatment is given and withdrawn alternatively for a fixed duration. Whatever the effect of interaction between Selection and Maturation etc. on dependent variable takes place, it gets cancelled out at the time of analysing the data as it is present in all observations. Thus, Equivalent Time Samples Design is valid against the criterion of interaction of Selection and Maturation etc.

External Validity of Equivalent Time Samples Design

In Equivalent Time Samples Design, the pretest is followed by treatment for a fixed duration as decided by the researcher and the same test is administered again on the same set of students. The pretest sensitivity on the part of the students may influence the effect of the treatment. Now the treatment is withdrawn for a fixed duration as decided by the researcher and the same test is administered again on the same set of students. The assignment of treatment and withdrawal of treatment continues for a long period of time as decided by the researcher. The group on which the experiment is done does not represent the population. So it is not possible to generalise the results of such an experimental design. Thus, Equivalent Time Samples Design is not valid against the external validity criterion of interaction of Testing and Treatment.

You have noticed that in Equivalent Time Samples Design, the treatment has been given and withdrawn alternatively for a fixed duration as decided by the researcher. Also the subjects are assessed at the end of each periodic interval. This may sensitise the subjects to the experimental setting. So the knowledge of the subjects that they are participating in the experiment and their test sensitisation might have reacted with the treatment. Thus, effect of treatment is vitiated. The finding so obtained cannot be generalised to the natural setting. Therefore, Equivalent Time Samples Design is not valid against the external criterion of reactive arrangement.

You have noticed that in Equivalent Time Samples Design, the same set of subjects have been given the treatment at periodic intervals. The treatment may have carry over effect into those periods in which the treatment is withdrawn. This might vitiate the treatment effect. It may, therefore, be said that the finding can be generalised only to those conditions where treatment is present in repetitious and spaced form. Also the sample taken must represent the population to which the finding is to be generalised. In this design the intact group is taken which does not guaranty the representation of the population. So Equivalent Time Samples Design is not valid against the external validity criterion of Multiple Treatment Interference.

Analysis of Data of Equivalent Time Samples Design

The type of data generated by Equivalent Time Samples Design is such that a set of sampling unit (Time) is nested within other set of treatments. In other words, the occasions (Time) are nested within each treatment. Taking this into consideration, the data can be analysed through Nested Design of Analysis of Variance where occasions within treatment are represented.

Non-equivalent Control Group Design

There are many situations in Social and Behavioural Sciences where intact groups, as available in the field, are taken for experimentation. This design can be structured with One Experimental Group and One Control Group. The layout is as follows:

O X O

O O

The Layout of Non-equivalent Control Group Design with two Experimental Groups and One Control Group is as follows:

O X_1 O

O X_2 O

O O

From the above layout it is evident that there are two Experimental Groups with X_1 and X_2 Treatments and one Control Group. The researcher may have more than two Experimental Groups but there should always be one Control Group.

To understand Non-equivalent Control Group Design with one Experimental Group and One Control group, let us take one example. Suppose a researcher wants to compare Computer Aided Instruction and Lecture Method on the basis of Achievement in Physics of Class XI students of Government

Schools of Delhi. The researcher selects two sections of Class XI studying in one randomly selected Government School of Delhi. Both the groups are pretested by administering an Achievement in Physics Test developed by the researcher. The researcher randomly assigns the treatment. That is, the researcher selects one group randomly and teaches three topics of Physics (say) through already developed Computer Aided Instruction. Suppose the treatment continues for one month. At the end of one month, the same Achievement in Physics Test which was administered at the pretest stage is administered at the end of the treatment and is called posttest. During the time, the Experimental Group is taught three topics of Physics through Computer Aided Instruction, the same topics are taught to the subjects of Control Group through Lecture Method for one month. At the end, the same Achievement in Physics Test is administered to the Control Group which was administered to the Experimental Group. This will constitute the posttest.

From the above description, it is evident that that the school(s) is/are selected randomly but intact groups are taken from the selected school(s). All groups are pretested by using the same tool. One of the two groups is given the treatment. This is done randomly. At the end of the treatment, both the groups are tested using the same tool which was used in the beginning. This constitutes the posttest. Such type of design is called Non-equivalent Control Group Design

Internal Validity of Non-equivalent Control Group Design

From the above example it is evident that the researcher, after selecting the school randomly, took two groups as existed in the selected schools. During the treatment, if any special event, like, debate on topic of Physics, talk on Study Habits, demonstration of Yoga, etc. takes place in the institute, it may affect equally all students of both the groups. The occurrence of such special events is called History. Any change in the dependent variable due to History will be cancelled when both the groups are compared. Hence, the Non-equivalent Control Group Design is valid against the criterion of History.

From the above example, it is evident that all students are from same Class XI. The age of students may range between 15 to 17 years. The students are likely to have Biological and Psychological changes to the same extent. Biological and Psychological changes refers to maturation. That is, the subjects are likely to have same type of interest, fatigue, motivation, etc. These characteristics of subjects may bring change in the dependent variable along with the independent variable or the treatment but the degree of change may be to the same extent. On comparison whatever change will occur due to maturation, it will cancel out at the time of analysis. Thus, Non-equivalent Control Group Design is valid against the criterion of Maturation.

During the experimentation, both the groups are pretested as well as posttested with the help of the same tool or instrument under the same condition.

Due to pretest, there might be changes in the subjects of both the groups which may affect the performance of subjects on the posttest. The researcher will either compare the changes in the scores of dependent variable or take pretest as covariate. In both the cases, on comparing the changes in the dependent variable due to testing will cancel out. Thus, Non-equivalent Control Group Design is valid against the criterion of Testing.

It has been mentioned that for pretest as well as posttest the same tool or instrument is used. The characteristics of tool, such as, difficulty level, discrimination index, reliability, validity, objectivity, scoring procedure, etc. are the same for both the groups. So these characteristics of subjects may not change the responses. The change in responses is likely to be due to the treatment only. In case there is some change in the dependent variable due the characteristics of tool that will cancel out on comparison. Thus, Non-equivalent Control Group Design is valid against the criterion of Instrumentation.

It has been mentioned that intact groups are taken. The procedure of selection remains same for both the groups. The members of groups are not equivalent on all the major intervening variables. That is why the groups are Non-equivalent. The effect due to individual differences will be balanced when the groups are compared. So the effect of selection is internally controlled in this design. Thus, Non-equivalent Control Group Design is valid against the criterion of Selection.

In Non-equivalent Control Group Design the assessment or measurement of dependent variable is taken at Pre as well as Post stages with the help of the same tool. The data of all those students are analysed who were present at the time of Pre as well as Post testing. By chance if some students were not present either at Pretest stage or Posttest stage, their scores are not considered at the time of analysis. Those subjects whose data are not considered are referred as Mortality. The lost data, if any, are not considered at the time of analysis. So the Mortality factor does not affect the dependent variable. Thus, Non-equivalent Control Group Design is valid against the criterion of Mortality.

In Non-equivalent Control Group Design, intact groups are taken from the field. That means subjects are not selected randomly but the schools to which they belong were selected randomly. It is quite possible that subjects in one of the selected group may have better reasoning ability, study habits, better adjustment, better tolerance of ambiguity, etc. Due to these characteristics, the treatment given to this group may boost the results which ultimately vitiate the effect of treatment as the researcher may not be able to say with confidence that obtained results are due to treatment only. The obtained results might be due to the effect of interaction of Selection and Maturation. Thus, Non-equivalent Control Group Design is not valid against the criterion of interaction of Selection and Maturation, etc.

External Validity of Non-equivalent Control Group Design

In Non-equivalent Control Group Design all subjects of both the Groups are pretested. Due to pretesting, the subjects become aware of the type of questions, content coverage, difficulty level of questions, etc. It is possible that some students or subjects may like to know the answer of some questions which they could not answer during pretesting. Exposer to pretest of Subjects of Experimental Group as well as Control Group is likely to affect their performance at the posttest stage. During the period of treatment, some of the subjects may become attentive, may ask more questions, may do home assignment with better concentration, etc. In case the pretest is not given, subjects of Experimental Group as well as Control Group would not have been benefited from the testing. The benefit of testing may be the same in both the groups. The results obtained from Non-equivalent Control Group Design may not be generalised to those who did not take the pretest. Thus, the External Validity of Non-equivalent Control Group Design is vitiated because of the interaction of Testing and Treatment. Therefore, Non-equivalent Control Group Design is not valid against the External Validity Criterion of Interaction of Testing and Treatment.

Non-equivalent Control Group Design is limited by the lack of randomisation, it still has several strengths because it includes a pretest and Control Group. There is some control over History, Maturation, Testing, and Instrumentation, Selection and Mortality effects. The pretest scores can be used to test the assumption of initial equivalence on the dependent variable based on average scores and measures of variability. The major threat to Internal Validity is the interaction of Selection with History and Maturation.

Analysis of Data of Non-equivalent Control Group Design

For comparing gain scores, the data can be analysed with the help of t-test or One Way ANOVA. The data can also be analysed with the help of One Way ANCOVA by taking Pretest as a covariate. Ordinal Scale data can be analysed by using Mann-Whitney U Test. Depending on the wording of the objective, other statistical techniques may also be used. Nonparametric tests may be more appropriate with Non-equivalent Groups, as variances are likely to be unequal.

In nutshell the *Internal and External Validity* of all Experimental Designs belonging to Quasi-experimental Designs are as follows:

S. No.	*Name of Design*	*Source of Internal Validity*	*Source of External Validity*
1.	Time Series Design	Maturation, Testing, Regression, Selection, Mortality, Interaction of Selection and Maturation, etc.	----NIL----
2.	Equivalent Time Samples Design	History, Maturation, Testing, Instrumentation, Regression, Selection, Mortality, Interaction of Selection and Maturation, etc.	----NIL----
3.	Non-equivalent Control Group Design	History, Maturation, Testing, Instrumentation, Selection, Mortality	----NIL----

In nutshell the *Internal and External Invalidity* of all Quasi-experimental Designs are as follows:

S. No.	Name of Design	Source of Internal Invalidity	Source of External Invalidity
1.	Time Series Design	History	Interaction of Testing and Treatment
2.	Equivalent Time Samples Design	----NIL----	Interaction of Testing and Treatment, Reactive Arrangements, and Multiple Treatment Interference
3.	Non-equivalent Control Group Design	Interaction of Selection and Maturation, etc.	Interaction of Testing and Treatment

TRUE EXPERIMENTAL DESIGNS

Different types of True Experimental Design are Pretest-Posttest Control Group Design, Posttest Only Control Group Design and Solomon Four Group Design. Their details are given below:

Pretest-Posttest Control Group Design

It is the basic structure of an experiment. It is used to compare two or more groups that are formed by random assignment. One group receives the experimental treatment and the other acts as a control. Both groups are tested prior to and following the treatment. The groups differ solely on the basis of what occurs between pretest and posttest assessment. Therefore, changes from pretest to posttest that appear in the experimental group but not in the control group can be reasonably attributed to the treatment. The Pretest-Posttest Control Group Design can be of several form as given below:

Set I	R	O	X	O
	R	O		O
Set II	R	O	X_1	O
	R	O	X_2	O
Set III	R	O	X_1	O
	R	O	X_2	O
	R	O		O

From Set I, it is evident that subjects are selected randomly from the population of the experimental study. Randomly selected subjects are further divided randomly into two groups. Both randomly formed groups are pretested using the same tool. One of the groups is selected randomly and assigned treatment (X). The other group is not given any treatment but allowed to continue with their routine activities. Suppose the experiment continues for three months. At the end of the treatment or experiment, both groups are post-tested using the same tool which is used at the pretest stage.

From Set II it is evident that subjects are selected randomly from the population of the experimental study. Randomly selected subjects are further divided randomly into two groups. Both randomly formed groups are pretested using the same tool. There are two levels of treatment, namely, X_1 and X_2.These are assigned randomly to the selected groups. One group is assigned treatment (X_1) and another group is given treatment (X_2). Suppose the experiment continues for two months. At the end of the treatment or experiment, both groups are post-tested using the same tool which is used at the pretest stage.

From Set III it is evident that subjects are selected randomly from the population of the experimental study. Randomly selected subjects are further divided randomly into three groups. All randomly formed groups are pretested using the same tool. There are three levels of treatment, namely, X_1, X_2 and Control. These are assigned randomly to the selected groups. One group is assigned treatment (X_1) and another group is given treatment (X_2). The third group continues with the routine activities. Suppose the experiment continues for two months. At the end of the treatment or experiment, all the three groups are post-tested using the same tool which is used at the pretest stage.

From above description it is clear that in Pretest-Posttest Control Group Design, there should be minimum two groups and there is no upper limit of number of groups. There may or may not be a control group which is not given any specific treatment. All subjects are randomly selected and treatment is also assigned randomly. All groups are pretested as well as post-tested using the same tool. Experiment must continue for a longer period because treatment in Social Science is like homeopathy medicine. It takes time to show its result.

Internal Validity of Pretest-Posttest Control Group Design

In Pretest-Posttest Control Group Design, the subjects are selected randomly from the population and divided randomly into two or more groups as per the requirement of the design. Further the groups are assigned randomly to treatments with such restrictions as are required to achieve balanced representation of such highly likely sources of bias as experimenters, time of the day, day of the week, portion of academic session, nearness to examination, etc. All those in the same session share the same intra-session history, thus have sources of similarity other than the treatment (X). Thus, Pretest-Posttest Control Group Design is valid against internal criterion of History.

The subjects of Pretest-Posttest Control Group Design belong to the same population. Their maturity level is quite similar. During experiment, there are physical as well as psychological changes among the subjects of the groups. These changes get reflected in the posttest. The difference between Posttest and Pretest of experimental group reflects the effect of treatment as well as maturation. Similarly in the control group, the difference between Posttest and Pretest reflects the effect of no treatment as well as maturation. On comparing the groups, the maturation effect gets nullified and only treatment effect is obtained. Thus, Pretest-Posttest Control Group Design is valid against internal criterion of Maturation.

All groups of Pretest-Posttest Control Group Design are pretested. All groups of this design are quite similar. They get benefited equally from the pretest. Posttest reflects the experience of subjects of the groups with the pretest and treatment. The difference between Posttest and Pretest of experimental group reflects the effect of treatment as well as testing. Similarly in the control group, the difference between Posttest and Pretest reflects the effect of no treatment as well as testing. On comparing the groups, the testing effect gets nullified and only treatment effect is obtained. Thus, Pretest-Posttest Control Group Design is valid against internal criterion of Testing.

In Pretest-Posttest Control Group Design, the dependent variable is assessed with the help of appropriate instrument. The same instrument is used for assessing dependent variable both at pretest as well as posttest stages. Various characteristics, such as, instructions, difficulty level, discrimination index, scoring, testing time, etc. of instrument remain the same. The difference between Posttest and Pretest of experimental group reflects the effect of treatment as well as instrumentation. Similarly in the control group, the difference between Posttest and Pretest reflects the effect of no treatment as well as instrumentation. On comparing the groups, the instrumentation effect gets nullified and only treatment effect is obtained. Thus, Pretest-Posttest Control Group Design is valid against internal criterion of Instrumentation.

Regression is controlled as far as mean differences are concerned, no matter how extreme the group is on pretest scores, if both experimental and control groups are randomly assigned from this extreme pool. In such a case, the control group regresses as much as does the experimental group. Thus, Pretest-Posttest Control Group Design is valid against internal criterion of Regression.

In the Pretest-Posttest Control Group Design, groups are formed randomly and even the treatments are assigned randomly. Randomisation assures equality of groups. This is stated by sampling statistics. Thus, the assurance of equality is greater for large numbers of random assignments than for small. In this design there will occasionally be an apparently significant difference between the pretest scores. Thus, while simple or stratified randomisation assures unbiased assignments of subjects to groups, it is less than a perfect way of assuring the initial equivalence of such groups. It is nonetheless the only way of doing so, and the essential way. Thus, Pretest-Posttest Control Group Design is valid against internal criterion of Selection.

During experiment, it is possible that some subjects may dropout completely or some partial data are available. This refers to the mortality. Mortality occurs in short as well as long duration experiments. The chances of dropout are more in long duration experiments. If the dropouts are from all the groups so that the equivalency among the groups is not disturbed, than the mortality factor does not confound with the treatment. On the other hand if the dropouts are subjects who are less motivated, less interested, low achievers, less intelligence, less responsive to the treatment, etc. and belong to both Experimental as well as Control groups, then there is possibility that groups' equivalency is in danger. The same may ultimately vitiate the effect of the treatment. Under such conditions this design is succumbed to mortality effect. On the other hand, in short duration experiments the probability of dropout is less. Even if the dropouts are there, the number may be too small to interfere with the equivalence of the groups. In such a case the mortality may not jeopardize the treatment effect. Thus, Pretest-Posttest Control Group Design is valid against internal criterion of Mortality.

In Pretest-Posttest Control Group Design, the subjects are randomly selected as well as assigned to treatment randomly. This ensures the equivalence of groups with respect to variables such as, Intelligence, Interest, Motivation, Socio-economic Status, Stress, previous achievement in the subject, etc. During the process of experimentation, some special event (History), psychological changes of fatigue, cognitive development, interest, etc. (Maturation) may interact with the characteristics of subjects (Selection). Such interaction may alter the scores of posttest in both the groups. On comparing mean gain scores of groups, the interaction effect, if any, is nullified. This reflects the true effect of the treatment making this design valid against the criterion of interaction of Selection and Maturation, etc. Thus, Pretest-Posttest Control Group Design is valid against internal criterion of interaction of Selection and Maturation, etc.

External Validity of Pretest-Posttest Control Group Design

The findings of the experiment using Pretest-Posttest Control Group Design may be generalised to the group who is pretested but logically unable to generalise to the larger unpretested population about which one would prefer to be able to speak. The effect of the pretest upon Treatment (X) as it restricts external validity is of course a function of the extent to which such repeated measurements are characteristic of the population to which one wants to generalise. In the area of mass communications, the researcher's interview and attitude-test procedures are quite typical. But in research on teaching, one is interested in generalising to a setting in which testing is a regular phenomenon. Especially if the experimenter can use regular classroom examinations as test scores, but probably also if the experimental test scores are similar to those usually used, no undesirable interaction of testing and Treatment (X) would be present. Where highly unusual test procedures are used, or where the testing procedure involves deception, perceptual or cognitive restructuring, surprise, stress, anxiety, fear of failure, etc., experimental designs having no pretesting remain highly desirable if not essential. Generalisation in true sense is not justified logically. Thus, Pretest-Posttest Control Group Design does not have external valid against the criterion of interaction of Testing and Treatment.

In social science researches it is almost impossible to have sample which truly represents the population to which they belong. The results may hold good only for that unique population from which the experimental and control groups are jointly selected provided the subjects involved in the study represent the unique population. In reality the researcher cannot randomly select the subjects from the population. Of course one can assign the treatment randomly to the groups. The members of experimental and control groups differ with respect to variables, like, intelligent, study habits, anxiety, stress, motivation, interest, etc. Thus, it limits the generalisability of findings. Therefore, Pretest-Posttest Control Group Design may not have external validity against the criterion of interaction of Selection and Treatment.

In the usual psychological experiment, if not in educational research, a most prominent source of unrepresentativeness is the artificiality of the experimental setting and the student's knowledge that he is participating in an experiment. For human experimental subjects, in which the procedures and experimental treatment are reacted to not only for their simple stimulus values, but also for their role as clues in defining the experimenter's intent. The anxiety, stress, outguessing, up-for inspection, I'm-a-guinea-pig, or whatever attitudes so generated are unrepresentative of the school setting, and seem to be qualifiers of the effect of Treatment (X), seriously hampering generalisation where such reactive arrangements are unavoidable, but internally valid experiments of this type should by all means be continued. But if they can be avoided, they obviously should be. Further any aspect of the experimental procedure may produce reactive arrangements effect. The pretesting itself, apart from its contents, may do so, and part of the pretest interaction with Treatment (X) may be of this nature, although there are ample grounds to suspect the content features of the testing process. The process of randomisation and assignment to treatments may affect classroom when a randomly selected half of the pupils in a class are sent to a separate room. This action, plus the presence of the strange "teachers", must certainly create expectations of the unusual. The presentation of the treatment (X) could have a similar effect. The more obvious the connection between the experimental treatment and the posttest content, the more likely this effect becomes.

In the area of public opinion change, reactive arrangements may be very hard to avoid. But in research on teaching methods there is no need for the students to know that an experiment is going on. If the treatments are modified usual classroom events occurring at plausible periods in the curriculum calendar, then one-third of the battle is won when these treatments occur without special announcement. If the tests are similarly embedded as regular examinations, the second requirement is achieved. So the experimentation within schools must be conducted by regular staff of the schools concerned, whenever possible, especially when findings are to be generalised to other classroom situations. Thus, the Pretest-Posttest Control Group Design may or may not have external valid against the criterion of Reactive Arrangements as it depends on the situation under which it is conducted.

Hence Pretest-Posttest Control Group Design is having internal validity against criteria of History, Maturation, Testing, Instrumentation, Regression, Selection, Mortality, and interaction of Selection and Maturation, etc. On the other hand, this design lacks external validity against the criterion of interaction of Testing and Treatment but may or may not have external validity against the criteria of Selection and Treatment, and Reactive Arrangements.

Data Analysis of Pretest-Posttest Control Group Design

The data can be analysed by computing the change score (Posttest Score-Pretest Score) for each subject both in Experimental and Control Groups separately. Now the change mean scores of dependent variable of Experimental and Control Groups can be analysed with the help of t-test provided the assumptions of t-test are satisfied. If not then Mann-Whitney U Test can be used to compare two groups, and the Kruskal-Wallis Analysis of Variance by Ranks is used to compare three or more groups. The data can also be analysed using ANCOVA where Pretest can be used as covariate. Discriminant analysis can also be used to distinguish between groups with multiple outcome measures.

Posttest Only Control Group Design

The Posttest Only Control Group Design is identical to Pretest-Posttest Control Group Design, with the obvious exception that a Pretest is not administered to either group. The layout is as follows:

R	X	O
R		O

To understand it further, let us consider the title: "A study of effect of Computer Aided Instruction on Achievement in Mathematics of Class XII students of Government Schools of Delhi." One of the objectives of this experimental study can be—To compare mean scores of Achievement in Mathematics of students taught through Computer Aided Instruction and Lecture Method. For this study it is possible to have a frame of Class XII students studying in different Government Schools of Delhi. Suppose a group of 100 students of Class XII studying in Government Schools of Delhi is selected randomly. The students are further divided randomly in two groups and one of the groups is termed as Experimental Group and another Control Group. The Experimental Group is taught some topics of Mathematics through Computer Aided Instruction (CAI) and the same topics are taught to Control Group through Lecture Method. This experiment continued for two months. At the end of two months of treatment, both the groups were tested by administering Achievement in Mathematics Test. Thus, it is clear that the subjects are randomly selected, divided into groups randomly and randomly assigned to treatment. At the end of the treatment the testing is done with the help of appropriate tool, and is called Posttest.

Posttest Only Control Group Design involves randomisation and comparison groups, its internal validity is strong, even without a Pretest; that is, one can assume groups are equivalent prior to treatment because they have been randomly assigned to groups. As there is no Pretest to document the results of randomisation, this design is most successful when the number of subjects is large, so that the probability of truly balancing interpersonal characteristics is increased.

Internal Validity and External Validity of Posttest Only Control Group Design

As stated earlier, except Pretest, Posttest Only Control Group Design is quite similar to Pretest-Posttest Only Control Group Design. This is the reason that Posttest Only Control Group Design has Internal Validity and External Validity similar to Pretest-Posttest Only Control Group Design. Thus, Posttest Only Control Group Design has Internal Validity against criteria of History, Maturation, Testing, Instrumentation, Regression, Selection, Mortality, and interaction of Selection and Maturation, etc. On the other hand, this design has External Validity against the criterion of interaction of Testing and Treatment because there is no Pretest. But it may or may not have External Validity against the criteria of Interaction of Selection and Treatment, and Reactive Arrangements.

Data Analysis of Posttest Only Control Group Design

The posttest data can be analysed with the help of t-test if assumptions of t-test are met otherwise Mann-Whitney U Test can be used for analysing the data. With more than two groups, One Way ANOVA or Kruskal-Wallis Analysis of Variance by Ranks should be used to compare posttest means. An ANCOVA can be used when covariate data on relevant extraneous variables are available. Regression or Discriminant analysis procedures can also be used.

Solomon Four Group Design

Solomon Four Group Design was developed by Richard Solomon in 1949. It was designed to overcome the problem of pretest sensitisation. Pretest sensitisation occurs when subjects performance on the posttest are affected by the exposure to the pretest. The main feature of Solomon Four Group Design is that the subjects are randomly assigned to either administer or not to administer the pretest and then randomly assigned to either a treatment or control group. After that all subjects are administered posttest. Thus, it is a combination of

Pretest-Posttest Control Group Design and Posttest Only Control Group Design. The layout is given below:

$$\begin{array}{llll} R & O_1 & X & O_2 \\ R & O_3 & & O_4 \\ R & & X & O_5 \\ R & & & O_6 \end{array}$$

Suppose a researcher wants to compare Computer Aided Instruction and Lecture Method on the basis of Achievement in Physics of Class XI students of Government Schools of Delhi. Suppose the researcher selects randomly 200 Class XI students of Government Schools of Delhi. Students are further randomly divided into four groups. Two randomly selected groups are pretested by administering Achievement in Physics Test. Of these two groups, one of the randomly selected group is taught Physics through Computer Aided Instruction and other pretested group is taught the same topic of Physics through Lecture Method. Of the remaining two groups, one randomly selected group is taught same topics of Physics through Computer Aided Instruction and another is taught the same topics of Physics through Lecture Method. At the end of teaching all the topics, all the four groups are posttested using the same Achievement in Physics which was used at the pretest stage. From the layout it is evident that O_1 and O_3 represent Pre-Achievement in Physics while O_2 , O_4 , O_5 and O_6 represents Post-Achievement in Physics. From the layout, it is evident that there are two variables, namely, treatment and testing. The two levels of treatment are Computer Aided Instruction and Lecture Method while two levels of testing are Pretest and Posttest.

Internal Validity and External Validity of Solomon Four Group Design

As stated above, Solomon Four Group Design is a combination of Pretest-Posttest Control Group Design and Posttest Only Control Group Design. As mentioned before, Posttest Only Control Group Design has Internal Validity and External Validity similar to Pretest-Posttest Only Control Group Design. Thus, Solomon Four Group Design has Internal Validity against criteria of History, Maturation, Testing, Instrumentation, Regression, Selection, Mortality, and interaction of Selection and Maturation, etc. On the other hand, this design has External Validity against the criterion of interaction of testing and treatment because the researcher can study the effect of testing on Achievement in Physics as well as effect of interaction between treatment and testing on Achievement in Physics. But it may or may not have External Validity against the criteria of Interaction of Selection and Treatment, and Reactive Arrangements.

The main drawbacks of Solomon Four Group Design are its cost and feasibility. Also this design requires twice the number of subjects or participants, materials and resources to implement.

Data Analysis of Solomon Four Group Design

The data can be analysed with the help of 2 X 2 Factorial Design ANOVA.

In nutshell the *Internal and External Validity* of all Experimental Designs belonging to True-Experimental Designs are as follows:

S. No.	*Name of Design*	*Source of Internal Validity*	*Source of External Validity*
1.	Pretest-Posttest Control Group Design	History, Maturation, Testing, Instrumentation, Regression, Selection, Mortality, Interaction of Selection and Maturation, etc.	----NIL---
2.	Posttest Only Control Group Design	History, Maturation, Testing, Instrumentation, Regression, Selection, Mortality, Interaction of Selection and Maturation, etc.	Interaction of Testing and Treatment
3.	Solomon Four Group Design	History, Maturation, Testing, Instrumentation, Regression, Selection, Mortality, Interaction of Selection and Maturation, etc.	Interaction of Testing and Treatment

In nutshell the *Internal and External Invalidity* of all True Experimental Designs are as follows:

S. No.	*Name of Design*	*Source of Internal Invalidity*	*Source of External Invalidity*
1.	Pretest-Posttest Control Group Design	-----NIL-----	Interaction of Testing and Treatment
2.	Posttest Only Control Group Design	------NIL-----	----Doubt full----
3.	Solomon Four Group Design	------NIL------	----Doubt full----

Take a Test

1. Which of the following is NOT one of the main characteristic of a True Experimental Design?
   A) The Manipulation of a Variable
   B) The measurement of changes due to manipulation of a variable.
   C) Holding everything constant except the variable being manipulated.
   D) All subjects experience all experimental conditions.
2. In experimental research, the manipulated variable is called
   A) Dependent Variable B) Independent Variable
   C) Confounding Variable D) Concomitant Variable.
3. In experimental design, the variable being assessed is called
   A) Dependent Variable B) Criterion variable
   C) Independent Variable D) Confounding Variable.
4. Which of the following is NOT the strength of experimental researches?
   A) Replicability
   B) Narrow definition of concepts used in the research
   C) Establishment of Cause and Effect Relationship
   D) Control of intervening variables.

5. A variable that changes in a systematic way with the treatment and may also effect the dependent variable is known as a
   A) Independent variable B) Concomitant variable
   C) Confounding Variable D) All of the above.
6. Suppose neither the experimenter nor the subject knows which experimental condition has been assigned to the subject, this is known as
   A) Double-blind B) Experimental conditions
   C) Control condition D) Single-blind.
7. Field experiments and natural experiments are collectively called as
   A) True Experiments B) Pre-experiments
   C) Quasi-experiments D) False experiments.
8. Which of the following characteristics of True Experimental Designs is most often lacking in Quasi-experimental Designs?
   A) Implementation of some type of treatment.
   B) Appropriate comparison condition.
   C) Potential for contamination due to diffusion of treatments.
   D) High degree of control, specially the random selection of subjects.
9. Which of the following represents a threat to the internal validity of a study because differences exist between the individuals in the experimental and control groups at the start of the study?
   A) Maturation B) Subject mortality
   C) Selection D) Regression.
10. What is the main evidence for the effectiveness of a treatment that is tested using a Time Series Design?
    A) Clear discontinuity in the time graph at the point of the treatment or intervention.
    B) Increasing and decreasing trend in the graph around the point of treatment.
    C) Strong decreasing trend in the graph that continues through the point of treatment.
    D) High variable responses in the graph around the point of treatment.
11. In experimental research, the researcher manipulates
    A) At least one dependent variable
    B) All variables
    C) At least one independent variable
    D) At least one independent variable and one dependent variable.
12. In an experimental study of the effects of ETV Programme on academic achievement after controlling reasoning of students, the dependent variable is
    A) Reasoning B) Academic Achievement
    C) ETV Programme D) All of the above.
13. Which of the following is NOT a necessary step in conducting an experimental study?
    A) Manipulation of an independent variable
    B) Selection of tool
    C) Formulation of Hypothesis
    D) Dividing the sample into subgroups to control intervening variables.

14. In an experimental study of the effect of Talking Books in English on English Reading comprehension of students with special needs, the researcher is in control of
    A) The selection of subjects not their assignment to a treatment group.
    B) The selection and assignment of subjects
    C) The assignment of subjects to treatment but not their selection
    D) Neither the selection of group nor assignment of treatment.
15. The best way to control extraneous variables in experimental research is
    A) Randomisation
    B) Using Intact groups
    C) Avoid all threats to external validity
    D) Avoid all threats to internal validity
16. Which of the following would NOT NECESSARILY be an assigned variable?
    A) Reasoning
    B) Participation in extra-curricular activities
    C) Scientific attitude
    D) Mother's level of qualification
17. Which of the following is correct?
    A) A study can be externally valid but not internally valid
    B) A study must be both internally and externally valid
    C) A study can be internally valid but not externally valid
    D) The internal and external validity of researches are not related in any way.
18. The biggest threat to internal validity of research with intact groups is
    A) History B) Maturation
    C) Experimenter bias D) Different selection of subjects.
19. Testing can affect internal validity negatively when
    A) The information tested is attitudinal in nature
    B) Time between pretest and posttest is short
    C) The tools are unreliable
    D) Subjects are with very low scores.
20. Ecology validity refers to
    A) The subjects to whom results generalise
    B) The tool used to assess dependent variable
    C) The internal validity of the study
    D) The context to which the results generalise.
21. Mr. Sharma's Class IX was not chosen to participate in a new computer based programme. His students were furious that they were not selected so they decided to show to researcher that they were better anyway. The finding of this study would be confounded by the
    A) Hawthorne Effect B) Researcher Effect
    C) John Henry Effect D) Placebo Effect.
22. Control in an experimental study is BEST described as an attempt to
    A) Limit threats to internal validity
    B) Limit threats to external validity
    C) Increase the generalisability of findings
    D) Equate the subjects on the treatment variable.

23. Which of the following designs poses the greatest risk of internal validity?
    A) O O O O X O O O O
    B) O X O
    C) O X_1 O, O X_2 O
    D) R X_1 O; R X_2 O
24. Many researchers believe that research involves testing, treating and testing again to show gains. This is an example of
    A) comparison group research
    B) quasi-experimental research
    C) true experimental research
    D) pre-experimental research
25. Quasi-experimental design is used because
    A) Random selection of subjects is not possible
    B) Neither random selection nor random assignment is possible
    C) Random assignment is not possible
    D) Comparison groups are not available
26. Researcher thinks that the effects of treatment will be different for males and females. The best design to test this is
    A) Pretest-Posttest Single Group Design
    B) Factorial Design
    C) Time series Design
    D) Non-equivalent Control Group Design
27. The principle of experimental design is
    A) Maximisation of treatment variance only
    B) Minimisation of error variance only
    C) Maximisation of treatment variance and minimisation of error variance
    D) None of the above.
28. Which of the following experimental design is mostly applicable in Science?
    A) Pre-experimental Design B) Quasi-experimental Design
    C) True Experimental Design D) All the above.
29. Which of the following experimental design is mostly applicable in Social Sciences?
    A) Quasi-experimental Design B) Pre-experimental Design
    C) True Experimental Design D) All the above.
30. Non-equivalent Control Group Design has internal validity in respect of
    A) Testing B) Regression
    C) Selection D) All the above.
31. Which of the following statement is Incorrect?
    A) Time series Design has poor internal validity.
    B) Pretest-posttest Single Group Design has good external validity.
    C) Solomon Four Group Design has good external validity.
    D) All the above.
32. Which of the following is NOT the criterion of testing internal validity of experimental design?
    A) Interaction of Testing and Treatment
    B) Interaction of Selection and Maturation.

C) Instrumentation
D) Regression.

33. Which of the following criterion is used for testing internal validity of experimental design?
A) Mortality B) History
C) Maturation D) All the above.

34. The data obtained through the use of Non-equivalent Control Group Design can be analysed with the help of
A) t-test only
B) One Way ANCOVA only
C) Either t-test or One Way ANCOVA
D) None of the above.

35. Which of the following is/are methods of controlling intervening variables?
A) Selective Manipulation B) Statistical Manipulation
C) Physical Manipulation D) All of the above.

36. Which of the following is NOT the method of counter balancing?
A) Incomplete Counter Balancing
B) Selecting Counter Balancing
C) Complete Counter Balancing
D) Randomise Counter Balancing.

37. Different methods of Counter Balancing are
A) Random assignment of subjects to groups.
B) Having groups where individuals are matched case by case.
C) Having groups matched on intervening variables.
D) All of the above.

38. Which of the following is NOT the characteristic of Experimental Method?
A) Presence of Independent Variable and Criterion Variable.
B) Manipulation of Variable
C) Control of Intervening Variables
D) Random assignment of treatment to groups.

39. Which of the following experimental design has the best internal validity?
A) Pre-experimental Designs B) Quasi-experimental Designs
C) True Experimental Designs D) All of the above.

40. Which of the following experimental design has the moderate internal validity?
A) Pre-experimental Designs B) Quasi-experimental Designs
C) True Experimental Designs D) None of the above.

8
Basics of Statistics

INTRODUCTION

By now it must have been clear that Data Collection is one of the steps of Research. The Data should be collected with the help of tools and/or instruments. The collected data might be qualitative and/or quantitative. Both qualitative as well as quantitative data have to be analysed in order to answer questions written in the form of objectives or research questions. In some researches the qualitative data are converted into quantitative data. One of the reasons might be ease of analysis as analysis can be done with the help of statistical techniques using SPSS. Before analysing the quantitative data, it is important to understand some of the Basics of Statistics or Fundamentals of Statistics. In many researches it has been observed that Data Analysis is weak. This might be because the Basics of Statistics are not clear to the researchers. In this chapter an attempt is made to bring to the light of Basics of Statistics. After reading this chapter, the reader will be able to:

- Define Parameter and Statistic.
- Differentiate between Parameter and Statistic.
- List the difference between Parametric Statistics and Non-parametric Statistics.
- Name different Scales of Measurement.
- Differentiate among different types of Scale of Measurement.
- Name the Scale of Measurement for the given Variable.

DEFINITION OF PARAMETER AND STATISTIC

Parameter

A fixed characteristic of population based on all the subjects/elements of the population is termed as the parameter. Here population refers to an aggregate of all units under consideration, which share common characteristics. It is a numerical value that remains unchanged, as every member of the population is surveyed in order to know the parameter. It indicates true value, which is obtained after the census is conducted.

Statistic

A statistic is defined as a numerical value, which is obtained from a sample of data. It is a descriptive statistical measure and function of sample observation. A sample is described as a fraction of the population, which represents the entire population in all its characteristics. The common use of statistic is to estimate a particular population parameter.

From the given population, it is possible to draw multiple samples, and the result (statistic) obtained from different samples will vary, which depends on the characteristics of samples.

DIFFERENCE BETWEEN STATISTIC AND PARAMETER

The difference between statistic and parameter can be drawn clearly on the following grounds:

1. A Statistic is a characteristic of a small portion of the population, i.e. sample. The parameter is a fixed measure which describes the target population.
2. The Statistic is a variable and known number which depend on the sample of the population while the parameter is a fixed and unknown numerical value.
3. Statistical notations are different for Population Parameters and Sample Statistics, which are given as under:
    - In Population Parameter, μ (Greek letter mu) represents mean, P denotes Population Proportion, Standard Deviation is labeled as σ (Greek letter sigma), Variance is represented by σ^2, Population size is indicated by N, Standard Error of mean is represented by $\sigma_{\bar{x}}$, Standard Error of Proportion is labeled as σ_p, Coefficient of variation is denoted by σ/μ.
    - In Sample Statistics, $\bar{x}$ (x-bar) represents mean, $\hat{p}$ (p-hat) denotes Sample Proportion, Standard Deviation is labeled as s, Variance is represented by s^2, n denotes Sample Size, Standard Error of mean is represented by $s_{\bar{x}}$, Standard Error of proportion is labeled as s_p, Coefficient of Variation is denoted by $s/(\bar{x})$.

DIFFERENCE BETWEEN PARAMETRIC STATISTICS AND NON-PARAMETRIC STATISTICS

Non-parametric statistics are also called distribution-free statistics because the data do not follow a specific distribution. *Non-parametric* statistics are used when data don't meet the assumptions of the *parametric* statistics, especially the assumption about normal distribution of data.

Basis for Comparison	*Parametric Statistics*	*Non-parametric Statistics*
Distribution	Normal Distribution	Any Distribution
Scale of Measurement	Interval Scale or Ratio Scale	Any Scale of Measurement
Power of Test	More Powerful	Less Powerful
Measure of Central Tendency	Mean	Mode

SCALES OF MEASUREMENT

By now it is clear that research cannot be conducted without the variable(s). In all subjects, there are variables but names differ from subject to subject and also from research to research. The researcher has to have information or data for each variable. The information may be either qualitative or quantitative in nature. The information related to a variable has to be at least on any one Scale of Measurement. There are four Scales of Measurement. These are Nominal Scale, Ordinal Scale, Interval Scale and Ratio Scale. Each Scale of Measurement is explained below:

Nominal Scale

Nominal Scale is the lowest level of measurement and also referred to as the classificatory scale. The main characteristic of Nominal Scale is count or frequency. Objects or people are assigned to categories or groups according to some criteria. Categories or groups may be coded by name, number, letter, or symbol, although none of these have any quantitative value. They are used purely as labels for identification, such as, Gender, Locale, Types of School, Marital Status, Caste, Colour, Discipline, Blood Group, RBC, Books in the Library, etc. Nominal categories are mutually exclusive, so that no object or person can logically be assigned to more than one category or group. It is also assumed that the rules for classifying a set of attributes or characteristics are exhaustive; that is, every subject can be accurately assigned to one category. Classifying Gender as Male and Female would follow these rules. Classifying hair colour as blonde or brunette would not. The numbers or symbols used to designate groups on a nominal scale can be altered without changing the values or characteristics they identify. The categories cannot, therefore, be put in some order or sequence on the basis of their assigned numerals. The only permissible mathematical operation is counting the number of subjects within each category, such as, 40 Males and 30 Females. Statements can then be made concerning the frequency of occurrence of a particular characteristic or the proportions of a total group that fall within each category. Data on Nominal Scale can be analysed by computing percentage, using Chi-square Test, Sign Test, Median Test, McNemar Test for the Significance of changes, Contingency Coefficient, etc. provided their assumptions are satisfied by data which is to be analysed.

Ordinal Scale

Measurement on an Ordinal Scale requires that categories be rank-ordered or put in some sequence on the basis of an operationally defined characteristic or property. Data are organised into adjacent categories exhibiting "greater than–less than" relationship. The intervals between ranks on an Ordinal Scale may not be consistent and indeed may not be known. This means that although objects assigned to one rank are considered equivalent on the rank criterion, they may not actually be of equal value along the continuum that underlies the scale. Therefore, Ordinal Scale often record ties even when true values are unequal. For example, Military rank is ordinal but has no zero rank. Assistant Professor, Associate Professor and Professor Designation are on Ordinal Scale. One can arrange the paintings, handwritings, beauty, smell, taste, size of shoes, attractiveness, etc. in some order, and thus constitutes the Ordinal Scale. Data on Ordinal Scale can be analysed with the help of Rank Difference Method of Correlation, Mann-Whiney U Test, Kendall Coefficient of Concordance, Kendall Rank Correlation Coefficient, etc. provided their assumptions are satisfied by data which is to be analysed.

Interval Scale

Interval Scale has a reference point or non-fixed zero and intervals of equal length. The reference point is not true zero. Therefore, relative differences and equivalence within a scale can be determined but absolute magnitude of an attribute or characteristic is unknown, because interval measures are not related to true zero. This means that negative values may represent lesser amount of an attribute or characteristic. Year 1 was an arbitrary historical designation, but not the beginning of time. Measurement of temperature using Fahrenheit and Celsius scale is also at the Interval Scale. Both have artificial zero point that do not represent a total absence of heat and can indicate temperature in negative degrees. Within each temperature scale one can identify that the numerical difference between 5° and 10° is equal to the numerical difference between 40° and 45° (in each case 5°); however, these differences are based on the numerical values on the scale, not on the true nature of the variable itself. Therefore, the amount of heat or molecular motion generated between 5° and 10° is not necessarily the same as the difference between 40° and 45°.

Because of the nature of the Interval Scale, one must consider the practical implications for interpreting measured differences. Interval values can be added and subtracted, but these operations cannot be used to interpret actual quantities. Thus, ratio cannot be computed and also there is no true zero. The variables having data on Interval Scale are Heat, Temperature, Stress, Anxiety, Power of a lens, etc. Interval Scale data can be analysed with the help of strong statistics, like, t-test, One Way ANOVA, Two Way ANOVA, Three Way ANOVA, One Way ANCOVA, Two Way ANCOVA, Three Way ANCOVA, Correlation,

Partial Correlation, Multiple Correlation, Canonical Correlation, Regression Analysis, Factor Analysis, Discriminant Analysis, etc. provided their assumptions are satisfied by data which is to be analysed.

Ratio Scale

Ratio Scale has a fixed zero or reference point and ratios are of equal. This is the highest level of measurement. A score of zero on Ratio Scale represents a total absence of whatever property is being measured. Therefore, negative values are not possible. Examples of Ratio Scale are Range of Motion, Height, Weight, Age, Force, Salary, Birth Order, Blood Pressure, Energy, etc. Numbers on this scale reflect actual amounts of the variable being measured. It makes sense, then, to say that one person is twice as heavy as another, or that one person is half as tall as another. All mathematical and statistical operations are permissible with Ratio Scale data. Ratio Scale data can be analysed with the help of same Statistical techniques which are used to analyse Interval Scale data. Thus, for Interval Scale as well as Ratio Scale data the same Statistical Techniques are used but before using the Statistical Technique, one must make sure that the data satisfy the underlying assumptions of the technique.

> ***Caution***
>
> 1. Higher Scale data can be changed to Lower Scale but not vice-versa.
> 2. The data on Interval Scale or Ratio Scale are stronger than the data on Nominal Scale or Ordinal Scale.

Take a Test

1. Which of the following is a Parameter Symbol?
   A) m B) s
   C) μ D) None of the above.
2. Which of the following is a Statistics Symbol?
   A) σ B) Σ
   C) β D) m
3. The main characteristics of Interval Scale data are
   A) Only equal intervals B) Fixed reference point
   C) Only reference point D) Non fixed reference point as well as equal intervals.
4. Which of the following has measurement on Nominal Scale?
   A) Words in a line B) Books in the library
   C) Both A and B D) Price of pen.
5. Which of the following is the highest Scale of Measurement?
   A) Interval Scale B) Ordinal Scale
   C) Nominal Scale D) All of the above.
6. Which of the following variable has measurement on Nominal Scale?
   A) Fear of Failure B) Income
   C) Temperature D) Residential Background.

7. Which of the variable has measurement on Ordinal Scale?
   A) Fear of Crime B) Monthly Expenditure
   C) Gender D) Temperature.
8. Only Ratio Scale has
   A) Non fixed Zero B) Fixed Zero
   C) Both A and B D) Neither A nor B.
9. Ordinal Scale has the property of
   A) Metricity B) Variability
   C) Ranking D) Absolution.
10. Which of the following Scale of Measurement has the greatest limitations on Statistical manipulation?
    A) Ratio Scale B) Nominal Scale
    C) Ordinal Scale D) Interval Scale.
11. A typical linear, numeric scale yields data on
    A) Nominal Scale B) Ordinal Scale
    C) Interval Scale D) Ratio Scale.
12. The order in which the students complete the task is an example of
    A) Ratio Scale B) Interval Scale
    C) Nominal Scale D) Ordinal Scale.
13. What is the level of measurement if the participants are asked to choose their favourite picture from a set of six?
    A) Nominal B) Ratio
    C) Interval D) Ordinal.
14. What is the difference between data measured on an Interval Scale and data measured on Ratio Scale?
    A) A Ratio Scale puts scores into categories, while an interval scale measures on a continuous scale.
    B) A Ratio Scale has a true zero point, so zero on the scale corresponds to the zero of the concept being measured.
    C) An Interval Scale has a true zero point, so zero on the scale corresponds to the zero of the concept being measured.
    D) A Ratio Scale has equal intervals between the points on the scale, whereas Interval Scale does not.
15. A teacher records the height of each student of Class V. The Scale of Measurement for Height is
    A) Nominal Scale B) Ordinal Scale
    C) Interval Scale D) Ratio Scale.
16. The Scale of Measurement for Eye Colour is
    A) Nominal Scale B) Ordinal Scale
    C) Interval Scale D) Ratio Scale.
17. A teacher of Class IV records the percentage that each student got correct answer on the last Mathematics Test. In this case the Scale of Measurement is
    A) Nominal Scale B) Ordinal Scale
    C) Ratio Scale D) Interval Scale.
18. Place of Birth is the example of
    A) Nominal Scale B) Ordinal Scale
    C) Interval Scale D) Ratio Scale.

19. The birth order of the children in a family is the information on the
    A) Nominal Scale B) Ordinal Scale
    C) Interval Scale D) Ratio Scale.
20. Which of the following statements best relate to Ratio Scale data?
    A) Category membership
    B) Equal intervals and true zero point
    C) Hightest level of data
    D) Both B and C.
21. Which of the following statements best describes the relationship between a Parameter and a Statistic?
    A) A parameter has a sampling distribution with the statistic as its mean.
    B) A parameter has a sampling distribution that can be used to determine what values the statistic is likely to have in repeated samples.
    C) A parameter is used to estimate a statistic.
    D) A statistic is used to estimate a parameter.
22. Which of the following statements is correct?
    A) Parameter describes the population. B) Parameter describes the sample
    C) Both A and B D) Neither A nor B.
23. Which of the following statements is correct?
    A) Non-parametric Statistics are stronger than Parametric Statistics.
    B) Both Nonparametric Statistics and Parametric Statistics are equally strong.
    C) Non-parametric Statistics are less strong than Parametric Statistics.
    D) Parametric Statistics can be used with Ordinal Scale data.

9
t–Test

INTRODUCTION

As stated in earlier chapters, the researcher may collect quantitative data with the help of Test, Scale, or Inventory and may like to analyse the data with the help of appropriate Statistical Technique. There are large numbers of Statistical Techniques available to the researcher. He/she must know which Statistical Technique is the most appropriate for analysing the data related to objectives of her/his research. If a researcher is interested in comparing the means of a variable of two independent groups, then t-Test can be used. After reading this chapter, you will be able to:

- Tell other names of t-Test.
- Write assumptions underlying t-Test.
- Word research Objective correctly whose data can be analysed with the help of t-Test.
- Write Hypothesis correctly for the given Objective.
- Analyse data using SPSS.
- Put SPSS output in appropriate Table along with proper heading.
- Interpret the information given in the t-Test Table and test the given Hypothesis.

OTHER NAMES OF t-TEST

Other names of t-Test are Independent Samples t-Test and Student's t-Test.

ASSUMPTIONS UNDERLYING t-TEST

The data to be analysed with the help of t-Test must satisfy the following assumptions.

1. Normal Distribution: The data of criterion variable or dependent variable must be normally distributed in the population.
2. Homogeneity of Variance: The differences within one group must be equal to the differences within second group.

$$\sigma_1^2 = \sigma_2^2$$

3. The data must be either on Interval Scale or Ratio Scale.
4. There should be *no significant outliers* within each independent group.

WHEN TO USE t-TEST

t-Test or Independent Samples t-Test is to be used only when the researcher is interested in studying the significance of difference between mean scores of Dependent Variable or Criterion Variable of only two Independent Groups and the data must satisfy the Assumptions underlying t-Test.

Example-I

How To Write Objective For t-Test

The objective should be worded as given below so that data can be analysed with the help of t-Test:

- To compare mean scores of Self-efficacy of Male and Female Teachers.

How to Formulate Hypothesis

The Hypothesis which can be tested with the help of t-Test is formulated in the Null Form as given below:

- There is no significant difference between mean scores of Self-efficacy of Male and Female Teachers.

Which Statistical Technique to Use for Analysing Data

For testing the hypothesis, t-Test should be used and the data can be analysed using Statistical Package for the Social Sciences (SPSS). The outputs of SPSS are as given in Tables 9.1 and 9.2.

Table 9.1: Group Statistics

	2	*N*	*Mean*	*Std. Deviation*	*Std. Error Mean*
Self-efficacy	Males	150	57.1600	20.80400	1.69864
	Females	150	80.2000	23.47982	1.91712

How to Interpret the Results Given in Tables 9.1 and 9.2

The results of t-Test should be interpreted as given below:

The Objective was to compare mean scores of Self-efficacy of Male and Female Teachers. There were two levels of Gender, namely, Males and Females. The data were analysed with the help of t-Test and the results are given in Table 9.3.

From Table 9.3, it is evident that the t-value is 8.99 which is significant at 0.01 level with df = 298. It shows that the mean scores of Self-efficacy of Male

Table 9.2: Independent Samples Test

		Levene's Test for Equality of Variances		t-test for Equality of Means						
									95% Confidence Interval of the Difference	
		F	Sig.	t	df	Sig. (2-tailed)	Mean Difference	Std. Error Difference	Lower	Upper
Self-efficacy	Equal variances assumed	1.873	.172	-8.995	298	.000	-23.04000	2.56139	-28.08071	-17.99929
	Equal variances not assumed			-8.995	293.741	.000	-23.04000	2.56139	-28.08100	-17.99900

Caution: *The t-Values are shown as negative in Table 9.2 but it should always be reported as positive because it represents the difference between means of two groups. Difference is a Scalar quantity which has only magnitude but no direction.*

Table 9.3: Gender-wise M, SD, N, and t-Values of Self-efficacy of Teachers

Gender	M	SD	N	t-value	Remark
Males	57.16	20.80	150	8.99	p<0.01
Females	80.20	23.48	150		

and Female Teachers differ significantly. Thus, the null hypothesis that there is no significant difference between mean scores of Self-efficacy of Male and Female Teachers is rejected. Further, the mean score of Self-efficacy of Female Teachers is 80.20 which is significantly higher than that of Male Teachers whose mean score of Self-efficacy is 57.16. It may, therefore, be said that Female Teachers were found to believe significantly more in their own ability to succeed in a situation than their counter part Male Teachers.

Example-2

How to Write Objective for t-Test

The Objective should be worded as given below so that data can be analysed with the help of t-Test:

- To compare mean scores of Self-efficacy of Teachers of Primary Schools and Higher Secondary Schools.

How to Formulate Hypothesis

The hypothesis which can be tested with the help of t-Test is formulated in the

Null Form as given below:

- There is no significant difference between mean scores of Self-efficacy of Teachers of Primary Schools and Higher Secondary Schools.

Which Statistical Technique to Use for Analysing Data

For testing the hypothesis, t-Test should be used and the data can be analysed using Statistical Package for the Social Sciences (SPSS). The outputs of SPSS are as given in Tables 9.4 and 9.5.

Table 9.4: Group Statistics

	3	*N*	*Mean*	*Std. Deviation*	*Std. Error Mean*
Self-efficacy	Primary School	100	73.2900	26.52930	2.65293
	Higher Secondary School	100	73.4600	25.45720	2.54572

Table 9.5: Independent Samples Test

		Levene's Test for Equality of Variances		*t-test for Equality of Means*						
									95% Confidence Interval of the Difference	
		F	Sig.	t	df	Sig. (2-tailed)	Mean Difference	Std. Error Difference	Lower	Upper
Self-efficacy	Equal variances assumed	.119	.731	-.046	198	.963	-.17000	3.67678	-7.42068	7.08068
	Equal variances not assumed			-.046	197.664	.963	-.17000	3.67678	-7.42076	7.08076

How to Interpret the Results Given in Tables 9.4 and 9.5

The results of t-Test should be interpreted as given below:

The Objective was to compare mean scores of Self-efficacy of Teachers of Primary Schools and Higher Secondary Schools. There were teachers from two types of school, namely, Primary Schools and Higher Secondary Schools. The data were analysed with the help of t-Test and the results are given in Table 9.6.

Table 9.6: School-wise M, SD, N, and t-values of Self-efficacy of Teachers

Types of School	*M*	*SD*	*N*	*t-value*	*Remark*
Primary Schools	73.29	26.53	100	0.05	Not significant
Higher Secondary schools	73.46	25.46	100		

From Table 9.6, it is evident that the t-value is 0.05 which is not significant. It shows that the mean scores of Self-efficacy of Teachers of Primary Schools and Higher Secondary Schools did not differ significantly. Thus, the null hypothesis that there is no significant difference between mean scores of Self-efficacy of Teachers of Primary Schools and Higher Secondary Schools is not rejected. It may, therefore, be said that Teachers of Primary Schools and Higher Secondary Schools were found to believe to the same extent in their own ability to succeed in a situation.

Take a Test

1. The main difference between Z and t–tests is that
   A) For a t-test, the population mean and standard deviation are needed.
   B) For t-test only, the sample mean is needed.
   C) For Z-test, the population mean and standard deviation are needed.
   D) Z and t-tests are identical except for the size of the sample used.
2. How does the shape of the distribution change as the sample size increases?
   A) It becomes broader.
   B) It becomes more normal looking.
   C) It becomes skewed.
   D) It becomes flatter.
3. Which of the following would most likely cause the confidence interval to become smaller?
   A) Decreasing the Standard error.
   B) Decreasing N.
   C) Increasing mean.
   D) Increasing Alpha.
4. If all other factors are held constant, then as the error term of a t-statistics becomes greater,
   A) Between groups variance becomes greater.
   B) The probability of making a Type-I error increases.
   C) The probability of making a Type-II error increases.
   D) There is a greater likelihood of rejecting the Null Hypothesis.
5. An Independent Samples t-test can be used to assess
   A) Differences between two groups of participants.
   B) Differences between scores obtained on two separate occasions from the same participants.
   C) Relationship between two data sets.
   D) Goodness of fit.
6. Which of the following assumptions must be satisfied to use t-Test?
   A) The data from two cases are not linked in any way.
   B) The data of the dependent variable must be either on interval or ratio scale.
   C) The dependent variable data must be normally distributed.
   D) All the above.

7. Which of the following statistics are important when interpreting Independent Sample t-test?
   A) t-value
   B) Significance level
   C) Descriptive statistics
   D) All the above.
8. What should Leven's Test be in order to use the "equal variance assumed" row of a t-test?
   A) It should be significant at 0.01 level.
   B) It should not be significant.
   C) It should be significant at 0.05 level.
   D) None of the above.
9. What should Leven's Test be in order to use the "unequal variance assumed" row of a t-test?
   A) It should be significant at least at 0.05 level.
   B) It should not be significant.
   C) It has to be significant at 0.01 level.
   D) None of the above.

10
Correlated t-Test

INTRODUCTION

As mentioned earlier there are different types of researches. One of them is Experimental Research. Whenever an Experimental Research is done, it employs some Experimental Design. As mentioned earlier, there are three categories of Experimental Design. These are Pre-experimental Designs, Quasi-experimental Designs, and True Experimental Designs. Of these, Pre-experimental Designs are most weak designs as the Internal Validity and External Validity are very poor. It is advisable not to use Pre-experimental Designs because the researcher cannot say with confidence that whatever change has occurred in the Dependent Variable is entirely due to treatment. In spite of weakness, researchers do use Pre-experimental Design. There are many Pre-experimental Designs. The most popular Pre-experimental Design is Pretest-Posttest Single Group Design. In this Design, the researcher selects an intact group. This group is pretested on a variable. After pretesting, the treatment is given to the group for specific period of time. At the end of the treatment, the same group is posttested using the same tool which was used at the pretest stage. Thus, the researcher can get scores at Pretest Stage as well as Posttest Stage. These two stages means can be compared with the help of Correlated t-Test. After reading this chapter, the researcher will be able to:

- Tell another name of Correlated t-Test.
- List the assumption underlying correlated t-Test.
- Write the objective of research whose data can be analysed with the help of Correlated t-Test.
- Write Hypothesis for the given objective.
- Analyse data with the help of Correlated t-Test using SPSS.
- Put SPSS output in appropriate Table along with proper heading.
- Interpret the information given in the Correlated t-Test Table and test the given hypothesis.

ALTERNATIVE NAME OF CORRELATED t-TEST

The alternative name of Correlated t-Test is Paired Samples t-Test.

ASSUMPTIONS UNDERLYING CORRELATED t-TEST

The following are the assumptions underlying Correlated t-Test or Paired Samples t-Test.

1. Normal Distribution: The data of criterion variable or dependent variable must be normally distributed in the population.
2. *There should be two categorical, "related groups"* or *"matched pairs"*.
3. The data must be either on Interval Scale or Ratio Scale.
4. There should be *no significant outliers* in the *differences* between the two related groups.

WHEN TO USE CORRELATED t-TEST

Correlated t-Test should be used only if the researcher has a group and assessed the Dependent Variable before as well as after the treatment. Also the data must satisfy the assumptions underlying Correlated t-Test.

HOW TO WRITE OBJECTIVE FOR CORRELATED t-TEST

The objective should be worded as given below so that data can be analysed with the help of Correlated t-Test:

- To compare mean scores of Achievement in Physics at Pretest and Posttest Stages of group taught through Computer Aided Instruction.

HOW TO FORMULATE HYPOTHESIS

The hypothesis which can be tested with the help of Correlated t-Test is formulated in the Null Form as given below:

- There is no significant difference in mean scores of Achievement in Physics at Pretest and Posttest Stages of group taught through Computer Aided Instruction.

WHICH STATISTICAL TECHNIQUE TO USE FOR ANALYSING DATA

For testing the hypothesis, Correlated t-Test should be used and the data can be analysed using Statistical Package for the Social Sciences (SPSS). The outputs of SPSS are as given in Tables 10.1, 10.2 and 10.3.

Table 10.1: Paired Samples Statistics

		Mean	*N*	*Std. Deviation*	*Std. Error Mean*
Pair 1	pretest. scores	46.6333	30	9.65074	1.76198
	posttest. scores	63.6333	30	7.15100	1.30559

Table 10.2: Paired Samples Correlations

		N	Correlation	Sig.
Pair 1	pretest. scores & posttest. scores	30	.980	.000

Table 10.3: Paired Samples t-Test

		Paired Differences					t	df	Sig. (2-tailed)
		Mean	Std. Deviation	Std. Error Mean	95% Confidence Interval of the Difference				
					Lower	Upper			
Pair 1	Pretest Score Posttest Scores	-17.00000	2.99425	.54667	-18.11807	-15.88193	-31.097	29	.000

HOW TO INTERPRET THE RESULTS GIVEN IN TABLES 10.1, 10.2 AND 10.3

The results of Correlated t-Test should be interpreted as given below:

The objective was to compare mean scores of Achievement in Physics at Pretest and Posttest Stages of group taught through Computer Aided Instruction. The data were analysed with the help of Correlated t-test and the results are given in Table 10.4.

Table 10.4: Testing-wise M, SD, N, r, and correlated t-value of Achievement in Physics

Testing	M	SD	N	r	Correlated t-Test	Remark
Pretest Posttest	46.63 63.63	9.65 7.15	30	0.98	31.10	p<0.01

From Table 10.4, it can be seen that the Correlated t-Value is 31.10 which is significant at 0.01 level with df = 29. It indicates that mean scores of Achievement in Physics at Pretest and Posttest stages of group taught Physics with the help of Computer Aided Instruction differ significantly. Thus, the null hypothesis that there is no significant difference in mean scores of Achievement in Physics at Pretest and Posttest Stages of group taught through Computer Aided Instruction is rejected. Further, the mean score of Achievement in Physics after teaching Physics through Computer Aided Instruction is 63.63 which is significantly higher than Achievement in Physics before teaching whose mean score at Pretest is 46.63. It may, therefore, be said that Achievement in Physics of students improved significantly when taught through Computer Aided Instruction.

Take a Test

1. For calculating df, the formula to be used is
   A) N–1 B) N–2
   C) $N_1 + N_2 - 2$ D) None of the above.
2. Which of the following is not the assumption of Correlated t-test?
   A) Normal Distribution
   B) Data may be on any Scale of Measurement
   C) The data may be on Interval Scale.
   D) There should not be outliers.
3. The Correlated t-test can be used in
   A) Survey Research B) Case Study Research
   C) Historical Research D) Experimental Research
4. For Correlated t-test, the Objective should be worded as
   A) To study the difference in scores at Pre and Post stages of the study.
   B) To compare scores of variable at Pre and Post stages of the study.
   C) To compare mean scores of variable at Pre and Post stages of the study.
   D) To study the difference in mean scores at Pre and Post stages of the study.
5. Which of the following statement is correct?
   A) The assumptions of Correlated t-test and t-test are same.
   B) The assumptions of Correlated t-test and t-test are different.
   C) Another name of Correlated t-test is Student's t-test.
   D) In place of Correlated t-test, Independent Samples t-test can be used.
6. In which of the following cases would you use paired Samples t-Test?
   A) When comparing two separate groups.
   B) When comparing the same participants performance before and after training.
   C) When assessing goodness of fit.
   D) When comparing men and women's scores.
7. Which section of a paired samples t-test output can be ignored?
   A) The t, df and sig. columns. B) The paired differences.
   C) The paired-samples correlation. D) Descriptive Statistics

11
Analysis of Variance

INTRODUCTION

The researcher may come across a situation where there are more than two levels of a variable and he/she wants to study the significance of difference among the means scores of one variable of different levels. For example, types of school can have three levels, such as, Government Schools, Aided Schools, and Private Schools. One may divide students into three independent groups on the basis of Intelligence, such as, High Intelligent, Average Intelligent and Low Intelligent. In cases where there are more than two groups or levels of a variable, t-Test or independent samples t-Test cannot be used. One has to use another Statistical Technique called Analysis of Variance. If there is one variable having more than two levels, then researcher can compare means of more than two groups using One Way Analysis of Variance or One Way ANOVA. It is called One Way because there is one variable having more than two groups or levels. If there are two variables in a research, each having two or more levels, the data can be analysed with the help of Two Way ANOVA. Similarly, in case of three variables, each having two or more levels, data can be analysed with the help of Three Way ANOVA. Normally more than three variables each having two or more levels are not taken because it is difficult to plot graphs for interactions among four or more variables. So researchers plan a research where data can be analysed with the help of maximum Three Way of ANOVA. After reading this chapter, researcher will be able to:

- List different names of ANOVA.
- Write assumptions underlying Analysis of Variance.
- Word research objective correctly whose data can be analysed with the help of One Way ANOVA, Two Way ANOVA, or Three Way ANOVA.
- Write hypothesis correctly for the given objective.
- Analyse data using SPSS.
- Put SPSS out-put in an appropriate table along with proper heading.
- Interpret the information given in the One Way ANOVA Table, Two Way ANOVA Table, or Three Way ANOVA Table and test the given hypothesis.

DIFFERENT NAMES OF ANOVA

- One Way ANOVA means One Variable having more than two levels along with One dependent or criterion variable.
- Two Way ANOVA means Two Variables, each having two or more than two levels along with one dependent or criterion variable. If there are n levels of one variable and m levels of another variable, then it can be called n x m Factorial Design ANOVA.
- Three Way ANOVA means Three Variables, each having two or more than two levels along with one dependent or criterion variable. If there are n levels of one variable, m levels of second variable, and h levels of third variable, then it can be called n x m x h Factorial Design ANOVA.

ASSUMPTIONS UNDERLYING ANOVA

The dependent or criterion variable data to be analysed with the help of ANOVA must satisfy the following assumptions.

1. *Normal Distribution:* The data of criterion variable or dependent variable must be normally distributed in the Population.
2. *Homogeneity of Variance:* The differences within groups of more than two independent groups must be equal.

$$\sigma_1^2 = \sigma_2^2 = \sigma_3^2 \ldots\ldots\ldots = \sigma_n^2$$

3. The data must be either on Interval Scale or Ratio Scale.
4. There should be *no significant outliers* within each group.

WHEN TO USE

- *One Way ANOVA:* It is to be used when the researcher wants to compare mean scores of Dependent Variable or Criterion Variable of more than two Independent Groups, and data satisfy the assumptions underlying ANOVA.
- *Two-Way ANOVA:* It is to be used when researcher has two categorical variables each having two or more levels, wants to compare mean scores of Dependent Variable or Criterion Variable and data satisfy the assumptions underlying ANOVA.
- *Three-Way ANOVA:* It is to be used when researcher has three categorical variables each having two or more levels, wants to compare mean scores of Dependent Variable or Criterion Variable and data satisfy the assumptions underlying ANOVA.

Example-I

How to Write Objective for One Way ANOVA

The objective should be worded as given below so that data can be analysed with the help of One Way ANOVA:

- To compare mean scores of Self-efficacy of Teachers teaching in Primary Schools. Secondary Schools and Higher Secondary Schools.

How to Formulate Hypothesis

The hypothesis which can be tested with the help of One Way ANOVA is formulated in the Null Form as given below:

- There is no significant difference among mean scores of Self-efficacy of Teachers teaching in Primary Schools, Secondary Schools and Higher Secondary Schools.

Which Statistical Technique to Use for Analysing Data

For testing the Hypothesis, One Way ANOVA should be used and the data can be analysed using Statistical Package for the Social Sciences (SPSS). The outputs of SPSS are as given in Tables 11.1, 11.2 and 11.3.

Table 11.1: Descriptive

Self-efficacy								
	N	*Mean*	*Std. Deviation*	*Std. Error*	*95% Confidence Interval for Mean*		*Minimum*	*Maximum*
					Lower Bound	*Upper Bound*		
Primary School	100	73.2900	26.52930	2.65293	68.0260	78.5540	36.00	124.00
Secondary School	100	59.2900	19.94502	1.99450	55.3325	63.2475	32.00	93.00
Higher Secondary School	100	73.4600	25.45720	2.54572	68.4087	78.5113	40.00	117.00
Total	**300**	**68.6800**	**24.97124**	**1.44172**	**65.8428**	**71.5172**	**32.00**	**124.00**

Table 11.2: ANOVA

Self-efficacy					
	Sum of Squares	*df*	*Mean Square*	*F*	*Sig.*
Between Groups	13227.260	2	6613.630	11.340	.000
Within Groups	173218.020	297	583.226		
Total	**186445.280**	**299**			

Table 11.3: Post Hoc Tests

Self-efficacy			
Duncan[a]			
3	N	Subset for alpha = 0.05	
		1	2
Secondary School	100	59.2900	
Primary School	100		73.2900
Higher Secondary School	100		73.4600
Sig.		1.000	.960

Means for groups in homogeneous subsets are displayed.

a. Uses Harmonic Mean Sample Size = 100.000.

How to Interpret the Results Given in Tables 11.1, 11.2 and 11.3

The results of One Way ANOVA should be interpreted as given below:

The objective was to compare mean scores of Self-efficacy of Teachers teaching in Primary Schools, Secondary Schools, and Higher Secondary Schools. The Teachers belonged to three Types of Schools, such as, Primary Schools, Secondary Schools, and Higher Secondary Schools. Thus, the data were analysed with the help of One Way ANOVA and the results are given in Table 11.4.

Table 11.4: Summary of One way ANOVA of Self-efficacy of Teachers

Source of Variance	*df*	*SS*	*MSS*	*F-Value*	*Remark*
Types of Schools	2	13227.26	6613.63	11.34	p<0.01
Error	297	173218.02	583.23		
Total	299				

From Table 11.4, it is evident that the F-Value is 11.34 which is significant at 0.01 level with df = 2/297. It shows that the mean scores of Self-efficacy of Teachers teaching in Primary Schools, Secondary Schools, and Higher Secondary Schools differ significantly. Thus, the null hypothesis that there is no significant difference among mean scores of Self-efficacy of Teachers teaching in Primary Schools, Secondary Schools and Higher Secondary Schools is rejected. In order to know which Type of School Teachers had significantly higher mean score of Self-efficacy, the data were further analysed with the help of Duncan Multiple Range Test and the results are given in Table 11.5.

Table 11.5: School-wise Mean, N and Significance of Difference among Mean Scores of Self-Efficacy of Teachers

Types of School	*M*	*N*	*Secondary Schools*	*Higher Secondary School*
Primary Schools	73.29	100	*	Not significant
Secondary Schools	59.29	100		*
Higher Secondary Schools	73.46	100		

* Significant at 0.05 level

From Table 11.5, it can be seen that mean scores of Self-efficacy of Teachers of Primary Schools and Secondary Schools differ significantly. The mean score of Self-efficacy of Primary Schools Teachers is 73.29 which is significantly higher than those of Secondary Schools Teachers whose mean score of Self-efficacy is 59.29. It may, therefore, be said that Primary Schools Teachers were found to believe significantly more in their own ability to succeed in a situation than their counter part of Secondary Schools.

The mean scores of Self-efficacy of Teachers of Primary Schools and Higher Secondary Schools did not differ significantly (Vide Table 11.5). It may, therefore, be said that Teachers of Primary Schools and Higher Secondary Schools were found to believe to the same extent in their own ability to succeed in a situation.

From Table 11.5, it can be seen that mean scores of Self-efficacy of Teachers of Secondary Schools and Higher Secondary Schools differ significantly. The mean score of Self-efficacy of Teachers of Higher Secondary Schools is 73.46 which is significantly higher than those of Secondary Schools whose mean score of Self-efficacy is 59.29. It may, therefore, be said that Teachers of Higher Secondary Schools were found to believe significantly higher in their own ability to succeed in a situation than their counter part of Secondary Schools.

On the whole it may be said that Teachers of Primary Schools as well as Higher Secondary Schools were found to believe significantly more in their own ability to succeed in a situation than their counter part of Teachers of Secondary Schools.

Note: If F-Value is significant and the researcher decides to analyse data further with the help of t-Test, then interpretation of F-Value will remain same but in place of Duncan Multiple Range Test results interpretation, t-test results should be interpreted as given below. SPSS outputs of t-test are not given here. Only the results are given in the Table 11.6.

Table 11.6: Type of School-wise M, SD, N, and t-Values of Self-efficacy of Teachers

Type of School	*M*	*SD*	*N*	*Secondary Schools*	*Higher Secondary Schools*
Primary Schools	73.29	26.53	100	4.22**	0.05
Secondary Schools	59.29	19.94	100	—	4.38**
Higher Secondary Schools	73.46	25.46	100		

** Significant at 0.01 level

From Table 11.6, it can be seen that the t-value for Primary Schools and Secondary Schools is 4.22 which is significant at 0.01 level with df = 198. It shows that the mean scores of Self-efficacy of Primary Schools Teachers and Secondary Schools Teachers differ significantly. The mean score of Self-efficacy of Primary Schools Teachers is 73.29 which is significantly higher than that of Secondary Schools Teachers whose mean score of Self-efficacy is 59.29. It may, therefore, be said that Primary Schools Teachers were found to believe significantly more in their own ability to succeed in a situation than their counter part Teachers of Secondary Schools.

It can be seen that the t-value for Primary Schools and Higher Secondary Schools is 0.05 which is not significant (Vide Table 11.6). It shows that the mean scores of Self-efficacy of Primary Schools Teachers and Higher Secondary Schools Teachers did not differ significantly. It may, therefore, be said that both Primary Schools Teachers as well as Higher Secondary Schools Teachers were found to believe to the same extent in their own ability to succeed in a situation.

From Table 11.6, it can be seen that the t-value for Teachers of Secondary Schools and Higher Secondary Schools is 4.38 which is significant at 0.01 level with df = 198. It shows that the mean scores of Self-efficacy of Secondary Schools Teachers and Higher Secondary Schools Teachers differ significantly. The mean score of Self-efficacy of Secondary Schools Teachers is 59.29 which is significantly lower than that of Higher Secondary Schools Teachers whose mean score of Self-efficacy is 73.46. It may, therefore, be said that Higher Secondary Schools Teachers were found to believe significantly more in their own ability to succeed in a situation than their counter part Teachers of Secondary Schools.

On the whole it may be said that Teachers of Primary Schools as well as Higher Secondary Schools were found to believe significantly more in their own ability to succeed in a situation than their counter part Teachers of Secondary Schools.

Example-2

How to Write Objective for One Way ANOVA

The Objective should be worded as given below so that data can be analysed with the help of One Way ANOVA:

- To study the influence of Religious Affairs on Academic Achievement of Students.

How to Formulate Hypothesis

The hypothesis which can be tested with the help of One Way ANOVA is formulated in the Null Form as given below:

- There is no significant influence of Religious Affairs on Academic Achievement of students.

Which Statistical Technique to Use for Analysing Data

For testing the hypothesis, One Way ANOVA should be used and the data can be analysed by using Statistical Package for the Social Sciences (SPSS). The outputs of SPSS are as given in Tables 11.7 and 11.8.

Table 11.7: Descriptives

Academic Achievement								
	N	Mean	Std. Deviation	Std. Error	95% Confidence Interval for Mean: Lower Bound	95% Confidence Interval for Mean: Upper Bound	Minimum	Maximum
Catholic	21	67.4762	15.82599	3.45351	60.2723	74.6801	36.00	93.00
Protestant	20	76.4000	19.24468	4.30324	67.3932	85.4068	29.00	99.00
Jewish	9	69.3333	15.63650	5.21217	57.3141	81.3526	48.00	96.00
Total	**50**	**71.3800**	**17.41673**	**2.46310**	**66.4302**	**76.3298**	**29.00**	**99.00**

Table 11.8: ANOVA

Academic Achievement					
	Sum of Squares	df	Mean Square	F	Sig.
Between Groups	861.742	2	430.871	1.446	.246
Within Groups	14002.038	47	297.916		
Total	**14863.780**	**49**			

How to Interpret the Results Given in Tables 11.7 and 11.8

The results of One Way ANOVA should be interpreted as given below:

The objective was to study the influence of Religious Affairs on Academic Achievement of students. The students belonged to three Religious Affairs, such as, Catholic, Protestant and Jewish. Thus, the data were analysed with the help of One Way ANOVA and the results are given in Table 11.9.

Table 11.9: Summary of One way ANOVA of Academic Achievement of Students

Source of Variance	*df*	*SS*	*MSS*	*F-Value*
Religious Affairs	2	861.74	430.87	1.45
Error	47	14002.04	297.92	
Total	**49**			

From Table 11.9, it can be seen that the F-Value of 1.45 is not significant. It shows that mean scores of Academic Achievement of students belonging to Catholic, Protestant and Jewish religious groups did not differ significantly. So there is no significant influence of Religious Affairs on Academic Achievement of students. Thus, the null hypothesis that there is no significant influence of Religious Affairs on Academic Achievement of students is not rejected. It may, therefore, be said that Academic Achievement of students was found to be independent of Religious Affairs of students.

Example-3

How to Write Objective for Two Way ANOVA

The objective should be worded as given below so that data can be analysed with the help of Two Way ANOVA:

- 3: To study the influence of Locale of School, Types of Schools and their interaction on Self-efficacy of Teachers.

OR

- 3a: To study the influence of Locale of Schools on Self-efficacy of Teachers.
- 3b: To study the influence of Types of Schools on Self-efficacy of Teachers.
- 3c: To study the influence of interaction between Locale of Schools and Types of Schools on Self-efficacy of Teachers.

How to Formulate Hypothesis

The Hypothesis which can be tested with the help of Two Way ANOVA is formulated in the Null Form as given below:

- 3: There is no significant influence of Locale of Schools, Types of Schools and their interaction on Self-efficacy of Teachers.

OR

- 3a: There is no significant influence of Locale of Schools on Self-efficacy of Teachers.
- 3b: There is no significant influence of Types of Schools on Self-efficacy of Teachers.
- 3c: There is no significant influence of interaction between Locale of Schools and Types of Schools on Self-efficacy of Teachers.

Which Statistical Technique to Use for Analysing Data

In this study there were two Variables, namely, Locale of Schools and Types of Schools. There were two levels of Locale of Schools, namely, Urban Area and Rural Area. Primary Schools, Secondary Schools and Higher Secondary Schools were the three Types of Schools to which Teachers belong. Thus, the data were analysed with the help of Two Way ANOVA or 2 X 3 Factorial Design ANOVA using Statistical Package for the Social Sciences (SPSS). The outputs of SPSS are as given in Tables 11.10, 11.11 and 11.12.

Table 11.10: Descriptive Statistics

Dependent Variable: Self-efficacy

2	*3*	*Mean*	*Std. Deviation*	*N*
Rural Area	Primary School	80.8033	25.85461	61

	Secondary School	61.2167	19.76137	60
	Higher Secondary School	75.0333	26.10018	60
	Total	**72.3978**	**25.33853**	**181**
Urban Area	Primary School	61.5385	23.36196	39
	Secondary School	56.4000	20.11862	40
	Higher Secondary School	71.1000	24.59706	40
	Total	**63.0252**	**23.39255**	**119**
Total	Primary School	73.2900	26.52930	100
	Secondary School	59.2900	19.94502	100
	Higher Secondary School	73.4600	25.45720	100
	Total	**68.6800**	**24.97124**	**300**

Table 11.11: Tests of Between-Subjects Effects

Dependent Variable: Self-efficacy

Source	*Type III Sum of Squares*	*df*	*Mean Square*	*F*	*Sig.*
Corrected Model	22984.632a	5	4596.926	8.268	.000
Intercept	1315413.522	1	1315413.522	2365.900	.000
Locale of School	6260.220	1	6260.220	11.260	.001
Types of School	11500.991	2	5750.495	10.343	.000
Locale of School * Types of School	3535.917	2	1767.958	3.180	.043
Error	163460.648	294	555.989		
Total	1601528.000	300			
Corrected Total	186445.280	299			

a. R Squared = .123 (Adjusted R Squared = .108)

Table 11.12: Post Hoc Tests

Self-efficacy

Duncana, b

3	*N*	*Subset*	
		1	2
Secondary School	100	59.2900	
Primary School	100		73.2900
Higher Secondary School	100		73.4600
Sig.		1.000	.959

Means for groups in homogeneous subsets are displayed.
Based on observed means.
The error term is Mean Square (Error) = 555.989.

a. Uses Harmonic Mean Sample Size = 100.000.

b. Alpha = .05.

How To Interpret the Results Given in Tables 11.10, 11.11 and 11.12

The results of Two Way ANOVA should be interpreted as given below:

The Objective was to study the influence of Local of Schools, Type of Schools and their interaction on Self-efficacy of Teachers. There were two levels of Local of Schools, namely, Urban and Rural; while Teachers belonged to Primary Schools, Secondary Schools, and Higher Secondary Schools. Thus, the data were analysed with the help of Two Way ANOVA or 2 X 3 Factorial Design ANOVA; and the results are given in Table 11.13.

Table 11.13: Summary of 2 X 3 Factorial Design ANOVA of Self-efficacy of Teachers

Source of Variance	*df*	*SS*	*MSS*	*F-Value*	*Remark*
Locale of Schools (A)	1	6260.22	6260.22	11.26	p<0.01
Types of Schools (B)	2	11500.99	5750.49	10.34	p<0.01
A X B	2	3535.92	1767.96	3.18	p<0.05
Error	294	163460.65	555.99		
Total	**299**				

Influence of Locale of Schools on Self-efficacy

From Table 11.13, it is evident that the F-Value for Locale of Schools is 11.26 which is significant at 0.01 level with df = 1/294. It shows that mean scores of Self-efficacy of Teachers working in Urban Schools differ significantly from those working in Rural Schools. So there was a significant influence of Locale of Schools on Self-efficacy of Teachers. Thus, the null hypothesis that there is no significant influence of Locale of Schools on Self-efficacy of Teachers is rejected. Further, the mean score of Self-efficacy of Teachers working in Rural Schools is 72.40 which is significantly higher than those working in Urban Schools whose mean score of Self-efficacy is 63.02. It may, therefore, be said that Teachers working in Rural Schools were found to believe significantly more in their own ability to succeed in a situation than their counter part Teachers working in Urban Schools.

Influence of Types of Schools

The F-Value for Types of Schools is 10.34 which is significant at 0.01 level with df = 2/294 (Vide Table 11.13). It shows that mean scores of Self-efficacy of Teachers working in Primary Schools, Secondary Schools, and Higher Secondary Schools differ significantly among themselves. So there was a significant influence of Types of Schools on Self-efficacy of Teachers. Thus, the null hypothesis that there is no significant influence of Types of Schools on Self-efficacy of Teachers is rejected. In order to know Teachers working in which Type of Schools had significantly higher Self-efficacy, the data were further analysed with the help of Duncan's Multiple Range Test and the results are given in Table 11.14.

Table 11.14: Types of School-wise Mean, N and significance of difference among mean scores of Self-efficacy of Teachers

Types of School	*M*	*N*	*Secondary Schools*	*Higher Secondary School*
Primary Schools	73.29	100	*	Not significant
Secondary Schools	59.29	100		
Higher Secondary Schools	73.46	100		*

* Significant at 0.05 level

From Table 11.14, it can be seen that mean scores of Self-efficacy of Teachers of Primary Schools and Secondary Schools differ significantly. The mean score of Self-efficacy of Primary Schools Teachers is 73.29 which is significantly higher than those of Secondary Schools Teachers whose mean score of Self-efficacy is 59.29. It may, therefore, be said that Primary Schools Teachers were found to believe significantly more in their own ability to succeed in a situation than their counter part of Secondary Schools Teachers.

The mean scores of Self-efficacy of Teachers of Primary Schools and Higher Secondary Schools did not differ significantly (Vide Table 11.14). It may, therefore, be said that Teachers of Primary Schools and Higher Secondary Schools were found to believe to the same extent in their own ability to succeed in a situation.

From Table 11.14, it can be seen that mean scores of Self-efficacy of Teachers of Secondary Schools and Higher Secondary Schools differ significantly. The mean score of Self-efficacy of Higher Secondary Schools Teachers is 73.46 which is significantly higher than those of Secondary Schools Teachers whose mean score of Self-efficacy is 59.29. It may, therefore, be said that Higher Secondary Schools Teachers were found to believe significantly more in their own ability to succeed in a situation than their counter part of Secondary Schools Teachers.

On the whole it may be said that Teachers of Primary Schools as well as Higher Secondary Schools were found to believe significantly more in their own ability to succeed in a situation than their counter part Teachers of Secondary Schools.

Influence of Interaction between Locale of Schools and Types of Schools on Self-efficacy of Teachers

The F-Value for interaction between Locale of Schools and Types of Schools is 3.18 which is significant at 0.05 level with df = 2/294 (Vide Table 11.13). It shows that the mean scores of Self-efficacy of Teachers from Urban Schools and Rural Schools teaching in Primary Schools, Secondary Schools and Higher Secondary Schools differ significantly. It means that there was a significant influence of interaction between Locale of Schools and Types of Schools on Self-efficacy of Teachers. Thus, the null hypothesis that there is no significant influence of interaction between Locale of Schools and Types of Schools on Self-efficacy of Teachers is rejected. In order to know the trend of influence of interaction between

Locale of Schools and Types of Schools, Graph 1, has been plotted.

From Graph 1, it can be seen that irrespective of Locale of Schools, the trend of Self-efficacy across Types of Schools remains the same. In case of teachers working in Schools of Rural Area, there is a sharp decline in Self-efficacy of Teachers as schools change from Primary to Secondary; but there is sharp increase in Self-efficacy of Teachers as schools change from Secondary to Higher Secondary. On the other hand, in case of teachers working

Graph 1: Trend of influence of interaction between Locale of Schools and Types of Schools on Self-efficacy of Teachers

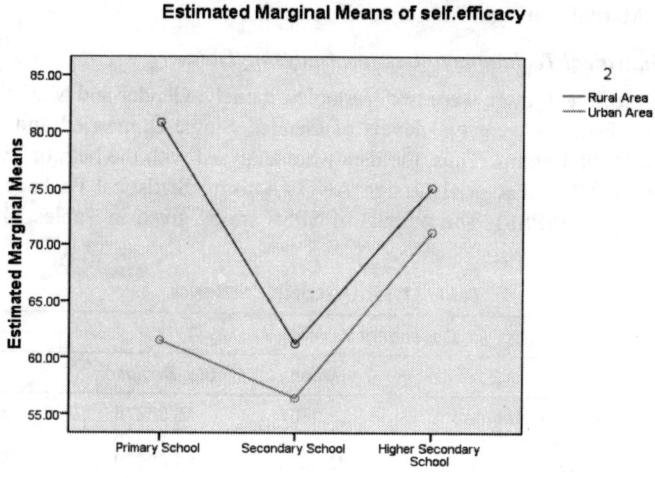

in schools of urban area, there is a decline in Self-efficacy of Teachers as schools change from Primary to Secondary, but there is sharp increase in Self-efficacy of Teachers as schools change from Secondary to Higher Secondary. Further Primary Schools Teachers of Rural area had higher Self-efficacy as compared to those of Urban Area.

Example-4

How to Write Objective for Two Way ANOVA

The Objective should be worded as given below so that data can be analysed with the help of Two Way ANOVA:

- 4: To study the influence of Gender, Marital Status and their interaction on Anxiety of Teachers.

OR

- 4a: To study the influence of Gender on Anxiety of Teachers.
- 4b: To study the influence of Marital Status on Anxiety of Teachers.
- 4c: To study the influence of interaction between Gender and Marital Status on Anxiety of Teachers.

How to Formulate Hypothesis

The Hypothesis which can be tested with the help of Two Way ANOVA is formulated in the Null Form as given below:

- 4: There is no significant influence of Gender, Marital Status and their interaction on Anxiety of Teachers. OR
- 4a: There is no significant influence of Gender on Anxiety of Teachers.
- 4b: There is no significant influence of Marital Status on Anxiety of Teachers.
- 4c: There is no significant influence of interaction between Gender and Marital Status on Anxiety of Teachers.

Which Statistical Technique to Use for Analysing Data

As per Objective-4, there were two Variables, namely, Gender and Marital Status. Males and Females were two levels of Gender. Single-Unmarried and Married were two Marital Status. Thus, the data were analysed with the help of Two Way ANOVA or 2 X 2 Factorial Design ANOVA using Statistical Package for the Social Sciences (SPSS). The outputs of SPSS are as given in Tables 11.15 and 11.16.

Table 11.15: Descriptive Statistics

Dependent Variable: Anxiety

2	2	Mean	Std. Deviation	N
Male	Single-Unmarried	23.0667	15.58278	30
	Married	19.8175	14.47226	126
	Total	**20.4423**	**14.69660**	**156**
Female	Single-Unmarried	24.1286	13.95430	70
	Married	21.0274	12.50707	146
	Total	**22.0324**	**13.04247**	**216**
Total	Single-Unmarried	23.8100	14.39044	100
	Married	20.4669	13.44137	272
	Total	**21.3656**	**13.76353**	**372**

Table 11.16: Tests of Between-Subjects Effects

Dependent Variable: Anxiety

Source	Type III Sum of Squares	df	Mean Square	F	Sig.
Corrected Model	939.878[a]	3	313.293	1.663	.175
Intercept	124205.985	1	124205.985	659.180	.000
Gender	82.706	1	82.706	.439	.508
Marital Status	646.221	1	646.221	3.430	.065
Gender * Marital Status	.351	1	.351	.002	.966
Error	69340.402	368	188.425		
Total	**240094.000**	**372**			
Corrected Total	**70280.280**	**371**			

a. R Squared = .013 (Adjusted R Squared = .005)

How to Interpret the Results Given in Tables 11.15 and 11.16

The results of Two Way ANOVA should be interpreted as given below:

The Objective was to study the influence of Gender, Marital Status and their interaction on Anxiety of Teachers. There were two levels of Gender, namely, Males and Females; while Single-Unmarried and Married were the two levels of Marital Status. Thus, the data were analysed with the help of Two Way ANOVA or 2 X 2 Factorial Design ANOVA; and the results are given in Table 11.17.

Table 11.17: Summary of 2 × 2 Factorial Design ANOVA of Anxiety of Teachers

Source of Variance	*df*	*SS*	*MSS*	*F-Value*
Gender (A)	1	82.71	82.71	0.44
Marital Status (B)	1	646.22	646.22	3.43
A X B	1	0.35	0.35	0.002
Error	368	69340.40	188.42	
Total	371			

Influence of Gender on Anxiety of Teachers

From Table 11.17, it can be seen that the F-Value for Gender is 0.44 which is not significant. It indicates that the mean scores of Anxiety of Male Teachers and Female Teachers did not differ significantly. That is, there was no significant influence of Gender on Anxiety of Teachers. Thus, the null hypothesis that there is no significant influence of Gender on Anxiety of Teachers is not rejected. It may, therefore, be said that both Male Teachers and Female Teachers were found to have Anxiety to the same extent.

Influence of Marital Status on Anxiety of Teachers

The F-Value for Marital Status is 3.43 which is not significant (Vide Table 11.17). It indicates that the mean scores of Anxiety of Single-Unmarried Teachers and Married Teachers did not differ significantly. That is, there was no significant influence of Marital Status on Anxiety of Teachers. Thus, the null hypothesis that there is no significant influence of Marital Status on Anxiety of Teachers is not rejected. It may, therefore, be said that both Single-Unmarried Teachers and Married Teachers were found to have Anxiety to the same extent.

Influence of Interaction between Gender and Marital Status on Anxiety of Teachers

From Table 11.17, it can be seen that the F-Value for interaction between Gender and Marital Status of Teachers is 0.002 which is not significant. It indicates that the mean scores of Anxiety of Male and Female Teachers with Single-Unmarried status and Married status did not differ significantly. That is, there was no significant influence of interaction between Gender and Marital Status on Anxiety of Teachers. Thus, the null hypothesis that there is no significant influence of interaction between Gender and Marital Status on Anxiety of Teachers is not rejected. It may, therefore, be said that Anxiety was found to be independent of influence of interaction between Gender and Marital Status of Teachers.

Example-5

How to Write Objective for Three Way ANOVA

The Objective should be worded as given below so that data can be analysed with the help of Three Way ANOVA:

- 5: To study the influence of Locale of Schools, Gender, Types of School, and their various interactions on Emotional Competence of Teachers.

Or

- 5a: To study the influence of Locale of Schools on Emotional Competence of Teachers.
- 5b: To study the influence of Gender on Emotional Competence of Teachers.
- 5c: To study the influence of Types of School on Emotional Competence of Teachers.
- 5d: To study the influence of interaction between Locale of Schools and Gender on Emotional Competence of Teachers.
- 5e: To study the influence of interaction between Locale of Schools and Types of School on Emotional Competence of Teachers.
- 5f: To study the influence of interaction between Gender and Types of School on Emotional Competence of Teachers.
- 5g: To study the influence of interaction among Locale of Schools, Gender and Types of School on Emotional Competence of Teachers.

How to Formulate Hypothesis

The hypothesis which can be tested with the help of Three Way ANOVA is formulated in the Null Form as given below:

- 5: There is no significant influence of Locale of Schools, Gender, Types of School, and their various interactions on Emotional Competence of Teachers.

Or

- 5a: There is no significant influence of Locale of Schools on Emotional Competence of Teachers.
- 5b: There is no significant influence of Gender on Emotional Competence of Teachers.
- 5c: There is no significant influence of Types of School on Emotional Competence of Teachers.
- 5d: There is no significant influence of interaction between Locale of Schools and Gender on Emotional Competence of Teachers.
- 5e: There is no significant influence of interaction between Locale of Schools and Types of School on Emotional Competence of Teachers.

- 5f: There is no significant influence of interaction between Gender and Types of School on Emotional Competence of Teachers.
- 5g: There is no significant influence of interaction among Locale of Schools, Gender and Types of School on Emotional Competence of Teachers.

Which Statistical Technique to Use for Analysing Data

As per Objective-5, there were three Variables, namely, Locale of Schools, Gender and Types of School. Urban Area and Rural Area were the two levels of Locale of Schools. Males and Females were two levels of Gender. Government Schools and Private Schools were two Types of School. Thus, the data were analysed with the help of Three Way ANOVA or 2 X 2 X 2 Factorial Design ANOVA using Statistical Package for the Social Sciences (SPSS). The outputs of SPSS are as given in Tables 11.18 and 11.19.

Table 11.18: Descriptive Statistics

Dependent Variable: emotional competence

2	2	2	Mean	Std. Deviation	N
Rural Area	Males	Government School	179.8378	27.72135	37
		Private School	81.5556	4.68907	54
		Total	**121.5165**	**51.73788**	**91**
	Females	Government School	146.6667	79.84986	36
		Private School	116.3333	3.92380	54
		Total	**128.4667**	**52.34398**	**90**
	Total	Government School	163.4795	61.33947	73
		Private School	98.9444	17.99212	108
		Total	**124.9724**	**52.01222**	**181**
Urban Area	Males	Government School	150.0870	13.63122	23
		Private School	87.3333	13.77368	36
		Total	**111.7966**	**33.73159**	**59**
	Females	Government School	187.3333	12.54788	24
		Private School	120.3333	13.44619	36
		Total	**147.1333**	**35.55634**	**60**
	Total	Government School	169.1064	22.84278	47
		Private School	103.8333	21.41804	72
		Total	**129.6134**	**38.80964**	**119**
Total	Males	Government School	168.4333	27.40368	60
		Private School	83.8667	9.78786	90
		Total	**117.6933**	**45.63408**	**150**
	Females	Government School	162.9333	65.17197	60
		Private School	117.9333	9.17348	90
		Total	**135.9333**	**47.13150**	**150**
	Total	Government School	165.6833	49.85778	120
		Private School	100.9000	19.52512	180
		Total	**126.8133**	**47.20359**	**300**

Table 11.19: Tests of Between-Subjects Effects

Dependent Variable: emotional competence

Source	*Type III Sum of Squares*	*df*	*Mean Square*	*F*	*Sig.*
Corrected Model	392742.027[a]	7	56106.004	59.905	.000
Intercept	4918623.821	1	4918623.821	5251.644	.000
Locale of school	1841.487	1	1841.487	1.966	.162
Gender	22201.770	1	22201.770	23.705	.000
Types of School	287064.574	1	287064.574	306.501	.000
Locale of School * Gender	20260.475	1	20260.475	21.632	.000
Locale of School * Types of School	5.569	1	5.569	.006	.939
Gender * Types of School	17450.663	1	17450.663	18.632	.000
Locale of School * Gender * Types of School	22413.834	1	22413.834	23.931	.000
Error	273483.520	292	936.587		
Total	5490712.000	300			
Corrected Total	666225.547	299			

a. R Squared = .590 (Adjusted R Squared = .580)

How to Interpret the Results Given in Tables 11.18 and 11.19

The results of Three Way ANOVA should be interpreted as given below:

The Objective was to study the influence of Locale of Schools, Gender, Types of School, and their various interactions on Emotional Competence of Teachers. There were two levels of Locale of Schools, namely, Rural Area and Urban Area. Males and Females were the two levels of Gender. Types of School were Government Schools and Private Schools. Thus, the data were analysed with the help of Three Way ANOVA or 2 X 2 X 2 Factorial Design ANOVA; and the results are given in Table 11.20.

Table 11.20: Summary of 2 X 2 X 2 Factorial Design ANOVA of Emotional Competence of Teachers

Source of Variance	*df*	*SS*	*MSS*	*F-Value*
Locale of School (A)	1	1841.49	1841.49	1.97
Gender (B)	1	22201.77	22201.77	23.71**
Types of School (C)	1	287064.57	287064.57	306.50**
A X B	1	20260.47	20260.47	21.63**
A X C	1	5.57	5.57	0.01
B X C	1	17450.66	17450.66	18.63**
A X B X C	1	22413.83	22413.83	23.93**
Error	292	273483.52	936.59	
Total	**299**			

** Significant at 0.01 level.

Influence of Locale of School on Emotional Competence of Teachers

From Table 11.20, it can be seen that the F-Value of 1.97 for Locale of School is not significant. It indicates that the mean scores of Emotional Competence of Teachers working in Rural and Urban Area schools did not differ significantly. So there was no significant influence of Locale of School on Emotional

Competence of Teachers. Thus, the null hypothesis that there is no significant influence of Locale of School on Emotional Competence of Teacher is not rejected. It may, therefore, be said that Teachers working in Rural and Urban Area schools were found to have Emotional Competence to the same extent.

Influence of Gender on Emotional Competence of Teachers

The F-Value for Gender is 27.31 which is significant at 0.01 level with df = 1/292 (Vide Table 11.20). It indicates that the mean scores of Emotional Competence of Male and Female Teachers differ significantly. So there was a significant influence of Gender on Emotional Competence of Teachers. Thus, the null hypothesis that there is no significant influence of Gender on Emotional Competence of Teacher is rejected. Further the mean score of Emotional Competence of Male Teachers is 117.69 which is significantly lower than that of Female Teachers whose mean score of Emotional Competence is 135.93. It may, therefore, be said that Female Teachers were found to have higher Emotional Competence as compared to Male Teachers.

Influence of Types of School on Emotional Competence of Teachers

The F-Value for Types of School is 306.50 which is significant at 0.01 level with df = 1/292 (Vide Table 11.20). It indicates that the mean scores of Emotional Competence of Government Schools and Private Schools Teachers differ significantly. So there was a significant influence of Types of School on Emotional Competence of Teachers. Thus, the null hypothesis that there is no significant influence of Types of School on Emotional Competence of Teacher is rejected. Further the mean score of Emotional Competence of Government Schools Teachers is 165.68 which is significantly higher than those of Private Schools Teachers whose mean score of Emotional Competence is 100.90. It may, therefore, be said that Government Schools Teachers were found to have higher Emotional Competence as compared to Private Schools Teachers.

Influence of Interaction between Locale of School and Gender on Emotional Competency of Teachers

The F-Value for interaction between Local of School and Gender is 21.63 which is significant at 0.01 level with df = 1/292 (Vide Table 11.20). It indicates that the mean scores of Emotional Competence of Male and Female Teachers belonging to schools situated in Rural and Urban area differ significantly. So there was a significant influence of interaction between Local of School and Gender on Emotional Competence of Teachers. Thus, the null hypothesis that there is no significant influence of interaction between Local of School and Gender on Emotional Competence of Teacher is rejected. In order to know the trend of influence of interaction between Local of School and Gender on Emotional Competence of Teachers, Graph 2 has been plotted.

Graph 2: Trend of influence of interaction between Locale of Schools and Gender on Emotional Competence of Teachers

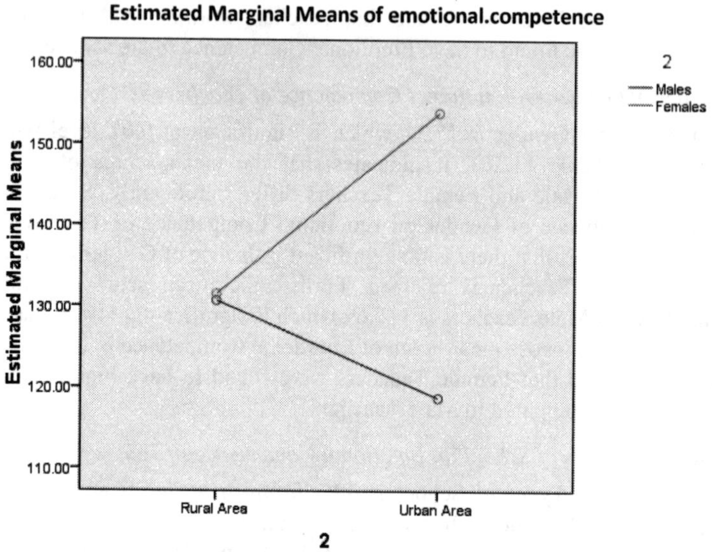

From Graph 2, it can be seen that both Male and Female Teachers working in Rural Area schools had Emotional Competence to the same extent. On the other hand, Female Teachers working in Urban Area schools had higher Emotional Competency as compared to Male Teachers from the same area. It may, therefore, be said that amongst Urban Area schools Female Teachers had higher Emotional Competence than Male Teachers but Male Teachers as well as Female Teachers working in Rural Area schools had Emotional Competency to the same extent.

Influence of Interaction between Locale of School and Types of School on Emotional Competency of Teachers

The F-Value for interaction between Local of School and Types of School is 0.01 which is not significant (Vide Table 11.20). It indicates that the mean scores of Emotional Competence of Government Schools and Private Schools Teachers teaching in schools situated in Rural and Urban Area did not differ significantly. So there was no significant influence of interaction between Local of School and Types of School on Emotional Competence of Teachers. Thus, the null hypothesis that there is no significant influence of interaction between Local of School and Types of School on Emotional Competence of Teacher is not rejected. It may, therefore, be said that Emotional Competence was found to be independent of interaction between Local of School and Types of School.

Influence of Interaction between Gender and Types of School on Emotional Competency of Teachers

The F-Value for interaction between Gender and Types of School is 18.63 which is significant at 0.01 level with df = 1/292 (Vide Table 11.20). It indicates that the mean scores of Emotional Competence of Male and Female Teachers teaching in Government and Private Schools differ significantly. So there was a significant influence of interaction between Gender and Types of School on Emotional Competence of Teachers. Thus, the null hypothesis that there is no significant influence of interaction between Gender and Types of School on Emotional Competence of Teacher is rejected. In order to know the trend of influence of interaction between Gender and Types of School on Emotional Competence of Teachers, Graph 3 has been plotted.

Graph 3: Trend of influence of interaction between Gender and Types of Schools on Emotional Competence of Teachers

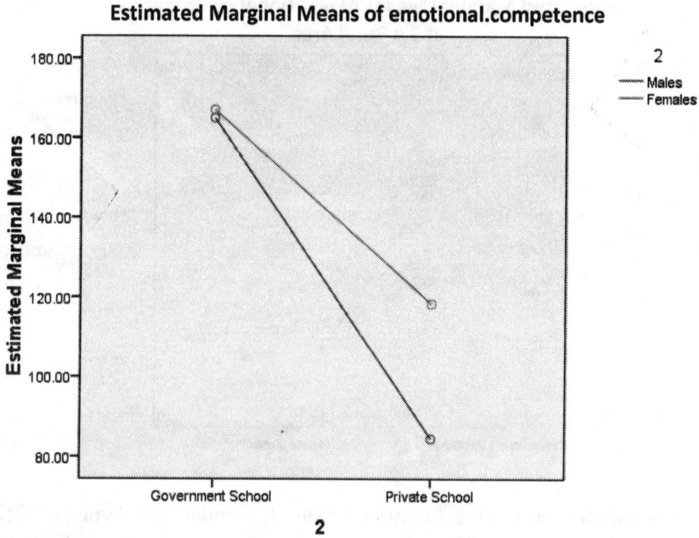

From Graph 3, it can be seen that both Male and Female Teachers working in Government Schools were found to have higher Emotional Competence as compared to Teachers working in Private Schools. Further, both Male and Female Teachers working in Government Schools were found to have Emotional Competence to the same extent. On the other hand, amogst Teachers of Private Schools, Female Teachers were found to have higher Emotional Competence as compared to Male Teachers. Lastly, as the Type of School changes from Government to Private, there is a sharp decline in Emotional Competence of both Male and Female Teachers. It may, therefore, be said that both Male and Female Teachers of Government Schools had higher Emotional

Competence and it decreases sharply as Type of School changes from Government to Private.

Influence of Interaction among Locale of School, Gender and Types of School on Emotional Competency of Teachers

The F-Value for interaction among Locale of School, Gender and Types of School is 23.93 which is significant at 0.01 level with df = 1/292 (Vide Table 11.20). It indicates that the mean scores of Emotional Competence of Male and Female Teachers teaching in Government and Private Schools situated in Rural Area and Urban Area differ significantly. So there was a significant influence of interaction among Locale of School, Gender and Types of School on Emotional Competence of Teachers. Thus, the null hypothesis that there is no significant

Graph 4: Trend of influence of interaction between Types of Schools and Gender on Emotional Competence of Teachers teaching in schools situated in Rural Area

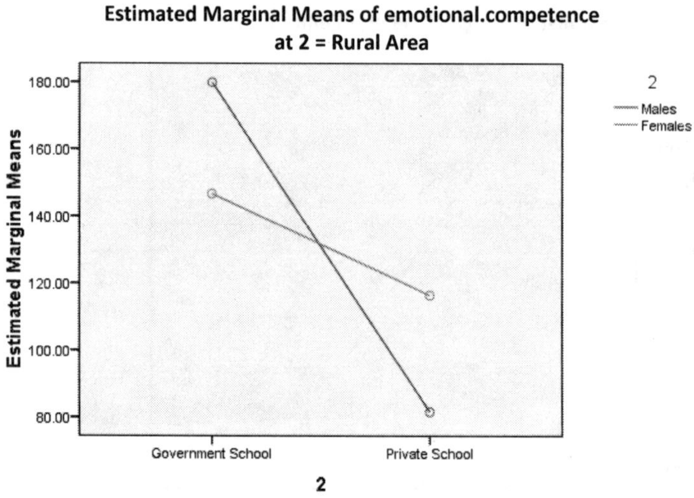

influence of interaction among Locale of School, Gender and Types of School on Emotional Competence of Teacher is rejected. In order to know the trend of influence of interaction among Locale of School, Gender and Types of School on Emotional Competence of Teachers, Graphs 4 and 5 have been plotted.

It is evident from Graph 4 that Teachers teaching in Schools situated in Rural Area, as the Type of School changes from Government Schools to Private Schools, there is a decline in Emotional Competence of both Male and Female Teachers but it is sharper in case of Male Teachers than Female Teachers. The Male Teachers teaching in Government Schools had higher Emotional Competence as compared to their counterpart of Female Teachers. On the other hand, Female Teachers teaching in Private Schools had higher Emotional Competence as compared to their counter part of Male Teachers. It may,

Graph 5: Trend of influence of interaction between Types of Schools and Gender on Emotional Competence of Teachers teaching in Schools situated in Urban Area

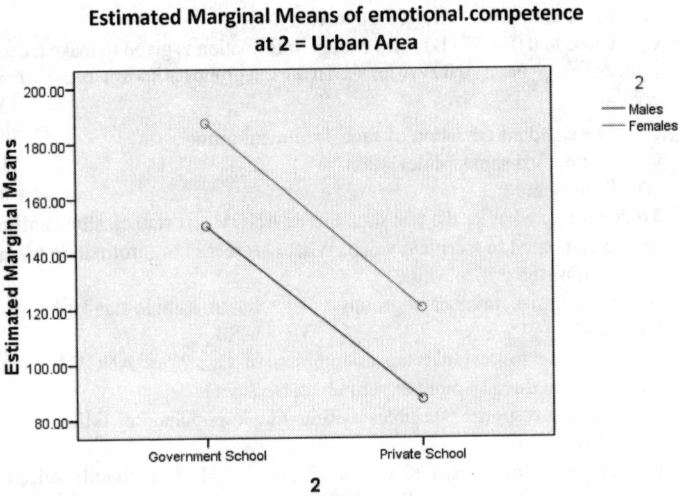

therefore, be said that Male Teachers of Government Schools and Female Teachers of Private Schools had higher Emotional Competence.

On the other hand, in case of teachers working in schools situated in Urban Area, both Male as well as Female Teachers from Government Schools had higher Emotional Competence than those working in Private Schools (as per Graph 5). Irrespective of Types of School, Female Teachers had higher Emotional Competence. Lastly, Female Teachers teaching in Government Schools had higher Emotional Competence. It may, therefore, be said that Irrespective of Types of School, Female Teachers had higher Emotional Competence. Lastly, Female Teachers teaching in Government Schools had higher Emotional Competence as compared to those of Private Schools.

Take a Test

1. The Analysis of variance is a statistical technique of comparing the .... of several populations.
   A) Standard Deviations B) Variations
   C) Means D) Proportions.
2. The .... sum of square measures the variability of the observed values around their respective treatment means.
   A) Treatment B) Error
   C) Total D) All of the above.
3. The .... sum of square measures the variability of the sample Treatment means around the overall mean.
   A) Treatment B) Error
   C) Total D) All of the above.

4. If the True means of the populations are equal, then $MSS_{Treatment}/MSS_{Error}$ should be
   A) More than 1.00 B) Close to 1.0
   C) Close to 0.0 D) Not enough information is given to make a decision.
5. If the MSS_{Error} of an ANOVA for six Treatment groups is known, one can compute
   A) df_1
   B) The standard deviation of each Treatment group.
   C) The pooled standard deviation.
   D) Both B and C.
6. To determine whether the test statistics of ANOVA is statistically significant, it can be compared to a critical value. What two pieces of information are needed to determine the critical value?
   A) Sample size, number of groups B) Mean, sample standard deviation
   C) $MSS_{Treatment}$ D) MSS_{Error}.
7. Which of the following is an assumption of One Way ANOVA comparing samples from three or more experimental treatments?
   A) All the response variables within the k populations follow a Normal Distribution.
   B) The samples associated with each population are randomly selected and are independent from all other samples.
   C) The response variables within each of the k population have equal variances.
   D) All the above.
8. The error deviation within the SS_{Error} statistic measure distances
   A) Within groups B) Between groups
   C) Both A and B D) None of the above.
9. As variability due to chance decreases, the value of F will
   A) Increase B) Decrease
   C) Stay the same D) Cannot tell from the given information.
10. In One Way ANOVA which of the following is used within the F-ratio as a measurement of the variance of individual observations.
    A) $SS_{Treatment}$ B) $MSS_{Treatment}$
    C) SS_{Error} D) MSS_{Error}.
11. What do ANOVA calculate?
    A) R-Ratio B) t-Ratio
    C) Z-Ratio D) F-Ratio.
12. What is listed in the first column of output of One Way ANOVA table?
    A) Source of variation B) Degrees of freedom
    C) Sum of squares D) Significance level.
13. How many dependent variables are there in Two Way ANOVA?
    A) 2 B) 1
    C) 3 D) 4.
14. The Two Way ANOVA
    A) allows the assessment of interaction between two independent variables.
    B) results in the calculation of three F-Ratios.
    C) assesses the effects of two independent variables in one experiment.
    D) does all of the above.

15. An easy way to determine if there is likely to be a main effect of a factor is to
    A) look at all the cell means separately.
    B) look at the grand mean.
    C) look at the row and column means.
    D) look at the difference between the row and the column means.
16. In Two Way ANOVA, a significant interaction effect occurs whenever
    A) there are no main effects.
    B) variable A has a main effect and variable B has a main effect.
    C) the effect of one variable is the same at all levels of the other variable.
    D) the effect of one variable in not the same at all levels of the other variable.
17. What term refers to the situation where two independent variables have an effect when they are in combination?
    A) Artifact B) Confounding variable
    C) Interaction D) Dependency.
18. A 2 X 2 factorial design
    A) Is called a One Way ANOVA.
    B) Results in a four cell matrix.
    C) Cannot yield interactions.
    D) Must include an organismic independent variable.
19. What does A X B mean in two way ANOVA?
    A) There must be significant main effects for Factors A & B.
    B) The main effects for Factors A and B must be short of significance.
    C) The effect of Factor A depends on levels of Factor B.
    D) If there are significant main effects, they must be interpreted first before interpreting the interaction.
20. Factorial experiments
    A) Include two or more dependent variables.
    B) Include two or more independent variables.
    C) Focus on unmeasured factors.
    D) Focus on organismic factors.
21. Factorial Designs allow us to study both———effects of independent variables on dependent variables.
    A) Main and interactive. B) Dependent and independent.
    C) Symbiotic and dichotomous. D) Rank order and correlational.
22. Which of the following statements is correct about interactions?
    A) They are enhancement of main effect.
    B) They are additive effects.
    C) They are spurious effects.
    D) They occur only in interaction with organismic variables.
23. What are the factors in factorial design?
    A) The independent variables. B) The dependent variables.
    C) The organismic variables. D) The experimental variables.
24. Factorial designs
    A) Include no more than one research hypothesis.
    B) Cannot test participants across more than one condition.
    C) Are ineffective when matched participants are included.
    D) Contain more than one null hypothesis.

25. What information is given in the factorial notation, 2 X 3 X 2?
    A) Interactions will be found.
    B) The design has 12 independent variables.
    C) The design has three independent variables, 2 levels of A variable, 3 levels of B variable and 2 levels of C variable.
    D) The design has two independent variables, three dependent variables and two intervening variables.
26. What is listed in the first column of three way ANOVA table?
    A) Source of variation B) Degrees of freedom
    C) Sum of squares D) Significance level.
27. Which of the following statements is true?
    A) No more than four factors can be included in a Factorial Design.
    B) Interactions up to ten factors can be easily interpreted.
    C) Any number of factors can be included but the interpretation of interactions is more difficult as the number of factors increases.
    D) The number of factors has no bearing on the interpretation of results.
28. In Three Way ANOVA , the total interactions are
    A) Two B) Three
    C) Four D) Five.
29. What is listed in the first column of Three Way ANOVA Table which researcher makes for interpreting the results?
    A) Degree of freedom B) Sum of squares
    C) Significance level D) Source of Variation.
30. If a researcher reports F (3, 40) = 9.56, p = 0.01, what is the F-value?
    A) 9.56 B) 40
    C) 3 D) 0.01.
31. Which of the following is true in a 3 X 4 X 5 factorial design?
    A) The first independent variable has 4 levels.
    B) There are five independent variables.
    C) The interaction has five levels.
    D) The second independent variable has four levels.
32. A three way ANOVA will yield —— F-values.
    A) 7 B) 3
    C) 6 D) 4.
33. When a ANOVA is performed on samples drawn from K population, mean sum of square between Treatments (MSSTR) is
    A) SSTR/N B) SSTR/N–1
    C) SSTR/K D) SSTR/K–1.
34. How many dependent variables are there in Three Way ANOVA?
    A) 3 B) 5
    C) 1 D) 7.
35. Which one of the following indicates how "accurate" results from Sample Surveys may be?
    A) Correlation Test B) Significance Test
    C) Regression Test D) Multiple Correlation Test.

12
Analysis of Covariance

INTRODUCTION

By now you know that there might be many Intervening Variables both in survey as well as experimental researches which you may like to control. There are different ways of Controlling Intervening Variables about which you might have studied in a chapter on Experimental Design. There it is mentioned that one of the ways of controlling intervening variables is by analysing the data through Analysis of Covariance. In a research there might be many intervening variables. For some of the intervening variables, one may get quantitative data while for some other variables data may be qualitative in nature. In case the qualitative data cannot be converted into quantitative data than that variable cannot be controlled through the use of Statistical Technique. The researcher may use other ways to control such variables in experimental as well as survey researches. For controlling intervening variables having quantitative data, Analysis of Covariance can be used. There must be minimum one covariate.

In each survey as well as experimental research, one must have at least One Criterion Variable or Dependent Variable. Further if there is one variable having two or more levels and at least one Covariate, then researcher can compare adjusted mean scores of dependent or criterion variable of two or more groups by using One Way Analysis of Covariance or One Way ANCOVA. It is called One Way because there is one variable having two or more levels. If there are two variables in a research, each having two or more levels, along with dependent or criterion variable and at least One Covariate, the data can be analysed with the help of Two Way ANCOVA. Similarly, in case of three variables, each having two or more levels and a dependent or criterion variable along with at least One Covariate, data can be analysed with the help of Three Way ANCOVA. Normally more than three variables each having two or more levels are not taken because it is difficult to plot graphs for interactions among four or more variables. So researchers plan a research where data can be analysed with the help of maximum Three Way of ANCOVA. After reading this chapter, researcher will be able to:

- List different names of ANCOVA.
- Write assumptions underlying Analysis of Covariance.
- Word research objective correctly whose data can be analysed with the help of One Way ANCOVA, Two Way ANCOVA, or Three Way ANCOVA.
- Write Hypothesis correctly for the given objective.
- Analyse data using SPSS.
- Put SPSS out-put in an appropriate Table along with proper heading.
- Interpret the information given in the One Way ANCOV Table, Two Way ANCOVA Table, or Three Way ANCOVA Table and test the given hypothesis.

DIFFERENT NAMES OF ANCOVA

- One Way ANCOVA means one Variable having two or more levels along with dependent or criterion variable and at least one Covariate.
- Two Way ANCOVA means two Variables, each having two or more than two levels. If there are n levels of one variable and m levels of another variable along with dependent or criterion variable and at least one Covariate, then it can be called n X m Factorial Design ANCOVA.
- Three Way ANCOVA means three Variables, each having two or more than two levels along with at least one Covariate. If there are n levels of one variable, m levels of second variable, and h levels of third variable and dependent or criterion variable and one Covariate, then it can be called n X m X h Factorial Design ANCOVA.

ASSUMPTIONS UNDERLYING ANCOVA

The dependent or criterion variable data to be analysed with the help of ANCOVA must satisfy the following assumptions.

1. Normal Distribution: The data of Criterion Variable or Dependent Variable must be normally distributed in the population.
2. Homogeneity of Variance: The differences within groups of more than two independent groups must be equal.
$$\sigma_1^2 = \sigma_2^2 = \sigma_3^2 \ldots\ldots\ldots = \sigma_n^2$$
3. The data of Dependent Variable or Criterion Variable must be either on Interval Scale or Ratio Scale.
4. There should be *no significant outliers* within each group.
5. There must be minimum one Covariate and its scale of measurement must be either Interval Scale or Ratio Scale.
6. In Experimental Research, the Independent Variable and Covariate are independent of each other.
7. There must be linear correlation between Dependent Variable or Criterion Variable and Covariate.

WHEN TO USE

- *One Way ANCOVA:* It is to be used when the researcher wants to compare adjusted mean scores of Dependent Variable or Criterion Variable of two or more than two groups; there is at least one Covariate; and data satisfy the assumptions underlying ANCOVA.
- *Two Way ANCOVA:* It is to be used when researcher has two categorical variables each having two or more levels, wants to compare adjusted mean scores of Dependent Variable or Criterion Variable of two or more than two groups; there is at least one Covariate; and data satisfy the assumptions underlying ANCOVA.
- *Three Way ANOVA:* It is to be used when researcher has three categorical variables each having two or more levels, wants to compare adjusted means scores of Dependent Variable or Criterion Variable of two or more than two groups; there is at least one Covariate; and data satisfy the assumptions underlying ANCOVA.

Example-I

How to Write Objective for One Way ANCOVA with one Covariate

The Objective should be worded as given below so that data can be analysed with the help of One Way ANCOVA:

- To compare adjusted mean scores of Achievement of students of Computer Aided Instruction Group and Lecture Method Group by considering their Pre-Achievement as covariate.

How to Formulate Hypothesis

The Hypothesis which can be tested with the help of One Way ANCOVA is formulated in the Null Form as given below:

- There is no significant difference between adjusted mean scores of Achievement of students of Computer Aided Instruction Group and Lecture Method Group by considering their Pre-Achievement as covariate.

Which Statistical Technique to Use for Analysing Data

As per Objective-1, Strategy of Teaching was One Independent Variable having two levels, namely, Computer Aided Instruction and Lecture Method. Pre-Achievement was one Covariate, and Post-Achievement was the Dependent Variable. Thus, the data were analysed with the help of One Way ANCOVA using Statistical Package for the Social Sciences (SPSS). The outputs of SPSS are as given in Tables 12.1, 12.2 and 12.3.

Table 12.1: Descriptive Statistics

Dependent Variable: Posttest Scores

2	Mean	Std. Deviation	N
Experimental Group	63.6333	7.15100	30
Control Group	48.9667	10.09433	30
Total	**56.3000**	**11.39774**	**60**

Table 12.2: Tests of Between-Subjects Effects

Dependent Variable: Posttest .Scores

Source	*Type III Sum of Squares*	*df*	*Mean Square*	*F*	*Sig.*
Corrected Model	7335.904[a]	2	3667.952	636.069	.000
Intercept	667.869	1	667.869	115.817	.000
Pretest Scores	4109.237	1	4109.237	712.593	.000
Treatment	2147.356	1	2147.356	372.379	.000
Error	328.696	57	5.767		
Total	197846.000	60			
Corrected Total	7664.600	59			

a. R Squared = .957 (Adjusted R Squared = .956)

Table 12.3: Adjusted Mean Scores of Achievement

Dependent Variable: Posttest Scores

2	Mean	Std. Error	95% Confidence Interval	
			Lower Bound	Upper Bound
Experimental Group	62.354[a]	.441	61.470	63.237
Control Group	50.246[a]	.441	49.363	51.130

a. Covariates appearing in the model are evaluated at the following values: pretest.scores = 45.1833.

How to Interpret the Results Given in Tables 12.1, 12.2 and 12.3

The results of One Way ANCOVA should be interpreted as given below:

The Objective was to compare adjusted mean scores of Achievement of students of Computer Aided Instruction Group and Lecture Method Group by considering their Pre-Achievement as covariate. Here Strategy of Teaching was One Independent Variable having two levels, namely, Computer Aided Instruction and Lecture Method. Pre-Achievement was one Covariate, and Post-Achievement was the Dependent Variable. Thus, the data were analysed with the help of One Way ANCOVA and the results are given in Table 12.4.

Table 12.4: Summary of One Way ANCOVA of Achievement of students by taking their Pre-Achievement as Covariate

Source of Variance	*df*	*SSy.x*	*MSSy.x*	*Fy.x*	*Remark*
Strategy of Teaching	1	2147.36	2147.36	372.38	p<0.01
Error	57	328.70	5.77		
Total	**59**				

From Table 12.4, it can be seen that the adjusted F-Value is 372.38 which is significant at 0.01 level with df = 1/57. It indicates that the adjusted mean scores of Achievement of students of Computer Aided Instruction and Lecture Method Groups differ significantly when their Pre-Achievement was taken as Covariate. Thus, the null hypothesis that there is no significant difference between adjusted mean scores of Achievement of students of Computer Aided Instruction Group and Lecture Method Group by considering their Pre-Achievement as covariate is rejected. Further, the adjusted mean score of Achievement of students of Computer Aided Instruction Group is 62.35 which is significantly higher than those of Lecture Method Group whose adjusted mean score of Achievement is 50.25. It may, therefore, be said that Achievement of students treated through Computer Aided Instruction was found to be significantly superior to Lecture Method when groups were matched in respect of their Pre-Achievement.

Example-2

How to Write Objective for One Way ANCOVA with one Covariate

The Objective should be worded as given below so that data can be analysed with the help of One Way ANCOVA:

- To compare adjusted mean scores of Self-confidence of Male and Female students by considering their Intelligence as covariate.

How to Formulate Hypothesis

The Hypothesis which can be tested with the help of One Way ANCOVA is formulated in the Null Form as given below:

- There is no significant difference in adjusted mean scores of Self-confidence of Male and Female students by considering their Intelligence as covariate.

Which Statistical Technique to Use for Analysing Data

As per Objective of Example-2, Males and Females were the two levels of Gender. Intelligence was one Covariate, and Self-confidence was the Criterion Variable. Thus, the data were analysed with the help of One Way ANCOVA using Statistical Package for the Social Sciences (SPSS). The outputs of SPSS are as given in Table 12.5.

Table 12.5: Tests of Between-Subjects Effects

Dependent Variable: Self Confidence					
Source	*Type III Sum of Squares*	*df*	*Mean Square*	*F*	*Sig.*
Corrected Model	4515.394[a]	2	2257.697	81.174	.000
Intercept	71.476	1	71.476	2.570	.114
Intelligent	4442.794	1	4442.794	159.738	.000
Gender	45.277	1	45.277	1.628	.207
Error	1585.340	57	27.813		
Total	146848.000	60			
Corrected Total	6100.733	59			

a. R Squared = .740 (Adjusted R Squared = .731)

How to Interpret the Results Given in Table 12.5

The results of One Way ANCOVA should be interpreted as given below:

The Objective was to compare adjusted mean scores of Self-confidence of Male and Female students by considering their Intelligence as Covariate. Here Gender was one variable having two levels, namely, Males and Females. Intelligence was one Covariate, and Self-confidence was the Criterion Variable. Thus, the data were analysed with the help of One Way ANCOVA and the results are given in Table 12.6.

Table 12.6: Summary of One Way ANCOVA of Self-confidence of students by taking their Intelligence as Covariate

Source of Variance	*df*	*SSy.x*	*MSSy.x*	*Fy.x*
Gender	1	45.28	45.28	1.63
Error	57	1585.34	27.81	
Total	**59**			

From Table 12.6, it can be seen that the adjusted F-Value is 1.63 which is not significant. It indicates that there is no significant difference in adjusted mean scores of Self-confidence of Male and Female students when their Intelligence was taken as Covariate. Thus, the null hypothesis that there is no significant difference in adjusted mean scores of Self-confidence of Male and Female students by considering their intelligence as covariate is not rejected. It may, therefore, be said that both Male and Female students were found to have Self-confidence to the same extent when intelligence was taken as Covariate.

Example-3

How to Write Objective For One Way ANCOVA with two Covariates

The Objective should be worded as given below so that data can be analysed with the help of One Way ANCOVA:

- To compare adjusted mean scores of Achievement of students of Computer Aided Instruction Group and Lecture Method Group by considering their Pre-Achievement and Intelligence as covariates.

How to Formulate Hypothesis

The Hypothesis which can be tested with the help of One Way ANCOVA is formulated in the Null Form as given below:

- There is no significant difference between adjusted mean scores of Achievement of students of Computer Aided Instruction Group and Lecture Method Group by considering their Pre-Achievement and Intelligence as covariates.

Which Statistical Technique to Use for Analysing Data

As per Objective given in Example-3, Strategy of Teaching was One Independent Variable having two levels, namely, Computer Aided Instruction and Lecture Method. Pre-Achievement and Intelligence were two Covariates, and Post-Achievement was the Dependent Variable. Thus, the data were analysed with the help of One Way ANCOVA using Statistical Package for the Social Sciences (SPSS). The outputs of SPSS are as given in Tables 12.7, 12.8 and 12.9.

Table 12.7: Descriptive Statistics

Dependent Variable: Posttest Scores

2	Mean	Std. Deviation	N
Experimental Group	63.6333	7.15100	30
Control Group	48.9667	10.09433	30
Total	**56.3000**	**11.39774**	**60**

Table 12.8: Tests of Between-Subjects Effects

Dependent Variable : Posttest Scores

Source	*Type III Sum of Squares*	*df*	*Mean Square*	*F*	*Sig.*
Corrected Model	7338.943[a]	3	2446.314	420.668	.000
Intercept	559.789	1	559.789	96.261	.000
Pretest Scores	1248.406	1	1248.406	214.676	.000
Intelligent	3.039	1	3.039	.523	.473
Treatment	2112.695	1	2112.695	363.299	.000
Error	325.657	56	5.815		
Total	197846.000	60			
Corrected Total	7664.600	59			

a. R Squared = .958 (Adjusted R Squared = .955)

Table 12.9: Adjusted mean scores of Achievement of Experimental and Control groups

Dependent Variable: Posttest Scores

2	Mean	Std. Error	95% Confidence Interval	
			Lower Bound	Upper Bound
Experimental Group	62.393[a]	.446	61.499	63.287
Control Group	50.207[a]	.446	49.313	51.101

a. Covariates appearing in the model are evaluated at the following values: pretest.scores = 45.1833, intelligent = 105.2000.

How to Interpret the Results Given in Tables 12.7, 12.8 and 12.9

The results of One Way ANCOVA should be interpreted as given below:

The Objective was to compare adjusted mean scores of Achievement of students of Computer Aided Instruction Group and Lecture Method Group by considering their Pre-Achievement and Intelligence as covariates. Here Strategy of Teaching was One Independent Variable having two levels, namely, Computer Aided Instruction and Lecture Method. Pre-Achievement and Intelligence were two Covariates, and Post-Achievement was the Dependent Variable. Thus, the data were analysed with the help of One Way ANCOVA and the results are given in Table 12.10.

Table 12.10: Summary of One Way ANCOVA of Achievement of students by taking their Pre-Achievement and Intelligence as Covariates

Source of Variance	*df*	*SSy.x*	*MSSy.x*	*Fy.x*	*Remark*
Strategy of Teaching	1	2112.69	2112.69	363.30	p<0.01
Error	56	325.66	5.81		
Total	**59**				

From Table 12.10, it can be seen that the adjusted F-Value is 363.30 which is significant at 0.01 level with df = 1/56. It indicates that the adjusted mean scores of Achievement of students of Computer Aided Instruction and Lecture Method Groups differ significantly when their Pre-Achievement and Intelligence were taken as Covariates. Thus, the null hypothesis that there is no significant difference between adjusted mean scores of Achievement of students of Computer Aided Instruction Group and Lecture Method Group by considering their Pre-Achievement and Intelligence as covariates is rejected. Further, the adjusted mean score of Achievement of students of Computer Aided Instruction Group is 62.39 which is significantly higher than that of Lecture Method Group whose adjusted mean score of Achievement of students is 50.21. It may, therefore, be said that Computer Aided Instruction was found to be significantly superior to Lecture Method in terms of Achievement of students when groups were matched in respect of Pre-Achievement and Intelligence of students.

Example-4

How to Write Objective for Two Way ANCOVA with Two Covariates

The Objective should be worded as given below so that data can be analysed with the help of Two Way ANCOVA:

- To study the influence of Gender, Marital Status and their interaction on Anxiety of teachers by considering their Psychological Risk Factor and Verbal Inteliigence as covariates.

How to Formulate Hypothesis

The Hypothesis which can be tested with the help of Two Way ANCOVA is formulated in the Null Form as given below:

- There is no significant influence of Gender, Marital Status and their interaction on Anxiety of teachers by considering their Psychological Risk Factor and Verbal Intelligence as covariates.

Which Statistical Technique to Use for Analysing Data

As per Objective given in Example-4, Gender had two levels, namely, Males and Females. Single/Unmarried and Married were the two levels of Marital Status. Psychological Risk Factor and Verbal Intelligence were two Covariates. Anxiety was the Criterion Variable. Thus, the data were analysed with the help of Two Way ANCOVA or 2 X 2 Factorial Design ANCOVA by using Statistical Package for the Social Sciences (SPSS). The outputs of SPSS are as given in Tables 12.11, and 12.12.

Table 12.11: Descriptive Statistics

Dependent Variable: Anxiety

2	2	*Mean*	*Std. Deviation*	*N*
Male	Single-Unmarried	23.0667	15.58278	30
	Married	19.8175	14.47226	126
	Total	**20.4423**	**14.69660**	**156**
Female	Single-Unmarried	24.1286	13.95430	70
	Married	21.0274	12.50707	146
	Total	**22.0324**	**13.04247**	**216**
Total	Single-Unmarried	23.8100	14.39044	100
	Married	20.4669	13.44137	272
	Total	**21.3656**	**13.76353**	**372**

Table 12.12: Tests of Between-Subjects Effects

Dependent Variable: Anxiety

Source	*Type III Sum of Squares*	*df*	*Mean Square*	*F*	*Sig.*
Corrected Model	30901.828[a]	5	6180.366	57.443	.000
Intercept	2063.637	1	2063.637	19.180	.000
Psychological Risk Factor	28798.237	1	28798.237	267.663	.000
Verbal Intelligence	571.147	1	571.147	5.308	.022
Gender	420.060	1	420.060	3.904	.049
Marital Status	52.250	1	52.250	.486	.486
Gender * Marital Status	198.754	1	198.754	1.847	.175
Error	39378.451	366	107.591		
Total	240094.000	372			
Corrected Total	70280.280	371			

a. R Squared = .440 (Adjusted R Squared = .432)

How to Interpret the Results Given in Tables 12.11 and 12.12

The results of Two Way ANCOVA should be interpreted as given below:

The Objective was to study the influence of Gender, Marital Status and their interaction on Anxiety of teachers by considering their Psychological Risk Factor and Verbal Intelligence as covariates. Males and Females were the two levels of Gender. Single/Unmarried and Married were the two levels of Marital Status. Psychological Risk Factor and Verbal Intelligence were covariates The Criterion Variable was Anxiety. Thus, the data were analysed with the help of Two Way ANCOVA or 2 X 2 Factorial design ANCOVA and the results are given in Table 12.13.

Table 12.13: Summary of Two Way ANCOVA of Anxiety of teachers by taking their Psychological Risk Factor and Verbal Intelligence as Covariates

Source of Variance	*df*	*SSy.x*	*MSSy.x*	*Fy.x*	*Remark*
Gender (A)	1	420.06	420.06	3.90	p<0.05
Marital Status (B)	1	52.25	52.25	0.49	
A X B	1	198.75	198.75	1.85	
Error	366	39378.45	107.59		
Total	**371**				

Influence of Gender on Anxiety of Teachers by taking their Psychological Risk Factor and Verbal Intelligence as Covariates

From Table 12.13 it is evident that the adjusted F-Value for Gender is 3.90 which is significance at 0.05 level with df = 1/366. It indicates that the adjusted mean scores of Anxiety of Male and Female Teachers differ significantly when their Psychological Risk Factor and Verbal Intelligence were taken as

Covariates. So there was a significant influence of Gender on Anxiety of Teachers when groups were matched with respect to their Psychological Risk Factor and Verbal Intelligence. Thus, the null hypothesis that there is no significant influence of Gender on Anxiety of Teachers by considering their Psychological Risk Factor and Verbal Intelligence as covariates is rejected. Further the adjusted mean score of Anxiety of Male Teachers is 20.01 which is significantly lower than those of Female Teachers whose adjusted mean score of Anxiety is 22.63. It may, therefore, be said that Female Teachers were found to higher Anxiety as compared to Male Teachers when their Psychological Risk Factor and Verbal Intelligence were taken as Covariates.

Influence of Marital Status on Anxiety of Teachers by taking their Psychological Risk Factor and Verbal Intelligence as Covariates

The adjusted F-Value for Marital Status is 0.49 which is not significant (Vide Table 12.13). It shows that the adjusted mean scores of Anxiety of Single/Unmarried and Married Teachers did not differ significantly when Psychological Risk Factor and Verbal Intelligence were taken as Covariates. So there was no significant influence of Marital Status on Anxiety of Teachers when their Psychological Risk Factor and Verbal Intelligence were taken as Covariates. Thus, the null hypothesis that there is no significant influence of Marital Status on Anxiety of Teachers when their Psychological Risk Factor and Verbal Intelligence were taken as Covariates is not rejected. It may, therefore, be said that Anxiety of Teachers was found to be independent of their Marital Status when their Psychological Risk Factor and Verbal Intelligence were taken as Covariates.

Influence of Interaction between Gender and Marital Status on Anxiety of Teachers by taking their Psychological Risk Factor and Verbal Intelligence as Covariates

From Table 12.13 it is evident that the adjusted F-Value for interaction between Gender and Marital Status is 1.85 which is not significant. It reflects that adjusted mean scores of Anxiety of Single/Unmarried and Married Male and Female Teachers did not differ significantly when their Psychological Risk Factor and Verbal Intelligence were taken as Covariates. So there was no significant influence of interaction between Gender and Marital Status on Anxiety of Teachers when their Psychological Risk Factor and Verbal Intelligence were taken as Covariates. Thus, the null hypothesis that there is no significant influence of interaction between Gender and Marital Status on Anxiety of Teachers when their Psychological Risk Factor and Verbal Intelligence were taken as Covariates is not rejected. It may, therefore, be said that Anxiety was found to be independent of interaction between Gender and Marital Status of teachers when their Psychological Risk Factor and Verbal Intelligence were taken as Covariates.

Example-5

How to Write Objective for Three Way ANCOVA with One Covariate

The Objective should be worded as given below so that data can be analysed with the help of Three Way ANCOVA:

- To study the influence of Gender, Marital Status, Caste and their various interactions on Change Proness of teachers by considering their Verbal Intelligence as covariate.

How to Formulate Hypothesis

The Hypothesis which can be tested with the help of Three Way ANCOVA is formulated in the Null Form as given below:

- There is no significant influence of Gender, Marital Status, Caste and their various interactions on Change Proness of teachers by considering their Verbal Intelligence as covariate.

Which Statistical Technique to Use for Analysing Data

As per Objective given in Example-5, Gender had two levels, namely, Males and Females. Single/Unmarried and Married were the two levels of Marital Status. There were two levels of Caste, namely, General and Others. Verbal Intelligence was the Covariate. Change Proness was the Criterion Variable. Thus, the data were analysed with the help of Three Way ANCOVA or 2 X 2 X 2 Factorial Design ANCOVA using Statistical Package for the Social Sciences (SPSS). The outputs of SPSS are as given in Tables 12.14.

Table 12.14: Tests of Between-Subjects Effects

Dependent Variable: Change Proness

Source	*Type III Sum of Squares*	*df*	*Mean Square*	*F*	*Sig.*
Corrected Model	2217.909[a]	8	277.239	1.034	.410
Intercept	238516.605	1	238516.605	889.167	.000
Verbal Intelligence	544.256	1	544.256	2.029	.155
Gender	41.703	1	41.703	.155	.694
Marital status	3.439	1	3.439	.013	.910
Cast	264.343	1	264.343	.985	.322
Gender * Marital status	84.300	1	84.300	.314	.575
Gender * Cast	7.994	1	7.994	.030	.863
Marital Status * Cast	147.565	1	147.565	.550	.459
Gender * Marital Status * Cast	7.041	1	7.041	.026	.871
Error	97373.703	363	268.247		
Total	4763272.000	372			
Corrected Total	99591.613	371			

a. R Squared = .022 (Adjusted R Squared = .001)

How to Interpret the Results Given in Table 12.14

The results of Three Way ANCOVA should be interpreted as given below:

The Objective was to study the influence of Gender, Marital Status, Caste and their various interactions on Change Proness of teachers by considering their Verbal Intelligence as covariate. Males and Females were the two levels of Gender. Single/Unmarried and Married were the two levels of Marital Status. There were two levels of Caste, namely, General and Others. Verbal Intelligence was covariate. The Criterion Variable was Change Proness. Thus, the data were analysed with the help of Three Way ANCOVA or 2 X 2 X 2 Factorial design ANCOVA and the results are given in Table 12.15.

Table 12.15: Summary of 2 X 2 X 2 Factorial Design ANCOVA of Change Proness of Teachers by taking their Verbal Intelligence as Covariate

Source of Variance	*df*	*SSy.x*	*MSSy.x*	*Fy.x*
Gender (A)	1	41.70	41.70	0.15
Marital Status (B)	1	3.44	3.44	0.01
Caste (C)	1	264.34	264.34	0.98
A X B	1	84.30	84.30	0.31
A X C	1	7.99	7.99	0.03
B X C	1	147.56	147.56	0.55
A X B X C	1	7.04	7.04	0.03
Error	363	97373.70	268.25	
Total	**371**			

Influence of Gender on Change Proness of Teachers by Taking Verbal Intelligence as Covariate

From Table 12.15 it is evident that adjusted F-Value for Gender is 0.15 which is not significant. It shows that adjusted mean scores of Change Proness of Male and Female Teachers did not differ significantly when their Verbal Intelligence was taken as Covariate. So there was no significant influence of Gender on Change Proness of Teachers when their Verbal Intelligence was taken as Covariate. Thus, the null hypothesis that there is no significance influence of Gender on Change Proness of Teachers when their Verbal Intelligence was taken as Covariate is not rejected. It may, therefore, be said that Change Proness was found to be independent of Gender of Teachers when their Verbal Intelligence was taken as Covariate.

Influence of Marital Status on Change Proness of Teachers by Taking Verbal Intelligence as Covariate

From Table 12.15 it is evident that adjusted F-Value for Marital Status is 0.01 which is not significant. It shows that adjusted mean scores of Change Proness of Single/Unmarried and Married Teachers did not differ significantly when their Verbal Intelligence was taken as Covariate. So there was no significant influence of Marital Status on Change Proness of Teachers when their Verbal

Intelligence was taken as Covariate. Thus, the null hypothesis that there is no significance influence of Marital Status on Change Proness of Teachers when their Verbal Intelligence was taken as Covariate is not rejected. It may, therefore, be said that Change Proness was found to be independent of Marital Status of Teachers when their Verbal Intelligence was taken as Covariate.

Influence of Caste on Change Proness of Teachers by Taking their Verbal Intelligence as Covariate

The adjusted F-Value for Caste is 0.98 which is not significant (Vide Table 12.15). It shows that adjusted mean scores of Change Proness of teachers belonging to General and Other caste Teachers did not differ significantly when their Verbal Intelligence was taken as Covariate. So there was no significant influence of Caste on Change Proness of Teachers when their Verbal Intelligence was taken as Covariate. Thus, the null hypothesis that there is no significance influence of Caste on Change Proness of Teachers when their Verbal Intelligence was taken as Covariate is not rejected. It may, therefore, be said that Change Proness was found to be independent of Caste of Teachers when their Verbal Intelligence was taken as Covariate.

Influence of Interaction between Gender and Marital Status on Change Proness of Teachers by Taking their Verbal Intelligence as Covariate

From Table 12.15 it is evident that adjusted F-Value for interaction between Gender and Marital Status is 0.31 which is not significant. It shows that adjusted mean scores of Change Proness of Single/Unmarried and Married Male and Female Teachers did not differ significantly when their Verbal Intelligence was taken as Covariate. So there was no significant influence of interaction between Gender and Marital Status on Change Proness of Teachers when their Verbal Intelligence was taken as Covariate. Thus, the null hypothesis that there is no significance influence of interaction between Gender and Marital Status on Change Proness of Teachers when their Verbal Intelligence was taken as Covariate is not rejected. It may, therefore, be said that Change Proness was found to be independent of interaction between Gender and Marital Status of Teachers when their Verbal Intelligence was taken as Covariate.

Influence of Interaction between Gender and Caste on Change Proness of Teachers by Taking their Verbal Intelligence as Covariate

The adjusted F-Value for interaction between Gender and Caste is 0.03 which is not significant (Vide Table 12.15). It shows that adjusted mean scores of Change Proness of Male and Female Teachers belonging to General and Others Castes did not differ significantly when their Verbal Intelligence was taken as Covariate. So there was no significant influence of interaction between Gender and Caste on Change Proness of Teachers when their Verbal Intelligence was taken as Covariate. Thus, the null hypothesis that there is no significance influence of interaction between Gender and Caste on Change Proness of Teachers when their Verbal Intelligence was taken as Covariate is not rejected. It may, therefore, be said that Change Proness was found to be independent of interaction between Gender and Caste of Teachers when their Verbal Intelligence was taken as Covariate.

Influence of Interaction between Marital Status and Caste on Change Proness of Teachers By Taking their Verbal Intelligence as Covariate

From Table 12.15 it is evident that adjusted F-Value for interaction between Marital Status and Caste is 0.55 which is not significant. It shows that adjusted mean scores of Change Proness of Single/Unmarried and Married Teachers belonging to General and Other Castes did not differ significantly when their Verbal Intelligence was taken as Covariate. So there was no significant influence of interaction between Marital Status and Caste on Change Proness of Teachers when their Verbal Intelligence was taken as Covariate. Thus, the null hypothesis that there is no significance influence of interaction between Marital Status and Caste on Change Proness of Teachers when their Verbal Intelligence was taken as Covariate is not rejected. It may, therefore, be said that Change Proness was found to be independent of interaction between Marital Status and Caste of Teachers when their Verbal Intelligence was taken as Covariate.

Influence of Interaction among Gender, Marital Status and Caste on Change Proness of Teachers By Taking their Verbal Intelligence as Covariate

From Table 12.15 it is evident that adjusted F-Value for interaction among Gender, Marital Status and Caste is 0.03 which is not significant. It shows that adjusted mean scores of Change Proness of Single/Unmarried and Married Male and Female Teachers belonging to General and Other Castes did not differ significantly when their Verbal Intelligence was taken as Covariate. So there was no significant influence of interaction among Gender, Marital Status and Caste on Change Proness of Teachers when their Verbal Intelligence was taken as Covariate. Thus, the null hypothesis that there is no significance influence of interaction among Gender, Marital Status and Caste on Change Proness of Teachers when their Verbal Intelligence was taken as Covariate is not rejected. It may, therefore, be said that Change Proness was found to be independent of interaction among Gender, Marital Status and Caste of Teachers when their Verbal Intelligence was taken as Covariate.

Example-6

How to Write Objective for Three Way ANCOVA with One Covariate

The Objective should be worded as given below so that data can be analysed with the help of Three Way ANCOVA:

- To study the influence of Gender, Locale of Schools, Management of

Schools and their various interactions on Self-efficacy of students by considering their Resilience as covariate.

How to Formulate Hypothesis

The Hypothesis which can be tested with the help of Three Way ANCOVA is formulated in the Null Form as given below:

- There is no significant influence of Gender, Locale of Schools, Management of Schools and their various interactions on Self-efficacy of students by considering their Resilience as covariate.

Which Statistical Technique to Use for Analysing Data

As per Objective given in Example-6, Gender had two levels, namely, Males and Females. Urban Area and Rural Area were the two levels of Locale of Schools. There were two levels of Management of Schools, namely, Government and Private. Resilience was the Covariate. Self-efficacy was the Criterion Variable. Thus, the data were analysed with the help of Three Way ANCOVA or 2 X 2 X 2 Factorial Design ANCOVA using Statistical Package for the Social Sciences (SPSS). The outputs of SPSS are as given in Tables 12.16, 12.17, 12.18, 12.19 and 12.20.

Table 12.16: Descriptive Statistics

Dependent Variable: Self Efficacy

2	2	2	Mean	Std. Deviation	N
Males	Rural Area	Government School	85.4595	9.84771	37
		Private School	44.2222	4.89384	54
		Total	60.9890	21.62740	91
	Urban Area	Government School	72.5217	8.28399	23
		Private School	37.6667	3.54562	36
		Total	51.2542	18.09896	59
	Total	Government School	80.5000	11.18034	60
		Private School	41.6000	5.44389	90
		Total	57.1600	20.80400	150
Females	Rural Area	Government School	109.3333	13.61512	36
		Private School	67.0000	9.16515	54
		Total	83.9333	23.61907	90
	Urban Area	Government School	100.0000	8.58715	24
		Private School	57.6667	7.28207	36
		Total	74.6000	22.30695	60
	Total	Government School	105.6000	12.64804	60
		Private School	63.2667	9.59260	90
		Total	80.2000	23.47982	150

Total	Rural Area	Government School	97.2329	16.82386	73
		Private School	55.6111	13.57901	108
		Total	72.3978	25.33853	181
	Urban Area	Government School	86.5532	16.20092	47
		Private School	47.6667	11.56488	72
		Total	63.0252	23.39255	119
	Total	Government School	93.0500	17.32383	120
		Private School	52.4333	13.36054	180
		Total	68.6800	24.97124	300

Table 12.17: Tests of Between-Subjects Effects

Dependent Variable: Self-efficacy

Source	*Type III Sum of Squares*	*df*	*Mean Square*	*F*	*Sig.*
Corrected Model	176547.732[a]	8	22068.467	648.840	.000
Intercept	58.301	1	58.301	1.714	.191
Resilience	11304.714	1	11304.714	332.372	.000
Gender	982.730	1	982.730	28.893	.000
Locale of School	158.715	1	158.715	4.666	.032
Management of School	5503.960	1	5503.960	161.823	.000
Gender * Locale of School	281.757	1	281.757	8.284	.004
Gender * Management of School	94.253	1	94.253	2.771	.097
Locale of School * Management of School	634.992	1	634.992	18.670	.000
Gender * Locale of School * Management of School	559.910	1	559.910	16.462	.000
Error	9897.548	291	34.012		
Total	1601528.000	300			
Corrected Total	186445.280	299			

a. R Squared = .947 (Adjusted R Squared = .945)

Table 12.18: Gender-wise Adjusted mean scores of Self-efficacy

Dependent Variable: Self-efficacy

2	*Mean*	*Std. Error*	*95% Confidence Interval*	
			Lower Bound	*Upper Bound*
Males	67.069a	.632	65.824	68.314
Females	73.395a	.744	71.931	74.859

a. Covariates appearing in the model are evaluated at the following values: resilience = 106.9733.

Table 12.19: Locale of School-wise Adjusted mean scores of Self-efficacy

Dependent Variable: Self-efficacy				
			95% Confidence Interval	
2	*Mean*	*Std. Error*	*Lower Bound*	*Upper Bound*
Rural Area	71.120[a]	.531	70.074	72.166
Urban Area	69.344[a]	.562	68.238	70.451

a. Covariates appearing in the model are evaluated at the following values: resilience = 106.9733.

Table 12.20: Management of School-wise Adjusted mean scores of Self-efficacy

Dependent Variable: Self-efficacy				
			95% Confidence Interval	
2	*Mean*	*Std. Error*	*Lower Bound*	*Upper Bound*
Government School	79.195[a]	.882	77.459	80.931
Private School	61.269[a]	.690	59.912	62.627

a. Covariates appearing in the model are evaluated at the following values: resilience = 106.9733.

How to Interpret the Results Given in Table 12.17

The results of Three Way ANCOVA should be interpreted as given below:

The objective was to study the influence of Gender, Locale of Schools, Management of Schools and their various interactions on Self-efficacy of students by considering their Resilience as covariate. Gender had two levels, namely, Males and Females. Urban Area and Rural Area were the two levels of Locale of Schools. There were two levels of Management of Schools, namely, Government and Private. Resilience was the Covariate. Self-efficacy was the Criterion Variable. Thus, the data were analysed with the help of Three Way ANCOVA or 2 X 2 X 2 Factorial Design ANCOVA and the results are given in Table 12.21.

Table 12.21: Summary of Three Way ANCOVA of Self-efficacy of students by taking their Resilience as Covariate

Source of Variance	*df*	*$SS_{y.x}$*	*$MSS_{y.x}$*	*$F_{y.x}$*	*Remark*
Gender (A)	1	982.73	982.73	28.89	p<0.01
Locale of Schools (B)	1	158.71	158.71	4.67	p<0.05
Management of Schools (C)	1	5503.96	5503.96	161.82	p<0.01
A X B	1	281.76	281.76	8.28	p<0.01
A X C	1	94.25	94.25	2.77	ns
B X C	1	634.99	634.99	18.67	p<0.01
A X B X C	1	559.91	559.91	16.46	p<0.01
Error	291	9897.55	34.01		
Total	**299**				

ns: Not Significant

Influence of Gender on Self-efficacy of Students by Taking their Resilience as Covariate

From Table 12.21 it can be seen that the adjusted F-Value for Gender is 28.89 which is significant at 0.01 level with df = 1/291. It indicates that the adjusted mean scores of Self-efficacy of Male and Female students differ significantly when their Resilience was taken as Covariate. So there was a significant influence of Gender on Self-efficacy of students when their Resilience was taken as Covariate. Thus, the null hypothesis that there is no significant influence of Gender on Self-efficacy of students when their Resilience was taken as Covariate is rejected. Further the adjusted mean score of Self-efficacy of Male students is 67.07 which is significantly lower than those of Female students whose adjusted mean score of Self-efficacy is 73.39. It may, therefore, be said that Female students were found to have higher Self-efficacy as compared to their counter parts of Male students when their Resilience was taken as Covariate.

Influence of Locale of Schools on Self-efficacy of Students by Taking their Resilience as Covariate

The adjusted F-Value for Locale of Schools is 4.67 which is significant at 0.05 level with df = 1/291 (Vide Table 12.21). It indicates that the adjusted mean scores of Self-efficacy of students studying in schools situated in Rural Area and Urban Area differ significantly when their Resilience was taken as Covariate. So there was a significant influence of Locale of School on Self-efficacy of students when their Resilience was taken as Covariate. Thus, the null hypothesis that there is no significant influence of Locale of Schools on Self-efficacy of students when their Resilience was taken as Covariate is rejected. Further the adjusted mean score of Self-efficacy of students studying in schools situated in Rural Area is 71.12 which is significantly higher than those students studying in schools situated in Urban Area whose adjusted mean score of Self-efficacy is 69.34. It may, therefore, be said that students studying in schools situated in Rural Area were found to have higher Self-efficacy as compared to their counter parts of students studying in schools situated in Urban Area when their Resilience was taken as Covariate.

Influence of Management of Schools on Self-efficacy of Students by Taking their Resilience as Covariate

The adjusted F-Value for Management of Schools is 161.82 which is significant at 0.01 level with df = 1/291 (Vide Table 12.21). It indicates that the adjusted mean scores of Self-efficacy of students studying in Government schools and Private schools differ significantly when their Resilience was taken as Covariate. So there was a significant influence of Management of School on Self-efficacy of students when their Resilience was taken as Covariate. Thus, the null hypothesis that there is no significant influence of Management of Schools on Self-efficacy of students when their Resilience was taken as Covariate is rejected. Further the adjusted mean score of Self-efficacy of students studying in Government schools is 79.19 which is significantly higher than those students studying in Private schools whose adjusted mean score of Self-efficacy is 61.27. It may, therefore, be said that students studying in Government schools were found to have higher Self-efficacy as compared to their counter parts of students studying in Private schools when their Resilience was taken as Covariate.

Influence of Interaction between Gender and Locale of Schools on Self-efficacy of students by taking their Resilience as Covariate

From Table 12.21 it is evident that the adjusted F-Value for interaction between Gender and Locale of Schools is 8.28 which is significant at 0.01 level with df = 1/291. It reflects that the adjusted mean scores of Self-efficacy of Males and Females studying in Schools situated in Rural and Urban Areas differ significantly when their Resilience was taken as Covariate. So there was a significant influence of interaction between Gender and Locale of Schools on Self-efficacy of students when their Resilience was taken as Covariate. Thus, the null hypothesis that there is no significant influence of interaction between Gender and Locale of Schools on Self-efficacy of students when their Resilience was taken as Covariate is rejected. In order to know the trend of influence of interaction between Gender and Locale of Schools on Self-efficacy of students when their Resilience was taken as Covariate, the Graph 12.1 has been plotted.

From Graph 12.1, it can be seen that Male students studying in schools situated in Rural as well as Urban areas were found to have Self-efficacy to the same extent when their Resilience was taken as Covariate. On the other hand Female students studying in Rural Area had higher Self-efficacy than those studying in schools situated in Urban Area. Further in case of students studying in Schools situated in Rural Area, there is a sharp increase in Self-efficacy as Gender changes from Males to Females than those studying in Schools situated in Urban Area by considering their Resilience as Covariate.

Influence of Interaction between Gender and Management of Schools on Self-efficacy of students by taking their Resilience as Covariate

The adjusted F-Value for interaction between Gender and Management of Schools is 2.77 which is not significant (Vide Table 12.21). It reveals that adjusted mean scores of Self-efficacy of Male and Female students studying in Government Schools and Private Schools did not differ significantly when their Resilience was taken as Covariate. So there was no significant influence of interaction between Gender and Management of Schools on Self-efficacy of students when their Resilience was taken as Covariate. Thus, the null hypothesis that there is no significant influence of interaction between Gender and Management of Schools on Self-efficacy of students by taking their Resilience

Graph 12.1: Trend of influence of interaction between Gender and Locale of Schools on Self-efficacy of students by taking their Resilience as covariance

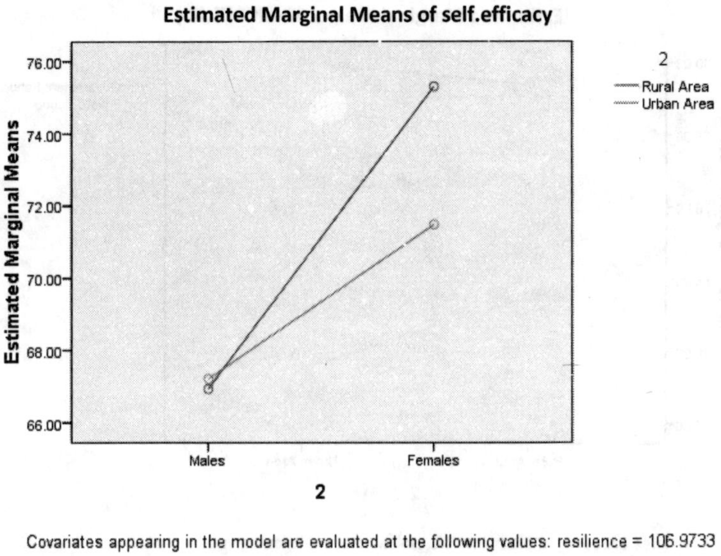

as Covariate is not rejected. It may, therefore, be said that Self-efficacy of students was found to be independent of interaction between Gender and Management of Schools when their Resilience was taken as Covariate.

Influence of Interaction between Locale of Schools and Management of Schools on Self-efficacy of students by taking their Resilience as Covariate

From Table 12.21 it is evident that the adjusted F-Value for interaction between Locale of Schools and Management of Schools is 18.67 which is significant at 0.01 level with df = 1/291. It reflects that the adjusted mean scores of Self-efficacy of students studying in Government Schools and Private Schools situated in Rural and Urban Areas differ significantly when their Resilience was taken as Covariate. So there was a significant influence of interaction between Locale of Schools and Management of Schools on Self-efficacy of students when their Resilience was taken as Covariate. Thus, the null hypothesis that there is no significant influence of interaction between Locale of Schools and Management of Schools on Self-efficacy of students when their Resilience was taken as Covariate is rejected. In order to know the trend of influence of interaction between Locale of Schools and Management of Schools on Self-efficacy of students when their Resilience was taken as Covariate, the Graph 12.2 has been plotted.

Graph 12.2: Trend of influence of interaction between Locale of Schools and Management of Schools on Self-efficacy of students by taking their Resilience as covariate

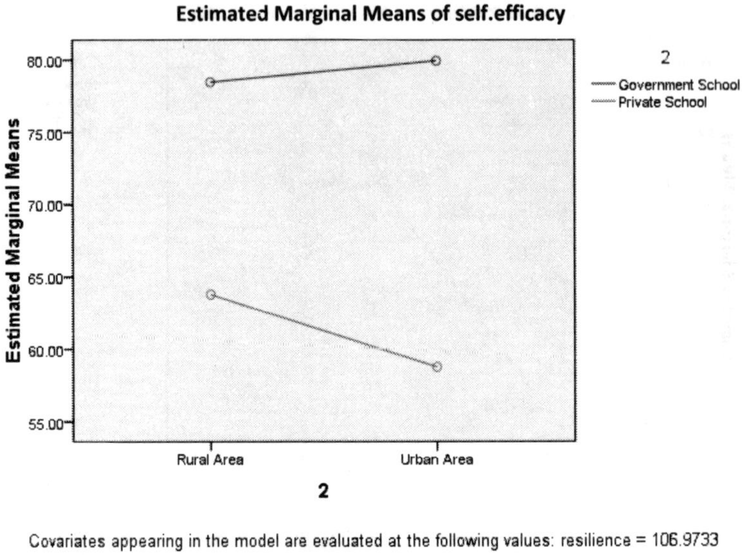

From Graph 12.2 it can be seen that irrespective of Locale of Schools, students studying in Government Schools had higher Self-efficacy as compared to those of Private Schools. Further there is slight increase in Self-efficacy of students of Government Schools as Locale of Schools changes from Rural Area to Urban Area. On the other hand, there is a decline in Self-efficacy of students of Private Schools as Locale of Schools changes from Rural Area to Urban Area.

Influence of Interaction among Gender, Locale of Schools and Management of Schools on Self-efficacy of students by taking their Resilience as Covariate

The adjusted F-Value for interaction among Gender, Locale of Schools and Management of Schools is 16.46 which is significant at 0.01 level with df = 1/291 (Vide Table 12.21). It reflects that the adjusted mean scores of Self-efficacy of Male and Female students studying in Government Schools and Private Schools situated in Rural and Urban Areas differ significantly when their Resilience was taken as Covariate. So there was a significant influence of interaction among Gender, Locale of Schools and Management of Schools on Self-efficacy of students when their Resilience was taken as Covariate. Thus, the null hypothesis that there is no significant influence of interaction among Gender, Locale of Schools and Management of Schools on Self-efficacy of students when their Resilience was taken as Covariate is rejected. In order to know the trend of influence of interaction among Gender, Locale of Schools and Management of Schools on Self-efficacy of students when their Resilience was taken as Covariate, the Graph 12.3 has been plotted.

Graph 12.3: Trend of influence of interaction among Gender, Locale of Schools and Management of Schools on Self-efficacy of students when their Resilience was taken as Covariate

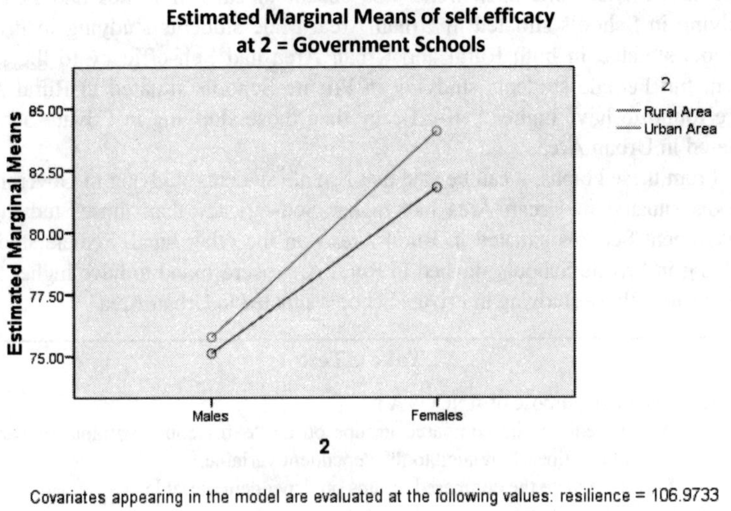

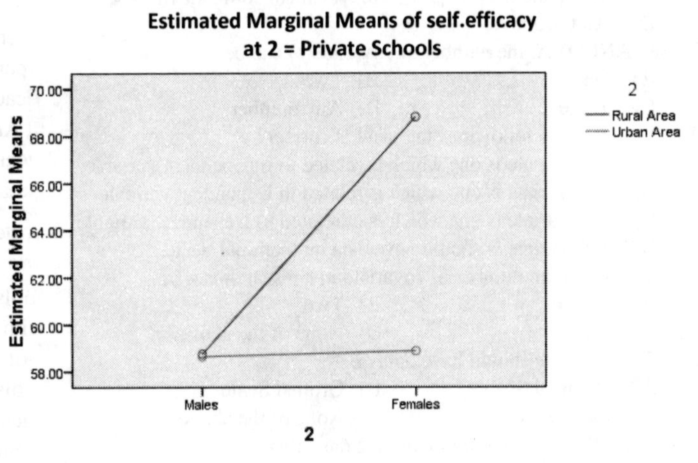

From Graph 12.3, in case of students studying in Government School, it can be observed that with change in Gender from Male to Female Self-efficacy of students studying in Government Schools situated in Rural and Urban Area increased. Female students studying in Government Schools situated in Rural as well as Urban area had higher Self-efficacy as compared to those of Male students. Lastly, Female students studying in Government schools situated in Urban Area had higher Self-efficacy than those studying in Government Schools situated in Rural Area.

In case of Private Schools, there is a sharp increase in Self-efficacy of students studying in schools situated in Rural Area as the Gender changes from Male to Female while such trend was absent in case of Males and Females studying in Schools situated in Urban Area. Male students studying in Private Schools situated in both Rural and Urban Area had Self-efficacy to the same extent but Female students studying in Private Schools situated in Rural Area were found to have higher Self-efficacy than those studying in Private Schools situated in Urban Area.

From these graphs, it can be said that Female students studying in Government schools situated in Urban Area had higher Self-efficacy than those studying in Government Schools situated in Rural Area. On the other hand, Female students studying in Private Schools situated in Rural Area were found to have higher Self-efficacy than those studying in Private Schools situated in Urban Area.

Take a Test

1. The main purpose of ANCOVA is
   A) To equate the compared groups on an "extraneous" variable (covariate) that is linearly related to the dependent variable.
   B) To equate the compared groups on dependent variable.
   C) To equate the compared groups on concomitant variable.
   D) All the above.
2. In ANCOVA, the number of covariate(s) can be
   A) One B) Two
   C) Three D) Any number.
3. Which of the following statement is correct?
   A) A covariate is one which is related to Independent variable.
   B) A covariate is one which is related to Dependent variable.
   C) A covariate is one which is unrelated to Dependent variable.
   D) A covariate is should have data on Nominal Scale.
4. The minimum number of covariate in a research can be
   A) One B) Two
   C) Three D) None of the above.
5. The covariate should have data on
   A) Nominal Scale B) Ordinal Scale
   C) Interval Scale D) None of the above.
6. ANCOVA can be used to analyse data obtained from
   A) Experimental Research B) Historical Research
   C) Survey Research D) Both A and C.
7. Which of the following is the underlying assumption of ANCOVA?
   A) There is linear relationship between covariate and Dependent variable.
   B) There is linear relationship between covariate and Independent variable.
   C) There is linear relationship between Independent variable and Dependent variable.
   D) There is curvilinear relationship between covariate and Dependent variable.

8. Which of the following statement is true?
   A) The covariate should be meaningfully related to Independent variable.
   B) The covariate should be meaningfully related to any variable of the study.
   C) The covariate should be meaningfully related to Dependent variable.
   D) The covariate should be meaningfully related to other covariates of the study.
9. Which of the following statement is not incorrect?
   A) In ANCOVA the groups should be formed on the basis of covariate scores.
   B) In ANCOVA the groups should not be formed on the basis of covariate scores.
   C) One of the covariate may have data on Ordinal Scale.
   D) ANCOVA may also be called ANOVA.
10. Which of the following statement is not incorrect?
    A) The assumptions underlying ANOVA and ANCOVA are same.
    B) The assumptions underlying ANCOVA are more than that of ANOVA.
    C) The Objective wording is same for ANOVA and ANCOVA.
    D) There may not be a hypothesis in a research where data are analyzed with the help of ANCOVA.
11. In Two-Way ANCOVA, there is
    A) One covariate at least. B) Two covariates at least.
    C) Three covariates at least. D) No restriction on number of covariate.
12. Which of the following statement is correct in the context of Two Way ANCOVA?
    A) There must be at least One variable with two levels.
    B) There must be at least two variables, each having two levels.
    C) There must be at least three variables, each having two levels.
    D) Any number of variables having only two levels of each.
13. Which of the following statement is correct in the context of Two Way ANCOVA?
    A) Two-Way ANCOVA can also be called 2x2 Factorial Design ANCOVA.
    B) Two-Way ANCOVA can also be called 2x4 Factorial Design ANCOVA.
    C) Two-Way ANCOVA can also be called 4x3 Factorial Design ANCOVA.
    D) Any one of the above depending on levels of Independent Variables.
14. Which of the following statement is correct in the context of Two-Way ANCOVA?
    A) The assumptions underlying One Way ANCOVA and Two-Way ANCOVA are different.
    B) The assumptions underlying One Way ANCOVA and Two-Way ANCOVA are same.
    C) The assumptions underlying One Way ANOVA and Two-Way ANCOVA are not different.
    D) None of the above.
15. Two-Way ANCOVA can be used to analyse data obtained through
    A) Survey research only. B) Experimental research only.
    C) Both A and B. D) None of the above.
16. In Two-Way ANCOVA with two Covariates, there must
    A) Not be any interaction. B) At least one interaction.
    C) At least two interactions. D) Any number of interactions.

17. Which of the following wording of Objective for Two-Way ANCOVA is correct?
    A) To compare mean scores of Study Habits of students studying in Government and Private Schools.
    B) To compare mean scores of Study Habits of students studying in Government and Private Schools by taking Intelligence of students as covariate.
    C) To study the influence of Types of School, Locale and their interaction on Study Habits of students by considering their Intelligence as covariate.
    D) To study the influence of Types of School, Locale and their interaction on Study Habits of students.
18. In Two-Way ANCOVA, each covariate data must be on
    A) Nominal Scale. B) Ordinal Scale.
    C) Interval Scale. D) Either on Interval Scale or Ratio Scale.
19. Which of the following is the underlying assumption of Two-Way ANCOVA?
    A) There is linear relationship between covariate and Dependent variable.
    B) There is linear relationship between covariate and Independent variable.
    C) There is linear relationship between Independent variable and Dependent variable.
    D) There is curvilinear relationship between covariate and Dependent variable.
20. Which of the following ANCOVA technique is the best?
    A) One Way ANCOVA. B) Two-Way ANCOVA.
    C) Three-Way ANCOVA. D) All the above.
21. Which of the following statement is correct?
    A) Assumptions underlying One Way ANCOVA and Two-Way ANCOVA are the same.
    B) Some of the assumptions of ANOVA and ANCOVA are same.
    C) The data of covariate must be either on Interval scale or Ratio Scale.
    D) All of the above.
22. Three-Way ANCOVA analysis will help the researcher in answering ……questions in one research.
    A) Seven B) Six
    C) Eight D) Five.
23. In Three-Way ANCOVA, it is essential to have minimum …….. Covariate(s).
    A) One B) Two
    C) Three D) Any number.
24. Which of the following is the correct wording of Objective whose data can be analysed with the help of Three-Way ANCOVA?
    A) To study the effect of Medium of Instruction, Gender, Locale and interaction on Achievement in Science of students.
    B) To study the effect of Medium of Instruction, Gender, Locale and their various interactions on Achievement in Science of students by taking Intelligence of students as covariate.
    C) To study the effect of Medium of Instruction, Gender and interaction on Achievement in Science of students by taking Intelligence of students as covariate.

D) To study the effect of Medium of Instruction, Gender, Locale and their interaction on Achievement in Science of students.

25. Which of the following is the correct wording of Hypothesis whose data can be analysed with the help of Three-Way ANCOVA?
    A) There is no significant effect of Medium of Instruction, Gender, Locale and interaction on Achievement in Science of students by taking their Study Habits as covariate.
    B) There is no effect of Medium of Instruction, Gender, Locale and their various interactions on Achievement in Science of students by taking their Study Habits as covariate.
    C) There is no significant effect of Medium of Instruction, Gender, Locale and their various interactions on Achievement in Science of students by taking Study Habits as covariate.
    D) There is no significant influence of Medium of Instruction, Gender, Locale and their interaction on Achievement in Science of students.
26. Which of the following statement is correct?
    A) The Hypothesis can be expressed in any sentence one likes.
    B) In formulation Hypothesis "Should" word must be used.
    C) The Hypothesis is to be written in future tense only.
    D) The Hypothesis is to be written always in present tense.
27. In Three-Way ANCOVA, the total interactions are
    A) 2 B) 3
    C) 4 D) 5.
28. Which of the following statement is correct?
    A) Total $SS_{y.x}$ may be negative.
    B) Treatment $SS_{y.x}$ may be negative.
    C) Error $SS_{y.x}$ may be negative
    D) None of the above.

13
Correlation

INTRODUCTION

All of us are aware about the word relationship. Relationship is a general word. There are two technical words, namely, Correlation and Association which shows relationship. Correlation and Association are technical terms used in Statistics but normally misunderstood by researchers. In order to use these words correctly one should understand the difference between them. Only after that one is in a position to select appropriate Statistical Technique. There are different methods of computing Correlation and all these are given in a book entitled "*Statistics in Psychology and Education*" by Henry E. Garrett. Further different Statistical Techniques used for computing Association are given in Non-parametric Statistics by Sidney Siegel and a few are given in "*Statistics in Psychology and Education*" by Henry E. Garrett. After reading this chapter, researchers will be in a position to:

- Differentiate between Correlation and Association.
- Name different methods of computing Correlation and Association.
- List Advantages and Disadvantages of Correlation.
- Tell another name of Product Moment Correlation.
- Write Objective of research whose data can be analysed with the help of Product Moment Correlation.
- Formulate Hypothesis correctly for the given Objective.
- Analyse data using SPSS.
- Put SPSS out-put in appropriate table along with proper heading.
- Interpret the information given in the Product Moment Correlation Table and test the given Hypothesis.

DIFFERENCE BETWEEN CORRELATION AND ASSOCIATION

The difference between Correlation and Association is given in the following table.

Basis	*Correlation*	*Association*
Distribution	Either both Variables or at least one Variable distribution should be Normal.	Variables may not have Normal distribution.
Commonness	It tells the percentage of commonness between two Variables.	It does not indicate commonness.
Direction	It can be positive or negative.	It does not indicate any direction.
Range of Value	Its' value can range between-1 and +1.	Its' value can also range between-1 and +1.
Strength	It tells whether the computed correlation is strong or weak.	It does not tell about the strength of Association.
Scale of Measurement	Either both or at least one Variable should have either Interval Scale or Ratio Scale.	Any Scale of Measurement.

DIFFERENT METHODS OF COMPUTING CORRELATION AND ASSOCIATION

Different methods of computing Correlation and Association between two Variables are given below:

Name	*Symbol*	*Assumptions*	*Type of Statistics*
Product Moment Correlation	r	1. Both the Variables should have Normal distribution. 2. The data of both Variables must be either on Interval Scale or Ratio Scale.	Parametric Statistics
Biserial Correlation	r_{bis}	1. One Variable distribution is Normal and its data must be either on Interval Scale or Ratio Scale. 2. The other Variable is classified into two categories or Dichotomous Variable. Dichotomous means cut into two parts.	Parametric Statistics
Point Biserial Correlation	r_{pbis}	1. One Variable distribution is Normal and its data must be either on Interval Scale or Ratio Scale. 2. The other Variable is classified into two true categories or Dichotomies Variable.	Parametric Statistics
Rank Difference Method of Correlation	ρ	1. The two Variables under study are not normally distributed. 2. Both the Variables should have Ordinal Scale data.	Non-Parametric Statistics
Tetrachoric Correlation	r_t	1. The two Variables under study are essentially continuous or have data on either Interval Scale or Ratio Scale and	Non-parametric Statistics

		normally distributed. 2. Each Variable is classified into only two artificial categories.	
The Phi Coefficient	φ	1. The two Variables under study are not normally distributed. 2. Each Variable is classified into only two genuine categories. In other words, when the classification is truly discrete and the variables can take only one of two values. 3. The data must be on Nominal Scale.	Non-parametric Statistics
The Contingency Coefficient	C	1. The two Variables under study are not normally distributed. 2. Each Variable is classified into more than two categories. 3. The data must be on Nominal Scale.	Non-parametric Statistics

ADVANTAGES OF CORRELTION

The following are the advantages of Correlation:

1. The researcher may collect data from larger portion of the population of the study.
2. The results tend to be more applicable to everyday life.
3. Correlation opens up a great deal of further research to other scholars.
4. Correlation allows researchers to determine the strength and direction of a relationship so that later studies can narrow down the findings and, if possible, determine causation experimentally.
5. Correlation allows the researcher to investigate naturally occurring Variables that may be unethical to test experimentally.
6. Correlation allows the researcher to clearly and easily see if there is a relationship between variables.

DISADVANTAGES OF CORRELTION

The disadvantages of Correlation might be as follows:

1. The most used Correlation coefficients only assess the linear relationship. It is, therefore, possible that while there is a strong non-linear relationship between the variables, the correlation value is close to Zero or even Zero. In such a case, a scatter diagram can roughly indicate the existence or otherwise a non-linear relationship.
2. One has to be careful in interpreting the value of 'r'. For example one can compute 'r' between size of shoe and Achievement in Mathematics. Irrespective of the value of 'r', it makes no sense and is termed as chance or non-sense correlation. It is also called as spurious correlation.

3. Correlation value does not say anything about the cause and effect relationship. The Correlation value only indicates that the two variables are related but it does not indicate that one variable influences the other or vice-versa. So statistical correlation should not be used to study causation because of the problem of third variable.
4. Correlation does not allow the researcher to go beyond the given data.

ANOTHER NAME OF PRODUCT MOMENT CORRELATION

- Product Moment Method was developed by Prof. Karl Pearson, so it is also called Pearson Product Moment Correlation.

WHEN TO USE

Example-I

How to Write Objective for Product Moment Correlation

The Objective should be worded as given below so that data can be analysed with the help of Product Moment Correlation:

To study the Correlation between Intelligence and Achievement in Mathematics of students.

How to Formulate Hypothesis

The Hypothesis which can be tested with the help of Product Moment Correlation is formulated in the Null Form as given below:

There is no significant correlation between Intelligence and Achievement in Mathematics of students.

Which Statistical Technique to use for Analysing Data

For testing the Hypothesis, Product Moment Correlation should be used and the data can be analysed using Statistical Package for the Social Sciences (SPSS). The output of SPSS is as given in Table 13.1.

Table 13.1: Correlations

		intelligent	*Achievement in Mathematics*
Intelligent	Pearson Correlation	1	.628**
	Sig. (2-tailed)		.000
	N	60	60
Achievement in Mathematics	Pearson Correlation	.628**	1
	Sig. (2-tailed)	.000	
	N	60	60

**. Correlation is significant at the 0.01 level (2-tailed).

How to Interpret the Results Given in Table 13.1

The results of correlation should be interpreted as given below:

The Objective was to study the correlation between Intelligence and Achievement in Mathematics of students. The data were analysed with the help of Product Moment Correlation and the results are given in Table 13.2.

Table 13.2: Correlation coefficient between Intelligence and Achievement in Mathematics of students

Variable	*Achievement in Mathematics*	*Remark*
Intelligence	0.628	p<0.01

From Table 13.2, it is evident that the correlation coefficient between Intelligence and Achievement in Mathematics is 0.628 which is positive and significant at 0.01 level with df = 58. It shows that Intelligence and Achievement in Mathematics were positively and significantly correlated. Thus, the null hypothesis that there is no significant correlation between Intelligence and Achievement in Mathematics of students is rejected. Further the percentage of commonness between Intelligence and Achievement in Mathematics is 39.44 which is moderate. It may, therefore, be said that Intelligence and Achievement in Mathematics were found to be moderately related.

Example-2

How to Write Objective for Product Moment Correlation

The Objective should be worded as given below so that data can be analysed with the help of Product Moment Correlation:

To study the correlation between Self-efficacy and Burnout of teachers.

How to Formulate Hypothesis

The Hypothesis which can be tested with the help of Product Moment Correlation is formulated in the Null Form as given below:

There is no significant correlation between Self-efficacy and Burnout of Teachers.

Which Statistical Technique to Use for Analysing Data

For testing the Hypothesis, Product Moment Correlation should be used and the data can be analysed using Statistical Package for the Social Sciences (SPSS). The output of SPSS is as given in Table 13.3.

Table 13.3: Correlations

		Self-efficacy	*burnout*
Self-efficacy	Pearson Correlation	1	-.976**
	Sig. (2-tailed)		.000
	N	300	300
Burnout	Pearson Correlation	–.976**	1
	Sig. (2-tailed)	.000	
	N	300	300

**. Correlation is significant at the 0.01 level (2-tailed).

How to Interpret the Results Given in Table 13.3

The results of correlation should be interpreted as given below:

The Objective was to study the correlation between Self-efficacy and Burnout of teachers. The data were analysed with the help of Product Moment Correlation and the results are given Table 13.4.

Table 13.4: Correlation Coefficient between Self-efficacy and Burnout of Teachers

Variable	*Burnout*	*Remark*
Self-efficacy	-0.976	p<0.01

From Table 13.4, it is evident that the correlation coefficient is-0.976 which is negative and significant at 0.01 level with df = 298. It reflects that Self-efficacy and Burnout were negatively and significantly correlated. Thus, the null hypothesis that there is no significant correlation between Self-efficacy and Burnout of Teachers is rejected. Further the percentage of commonness between Self-efficacy and Burnout is 95.26 which is high. It may, therefore, be said that Self-efficacy and Burnout were found to be inversely and strongly related. That is, higher the Burnout, lower is likely to be the Self-efficacy of Teachers.

Example-3

How to Write Objective for Product Moment Correlation

The Objective should be worded as given below so that data can be analysed with the help of Product Moment Correlation:

To study the correlation between Teaching Experience and Anxiety of teachers.

How to Formulate Hypothesis

The Hypothesis which can be tested with the help of Product Moment Correlation is formulated in the Null Form as given below:

There is no significant correlation between Teaching Experience and Anxiety of teachers.

Which Statistical Technique to Use for Analysing Data

For testing the Hypothesis, Product Moment Correlation should be used and the data can be analysed using Statistical Package for the Social Sciences (SPSS). The output of SPSS is as given in Table 13.5.

Table 13.5: Correlations

		Teaching Experience	*anxiety*
Teaching Experience	Pearson Correlation	1	-.140**
	Sig. (2-tailed)		.007
	N	372	372
Anxiety	Pearson Correlation	-.140**	1
	Sig. (2-tailed)	.007	
	N	372	372

**. Correlation is significant at the 0.01 level (2-tailed).

How to Interpret the Results Given in Table 13.5

The results of correlation should be interpreted as given below:

The Objective was to study the correlation between Teaching Experience and Anxiety of teachers. The data were analysed with the help of Product Moment Correlation and the results are given in Table 13.6.

Table 13.6: Correlation Cefficient between Teaching Experience and Anxiety of Teachers

Variable	*Anxiety*	*Remark*
Teaching Experience	-0.14	p<0.01

From Table 13.6, it is evident that the correlation coefficient is-0.14 which is negative and significant at 0.01 level with df = 370. It reflects that Teaching Experience and Anxiety were negatively and significantly correlated. Thus, the null hypothesis that there is no significant correlation between Teaching Experience and Anxiety of Teachers is rejected. Further the percentage of commonness between Teaching Experience and Anxiety of Teachers is 1.96 which is too low. It may, therefore, be said that higher Teaching Experience may not necessarily lead to lower Anxiety of Teachers.

> ***Caution:*** *The Correlation coefficients should be interpreted carefully and its value may be affected due to the other variables which have not been taken into consideration while computing Correlation.*

Take a Test

1. The more hot and humid the weather, the less clothing a person wears is an example of
   A) Moderate correlation B) Low correlation
   C) Negative correlation D) High positive correlation.
2. Correlation refers to
   A) The causal relationship between two variables.
   B) The relationship between two variables.
   C) The proportion of variance that two variables share.
   D) A statistical method that only can be used with a correlational research design.
3. If two variables are highly correlated, what do you know?
   A) That they always go together.
   B) That high values on one variable lead to high values on other variable.
   C) That there are no other variables responsible for the relationship.
   D) That changes in one variable are accompanied by predictable changes in the other.
4. If paired scores occupy the same positions with their own distributions (high with high and low with low)
   A) Pearson r will be low and negative. B) Pearson r will be high and positive.
   C) Standard deviation will be high. D) Pearson r will be close to zero.

5. Which of the following indicates the strongest relationship?
   A) r = 0.5 B) r = 0.09
   C) r = –0.6 D) r^2 = 0.2
6. A researcher finds the correlation of 0.4 between personal income and the number of years of college completed. Based upon this finding he can conclude that
   A) A person who attended four years of college will have an annual income of Rs. 5000.
   B) more years of education causes higher income.
   C) personal income is a positively skewed variable.
   D) more years of education are associated with higher income.
7. In calculating r with raw scores, the numerator of r represents
   A) the variance of X.
   B) the variance of Y.
   C) the variance of X multiplied by the variance of Y.
   D) the covariance of X and Y.
8. The coefficient of determination tells us
   A) the proportion of variance in X accounted for by the mean of Y.
   B) the proportion of variance in Y accounted for by X.
   C) the mean value of Y.
   D) the mean value of X.
9. Which of the following may have an adverse effect on a correlation coefficient?
   A) too many people in your survey.
   B) restricting the range of possible scores.
   C) the scores on one variable have larger numbers than the other variable.
   D) a negative relationship between your X and Y variables.
10. Which of the following would not allow you to calculate a correlation?
    A) a negative relationship between X and Y.
    B) a positive relationship between X and Y.
    C) a curvilinear relationship between X and Y.
    D) a linear relationship between X and Y.
11. Which of the following is not the use of r?
    A) Reliability B) Correlation
    C) Power analysis D) Validity.

14
Partial Correlation

INTRODUCTION

Now it is clear that the Correlation is computed between two Variables only. There are different methods of computing correlation. The method of computing correlation should be selected keeping in mind the stated assumptions. In reality there are many variables which might be interrelated. Due to this, it is difficult to say about the real commonness shared by the two variables. Thus, if there are more than two variables and the researcher is interested in computing correlation between two variables by partialling out the effect of other variables, Partial Correlation should be computed. All variables of the Partial Correlation should be interrelated, if not, than Partial Correlation should not be used for studying the correlation between two variables when the effects of other Variables are partialled out. After reading this chapter, the researcher will be able to:

- Define Partial Correlation.
- Write assumptions underlying Partial Correlation.
- Write research Objective correctly whose data can be analysed with the help of Partial Correlation.
- Formulate Hypothesis correctly for the given Objective.
- Analyse data using SPSS.
- Put SPSS out-put in appropriate Table along with proper heading.
- Interpret the information given in the Partial Correlation Table and test the given Hypothesis.

DEFINITION OF PARTIAL CORRELATION

Partial Correlation is a measure of the strength and direction of a linear relationship between two continuous variables whilst controlling for the effect of one or more other continuous variables (also known as 'control' variables).

ASSUMPTIONS UNDERLYING PARTIAL CORRELATION

The following are the assumptions to be satisfied if Partial Correlation is to be used for analysing the data.

1. There must be at least three variables or more so that correlation can be computed between two variables by partialling out the effect of the third variable or more.
2. The Scale of Measurement of all variables must be either Interval Scale or Ratio Scale.
3. Each variable of the Partial Correlation should have approximately Normal Distribution.
4. There must be linear relationship among the variables taken for Partial Correlation.
5. There should be no significant outliers.

WHEN TO USE

Example-I

How to Write Objective for Partial Correlation

The Objective can be worded as given below:

- To study the correlation between Self-efficacy and Emotional Competence by partialling out the effect of Burnout of Teachers.

How to Formulate Hypothesis

The Hypothesis may be stated in the Null Form as follows:

- There is no significant correlation between Self-efficacy and Emotional Competence when the effect of Burnout of Teachers is partialled out.

Statistical Technique Used for Analysing Data

For testing the Hypothesis, Partial Correlation Technique should be used and the data can be analysed using Statistical Package for the Social Sciences (SPSS).The SPSS out-puts are given in Tables 14.1 and 14.2.

Table 14.1: Correlations

		Self-efficacy	*Emotional Competence*	*Burnout*
Self-efficacy	Pearson Correlation	1	.610**	-.976**
	Sig. (2-tailed)		.000	.000
	N	300	300	300
Emotional Competence	Pearson Correlation	.610**	1	-.657**
	Sig. (2-tailed)	.000		.000
	N	300	300	300
Burnout	Pearson Correlation	-.976**	-.657**	1
	Sig. (2-tailed)	.000	.000	
	N	300	300	300

**. Correlation is significant at the 0.01 level (2-tailed).

From Table 14.1, it is evident that the correlation coefficients between Self-efficacy and Emotional Competence; Self-efficacy and Burnout; and Burnout and Emotional Competence are 0.610, – .976, and – 0.657 respectively. All these Correlation coefficients are high and significant at 0.01 level with df = 300. In such a situation Partial Correlation technique is the most appropriate for studying the Correlation between Self-efficacy and Emotional Competence by partialling out the effect of Burnout. The results of Partial Correlation are given in Table 14.2.

Table 14.2: Correlations

Control Variables			*Self-efficacy*	*Emotional Competence*
Burnout	Self-efficacy	Correlation	1.000	-.187
		Significance (2-tailed)	.	.001
		df	0	297
	Emotional Competence	Correlation	-.187	1.000
		Significance (2-tailed)	.001	.
		df	297	0

How to Interpret the Result given in Table 14.2

The result of Partial Correlation should be interpreted as given below:

The Objective was to study the Correlation between Self-efficacy and Emotional Competence by partialling out the effect of Burnout of Teachers. The data were analysed with the help of Partial Correlation and the results are given in Table 14.3.

Table 14.3: Partial Correlation coefficient between Self-efficacy and Emotional Competence by partialling out the effect of Burnout of Teachers

Variables	*Remark*
$r_{12.3} = -0.187$	$p<0.01$
1: Self-efficacy 2: Emotional Competence 3: Burnout	

From Table 14.3, it is evident that the Partial Correlation coefficient value is -0.187 which is negative and significant at 0.01 level with df = 297. It indicates the Self-efficacy and Emotional Competence were found to be negatively and significantly related when the effect of Burnout was partialled out. Thus, the null hypothesis that there is no significant Correlation between Self-efficacy and Emotional Competence when the effect of Burnout of Teachers is partialled out is rejected. The Partial Correlation value is too weak as it shares only 3.50% commonness. It may, therefore, be said that the relationship between Self-efficacy and Emotional Competence was weak when the effect of Burnout was partialled out.

Example-2

How to Write Objective for Partial Correlation

The Objective can be worded as given below:

- To study the correlation between Anxiety and Psychological Risk Factor by partialling out the effect of Emotional Quotient of Teachers.

How to Formulate Hypothesis

The Hypothesis may be stated in the Null Form as follows:

- There is no significant correlation between Anxiety and Psychological Risk Factor when the effect of Emotional Quotient of Teachers is partialled out.

Statistical Technique Used for Analysing Data

For testing the Hypothesis, Partial Correlation Technique should be used and the data can be analysed using Statistical Package for the Social Sciences (SPSS).The SPSS outputs are given in Tables 14.4 and 14.5.

Table 14.4: Correlations

		Anxiety	*Psychological Risk Factor*	*Total Emotional Quotient*
Anxiety	Pearson Correlation	1	.651**	-.290**
	Sig. (2-tailed)		.000	.000
	N	372	372	372
Psychological Risk Factor	Pearson Correlation	.651**	1	-.204**
	Sig. (2-tailed)	.000		.000
	N	372	372	372
Total Emotional Quotient	Pearson Correlation	-.290**	-.204**	1
	Sig. (2-tailed)	.000	.000	
	N	372	372	372

**. Correlation is significant at the 0.01 level (2-tailed).

Table 14.5: Correlations

Control Variables			*Anxiety*	*Psychological Risk Factor*
Total Emotional Quotient	Anxiety	Correlation	1.000	.632
		Significance (2-tailed)	.	.000
		df	0	369
	Psychological Risk Factor	Correlation	.632	1.000
		Significance (2-tailed)	.000	.
		df	369	0

From Table 14.4, it is evident that the correlation coefficients between Anxiety and Psychological Risk Factor; Anxiety and Emotional Quotient; and

Psychological Risk Factor and Emotional Quotient are 0.651,-.290, and-.204 respectively. All these Correlation coefficients are high and significant at 0.01 level with df = 372. In such a situation Partial Correlation technique is the most appropriate for studying the correlation between Anxiety and Psychological Risk Factor by partialling out the effect of Emotional Quotient. The results of Partial Correlation are given in Table 14.5.

How to Interpret the Result Given in Table 14.5

The results of Partial Correlation should be interpreted as given below:

The Objective was to study the Correlation between Anxiety and Psychological Risk Factor by partialling out the effect of Emotional Quotient of Teachers. The data were analysed with the help of Partial Correlation and the results are given in Table 14.6.

Table 14.6: Partial Correlation coefficient between Anxiety and Psychological Risk Factor by partialling out the effect of Emotional Quotient of Teachers

Variables	*Remark*
$r_{12.3} = 0.632$	$p<0.01$
1: Anxiety 2: Psychological Risk Factor 3: Emotional Quotient	

From Table 14.6, it is evident that the Partial Correlation coefficient value is 0.632 which is positive and significant at 0.01 level with df = 369. It indicates that the Anxiety and Psychological Risk Factor were found to be positively and significantly related when the effect of Emotional Quotient was partialled out. Thus, the null hypothesis that there is no significant correlation between Anxiety and Psychological Risk Factor when the effect of Emotional Quotient of Teachers is partialled out is rejected. The Partial Correlation value is moderate as it shares only 39.94% commonness. It may, therefore, be said that the relationship between Anxiety and Psychological Risk Factor was moderate when the effect of Emotional Quotient of Teachers was partialled out.

NOTE: As evident from Table 14.4, the Correlation coefficient between Anxiety and Emotional Quotient, and Psychological Risk Factor and Emotional Quotient are-0.290 and-0.204 respectively which are low. Due to low Correlation of Emotional Quotient with Anxiety and Psychological Risk Factor, partialling out the effect of Emotional Quotient did not change much the Partial Correlation coefficient between Anxiety and Psychological Risk Factor which was found to be 0.632. Thus, effect of Emotional Quotient should not have been partialled out as its presence or absence did not make much difference.

Example-3

How to Write Objective for Partial Correlation

The Objective can be worded as given below:

- To study the correlation between Classroom Teaching and Child Centered Practice by partialling out the effect of Attitude towards Teaching of Teachers.

How to Formulate Hypothesis

The Hypothesis may be stated in the Null Form as follows:

- There is no significant correlation between Classroom Teaching and Child Centered Practice by partialling out the effect of Attitude towards Teaching of Teachers.

Statistical Technique Used for Analysing Data

For testing the Hypothesis, Partial Correlation Technique should be used and the data can be analysed using Statistical Package for the Social Sciences (SPSS).The SPSS out-puts are given in Tables 14.7 and 14.8.

Table 14.7: Correlations

		Overall Attitude	*Classroom Teaching*	*Child Centred Practice*
Overall Attitude	Pearson Correlation	1	.743**	.683**
	Sig. (2-tailed)		.000	.000
	N	372	372	372
Classroom Teaching	Pearson Correlation	.743**	1	.553**
	Sig. (2-tailed)	.000		.000
	N	372	372	372
Child Centred Practice	Pearson Correlation	.683**	.553**	1
	Sig. (2-tailed)	.000	.000	
	N	372	372	372

**. Correlation is significant at the 0.01 level (2-tailed).

From Table 14.7, it is evident that the correlation coefficients between Attitude towards Teaching and Classroom Teaching; Attitude towards Teaching and Child Centered Practice; and Classroom Teaching and Child Centered Practice are 0.743, 0.683, and 0.553 respectively. All these correlation coefficients are high and significant at 0.01 level with df = 369. In such a situation Partial Correlation technique is the most appropriate for studying the correlation between Classroom Teaching and Child Centered Practice by partialling out the effect of Attitude towards Teaching. The results of Partial Correlation are given in Table 14.8.

Table 14.8: Correlations

Control Variables			*Classroom teaching*	*child Centred Practice*
Overall Attitude	classroom Teaching	Correlation	1.000	.094
		Significance (2-tailed)	.	.072
		df	0	369
	Child Centred Practice	Correlation	.094	1.000
		Significance (2-tailed)	.072	.
		df	369	0

How to Interpret the Result Given in Table 14.8

The results of Partial Correlation should be interpreted as given below:

The Objective was to study the correlation between Classroom Teaching and Child Centered Practice by partialling out the effect of Attitude towards Teaching of Teachers. The data were analysed with the help of Partial Correlation and the results are given in Table 14.8.

Table 14.8: Partial Correlation coefficient between Classroom Teaching and Child Centered Practice by partialling out the effect of Attitude towards Teaching of Teachers

Variables	*Remark*
$r_{12.3}$ = 0.094	Not significant
1: Classroom Teaching 2: Child Centered Practice 3: Attitude towards Teaching	

From Table 14.8, it is evident that the Partial Correlation coefficient value is 0.094 which is positive but not significant. It indicates that the Classroom Teaching and Child Centered Practice were not found to be significantly related when the effect of Attitude towards Teaching was partialled out. Thus, the null hypothesis that there is no significant correlation between Classroom Teaching and Child Centered Practice when the effect of Attitude towards Teaching of Teachers is partialled out is not rejected. The Partial Correlation value is low as it shares only 0.88% commonness. It may, therefore, be said that there was too weak relationship between Classroom Teaching and Child Centered Practice when the effect of Attitude towards Teaching of Teachers was partialled out.

Example-4

How to Write Objective for Partial Correlation

The Objective can be worded as given below:

- To study the correlation between Classroom Teaching and Child Centered Practice by partialling out the effect of Attitude towards Teaching and Emotional Intelligence of Teachers.

How to Formulate Hypothesis

The Hypothesis may be stated in the Null Form as follows:

- There is no significant correlation between Classroom Teaching and

Child Centered Practice by partialling out the effect of Attitude towards Teaching and Emotional Intelligence of Teachers.

Statistical Technique Used for Analysing Data

For testing the Hypothesis, Partial Correlation Technique should be used and the data can be analysed using Statistical Package for the Social Sciences (SPSS).The SPSS outputs are given in Tables 14.9 and 14.10.

Table 14.9: Correlations

		Overall Attitude	*Classroom Teaching*	*Child Centred Practice*	*Total Emotional Quotient*
Overall Attitude	Pearson Correlation	1	.743**	.683**	.264**
	Sig. (2-tailed)		.000	.000	.000
	N	372	372	372	372
Classroom Teaching	Pearson Correlation	.743**	1	.553**	.314**
	Sig. (2-tailed)	.000		.000	.000
	N	372	372	372	372
Child Centred Practice	Pearson Correlation	.683**	.553**	1	.175**
	Sig. (2-tailed)	.000	.000		.001
	N	372	372	372	372
Total Emotional Quotient	Pearson Correlation	.264**	.314**	.175**	1
	Sig. (2-tailed)	.000	.000	.001	
	N	372	372	372	372

**. Correlation is significant at the 0.01 level (2-tailed).

From Table 14.9 it can be seen that all inter-correlations among Attitude towards Teaching, Classroom Teaching, Child Centred Practices and Emotional Intelligence are significant at 0.01 level with df = 370. In such a situation it is appropriate to study the correlation between Classroom Teaching and Child Centered Practice by partialling out the effect of Attitude towards Teaching and Emotional Intelligence of Teachers.

NOTE: Since all inter-correlation coefficient are significant, so Partial Correlation is the best statistical technique to study the correlation between Classroom Teaching and Child Centred Practice by partialling out the effect of Attitude towards Teaching and Emotional Intelligence of Teachers.

Table 14.10: Correlations

Control Variables			*Classroom Teaching*	*Child Centred Practice*
Overall Attitude & Total Emotional Quotient	Classroom Teaching	Correlation	1.000	.097
		Significance (2-tailed)	.	.064
		df	0	368
	Child Centred Practice	Correlation	.097	1.000
		Significance (2-tailed)	.064	.
		df	368	0

How to Interpret the Result Given in Table 14.10

The results of Partial Correlation should be interpreted as given below:

The Objective was to study the correlation between Classroom Teaching and Child Centered Practice by partialling out the effect of Attitude towards Teaching and Emotional Intelligence of Teachers. The data were analysed with the help of Partial Correlation and the results are given in Table 14.11.

Table 14.11: Partial Correlation coefficient between Classroom Teaching and Child Centered Practice by partialling out the effect of Attitude towards Teaching and Emotional Intelligence of Teachers

Variables	*Remark*
$r_{12.34} = 0.097$	Not Significant
1: Classroom Teaching 2: Child Centered Practice 3: Attitude towards Teaching Emotional Intelligence	

From Table 14.11, it is evident that the Partial Correlation coefficient value is 0.097 which is positive but not significant. It indicates that the Classroom Teaching and Child Centered Practice were not found to be significantly related when the effect of Attitude towards Teaching and Emotional Intelligence of Teachers were partialled out. Thus, the null hypothesis that there is no significant Correlation between Classroom Teaching and Child Centered Practice when the effect of Attitude towards Teaching and Emotional Intelligence of Teachers are partialled out is not rejected. The Partial Correlation value is low as it shares only 0.94 % commonness. It may, therefore, be said that there was too weak relationship between Classroom Teaching and Child Centered Practice when the effect of Attitude towards Teaching and Emotional Intelligence of Teachers were partialled out.

NOTE: In Partial Correlation, there must be at least three or more Variables but the Correlation is to be computed between two variables by Partialling out the effect of other Variables. In the above four examples, one or two Variables have been partialled out and the results have been interpreted. Irrespective of Variables to be partialled out, the interpretation of Partial Correlation will be the same as given in above four examples.

Take a Test

1. Which of the following is the correct symbol of representing correlation between variables 2 and 4 by partialling out the effect of variables 1 and 3?

   A) $r_{14.23}$ B) $r_{24.13}$ C) $r_{13.24}$ D) $r_{43.12}$

2. The minimum number of variables required for Partial Correlation is

   A) 1 B) 2 C) 3 D) 4

3. Which of the following statement is correct?

   A) All variables must have measurement either on Interval Scale or Ratio Scale.

   B) At least one variable must have measurement on Ordinal Scale and rest on Ratio Scale.

   C) All variables must have measurement on Ordinal Scale.

   D) At least one variable must have measurement on Interval Scale and rest on Ordinal Scale.

4. Which of the following statement is correct?
   A) Partial Correlation is Non-Parametric Statistics.
   B) Partial Correlation may have one discrete variable out of the given variables.
   C) Partial Correlation is Parametric Statistics.
   D) Partial Correlation and Multiple Correlation are interpreted in the same way.
5. Which of the following statement is NOT correct?
   A) Partial Correlation can be computed among three variables without keeping any variable constant.
   B) In case of Partial Correlation, minimum three variables are required.
   C) No variable should have measurement on Nominal Scale.
   D) All variables must be continuous.
6. Which of the following is correct wording of objective involving Gender, Intelligence, Anxiety and Study Habits?
   A) To study partial correlation between Gender and Intelligence by keeping Anxiety and Study Habits of students constant.
   B) To study Gender-wise correlation between Anxiety and Intelligence by keeping Study Habits of students constant.
   C) To study correlation between Study Habits and Intelligence by keeping Anxiety and Gender of students constant.
   D) To study correlation between Anxiety and Intelligence by keeping Gender and Study Habits of students constant.
7. Which of the following is correct wording of Hypothesis involving Intelligence, Self-confidence and Study Habits?
   A) There is no significant correlation between Intelligence and Self-confidence by keeping Study Habits constant.
   B) There is no significant correlation between Intelligence and Study Habits by keeping Self-confidence constant.
   C) There is no significant correlation between Self-confidence and Study Habits by keeping Intelligence constant.
   D) All the above.
8. In Partial Correlation the total number of variables can be
   A) 3 B) 4
   C) 5 D) Any number of finite variables.
9. In case of Partial Correlation the variables under study must have
   A) Linear relationship B) Curvilinear relationship
   C) Rectangular relationship D) Exponential relationship
10. Which of the following is/are the assumption(s) of Partial Correlation?
    A) Each Variable of the Partial Correlation should have approximately Normal Distribution.
    B) There must be linear relationship among the Variables taken for Partial Correlation.
    C) There should be no significant outliers.
    D) All the above.

15
Multiple Correlation

INTRODUCTION

By now you must have understood the concept of Correlation and Partial Correlation. You must also have understood how to write Objectives, Formulate Hypothesis, Analyse data and interpret the results obtained using SPSS. All phenomena are complex in nature because each variable is related with many variables. In other words, there is a joint contribution of many variables in predicting a variable. This cannot be studied by analysing the data with the help of neither Correlation nor Partial Correlation. This can be studied only through the use of Multiple Correlation. After reading this chapter, the reader will be in a position to:

- Define Multiple Correlation.
- List Assumptions under lying Multiple Correlation.
- Write Objective whose data can be analysed with the help of Multiple Correlation.
- Formulate Hypothesis correctly for the given Objective.
- Analyse data using SPSS.
- Put SPSS out-put in appropriate Table along with proper heading.
- Interpret the information given in the Multiple Correlation Table and test the given Hypothesis.

DEFINITION OF MULTIPLE CORRELATION

Multiple Correlation reveals the joint contribution of two or more Variables in predicting a variable. It is denoted by R.

ASSUMPTIONS UNDERLYING MULTIPLE CORRELATION

The following assumptions must be satisfied if the data are to be analysed with the help of Multiple Correlation.

- There must be at least three Variables of which one should be Criterion or Dependent Variable and others should be the predictors.
- All predictors must be significantly correlated with the Criterion or

Dependent Variable and the Correlation must be linear.

- All Variables are Normally distributed.
- The Scale of Measurement of all Variables must be either Interval Scale or Ratio Scale.

WHEN TO USE

Example-I

How to Write Objective for Multiple Correlation

The Objective can be worded as given below:

- To study the joint contribution of Self-efficacy and Emotional Competence in predicting Burnout of Teachers.

How to Formulate Hypothesis

The Hypothesis should be formulated in the Null Form as given below:

- There is no significant joint contribution of Self-efficacy and Emotional Competence in predicting Burnout of Teachers.

Statistical Technique Used for Analysing Data

For testing the Hypothesis, Multiple Correlation Technique should be used and the data can be analysed using Statistical Package for the Social Sciences (SPSS). The SPSS outputs are given in Tables 15.1 and 15.2.

Table 15.1: Model Summary

Model	*R*	*R Square*	*Adjusted R Square*	*Std. Error of the Estimate*	*Change Statistics*				
					R Square Change	*F Change*	*df1*	*df2*	*Sig. F Change*
1	.979[a]	.958	.958	8.17102	.958	3372.776	2	297	.000

a. Predictors: (Constant), emotional competence, self-efficacy

Table 15.2: ANOVA[b]

Model		*Sum of Squares*	*df*	*Mean Square*	*F*	*Sig.*
1	Regression	450370.993	2	225185.497	3372.776	.000[a]
	Residual	19829.393	297	66.766		
	Total	470200.387	299			

a. Predictors: (Constant), emotional competence, self-efficacy

b. Dependent Variable: burnout

How to Interpret the Results Given in Table 15.1

The results of Multiple Correlation should be interpreted as given below:

The Objective was to study the joint contribution of Self-efficacy and Emotional Competence in predicting Burnout of Teachers. The data were analysed with the help of Multiple Correlation and the results are given in Table 15.3.

Table 15.3: Multiple Correlation Coefficient in predicting Burnout of Teachers on the basis of their Self-efficacy and Emotional Competence

Variables	*Remark*
$R_{1(23)} = 0.979$	$p < 0.01$
1: Burnout 2: Self-efficacy 3: Emotional Competence	

From Table 15.3, it is evident that Multiple Correlation Coefficient is 0.979 which is significant at 0.01 level with df = 2/297. It indicates that the joint contribution of Self-efficacy and Emotional Competence in predicting Burnout of Teachers is significant and high. Thus, the null hypothesis that there is no significant joint contribution of Self-efficacy and Emotional Competence in predicting Burnout of Teachers is rejected. Further the joint contribution of Self-efficacy and Emotional Competence in predicting Burnout of Teachers is 95.8% which is quite high. It may, therefore, be said that there was a high significant joint contribution of Self-efficacy and Emotional Competence in predicting Burnout of Teachers.

Example-2

How to Write Objective for Multiple Correlation

The Objective can be worded as given below:

- To study the joint contribution of Resilience, Emotional Competence and Burnout in predicting Self-efficacy of Teachers.

How to Formulate Hypothesis

The Hypothesis should be formulated in the Null Form as given below:

- There is no significant joint contribution of Resilience, Emotional Competence and Burnout in predicting Self-efficacy of Teachers.

Statistical Technique Used for Analysing Data

For testing the Hypothesis, Multiple Correlation Technique should be used and the data can be analysed using Statistical Package for the Social Sciences (SPSS).The SPSS outputs are given in Tables 15.4 and 15.5.

Table 15.4: Model Summary

Model	*R*	*R Square*	*Adjusted R Square*	*Std. Error of the Estimate*	*Change Statistics*				
					R Square Change	*F Change*	*df1*	*df2*	*Sig. F Change*
1	.984[a]	.969	.969	4.43024	.969	3067.806	3	296	.000

a. Predictors: (Constant), resilience, emotional competence, burnout

Table 15.5: ANOVA[b]

Model	Sum of Squares	df	Mean Square	F	Sig.
1 Regression	180635.682	3	60211.894	3067.806	.000a
Residual	5809.598	296	19.627		
Total	186445.280	299			

a. Predictors: (Constant), resilience, emotional competence, burnout
b. Dependent Variable: self-efficacy

How to Interpret the Result Given in Table 15.4

The results of Multiple Correlation should be interpreted as given below:

The Objective was to study the joint contribution of Resilience, Emotional Competence and Burnout in predicting Self-efficacy of Teachers. The data were analysed with the help of Multiple Correlation and the results are given in Table 15.6.

Table 15.6: Multiple Correlation Coefficient in predicting Self-efficacy of Teachers on the basis of their Resilience, Emotional Competence and Burnout

Variables	Remark
$R_{1(234)} = 0.984$ 1: Self-efficacy 2: Resilience 3: Emotional Competence 4. Burnout	p<0.01

From Table 15.6, it is evident that Multiple Correlation Coefficient is 0.984 which is significant at 0.01 level with df = 3/296. It indicates that the joint contribution of Resilience, Emotional Competence and Burnout in predicting Self-efficacy of Teachers is significant and high. Thus, the null hypothesis that there is no significant joint contribution of Resilience, Emotional Competence and Burnout in predicting Self-efficacy of Teachers is rejected. Further the joint contribution of Resilience, Emotional Competence and Burnout in predicting Self-efficacy of Teachers is 96.9% which is quite high. It may, therefore, be said that there was a high significant joint contribution of Resilience, Emotional Competence and Burnout in predicting Self-efficacy of Teachers.

Take a Test

1. The Multiple Correlation is represented by
   A) R B) r C) ρ D) None of the above.
2. Minimum number of variables required for Multiple Correlation is
   A) 2 B) 3 C) 4 D) Any number.
3. Which of the following is the correct wording of objective whose data may be analysed with the help of Multiple Correlation?
   A) To study the correlation among Intelligence, Study Habits and Achievement in Science of students.

B) To study the individual contribution of Intelligence and Study Habits in predicting Achievement in Science of students.
C) To study the joint contribution of Intelligence and Study Habits in predicting Achievement in Science of students.
D) To study the partial correlation between Intelligence and Achievement in Science by statistically controlling Study Habits of students.

4. In Multiple Correlation, the Scale of Measurement should be
   A) Nominal scale B) Ordinal scale
   C) Interval scale D) None of the above.
5. Which of the following is the correct wording of Null Hypothesis?
   A) There is no significant joint contribution of Intelligence and Study Habits in predicting Achievement in Science of students.
   B) There is contribution of Intelligence and Study Habits in predicting Achievement in Science of students.
   C) There is joint contribution of Intelligence and Study Habits in predicting Achievement in Science of students.
   D) All of the above.
6. Multiple Correlation can be used in
   A) Survey research. B) Experimental research.
   C) Historical research. D) Both A & B.
7. Which of the following statement is correct?
   A) In SPSS, the output of Regression Analysis gives the information about Multiple Correlation.
   B) In SPSS, the output of Correlation gives the information about Multiple Correlation.
   C) In SPSS, the output of Partial Correlation gives the information about Multiple Correlation.
   D) In SPSS, the output of One Way ANCOVA gives the information about Multiple Correlation.
8. Which of the following statement is NOT correct?
   A) Multiple Correlation Coefficient is always positive.
   B) The maximum value of Multiple Correlation coefficient is one.
   C) The maximum value of Multiple Correlation coefficient can be more than one.
   D) All of the above.
9. Which of the following statement is correct?
   A) Multiple Correlation indicates the correlation among variables.
   B) Multiple Correlation indicates the correlation of many variables separately with one variable.
   C) Multiple Correlation indicates the correlation of many variables together with one variable.
   D) None of the above
10. Which of the following is/are NOT the assumption(s) of Multiple Correlation?
   A) All predictors must be significantly correlated with the Criterion Variable.
   B) All Variables are Normally distributed.
   C) The Scale of Measurement of all Variables must be either Interval Scale or Ratio Scale.
   D) Correlation among variables may be curvilinear.

16
Regression Analysis

INTRODUCTION

By now it is evident that Multiple Correlation helps the researcher in studying the contribution of two or more variables in predicting a Dependent Variable or Criterion Variable. The researcher may be interested in finding out the individual contribution of each variable or predictor in predicting a Dependent Variable or Criterion Variable. This is very important from application point of view. In case the individual contribution of a variable in predicting the Criterion Variable is low than it may not be considered for prediction purpose. On the other hand, if the individual contribution of a Variable in predicting the Criterion Variable is high than it must be considered for prediction purpose. Take one example from daily life. It is well know that if a patient is having high BP, then doctor immediately ask him to reduce salt intake because intake of salt contributes maximum to BP. Further stress also contributes to BP but it is not easy to control. Thus, Regression Analysis can help researchers to isolate variables which contribute maximum in the prediction of a Criterion or Dependent variable. The individual contribution of each predictor in predicting the Criterion Variable or Dependent Variable is given by the Beta Coefficient. The significance of each Beta coefficient is indicated by the significance of its t-value. Hence, the significant t-value reflects that the variable contributes significantly in the prediction of the Criterion or Dependent Variable. Whenever the researcher wants to predict Criterion or Dependent Variable on the basis of two or more predictors the understanding of Regression Analysis is important. After reading this chapter, one will be able to:

- List Assumptions underlying Linear Regression Analysis.
- Write Objective whose data can be analysed with the help of Regression Analysis.
- Formulate Hypothesis correctly for the given Objective.
- Analyze data using SPSS.
- Put SPSS output in appropriate Table along with proper heading.

- Interpret the information given in the Regression Analysis Table and test the given Hypothesis.

ASSUMPTIONS OF LINEAR REGRESSION ANALYSIS

1. There must be at least two variables each having measurement either on Interval Scale or Ratio Scale.
2. For each variable, the sample size must be at least 20 subjects/cases.
3. The Dependent Variable or Criterion Variable should have linear correlation with each predictor.
4. There should be no outliers since Linear Regression is sensitive to outlier effects.
5. Each Variable taken up for Linear Regression should be normally distributed in the population.
6. There should be little or no multicollinearity in the data. In other words predictors should be independent of each other.
7. There should be little or no autocorrelation in the data.
8. There should be homoscedasticity. That is, the variance of error is the same across all levels of Predictors.

WHEN TO USE

Example-I

How to Write Objective for Regression Analysis

The Objective should be worded as given below so that data can be analysed with the help of Regression Analysis:

1. To study the individual contribution of Self-efficacy and Emotional Competence in predicting Burnout of Teachers.
2. To establish Regression Equation for predicting Burnout of Teachers on the basis of their Self-efficacy and Emotional Competence.

How to Formulate Hypothesis

The Hypothesis should be formulated in the Null Form as given below:

- There is no significant individual contribution of Self-efficacy and Emotional Competence in predicting Burnout of Teachers.

Note: *For Objective 2, there cannot be any hypothesis as Regression Equation is to be established but its significance cannot be judged or tested.*

Statistical Technique Used for Analysing Data

For testing the hypothesis, Regression Analysis Technique should be used and the data can be analysed using Statistical Package for the Social Sciences (SPSS). The SPSS outputs are given in Table 16.1.

Table 16.1: Coefficients[a]

Model	Unstandardized Coefficients		Standardized Coefficients	t	Sig.	Correlations		
	B	Std. Error	Beta			Zero-order	Partial	Part
1 (Constant)	221.939	1.508		147.207	.000			
Self-efficacy	-1.454	.024	-.915	-60.843	.000	-.976	-.962	-.725
Emotional Competence	-.083	.013	-.099	-6.561	.000	-.657	-.356	-.078

a. Dependent Variable: burnout

How to Interpret the Results Given in Table 16.1:

The results of Regression Analysis in respect of Objective 1, namely, individual contribution of Predictors in predicting Criterion Variable should be interpreted as given below:

Individual Contribution of Self-efficacy and Emotional Competence in predicting Burnout of Teachers

The Objective was to study the individual contribution of Self-efficacy and Emotional Competence in predicting Burnout of Teachers. The data were analysed with the help of Regression Analysis and the results are given in Table 16.2.

Table 16.2: Percentage of individual contribution of Self-efficacy and Emotional Competence in predicting Burnout of Teachers

Predictor	Beta Coefficient	t-value	% contribution
Self-efficacy	– 0.915	60.84**	89.30
Emotional Competence	– 0.099	6.56**	6.50

**Significant at 0.01 level.

From Table 16.2, it can be seen that Beta coefficients for Self-efficacy and Emotional Competence are – 0.915 and – 0.099 respectively which are negative and significant at 0.01 level. It indicates that Self-efficacy and Emotional Competence individually contribute significantly in the prediction of Burnout of Teachers. Thus, the null hypothesis that there is no significant individual contribution of Self-efficacy and Emotional Competence in predicting Burnout of Teachers is rejected. Since Beta Coefficients are negative, it shows that both Self-efficacy and Emotional Competence help in reducing Burnout of Teachers. Further the individual contribution of Self-efficacy and Emotional Competence in predicting Burnout of Teachers is 89.30% and 6.50%, respectively. The contribution of Emotional Competence in predicting Burnout of Teachers is 6.50% which is too small. It may, therefore, be said that the best predictor of Burnout of Teachers was found to be Self-efficacy of Teachers.

Regression Equation for predicting Burnout on the Basis of Self-efficacy and Emotional Competence of Teachers

The Objective was to establish Regression Equation for predicting Burnout on the basis Self-efficacy and Emotional Competence of Teachers. The data were analysed with the help of Regression Analysis and the results are given in Table 16.3.

Table 16.3: Regression Equation for predicting Burnout on the basis of Self-efficacy and Emotional Competence of Teachers

$$Y = -1.45\,X_1 - 0.08\,X_2 + 221.94$$

Y = Burnout of Teachers
X_1 = Self-efficacy of Teachers
X_2 = Emotional Competence of Teachers

The Regression Equation given in Table 16.3 can be used for predicting Burnout of Teachers on the basis of Self-efficacy and Emotional Competence of Teachers. For using this Regression Equation, the user should get scores of Teachers in respect of Self-efficacy and Emotional Competence by administering the same tools as used in this study.

Example–2

How to Write Objective for Regression Analysis

The Objective should be worded as given below so that data can be analysed with the help of Regression Analysis:

3. To study the individual contribution of Resilience, Emotional Competence and Burnout in predicting Self-efficacy of Teachers.
4. To establish Regression Equation for predicting Self-efficacy of Teachers on the basis of their Resilience, Emotional Competence and Burnout.

How to Formulate Hypothesis

The Hypothesis should be formulated in the Null Form as given below:

- There is no significant individual contribution of Resilience, Emotional Competence and Burnout in predicting Self-efficacy of Teachers.

NOTE: For objective 4, there cannot be any hypothesis as Regression Equation is to be established but its significance cannot be judged.

Statistical Technique Used for Analysing Data

For testing the Hypothesis, Regression Analysis Technique should be used and the data can be analysed using Statistical Package for the Social Sciences (SPSS). The SPSS outputs are given in Tables 16.4.

Table 16.4: Coefficients[a]

Model	Unstandardised Coefficients B	Unstandardised Coefficients Std. Error	Standardised Coefficients Beta	t	Sig.	Correlations Zero-order	Correlations Partial	Correlations Part
1 (Constant)	88.676	4.836		18.336	.000			
Emotional Competence	–.019	.007	–.037	–2.689	.008	.610	–.154	–.028
Burnout	–.447	.018	–.709	–24.963	.000	–.976	–.823	–.256
Resilience	.302	.025	.316	12.110	.000	.947	.576	.124

a. Dependent Variable: self-efficacy

How to Interpret the Results given in Table 16.4

The results of Regression Analysis in respect of Objective 3, namely, individual contribution of Predictors in predicting Criterion Variable should be interpreted as given below:

Individual Contribution of Resilience, Emotional Competence and Burnout in predicting Self-efficacy of Teachers

The Objective was to study the individual contribution of Resilience, Emotional Competence, and Burnout in predicting Self-efficacy of Teachers. The data were analysed with the help of Regression Analysis and the results are given in Table 16.5.

Table 16.5: Percentage of individual contribution of Resilience, Emotional Competence, and Burnout in predicting Self-efficacy of Teachers

Predictor	*Beta Coefficient*	*t-value*	*% contribution*
Resilience	–0.037	2.69**	–2.26
Emotional Competence	–0.709	24.96**	69.20
Burnout	0.316	12.11**	29.92

**Significant at 0.01 level

From Table 16.5, it can be seen that Beta coefficients for Resilience, Emotional Competence and Burnout are – 0.037, – 0.709 and 0.316 respectively which are significant at 0.01 level. The contribution of Resilience and Emotional Competence is negative while it is positive in case of Burnout. It indicates that Resilience, Emotional Competence and Burnout individually contribute significantly in the prediction of Self-efficacy of Teachers. Thus, the null hypothesis that there is no significant individual contribution of Resilience, Emotional Competence and Burnout in predicting Self-efficacy of Teachers is rejected. Since Beta Coefficients for Resilience and Emotional Competence are negative but it is positive in case of Burnout, it shows that both Resilience and Emotional Competence help in reducing

Self-efficacy of Teachers. The individual contribution of Resilience, Emotional Competence and Burnout in predicting Self-efficacy of Teachers is – 2.26 %, 69.20% and 29.92%, respectively. The contribution of Resilience in predicting Self-efficacy of Teachers is negative and too low. But the individual contribution of Emotional Competence in predicting Self-efficacy of Teachers is 69.20% which is the highest. Lastly, the individual contribution of Burnout in predicting Self-efficacy of Teachers is 29.92 which is moderate. It may, therefore, be said that the best predictor of Self-efficacy of Teachers was found to be Emotional Competence of Teachers followed by Burnout of Teachers.

Regression Equation for predicting Self-efficacy on the Basis of Resilience, Emotional Competence and Burnout of Teachers

The Objective was to establish Regression Equation for predicting *Self-efficacy* on the basis Resilience, Emotional Competence and Burnout of Teachers. The data were analysed with the help of Regression Analysis and the results are given in Table 16.6.

Table 16.6: Regression Equation for predicting Self-efficacy on the basis of Resilience, Emotional Competence and Burnout of Teachers

$$Y = 0.302\,X_1 - 0.019\,X_2 - 0.447\,X_3 + 88.676$$

Y = Self-efficacy of Teachers
X_1 = Resilience of Teachers
X_2 = Emotional Competence of Teachers
X_3 = Burnout of Teachers

The Regression Equation given in Table 16.6 can be used for predicting Self-efficacy of Teachers on the basis of Resilience, Emotional Competence and Burnout of Teachers. For using this Regression Equation, the user should get scores of teachers in respect of Resilience, Emotional Competence and Burnout by administering the same tools as used in this study.

Take a Test

1. In regression, the equation that describes how the response variable (y) is related to the explanatory variable (x) is:
   A) The Correlation model
   B) The Regression model
   C) Used to compute the correlation coefficient.
   D) None of the given alternative is correct.
2. In Regression equation, the variable that is being predicted is the
   A) Response or the dependent variable. B) Independent variable.
   C) Intervening variable. D) None of the above.
3. In Regression Analysis, the variable that is used to explain the change in the outcome of an experiment, or some natural process, is called
   A) Independent variable B) Predictor variable
   C) Explanatory variable D) All the above

4. In the case of an algebraic model for a straight line, if a value for the x variable is specified, then
   A) Exact value of the response variable can be computed.
   B) The computed response to the independent value will always give a minimal residual
   C) The computed value of y will always be the best estimate of the mean response.
   D) None of the above responses
5. A regression analysis is inappropriate when
   A) you have two variables that are measured on an interval or ratio scale.
   B) you want to make predictions for one variable based on information about another variable.
   C) the pattern of data points form a reasonably straight line.
   D) there is heteroscedasticity in the scatter plot.
6. The line described by the regression equation attempts to
   A) pass through as many points as possible.
   B) pass through as few points as possible.
   C) minimize the squared distance from the points.
   D) minimize the number of points it touches.
7. What does it mean to say that there is error in our regression?
   A) We calculated it wrong.
   B) There were data entry errors.
   C) We cannot predict Y perfectly.
   D) All data points fall on a straight line.
8. If we use more than one predictor to predict our criterion at the same time,
   A) we are no longer doing statistics.
   B) we are conducting multiple regression and there are established ways of determining which predictor is the best.
   C) we are conducting multiple regression and there are no established ways of determining which predictor is the best.
   D) the predictors will always suffer from heteroscedasticity.
9. For using Regression Analysis, one should have minimum——Variable(s)
   A) One B) Two C) Three D) Any number
10. Regression modeling is a statistical framework for developing a mathematical equation that describes how
    A) one explanatory and one or more response variables are related
    B) several explanatory and several response variables response are related
    C) one response and one or more explanatory variables are related
    D) All of these are correct.
11. A fitted least square regression line
    A) May be used to predict a value of y if the corresponding x value is given.
    B) Is evidence for a cause-effect relationship between x and y.
    C) Can only be computed if a strong linear relationship exists between x and y.
    D) None of these alternatives is correct.
12. A statistical technique that develops an equation that relates a dependent variable to one or more independent variables is called:
    A) Correlation analysis B) Regression analysis
    C) Partial correlation analysis D) All of the above.

17
Chi-Square Test

INTRODUCTION

Relationship is a general word. People use it in day-to-day life and they understand it. The statistical words for relationship are Correlation and Association. It is clear that correlation between variables exist because of commonness. In day-to-day life, the gray colour of hair is associated with the age of the person but there is no commonness between Colour of Hair and Age. In case one sees a lady with brown hair, he thinks that she is a foreigner. In this case the Hair Colour is associated with the Citizenship of the person. In research people may study the association between two variables. One of the Statistical Technique used for studying association between variables is Chi-Square Test. After reading this chapter, the reader will be able to:

- List Assumptions underlying Chi-Square Test.
- Name the year and person who invented Chi-Square Test.
- Tell the use of Chi-Square Goodness of fit test.
- List uses of Chi-Square Test.
- Write Objective whose data can be analysed with the help of Chi-Square Test.
- Formulate Hypothesis correctly for the given Objective.
- Analyze data using SPSS.
- Put SPSS output in appropriate Table along with proper heading.
- Interpret the information given in the Chi-Square Test Table and test the given Hypothesis.

ASSUMPTIONS OF CHI-SQUARE TEST

The data must satisfy the following assumptions of the Chi-Square Test:

1. The data in the cells should be frequencies, or counts of cases rather than percentages or some other transformation of the data.
2. The levels (or categories) of the variables are mutually exclusive. That is, a particular subject fits into one and only one level of each of the variables.
3. Each subject may contribute data to one and only one cell in the χ^2. If,

for example, the same subjects are tested over time such that the comparisons are of the same subjects at Time 1, Time 2, Time 3, etc., then χ^2 may not be used.

4. The study groups must be independent. This means that a different test must be used if the two groups are related. For example, a different test must be used if the researcher's data consists of paired samples, such as in studies in which a parent is paired with his or her child.
5. There are two variables, and both are measured as categories, usually at the nominal level. However, data may be ordinal data. Interval or ratio data that have been collapsed into ordinal categories may also be used. While Chi-square has no rule about limiting the number of cells (by limiting the number of categories for each variable), a very large number of cells (over 20) can make it difficult to meet assumption #6 below, and to interpret the meaning of the results.
6. The value of the cell *expected* should be 5 or more in at least 80% of the cells, and no cell should have an expected of less than one. This assumption is most likely to be met if the sample size equals at least the number of cells multiplied by 5. Essentially, this assumption specifies the number of cases (sample size) needed to use the χ^2.

NAME OF INVENTOR

One Statistical Technique that can be used when data are on Nominal Scale is Chi-Square Test. Chi-Square properties were first investigated by Karl Pearson in 1900. It can be used to study the association between variables whose data are on Nominal Scale. The *Chi-square* test is intended to test how likely it is that an observed distribution is due to chance. It is also called a "goodness of fit" statistic, because it measures how well the observed distribution of data fits with the distribution that is expected if the variables are independent. The *Chi-square test* is applied when there are two categorical variables from a single population. It is used to determine whether there is a significant association between the two variables. The Chi-Square is denoted by χ^2.

USE OF CHI-SQUARE GOODNESS OF FIT TEST

The purpose of Chi-square Goodness of Fit Test is used to decide whether there is any difference between the observed (experimental) value and the expected (theoretical) value. For example given a sample, one may like to test if it has been drawn from a normal population.

The Chi-square *goodness* of fit test is appropriate when the following conditions are met:

- The sampling method is Random Sampling.
- The variable under study is categorical.

- The expected value of the number of sample observations in each level of the variable is at least 5.

USES OF CHI-SQUARE TEST

The following are the uses of Chi-Square Test:

- A Chi-square (χ^2) statistic is used to investigate whether distributions of categorical variables differ from one another. Basically categorical variable yield data in the categories and numerical variables yield data in numerical form.
- The *Chi-square* test is intended to test how likely it is that an observed distribution is due to chance. It is also called a "goodness of fit" statistic, because it measures how well the observed distribution of data fits with the distribution that is expected if the variables are independent.
- The *Chi-Square test of Independence* is used to determine if there is a significant relationship between two nominal (categorical) variables. The frequency of one nominal variable is compared with different values of the second nominal variable.

WHEN TO USE

Example–I

How to Write Objective for Chi-Square Test

The Objective should be worded as given below so that data can be analysed with the help of Chi-Square Test:

- To study the association between Types of Hospital and Educational Qualification of Nurses.

How to Formulate Hypothesis

The Hypothesis should be formulated in the Null Form as given below:

- There is no significant association between Types of Hospital and Educational Qualification of Nurses.

Statistical Technique Used for Analysing Data

The data were analysed with the help of Chi-Square Test using SPSS. The SPSS outputs are given in Tables 17.1 and 17.2.

Table 17.1: 2 * 2 Cross Tabulation

Count

		2		*Total*
		Diploma	*Graduation*	
2	Government Hospital	109	41	150
	Private Hospital	104	46	150
Total		**213**	**87**	**300**

Table 17.2: Chi-Square Tests

	Value	*Df*	*Asymp. Sig. (2-sided)*	*Exact Sig. (2-sided)*	*Exact Sig. (1-sided)*
Pearson Chi-Square	.405[a]	1	.525		
Continuity Correction[b]	.259	1	.611		
Likelihood Ratio	.405	1	.525		
Fisher's Exact Test				.611	.305
Linear-by-Linear Association	.403	1	.525		
N of Valid Cases	300				

a. 0 cells (.0%) have expected count less than 5. The minimum expected count is 43.50.
b. Computed only for a 2x2 table

How to Interpret the Results Given in Table 17.2

The results of Chi-Square Test in respect of Objective 1, namely, to study the association between Types of Hospital and Educational Qualification of Nurses should be interpreted as given below:

Association between Types of Hospital and Educational Qualification of Nurses

The objective was to study association between Types of Hospital and Qualification of Nurses. There were two Types of Hospital, namely, Government Hospital and Private Hospital. There were two levels of Educational Qualification namely, Diploma Holders and Degree Holders. The data were analysed with the help of Chi-Square Test and the results are given in Table 17.3.

Table 17.3: Type of Hospital and Qualification-wise observed frequencies and Chi-Square value

Type of Hospital	*Diploma Holders*	*Degree Holders*	*Chi-Square Value*
Government Hospital	109	41	0.40
Private Hospital	104	46	

From Table 17.3, it can be seen that the Chi-Square value is 0.40 which is not significant. It indicates that there is no significant association between Types of Hospital and Qualification of Nurses. Thus, the Null Hypothesis that there is no significant association between Types of Hospital and Qualification of Nurses is not rejected. It may, therefore, be said the Types of Hospital and Qualification of Nurses were found to be independent of each other.

Example–2

The researcher teaches Mathematics through Computer Aided Instruction (CAI) to class IX students of Government Higher Secondary School, Qutab Minar, New Delhi. He wants to study the Reaction towards usefulness of CAI of Male as well as Female students. The Objective was worded as given below:

- To study association between Gender and Reaction towards usefulness of CAI of students.

How to Formulate Hypothesis

The Hypothesis should be formulated in the Null Form as given below:

- There is no significant association between Gender and Reaction towards usefulness of CAI of students.

Statistical Technique Used for Analysing Data

The data were analysed with the help of Chi-Square Test using SPSS. The SPSS outputs are given in Tables 17.4 and 17.5.

Table 17.4: 2 * 5 Cross Tabulation

Count

		5					*Total*
		Strongly Agree	*Agree*	*Undecided*	*Disagree*	*Strongly Disagree*	
2	Male students	24	34	7	15	11	91
	Female students	18	17	9	20	22	86
Total		**42**	**51**	**16**	**35**	**33**	**177**

Table 17.5: Chi-Square Tests

	Value	*df*	*Asymp. Sig. (2-sided)*
Pearson Chi-Square	11.022[a]	4	.026
Likelihood Ratio	11.201	4	.024
Linear-by-Linear Association	7.944	1	.005
N of Valid Cases	177		

a. 0 cells (.0%) have expected count less than 5. The minimum expected count is 7.77.

How to Interpret the Result Given in Table 17.5

The result of Chi-Square Test in respect of Objective 2, namely, to study association between Gender and Reaction towards usefulness of CAI of students should be interpreted as given below:

Association between Gender and Reaction towards usefulness of CAI of students

The objective was to study association between Gender and Reaction towards usefulness of CAI of students. There were two levels of Gender, namely, Male and Female. There were five levels of Reaction towards usefulness of CAI namely, Strongly Agree (SA), Agree (A), Undecided (U), Disagree (D) and Strongly Disagree (SD). The data were analysed with the help of Chi-Square Test and the results are given in Table 17.6.

Table 17.6: Gender and Reaction towards usefulness of CAI of students-wise observed frequencies and Chi-Square value

Gender	*SA*	*A*	*U*	*D*	*SD*	*Chi-Square Value*	*Remark*
Male	24	34	7	15	11	11.02	$p < 0.05$
Female	18	17	9	20	22		

From Table 17.6 it is evident that the Chi-Square value is 11.02 which is significant at 0.05 level with df = 4. It shows that Reaction towards usefulness of CAI of Male and Female students differ significantly. So there was a significant association between Gender and Reaction towards usefulness of CAI of students. Thus, the null hypothesis that there is no significant association between Gender and Reaction towards usefulness of CAI of students is rejected. Further majority of Male students had favourable Reaction towards usefulness of CAI as compared to Female students. It may, therefore, be said that Male students found CAI to more useful than Female students.

Take a Test

1. In SPSS, the output of Regression Analysis gives the information about Multiple Correlation and
   A) p-value B) Null Hypothesis
   C) Chi-square D) Alternative Hypothesis.
2. When they need an objective way to determine how well frequencies predicted by a theory match the observed data, researchers should utilise a(n) _____.
   A) ANCOVA B) Goodness-of-fit Test
   C) Negative inference D) Independent Samples t-Test.
3. Ram is getting ready to go home from the office. When deciding which of two routes to take home, he must consider issues such as traffic, construction, and mileage. In other words, Ram's decision will involve a(n) _____.
   A) Goodness-of-fit Test B) Negative inference
   C) Chi-Square Test D) Operational Definition.
4. The term "Statistical independence" means————.
   A) A study has more than one independent variable.
   B) The Null Hypothesis is correct.
   C) The Alternate Hypothesis is correct.
   D) There is no relationship between two variables.
5. In general, the expected frequencies per cell in the conduct of a Chi-Square test are those one would
   A) Expect to find in a given cell if the null hypothesis was actually true.
   B) Expect to find in a given cell if the alternative hypothesis was actually true.
   C) Expect to find in a given cell if null hypothesis was actually false.
   D) Expect to find in a given cell if either the null hypothesis or the alternate hypothesis was actually true.

6. The degree of freedom for Chi-Square test statistic when testing for independence in a contingency table with 4 rows and 4 columns is
   A) 9 B) 12
   C) 5 D) 7.
7. Each of the following accurately represents characteristics of the Chi-Square distribution except for
   A) As the degree of freedom increase, the critical value of Chi-Square distribution becomes larger.
   B) The region of rejection is always in the left-tail of the Chi-Square distribution.
   C) It is positively skewed distribution.
   D) Its shape depends on the number of degree of freedom.
8. The null hypothesis for the Chi-Square test of independence should specify
   A) That the two numerical variables are independent.
   B) That the two numerical variables are dependent.
   C) That the two categorical variables are independent.
   D) That the two categorical variables are dependent.
9. Which of the following value of the Chi-Square would be most likely to suggest that the null hypothesis is really true?
   A) 0.3251 B) 23.7183
   C) 14.9728 D) 18.4335.
10. To determine whether a set of observed frequencies differ from their corresponding expected frequency, one can apply
    A) t-test for independent samples B) Chi-Square test
    C) F-Test D) t-test for dependent samples.
11. The Chi-square test can be used for testing
    A) Independence B) Equality of proportions
    C) Equality of medians D) All of the above

18
Mann-Whitney U Test

INTRODUCTION

It has been explained that t-Test can be used to compare mean scores of a variable of two independent groups when the data satisfy the assumptions of normal distribution, homogeneity of variance and data should be either on Interval Scale or Ratio Scale. In case the data do not satisfy the assumption of Normal distribution, t-test cannot be used. The most appropriate statistical technique to use in such a situation is Mann-Whitney U Test. It is one of the most powerful non-parametric statistics, designed to test the null hypothesis that two independent samples come from the same population. This test is analogous to the parametric t-test for independent samples. Like the unpaired t-test, the U test does not require that groups be of the same size. It is, therefore, an excellent alternative to t-test when parametric assumptions are not met. After reading this chapter one will be able to:

- Tell when to use Mann-Whitney U test.
- List assumptions underlying Mann-Whitney U test.
- Write Objective whose data can be analysed with the help of Mann-Whitney U test.
- Formulate Hypothesis correctly for the given Objective.
- Analyse data using SPSS.
- Put SPSS output in appropriate Table along with proper heading.
- Interpret the information given in the Mann-Whitney U test Table and test the given Hypothesis.

WHEN TO USE MANN-WHITNEY U TEST

Thus, the *Mann-Whitney U test* is used to compare differences between two independent groups when the dependent variable or criterion variable is either ordinal or continuous, but not normally distributed. In statistics, the *Mann–Whitney U test* is also called the *Mann–Whitney*–Wilcoxon (MWW), Wilcoxon rank-sum *test*, or Wilcoxon–*Mann–Whitney test*. It is a Non-parametric test for testing the null hypothesis.

ASSUMPTIONS OF MANN-WHITNEY U TEST

The assumptions underlying the use of *Mann–Whitney U test* are as follows:

- One variable that consists of two categorical, independent groups (i.e., a dichotomous variable). For example Gender (two groups: "males" or "females"), employment status (two groups: "employed" or "unemployed"), transport type (two groups: "bus" or "car"), smoker (two groups: "yes" or "no"), trial (two groups: "intervention" or "control"), and so forth.
- One dependent or criterion variable that is measured at the continuous or ordinal level. Examples of continuous variables include revision time (measured in hours), intelligence (measured using IQ score), exam performance (measured from 0 to 100), weight (measured in kg), and so forth. Examples of ordinal variables include Likert items (e.g., a 5-point scale from "Strongly Agree" through to "Strongly Disagree"), amongst other ways of ranking categories (e.g., a 5-point scale explaining how much a customer liked a product, ranging from "Not very much" to "Yes, a lot").
- There should be no relationship between the observations in each group of the moderate variable or between the groups themselves. For example, there must be different participants in each group with no participant being in more than one group.
- Scale of measurement should be Ordinal.
- For maximum accuracy, there should be no ties, though this test—like others—has a way to handle ties

Example–I

How to Write Objective for Mann-Whitney U Test

The Objective should be worded as given below so that data can be analysed with the help of Mann-Whitney U Test:

- To compare mean ranks of Stress of Male and Female Parents.

How to Formulate Hypothesis

The Hypothesis should be formulated in the Null Form as given below:

- There is no significant difference between mean ranks of Stress of Male and Female Parents.

Statistical Technique Used for Analysing Data

The data were analysed with the help of Mann-Whitney U test using SPSS and the outputs are given in Tables 18.1 and 18.2.

Table 18.1: Ranks

	2	N	*Mean Rank*	*Sum of Ranks*
Total Stress	Male	14	24.21	339.00
	Female	43	30.56	1314.00
	Total	**57**		

Table 18.2: Test Statistics[a]

	Total Stress
Mann-Whitney U	234.000
Wilcoxon W	339.000
Z	–1.243
Asymp. Sig. (2-tailed)	.214

a. Grouping Variable: 2

How to Interpret the Results Given in Tables 18.1 and 18.2

The results of Mann-Whitney U Test in respect of Objective, namely, to compare mean ranks of Stress of Male and Female Parents should be interpreted as given below:

Gender-Wise Comparison of Mean Ranks of Stress

The Objective was to compare mean ranks of Stress of Male and Female Parents. The data were analysed with the help of Mann-Whitney U test. The results are given in Table 18.3.

Table 18.3: Gender-wise Mean Ranks, N and Mann-Whitney U-value of Stress Parents

Gender	*Mean Ranks*	*N*	*Mann-Whitney U-value*
Male	24.21	14	234.00
Female	30.56	43	

From Table 18.3, it can be seen that the Mann-Whitney U-value is 234.00 which is not significant. It indicates that the mean ranks of Stress of Male and Female Parents do not differ significantly. Thus, the Null Hypothesis that there is no significant difference in mean ranks of Stress of Male and Female Parents is not rejected. It may, therefore, be said that both Male and Female Parents were found to have stress to the same extent.

Example–2

How to Write Objective for Mann-Whitney U Test

The Objective should be worded as given below so that data can be analysed with the help of Mann-Whitney U Test:

- To compare mean ranks of Adaptive Behaviour of members belonging to Joint and Nuclear Families.

How to Formulate Hypothesis

The Hypothesis should be formulated in the Null Form as given below:

There is no significant difference between mean ranks of Adaptive Behaviour of members belonging to Joint and Nuclear Families.

Statistical Technique Used for Analysing Data

The data were analysed with the help of Mann-Whitney U test using SPSS and the outputs are given in Tables 18.4, and 18.5.

Table 18.4: Ranks

	2	*N*	*Mean Rank*	*Sum of Ranks*
Adaptive Behaviour	Joint Family	20	36.48	729.50
	Nuclear Family	37	24.96	923.50
	Total	**57**		

Table 18.5: Test Statistics[a]

	Adaptive Behaviour
Mann-Whitney U	220.500
Wilcoxon W	923.500
Z	-2.502
Asymp. Sig. (2-tailed)	.012

a. Grouping Variable: 2

How to Interpret the Result Given in Tables 18.4 and 18.5

The results of Mann-Whitney U Test in respect of Objective, namely, to compare mean ranks of Adaptive Behaviour of members belonging to Joint and Nuclear Families should be interpreted as given below:

Family Type-wise Comparison of Mean Ranks of Adaptive Behaviour

The Objective was to compare mean ranks of Adaptive Behaviour of members belonging to Joint and Nuclear Families. The data were analysed with the help of Mann-Whitney U test. The results are given in Table 18.6.

Table 18.6: Family Type-wise Mean Ranks, N and Mann-Whitney U-value of Adaptive Behaviour of Parents

Gender	*Mean Ranks*	*N*	*Mann-Whitney U-Value*	*Z-Value*	*Remark*
Joint Family	36.48	20	220.50	2.50	$p<0.01$
Nuclear Family	24.96	37			

From Table 18.6, it can be seen that the Mann-Whitney U-value is 220.50 which is significant at 0.01 level. It indicates that the mean ranks of Adaptive Behaviour of Parents of Joint Family and Nuclear Family differ significantly. Thus, the Null Hypothesis that there is no significant difference in mean ranks of

Adaptive Behaviour of Parents of Joint Family and Nuclear Family is rejected. Further, the mean rank score of Joint Family Parents is 36.48 which is significantly higher than those belonging to Nuclear Family whose mean rank score is 24.96. It may, therefore, be said that Parents of Joint Family were found to have better Adaptive Behaviour than those belonging to Nuclear Family.

Take a Test

1. The only assumptions required for the Mann-Whitney U Test are
   A) Independent Samples B) Random samples
   C) Normal population D) A and B.
2. Which of the following tests is not based on Ranks?
   A) Friedman Test B) Mann-Whitney U Test
   C) Wald-Wolfowitz Test D) Kruskal-Wallis Test.
3. Of the below Non-parametric tests, which relies on the calculation of ranks?
   A) Spearmen's Rho B) Mann-Whitney U Test
   C) Wilcoxon Matched Pair Test D) All of the above.
4. The ....test is calculated by ranking all of the participants scores from lowest to highest and adding up the ranks separately for each condition.
   A) Mann-Whitney U Test B) Spearman's Rho
   C) Friedman's One Way ANOVA D) Pearson's r.
5. The non-parametric equivalent of an unpaired samples t-test is
   A) Sign test B) Wilcoxon signed rank test
   C) Mann-Whitney U-Test D) Chi-square test
6. Mann-Whitney U Test is preferred to t-test when
   A) Data are paired.
   B) The assumption of normality is not met.
   C) Sample sizes are small.
   D) Samples are dependent.
7. In Mann-Whitney U Test the Scale of Measurement of dependent variable or criterion variable is
   A) Nominal Scale B) Ordinal Scale
   C) Interval scale D) B or C.
8. In Mann-Whitney U Test, one variable must be discontinuous having .... categories.
   A) 2 B) 3
   C) 4 D) 5.
9. Which of the following statements is correct?
   A) The assumptions of t-test and Mann-Whitney U Test are same.
   B) The assumptions of t-test and Mann-Whitney U Test are not same.
   C) Mann-Whitney U Test is parametric test.
   D) None of the above.
10. If you have independent samples of ranked data which non-parametric statistic should you use?
    A) One way ANOVA B) Chi-Square
    C) Spearman Rho D) Mann–Whitney U Test

19

Writing of Thesis or Research Report

INTRODUCTION

Researches are being conducted to find Solutions to Problems which may be of Social, Educational, Psychological, Physical, Biological etc. in nature. Solutions thus found add to the existing quantum of knowledge. This is how knowledge grows in a particular area. The researchers should not retain the findings to themself. They must disseminate the newer information through writing a research thesis or report or paper. Thus, writing a research thesis or report or paper is an essential part of any research through which a researcher tries to convey the findings of his research to his fellow researchers. But writing a thesis or report or paper is technical in nature which differs from other narrative writings. It follows certain set pattern, rules and conventions which the researcher must follow in order to communicate his ideas effectively. Although variations are found in these patterns from institution to institution and sometime from researcher to researcher but institutions or individuals should strictly follow the pattern set for them. A researcher who does not consistently follow one pattern adds only confusion to his communication. In this chapter, attempts are made to present a logical and popularly followed pattern of writing a research thesis or report. After reading this chapter the researcher will be able to:

- List the salient features involved in writing a Research Report or Thesis.
- Name different chapters in proper sequence.
- Write captions under which the information is to be given under different chapters.

SALIENT FEATURES OF WRITING RESEARCH REPORT OR THESIS

Before writing the actual Research Report or Thesis, the researcher should bear in mind the following points.

Language and Style

The primary virtues of scientific writing are simplicity, accuracy, conciseness, clarity and directness. Researcher should avoid unnecessary words. His presentation should be clear, intelligent, scholarly and economical. He should know what he has to say and then he should say it in most direct way possible and stop. The sentence should be exact and as simple as possible. Such as writing "… although the losses in the body weight were very small, there were some and they constitute about 2% of the initial weights" is incorrect. Scientifically it may be written as, "the losses in the body weight were 2% of the initial body weight." In scientific writing there is no place for a lot of words signifying little, because additional words only confuse the meaning that is to be conveyed. The researcher should avoid sophisticated expressions. Some examples are given below:

Incorrect	*Correct*
As far as researchers own observations are concerned, they show the treatment having being performed….	Researcher's observations show after treatment….
There can be little doubt that this is ….	This probably is….
Throughout the whole of the experiment ….	Throughout the experiment….
It is possible that the cause is the ….	The cause may be the….

Longer and unusual terms should be avoided when shorter and more commonly used terms are available. Such as:

Longer Term	*Shorter Term*
….during the time that….	….while….
….from the stand point of….	….according to….
….in all cases….	….always….
….in order to….	….to….
….in terms of….	….in….
….in view of the fact….	….since, because….
….for the reason that….	….because….
….at the present time….	….now or at present….

The researcher should avoid sentences containing several ideas. Brief sentence is preferable to one or two very long ones. When a complex sentence is unavoidable, the researcher should place the basic referent in the beginning. For example, one should not write: "In order to eradicate the ills of present teacher training programme, Microteaching Technique is being advocated." Here the referent is Microteaching technique so it should be placed in the beginning of the sentence and should be written as "Microteaching technique is advocated to eradicate the ills of present teacher training programme."

Precision

Another important aspect of research writing is precision. There is no place in research writing for indefinite antecedents or incomplete comparison. For example, in a research thesis or report comparing three methods of teaching, the researcher wrote "The students in the Programmed Learning Group achieved significantly, while the students in the Discussion Group lost significantly, and the students in the Control Group did not change." This is confusing. Here researcher should clearly write as: "The Programmed Learning Group achieved significantly higher in comparison to Discussion and Control Groups."

Indefinite terms of quality, quantity or frequency, like, many, often, good, normal, few, majority, etc. should not be used in the research writing. These words convey different meaning to different readers. Therefore, the researcher should use definite number or quantity.

Another aspect of precision is the selection of meaningful level of precision for presentation of quantitative information. The level of precision employed in the quantitative data should be appropriate to its level of the data and beyond. The level of precision should be meaningful and not increase decimal places for the sake of increasing decimal places. Restrain in use of significant figures is important in reporting significant findings. To report a mean = 7.500 when this represents the average of 7.410 is misleading. In Social Sciences, it is better to report results only up to two decimals but in pure science, it depends on the sensitivity of instrument. So in science the results may be reported up to three or more decimal points.

Consistency

Researcher should maintain consistency in the use of terminology. The researcher should select one term related to a concept and use it throughout the report. One should not for the sake of variety keep on using different synonyms available in the dictionary. For example, pupil teacher, student teacher, teacher trainee, trainee, etc. mean the same but one should not use them interchangeably. One term should be selected and used throughout the writing.

In addition to consistency in terminology, the researcher should try to maintain consistency in style. If the researcher presents generalisation first and references to individual set of data afterward while discussing the result, this pattern should be maintained throughout the report.

Further the researcher should use the same style of presenting the numerical information throughout the report. For example, if the researcher writes at one place "half of the students in ..." then one should keep on reporting one third, one seventh, one ninth, one tenth etc. but not as 1/3rd, 1/7th ,1/9th , 1/10th etc. In the use of main heading, subheading, italics, comma, semicolon, no full stop after a heading or subheading, consistency is required. In the same way, there must be consistency in presenting the numerical data. If the information of mean is given in two decimals, than the researcher should keep on giving information of mean in two decimals and not in three or more decimals. Also if mean is represented by M, Standard Deviation by SD, etc. than the same should be used throughout the report.

Continuity

The entire research report or thesis should be presented in an integrated fashion. The researcher should make an effort to use connecting sentences when one changes from one idea to another, one section to another, one aspect of data analysis to a second one so that the reader does not get a feeling of a sudden jerk without any preparation. The connecting sentence may be the last sentence of a section which acts an introduction for the forthcoming section or it may be the first sentence of the new caption/section.

The continuity must be maintained in respect of presentation of information related to an idea or aspect. The complete information related to an idea or aspect must be given under one caption. It helps the reader and avoids confusion.

Use of Third Person

The writing of a research report should be impersonal. The use of words, such as, I, my, we, he, they, etc. should be avoided. The convention is to use the third person like, researcher, investigator, experimenter, etc. the word "writer" should be avoided because his role is secondary in the research report writing. Instead of writing "I developed Programmed Learning Material on Research Methodology...." One should write it as "The investigator developed Programmed Learning Material on Research Methodology...." In order to avoid the temptation of using first person, it is advised to write the report in passive voice. The use of passive voice should only be made when necessary for emphasis as it requires extra words and may not convey the intended meaning. Compare "Fungi produce antibiotic" with "antibiotics are produced by Fundi".

The passive voice here requires 25% more space.

Use of Tense

The researcher writes the report only after completion of the study. One should use the past tense in writing the report. The present tense is to be used when the numbers from the table; the trend from the graph, etc. are to be referred. While writing a research proposal, future tense is to be used because the researcher is proposing to do that.

Use of Headings

The headings enable the reader to find quickly the required information. They make the researchers plan clear to reader when arranged in the table of contents. The use of headings helps the researcher to arrange the content in logical order. The researcher must not hesitate in using many headings. The heading should be concise consisting of words or phrases, but not sentence. The researcher should compose the sentence following a heading in such a manner that the sentence is complete in meaning without the heading. If necessary, the words used in writing the heading may be repeated. For example, if the heading is "Reversible Process", the sentence below the heading may begin as "A reversible process is one in which..." But not as "It is one in which..." because grammatically heading is not a part of the paragraph. There should be no "full stop" in headings as heading is not a complete sentence.

Table of Data or Results

Table should not appear physically until some reference is made to it in the text alerting the reader as to the nature of the data to be presented. Table should be integrated into the text rather than appearing on separate pages without integrating it with the text. Tables should appear as soon as possible they are first mentioned. Two simple tables are better than one complex table. As far as possible the researcher should not give data related to more than three variables in a table. The heading of the Table should reflect the information given in it.

Top Page of Thesis or Report

It should include the Title, Partial Fulfillment of Doctorate of Philosophy in Education, name of supervisor, name of candidate, name of University and year of submission. The layout of this page should be as given below:

EFFECTIVENESS OF VIDEO INSTUCTTIONAL MATERIAL ON RESEARCH METHODOLOGY IN TERMS OF ACHIEVEMENT AND REACTION TOWARDS IT OF POSTGRADUATE STUDENTS OF JAIPUR

A THESIS SUBMITTED TO
UNIVERSITY OF RAJASTHAN, JAIPUR
FOR THE AWARD OF DEGREE OF
DOCTOR OF PHILOSOPHY IN EDUCATION

SUPERVISOR INVESTIGATOR

DEPARTMENT OF EDUCATION
UNIVERSITY OF RAJASTHAN
JAIPUR
2020

An example of the Content page is as given below:

CONTENTS

CHAPTER–II: REVIEW OF RELATED LITERATURE

2.1.0 INTRODUCTION

2.2.0 PRINT MEDIA AND ACADEMIC ACHIEVEMENT

2.3.0 AUDIO MEDIA AND ACADEMIC ACHIEVEMENT

2.4.0 AUDIO-VISUAL MATERIAL AND ACADEMIC ACHIEVEMENT

2.5.0 SUM-UP

CHAPTER-III: METHODOLOGY

3.1.0 INTRODUCTION

3.3.0 SAMPLE

3.4.0 EXPERIMENTAL DESIGN

3.5.0 DEVELOPMENT OF VIDEO INSTRUCTIONAL MATERIAL

3.6.0 TOOLS

- 3.6.1 Intelligence
- 3.6.2 Personality
- 3.6.3 Achievement
- 3.6.4 Reaction towards Video Instructional Material scale

3.7.0 PROCEDURE OF DATA COLLECTION

3.8.0 DATA ANALYSIS

CHAPTER–IV: RESULTS AND INTERPRETATION

4.1.0 INTRODUCTION

4.2.0 EFFECTIVENESS OF VIDEO INSTRUCTIONAL MATERIAL IN TERMS OF ACHIEVEMENT IN RESEARCH METHODOLOGY OF STUDENTS

4.3.0 EFFECT OF TREATMENT, GENDER AND THEIR INTERACTION ON ACHIEVEMENT IN RESEARCH METHODOLOGY OF STUDENTS

CHAPTER–V: DISCUSSION

5.1.0 INTRODUCTION

5.2.0 FINDINGS

5.3.0 COMPARISION OF VIDEO INSTRUCTIONAL MATERIAL WITH TRADITIONAL METHOD

5.4.0 EFFECT OF GENDER ON ACHIEVEMENT OF STUDENTS

5.5.0 EFFECT OF INTERACTION BETWEEN TREATMENT AND GENDER ON ACHIEVEMENT OF STUDENTS

CHAPTER–VI: SUMMARY, FINDINGS AND IMPLICATIONS

6.1.0 INTRODUCTION

6.2.0 RATIONALE

6.3.0 STATEMENT OF PROBLEM

6.4.0 OBJECTIVES

6.5.0 HYPOTHESES

6.6.0 SAMPLE

6.7.0 EXPERIMENTAL DESIGN

6.8.0 TOOLS

6.9.0 PROCEDURE OF DATA COLLECTION
6.10.0 DATA ANALYSIS
6.11.0 FINDINGS
6.12.0 IMPLICATIONS
  6.12.1 Students
  6.12.2 Teachers
  6.12.3 Principals
  6.12.4 Parents
BIBLIOGRAPHY
APPENDIX–I: ACHIEVEMENT TESTS
APPENDIX–II: REACTION TOWARDS VIDEO INSTRUCTIONAL MATERIAL SCALE

Numbering of Main and Sub Captions

In case of Main Caption, the first digit refers to the chapter. The second digit refers to the first Main Caption while the third digit refers to the sub-caption. For example, 1.1.0 means that this caption belongs to First Chapter, First main Caption and there is no sub-caption. In this 3.3.5 example, First digit indicates the third chapter. Second digit indicates the third Main Caption while 5 indicates the fifth sub-caption of Main Caption 3.

CHAPTER WRITING

The chapters should be written as given below:

Chapter–I: Introduction

The first chapter of any research thesis or report is the INTRODUCTION. Normally it should give information in respect of Fundamentals related to the topic or theoretical frame work, Rationale of Study, Statement of Problem, Definitions of Key Words if applicable; Objectives, Hypotheses if applicable; and Delimitations.

The details regarding the Rationale of the study are unavoidable in a research thesis or report writing. The reader wants to know why the study was undertaken. The researcher taps different sources for writing the Rationale of his study. The analysis of Review of Related Literature helps in writing the Rationale of the study. When one goes through the researches conducted in a particular area, one may locate gaps, a few researches are conducted, and inconsistencies in the findings. In addition one may also find the same data may be analysed differently to answer some more questions.

After writing Rationale, the researcher should write the statement of Problem. It must be written in capital letters as this is one of the main captions. It should be as given in the proposal. This statement should come without any unnecessary introduction.

Sometimes there are certain terms which may be interpreted in different ways. In such a case it is better to give an operational definition to avoid vagueness and misinterpretation. It must match with the operational definition given by the researcher whose tool one is using. It is observed that most of the researchers give many definitions which are available in books. One must note that the thesis is not a book. The operational definition is given just to understand the variable which will help at the time of writing discussion. The operational definition makes the variable observable and measureable. It will help the reader in understanding the findings of the study.

The Objectives should be written in pin-pointed manner. It should be in the sentence form. In case the researcher decides to write them in question form, the caption heading should be Research Questions. There is no need of writing both in one research report or thesis. One must avoid the use of words, such as, 'To find out…." "To investigate…." "To analyse…." "To understand...." etc. It is better to use "To study…." "To compare….".

Hypotheses should be written after the Objectives. There might be researches where Hypotheses are not required because data are qualitative and cannot be converted into quantitative. In Philosophical Research, Historical Research and Descriptive Survey Research, the data are qualitative, so no Hypothesis can be formulated. In the absence of quantitative data, the statistical technique cannot be used for analysing the data. In Correlational Survey Research and Experimental Research researcher gets quantitative data so Hypothesis should be stated as it can be tested with the help of statistical techniques. The hypothesis must be written in the present tense but not in the future tense. Even in the research proposal, hypothesis should be formulated in the present tense. This is because hypothesis is stated either on the basis of Theory underlying the study or the Review of Related Literature.

Lastly, the Delimitations must be listed. In each and every research, there are limitations but it further gets limited. So the caption heading is Delimitation. The study may be delimited in respect of sample size, variables taken, nature of study, tools used, etc. It helps researchers in understanding the findings.

Chapter-II: Review of Related Literature

Normally Review of Related Literature is the second chapter but sometime it may be integrated with the First Chapter—Introduction. If the researcher decides to include Review of Related Literature in the First Chapter, it should be written before the Rationale of Study. The Zeist of it must be used in writing the Rationale of Study. This chapter should contain only those researches which are related to the problem of the study. It should be written in past tense because the researches being reported have already been conducted.

The Review of Related Literature is classified into different categories depending upon its nature and expected use. It is easy to trace the trend of the studies if these are presented in ascending order of publication rather than descending order of year in which these are published. These days some researchers have started presenting past researches in the descending order. If past researches are presented in descending order, than the reader may find it difficult to understand the trend related to the variable under consideration. After presenting the classified researches in ascending order of publication, one should write about the trend emerging from these studies. The Review of Related Literature should be as concise as possible. It should include the last name of the researcher followed by the year of publication in parenthesis, the relevant objectives of the study, the hypothesis if relevant, the sample—its size, sampling technique, and characteristics; Tools—its name along with name of developer, Reliability and Validity coefficients. If the study is of Experimental type, than the details regarding the name of design, name of treatment, duration of treatment, and method of controlling intervening variables. The statistical technique used in analysing the data, and the findings of the study should be presented in a way that they lead the reader rather the reader exerting to find out what he is reading about. All these information should be presented in one paragraph. The details of next research study should be presented in the next paragraph. That is, in case the researcher is presenting, say, 15 researches, then there must 15 paragraphs. At the end of this chapter, the Zeist must be presented. This Zeist is normally used in writing the Rationale of the study and also at the time of writing Discussion Chapter.

Chapter–III: Methodology

In this chapter, details regarding Sample; Tools/Instruments; Experimental Design, if applicable; Procedure of Data Collection, and Data Analysis used in the present research should be given. This chapter should be written in past tense because the details are being given after the research has been completed.

Under Sample the researcher must mention the Population from which the Sample was selected. The sample size along with the Sampling Technique must be written. At the end the main characteristics of Sample must be mentioned so that the reader understands the findings in the context.

While collecting the data the researcher either uses the available standardised tool or develops his/her own tool. In case the researcher decides to develop the tool, the separate chapter should be written where the details of its development must be given. In case the researcher has used already standardised tool, the name of the tool and the name of developer must be mentioned. Dimension-wise the number of items should be reported. The time allowed for giving responses must be mentioned if applicable. The scoring system to be used by the researcher should be mentioned. The Reliability and Validity Coefficients must be mentioned. The information about each tool must be given in one paragraph separately.

In case the Experimental research is conducted by researcher, the name of the Experimental Design along with the layout should be given. This is followed by the name and duration of Treatment. The information of Treatment must be detailed so that other researchers are able to replicate the study. There are different methods of controlling intervening variables. The method which the researcher has used in controlling intervening variables should be mentioned.

Procedure of Data Collection should be mentioned in such a manner so that it can be followed by another researcher who wants to replicate this study. It should clearly mention the instructions given, the sequence of administering the tools, the time allowed for each tool for responding, and the scoring procedure used by the researcher.

Lastly the data analysis should be mentioned. It must be given Objective-wise so that the reader is in a position to understand. There is no need of giving formula as these are available in books.

Chapter–IV: Results and Interpretation

This chapter should be written in the same sequence in which the Objectives are given in the First Chapter. The caption headings should be taken out from the wording of Objectives. The results should be integrated with the interpretation. The table in which the results are given should have appropriate title. While referring to the results, present sentence should be used else the rest part of this chapter should be written in the past tense. The findings emerged from the interpretation should be given in this chapter at the end.

Chapter–V: Discussion

Normally this chapter is quite weak in majority of studies. Discussion if written properly gives birth to new research problems. Different captions of this chapter should emerge from the findings. The findings should be discussed in the light of related researches. The researcher may find that the past researches either support or contradict the present research findings. In both the cases the researcher should give the reasons as why the present findings have emerged. This chapter normally decides the quality the research and must be written in past tense.

Chapter–VI: Summary, Findings And Implications

Majority content of this chapter will be taken from earlier chapters. In this chapter, the researcher must give information under various heads, such as, Rationale; Statement of Problem; Objectives; Hypotheses, if applicable; Sample; Tools; Experimental Design, if applicable; Procedure of Data Collection; Data Analysis; Findings; and Implications. The Implications should be written for different concerned people. If read, people must understand as how these findings can be used in the field to improve the quality. Depending on type of research, the implications can be written for Educational Planners; Principals, Teachers, Students, Parents, etc.

7. The information related to Data Analysis is to be given in
   A) Methodology Chapter.
   B) Introduction Chapter.
   C) Results and Interpretation Chapter.
   D) Discussion Chapter.
8. Which of the following should NOT be included in Paper?
   A) Bibliography B) References
   C) Discussion D) Both B and C
9. Which of the following is correct?
   A) et. al B) et. al.
   C) et al. D) et Al.
10. Which of the following reference is correctly written?
    A) Sansanwal (2008): Age and Research Competency. University News, 5 (2).
    B) Sansanwal, D.N. (2008): Age and Research Competency. University News, 5.
    C) Sansanwal, D.N. (2008): Age and Research Competency. University News, 5 (2), pp 14-20.
    D) Sansanwal (2008): Age and Research Competency. University News, 5, pp. 14-20.
11. Methodology chapter should give information related to
    A) Sample B) Tool
    C) Experimental Design D) All of the above
12. While writing Objective one should use
    A) To study B) To find out
    C) To investigate D) To survey
13. Which of the following statement is correct?
    A) Hypothesis is to be written in future tense in research proposal.
    B) Hypothesis is to be written in present tense in research proposal.
    C) Data analysis information is to be given under Procedure of Data Collection.
    D) Table heading should have verb in it.
14. Which of the following is correctly represented?
    A) Mean = 12.347 B) SD = 1.8372
    C) Correlation = 0.259 D) None of the above

Correct Answers

Chapter 1:

Correct Answer: 1) B, 2) A, 3) C, 4) D, 5) A, 6) D, 7) D, 8) B, 9) A, 10) D

Chapter 2:

Correct Answer: 1) C, 2) D, 3) D, 4) B, 5) C, 6) C, 7) D, 8) C, 9) A, 10) C, 11) B, 12) D, 13) D, 14) C, 15) C

Chapter 3:

Correct Answer: 1) B, 2) D, 3) A, 4) B, 5) C, 6) D, 7) C, 8) A, 9) B, 10) D, 11) C, 12) A, 13) C, 14) A, 15) D, 16) D, 17) B, 18) A, 19) C

Chapter 4:

Correct Answer: 1) C, 2) D, 3) B, 4) C, 5) A, 6) C, 7) B, 8) B, 9) B, 10) D, 11) A, 12) D, 13) A, 14) C, 15) A, 16) D, 17) A, 18) B, 19) D, 20) B, 21) C, 22) A, 23) D, 24) D, 25) C

Chapter 5:

Correct Answer: 1) D, 2) E 3) A, 4) D, 5) B, 6) C, 7) D, 8) C, 9) A, 10) C, 11) A, 12) C, 13) D, 14) B, 15) A, 16) C, 17) D, 18) A, 19) C, 20) B

Chapter 6:

Correct Answer: 1) B, 2) C, 3) A, 4) B, 5) A, 6) B, 7) D, 8) C, 9) D, 10) D

Chapter 7:

Correct Answers: 1) D, 2) B, 3) A, 4) B, 5) C, 6) A, 7) C, 8) D, 9) C, 10) A, 11) C, 12) B, 13) D, 14) B, 15) A, 16) B, 17) C, 18) D, 19) B, 20) D, 21) C, 22) A, 23) B, 24) D, 25) C, 26) B, 27) C, 28) C, 29) A, 30) D, 31) D, 32) A, 33) D, 34) C, 35) D, 36) B, 37) D, 38) A, 39) C, 40) B

Chapter 8:

Correct Answer: 1) C, 2) D, 3) D, 4) C, 5) A, 6) D, 7) A, 8) B, 9) C, 10) B, 11) C, 12) D, 13) A, 14) B, 15) D, 16) A, 17) C, 18) A, 19) D, 20) D, 21) D, 22) A, 23) C

Chapter 9:

Correct Answers; 1) C, 2) B, 3) A, 4) C, 5) A, 6) D, 7) D, 8) B, 9) A

Chapter 10:

Correct Answer: 1) A, 2) B, 3) D, 4) C, 5) A, 6) B, 7) C

Chapter 11:

Correct Answer: 1) C, 2) B, 3) A, 4) B, 5) C, 6) A, 7) D, 8) A, 9) A, 10) C, 11) D, 12) A, 13) B, 14) D, 15) C, 16) D, 17) C, 18) B, 19) C, 20) B, 21) A, 22) A, 23) A, 24) D, 25) C, 26) A, 27) C, 28) C, 29) D, 30) A, 31) D, 32) A, 33) D, 34) C, 35) B

Chapter 12:

Correct Answer: 1) A, 2) D, 3) B, 4) A, 5) C, 6) D, 7) A, 8) C, 9) B, 10) B, 11) D, 12) B, 13) D, 14) B, 15) C, 16) B, 17) C, 18) D, 19) A, 20) C, 21) D, 22) A, 23) A, 24) B, 25) C, 26) D, 27) C, 28) C

Chapter 13:

Correct answer: 1) C, 2) B, 3) D, 4) B, 5) C, 6) D, 7) D, 8) B, 9) B, 10) C, 11) C

Chapter 14:

Correct Answer: 1) B, 2) C, 3) A, 4) C, 5) A, 6) B, 7) D, 8) D, 9) A, 10) D

Chapter 15:

Correct Answer: 1) A, 2) B, 3) C, 4) C, 5) A, 6) D, 7) A, 8) C, 9) C, 10) D

Chapter 16:

Correct Answer: 1) B, 2) A, 3) D, 4) A, 5) D, 6) C, 7) C, 8) B, 9) B, 10) C, 11) A, 12) B

Chapter 17:

Correct Answer: 1) A, 2) B, 3) A, 4) D, 5) A, 6) A, 7) B, 8) C, 9) A, 10) B. 11) D

Chapter 18:

Correct Answer: 1) D, 2) C, 3) D, 4) A, 5) C, 6) B, 7) D, 8) A, 9) B, 10) D

Chapter 19:

Correct Answer: 1) B, 2) D, 3) C, 4) A, 5) D, 6) C, 7) A, 8) A, 9) C, 10) C, 11) D, 12) A, 13) B, 14) D

Table–1: t-Test

	Two Tailed 0.20	0.1	0.05	0.02	0.01
df	One Tailed 0.10	0.05	0.025	0.01	0.005
1	3.078	6.314	12.706	31.821	63.657
2	1.886	2.920	4.303	6.965	9.925
3	1.638	2.353	3.182	4.541	5.841
4	1.533	2.132	2.776	3.747	4.604
5	1.476	2.015	2.571	3.365	4.032
6	1.440	1.943	2.447	3.143	3.707
7	1.415	1.895	2.365	2.998	3.499
8	1.397	1.860	2.306	2.896	3.355
9	1.383	1.833	2.262	2.821	3.250
10	1.372	1.812	2.228	2.764	3.169
11	1.363	1.796	2.201	2.718	3.106
12	1.356	1.782	2.179	2.681	3.055
13	1.350	1.771	2.160	2.650	3.012
14	1.345	1.761	2.145	2.624	2.977
15	1.341	1.753	2.131	2.602	2.947
16	1.337	1.746	2.120	2.583	2.921
17	1.333	1.740	2.110	2.567	2.898
18	1.330	1.734	2.101	2.552	2.878
19	1.328	1.729	2.093	2.539	2.861
20	1.325	1.725	2.086	2.528	2.845
21	1.323	1.721	2.080	2.518	2.831
22	1.321	1.717	2.074	2.508	2.819
23	1.319	1.714	2.069	2.500	2.807
24	1.318	1.711	2.064	2.492	2.797
25	1.316	1.708	2.060	2.485	2.787
26	1.315	1.706	2.056	2.479	2.779
27	1.314	1.703	1.052	2.473	2.771
28	1.313	1.701	2.048	2.467	2.763
29	1.311	1.699	2.045	2.462	2.756
30	1.310	1.697	2.042	2.457	2.750
40	1.303	1.684	2.021	2.423	2.704
60	1.296	1.671	2.000	2.390	2.660
120	1.289	1.658	1.980	2.358	2.617
α	1.282	1.645	1.960	2.326	2.576

REFERENCE

1. Campbell, Donald T. and Stanley, Julian C. (1963): *Experimental and Quasi-Experimental Designs for Research.* Boston: Houghton Mifflin Company.
2. Joyce, Bruce and Weil, Marsha (1985): *Models of Teaching*, New Delhi: Prentice-Hall of India.
3. Lawshe, C.H. (1975). A quantitative approach to content validity. *Personnel Psychology*, 28, 563–575.
4. Sansanwal, D.N. (2015): Methodological Issues in Experimental Researches. *University News*, 9 March, 2015.
5. Simon, Anita and Boyer, E. Gil (1967): *Mirrors for Behaviour. Research for Better Schools*, Inc., Philadelphia, Pennsylvania.

Index

करके देखिये

''राम शब्द बहुत मीठा है कोई गाकर देखिये ।
आ सकते हैं राम जरा बुलाकर देखिये '' –अनूप जलोटा

मीठी वाणी से परायों को अपना बनाया जा सकता है ।
यकीन नहीं है तो आज़मा कर देखिये ।
आ सकते हैं राम जरा बुलाकर देखिये ।।

विद्यार्थी का पढ़ना अच्छा लगता है ।
अगर आज़माना है तो उन्हें पढ़ा कर देखिये ।
आ सकते हैं राम जरा बुलाकर देखिये ।।

कठिन विषय को सरल बनाया जा सकता है ।
यकीन नहीं है तो daily life से उदाहरण लेकर पढ़ाकर देखिये ।
आ सकते हैं राम जरा बुलाकर देखिये ।।

गणित और विज्ञान से विद्यार्थी को नफरत नहीं है ।
जरा इन्हें Teaching Aids के द्वारा पढ़ा कर देखिये ।
आ सकते हैं राम जरा बुलाकर देखिये ।।

Teaching को रोचक बनाया जा सकता है ।
अगर बनाना हो तो DNS की Jerk Technology का उपयोग करके देखिये ।
आ सकते हैं राम जरा बुलाकर देखिये ।।

Research Methodology और Statistics समझ में आ सकती है ।
यकीन नहीं है तो सनसनवाल से पढ़ कर देखिये ।
आ सकते हैं राम जरा बुलाकर देखिये ।।

– D.N. Sansanwal